Opera

Linda Hutcheon & Michael Hutcheon

Opera:
Desire,
Disease,
Death

University of Nebraska Press

Lincoln & London

Acknowledgments for the use of illustrations appear
on pages 287–88. © 1996 by the University of Nebraska
Press. All rights reserved. Manufactured in the United
States of America. ⊗ The paper in this book meets
the minimum requirements of American National
Standard for Information Sciences – Permanence of
Paper for Printed Library Materials, ANSI Z39.48-1984.
Library of Congress Cataloging in Publication Data
Hutcheon, Linda, 1947–
Opera : desire, disease, death / Linda Hutcheon and
Michael Hutcheon p. cm. Includes bibliographical
references and index. ISBN 0-8032-2367-6 (cl : alk. paper)
1. Sexuality in opera. 2. Diseases in opera. 3. Opera –
Social aspects. I. Hutcheon, Michael, 1945–. II. Title.
ML1700.H87 1996 782.1–dc20 95-18825 CIP MN
Text set in 10 pt. Cartier. Book design by R. Eckersley

Nothing is more punitive than to give a disease a meaning — that meaning being invariably a moralistic one. — Susan Sontag, Illness as Metaphor

Living after all is most felt at the pitch of pleasure or at the height of pain which can be overlapping areas of feeling as the romantic understanding of love as a sickness well illustrates. — David Steel

CONTENTS

List of Illustrations, ix

Acknowledgments, xi

Prologue: "All Concord's Born of Contraries," xiii

Collaborative Research, or Marital Methodologies, xiii

Interdisciplinary Work on the "Unnatural Beast," xv

A Note on the Notes, xvi

1. Melodies and Maladies: An Introduction, 1

Why Opera? 3

Why Disease and Opera? 11

Why These Diseases and These Operas? 18

2. Famous Last Breaths: The Tubercular Heroine, 29

Diagnosis Despite Mystery: Antonia, 30

The "Phthisic Beauty" and the Tubercle Bacillus, 36

The Consumptive Model: The "Tipo Traviata," 40

Poverty and Contagion: Mimì, 48

3. Syphilis, Suffering, and the Social Order: Richard Wagner's *Parsifal*, 61

Suffering and Sin, 62

Syphilis: The Medical Signs of the "Scourge of God," 68

Soldiers and Prostitutes, 76

Sexuality and Social Decline, 83

Redemption and the Sanctified Heterosexual Ideal, 85

The "Polyphony" of Wagner's Language, 87

4. The Pox Revisited: The "Pale Spirochete" in Twentieth-Century Opera, 95

The Femme Fatale as *Femme Malade*: *Lulu*, 95

The Terrors of Bedlam: "The Rake's Progress," 100

The Rake's Progress: Made in the U.S.A., 106

From the Top, This Time with Humor: *Candide*, 117

5. "Acoustic Contagion": Sexuality, Surveillance, and Epidemics, 123

Cholera: Danger, Shame, Social Unrest, 124

Lulu: Lesbian Love and Death, 130

Bourgeois Un-ease and Homosexual Dis-ease: *Death in Venice*, 133

Mario and the Magician: Fascism and the "Paralysis of Will," 149

6. Where There's Smoke, There's . . . , 161

Tobacco: A History of Double(d) Talk, 162

Male Bonding versus the Lone Rebel: *Les Contes d'Hoffmann* and *La Fanciulla del West*, 168

Sensual Pleasures and Their Dangers: *Il Segreto di Susanna* and *Il Tabarro*, 173

Sex, Smoking, and Violence: *Carmen*, 178

"No Smoking": Medical Knowledge and Social Change, 192

Epilogue. "Life-and-Death Passions": AIDS and the Stage, 195

Giving AIDS Meaning(s), 196

The "Gay Plague": *Angels in America*, 202

The Logic of Contagion: Cholera and AIDS, 210

"Polluted Blood": Syphilis and AIDS, 214

"Aesthetic" Epidemics: Tuberculosis and AIDS, 218

Gay Countermythologies, 220

Notes, 229

Photo Credits, 287

Index, 289

ILLUSTRATIONS

1. Dr. Miracle, *Les Contes d'Hoffmann*, 33

2. Antonia, *Les Contes d'Hoffmann*, 35

3. Violetta, *La Traviata*, 45

4. Rodolfo and Mimì, *La Bohème*, 51

5. Amfortas and Gurnemanz, *Parsifal*, 65

6. Syphilitic gumma, 70

7. Syphilis as the scourge of God against the sinful, 73

8. Tom Rakewell in the brothel, from William Hogarth, "The Rake's Progress," 104

9. Tom Rakewell in Bedlam, from William Hogarth, "The Rake's Progress," 105

10. Tom Rakewell with Mother Goose in the brothel, *The Rake's Progress*, 111

11. Tom Rakewell in Bedlam, final act of *The Rake's Progress*, 113

12. Lulu and the Countess Geschwitz, *Lulu*, 132

13. The dying Aschenbach and Tadzio, *Death in Venice*, 147

14. Cipolla hypnotizing Mario, *Mario and the Magician*, 157

15. Mario and Cipolla, *Mario and the Magician*, 158

16. English tobacco advertisement, 1832, 165

17. *Die Truckene Trunckenheit*, 1658, 166

18. Pipes sensual and deadly, 169

19. Male bonding over a smoke, 169

20. Jack Rance, *La Fanciulla del West*, 172

21. Chorus of cigarette makers, *Carmen*, 180

22. The angel of death striking during the plague, 207

23. The angel appearing to Prior Walter, *Angels in America*, 207

Acknowledgments

This book is dedicated to the undergraduate students in the Literary Studies Program at Victoria College at the University of Toronto. Neither of us has ever taught these students, but each year for four years they invited us to speak at their annual week-long conference, and each year we presented papers that eventually added up to the core of this book.

This study would not have been possible without the diligence, critical judgment, and investigative intelligence of Russell Kilbourn, more our coresearcher than our graduate assistant. Without the critical reading, scholarly example, stimulation, inspiration, and frankly, push of Sander Gilman, we would probably never have dreamed of turning those conference papers into a book. Without Herbert Lindenberger's early support for the proposal, that dream might never have become a reality. To all these we owe special gratitude. For their understanding and support of a project that appeared to diverge from both our research paths, we also thank our respective university departments and in particular Michael Baker and Eliot Phillipson.

To the Social Sciences and Humanities Research Council of Canada go our deep thanks for the generous financial support that made possible the hiring of our assistant and the necessary travel to research libraries and archives; to the Rockefeller Foundation goes our gratitude for the precious month at the Bellagio Study Centre, for it was during this time that much of the book came together and was made final.

Our research was assisted in numerous ways by the staff of the Wellcome Institute for the History of Medicine (especially Brenda Sutton), the New York Public Library (Arents Collection), the University of Toronto's John P. Robarts Library, especially the Fisher Library, Rare Books and Special Collections. To Shioban Mitchell of the Canadian Opera Company and to Joan Baillie and John Pennino, archivists of the Canadian Opera Company and of the Metropolitan Opera, go our thanks for assistance with the illustrations. Alice M. Bennett's meticulous and tactful copyediting was most appreciated.

Many friends, family, colleagues, and students have put up with our operatic-medical obsessions over the past few years. Some read or discussed parts of this book with critical attention for which we are thankful, and others offered suggestions for reading or listening. Even a short list of those we must thank would have to include (in random order): Alexander and Kathleen Hutcheon, Joanne and Christopher Adams, Elisa and Remo Bulfon, Gary Bortolotti and Heather Trueman, Marc Weiner, Peter Rabinowitz, Alan Bewell, Eva Geulen, Brian Corman, John Floras, Todd Gilman, Noe Zamel, Jerry Burrow, Raymond Grant, Walter Pache, Peter Dyson, David Stanley-Porter, Ed Cole, Adrienne Hood, Iain and Barbara Scott, Jenny Heathcote, Brad Bucknell, Shirley Neuman, Dorothy Piepke, Joseph So, Dick Whelan, Susan Quinn, Erik LaMont, Ellen Taaffe Zwilich, Fred Aman, Carol Greenhouse, and many, many others

The opportunity to try out the ideas in this book as they were developing, on live and "reactive" audiences, was a most valuable one for us, and we thank the organizers of the following conferences for giving us that chance: Semiotics of Culture (Toronto, 1990); Human Sciences in the Age of Theory (University of Western Ontario, 1993); Society for the Study of Narrative Literature (Vancouver, 1994); Cultural Studies in Canada (Toronto, 1994); Great Lakes Lung Conference (Niagara-on-the-Lake, 1994); Modern Language Association (Toronto, 1993; San Diego, 1994). In addition, we thank those who invited us to lecture to such diverse but equally critical and provocative audiences as those at the Toronto Wagner Society, the Royal Society of Canada, Medical Grand Rounds at the Toronto General, Toronto Western, Wellesley, and St. Michael's Hospitals, the Ontario Lung Association, University of Calgary, University of Alberta, University of Windsor, Laurentian University, and State University of New York at Binghamton.

To all these people go our thanks for encouragement and support, for correcting our errors and often misguided enthusiasms; whatever problems remain after all this assistance can only be blamed on us, we fear. Our many helpers, however, can live in hope that we'll remember and heed their advice even better in our next collaborative project.

Prologue

"All Concord's Born of Contraries"

The overture ought to apprise the spectators of the nature of the action that is to be represented and to form, so to speak, its argument.
— Christoph Willibald Gluck

A book about opera by a physician and a literary theorist calls for some explanation. Over the past few years our writing it has certainly provoked no little curiosity and even a bit of dismay (mostly from family and friends). These brief remarks are intended to answer some of the questions you too may have about this bizarre concord of apparent contraries (to borrow Ben Jonson's terms) and what it might hope to add to the study of opera.

Collaborative Research, or Marital Methodologies

Having met early in high school, we had already known each other about thirty years when this project began; we had been married for over twenty and thought we knew each other well. So much for those comfortable certainties that everyday life is based on. We were aware that we had been trained very differently: medical school and postgraduate work in respiratory physiology would obviously turn out a different kind of mind than a doctoral program in comparative literature. We were even aware that we thought and worked in "somewhat" different ways. But we hadn't counted on the extent or the force of what the French so rightly call *déformation professionnelle*. Since we both had some musical training and opera had always been a shared passion, we began our research assuming we would bring to it the different and varied skills of interpretation and analysis that both personality and education had developed.

Then one day we worked together, side by side, in a library. Much to our surprise, we discovered that we read in different ways and at different speeds, recording different things in different manners. Trained to read *and remember* every line, the physician worked with painstaking care and deliberate attention; he recorded each point made in sequential and logical order, taking detailed notes. The literary theorist, on the other hand, given the kind of research projects she had undertaken in the past, was accustomed to reading through large amounts of scholarly work to zero in on pertinent material; therefore she made her way through a number of books before gathering a series of what she considered relevant points on selected topics. Over the next few hours each of us grew more and more amazed at the other's pace, note-taking techniques, and choice of data to record, until we had to stop our work and talk through our astonishment. What we have learned in the years since that first day of shared research is that intellectual and professional "formation" (or deformation) has, over time, reinforced temperamental differences to the point that we now have the amusing distinction of possessing between us a collective obsessive-compulsive personality: in what has turned out to be a productive division of labor, he "obsesses" and she "compulses."

If anything can be said to have provoked this project, however, it was the (obsessive) eye for detail of the medically trained physician that kept noticing things about operas that no one seemed able to explain. Why was Rodolfo frightened by Mimi's consumptive coughing in *La Bohème* (1896), whereas Alfredo wasn't in the least upset by Violetta's in *La Traviata* (1853)? What had happened in those forty years in terms of knowledge about the disease? Why did no one mention that Amfortas's mysterious wound in Wagner's *Parsifal* would have been diagnosed quite easily at the time by both physicians and the lay public, who knew the signs of syphilis all too well? Why was the appearance of cholera in opera always directly associated with same-sex affection? Our attempts to answer these and other such questions led us not only into the history of both medicine and music, but into the words of the librettos themselves and even back to their literary source texts. This is where the compulsive's training in the techniques of interpreting narrative and poetic language, as well as in the history of French, German, Italian, and English literary culture, came in handy. (The translations offered alongside the original text are always our own and are always deliberately literal.)[1] The book you are about to read, then, is a hybrid of what very different temperaments and training have brought to bear on that most hybrid of art forms — opera.

Interdisciplinary Work on the "Unnatural Beast"

We have taken to heart the recent advice of a musicologist about opera: "To understand the complex and contradictory nature of this unnatural beast requires a flexible and varied arsenal of hermeneutical/interpretive instruments."[2] We are not musicologists, though we have of course drawn widely on the work of historians and analysts of opera in order to understand the conventions and technical aspects of the music both of opera in general and of specific operas. But as the first chapter explains in detail, our study should be seen as contributing to that current move to understand opera as part of the broader social context in which it is produced by composers and librettists, and also experienced by audiences. Embedded in the cultural life of its time and place, European and North American opera of the past two hundred years reveals much about the desires, anxieties, needs, and fears of those who created it and those who made it the popular and lasting art form it has turned out to be.

The audiences for whom we have written this book are multiple: people who are interested in medicine and its history; people who love opera and enjoy reading about it; people who study opera in academic fields as diverse as cultural studies, history, literary criticism, and of course musicology. What our interdisciplinary — medical and literary — work offers to all these various and even competing interests is a different way of explaining not only the power of opera but the way this particular artistic practice can reflect — and even alter — a cultural practice like medicine. In discussing opera as musical drama, we have not relied on simple assertions of music's ineffable power to move the emotions or, at the other extreme, on theories of its technical complexity that make sense only to composers and advanced students of musicology. Instead our aim has been to combine medical and cultural history with literary and dramatic analyses, each written to be intelligible to nonspecialists. We hope that this "concord" might add not only to the understanding of opera's social and artistic impact, in earlier times as well as now, but also to the enjoyment of the theatrical experience that is opera.

Our strong belief, from the start of this project, has been that opera commentary often lacks a sense of opera as itself a kind of promiscuously interdisciplinary and resolutely performative art form: it involves music, but music written especially for a particular text; that text in turn was designed especially to be put to music. Neither has meaning without the other. (This is why we have chosen throughout to refer to the creators of operas by the awkward but accurate double designation of composer/librettist—Verdi/Piave, or Britten/Piper, for example.) But just as important to opera's specific identity as an art form is that both the score and the libretto are only *scripts*, only instructions for *performances*, musical and dramatic. The notes of the score must be played according to certain specific instructions; the words of the libretto must be sung and acted out according to equally important directions that will govern the dramatic action, the characterization, and in the end the theatrical power and success of the opera as opera. (This is why dates given for operas are those of the premiere performances, and texts used are those of the standard sung versions.) Although psychoanalysts, linguists, literary critics, and cultural historians have all recently brought their talents to bear in exciting ways on the phenomenon of voice, that is not our main interest here.[3] Opera as a hybrid, complex, staged musical-theatrical experience, totally embedded in its culture, is.

A Note on the Notes

Because we have written this book with a wide audience in mind, we have placed the notes at the end so as not to interfere with the reading experience. It is never necessary to consult them while reading in order to understand the argument: the notes are supplementary or descriptive only and mainly provide references to the works consulted or cited. We have been thorough and detailed in our recording of scholarly research materials, not only out of obsessive-compulsive necessity, but so that readers with specialist interests (medical, musical, historical, literary) can follow up various points on their own.

Opera

Chapter 1

Melodies and Maladies: An Introduction

Music exalts each joy, allays each grief,
Expels diseases, softens every pain,
Subdues the rage of poison, and the plague.
— John Armstrong,
The Art of Preserving Health, 1744

La forme fatale.
— Aaron Copland on opera, 1975

It may be a truism that the stories we tell and the images we create to explain ourselves to ourselves are always loaded: cultural "representations"
are never innocent. This is a book about a particular set of stories and
images—those about illness and death as represented on the operatic
stage of Europe and North America in the nineteenth and twentieth
centuries. It is about what some readers will consider, at least at first, an
unlikely combination: medical history and musical history. If music has
been treasured for centuries as the purest of art forms, then music written for opera would have to be some of the most impure, for opera owes
its power—its considerable and well-documented power—to its com-
bining the musical and the dramatic, the aural and the visual, the emotional and the intellectual.

For us opera's commanding ability to overcome realist objections to
its artifice, to override purist concerns about its mixed artistic nature, to
overrule wary doubts about its financial or narrative excesses, and simply to overwhelm the imagination cannot come only from the score but
must also involve the dramatic story for which the music was especially
written—a story it incarnates in living, breathing, singing bodies on the
stage. It is in those intense and powerfully enacted tales that the medical

and the cultural meet. It would be an understatement of the first order to say that disease and mortality were concerns of art, as of life, well before the nineteenth and twentieth centuries. We have chosen to focus on these years because they also witnessed the birth and development of what we know today as "modern" medicine. It has been said that explaining sickness is "too significant — socially and emotionally — for it to be a value-free enterprise."[1] If this is true, then the way a society explains and represents illness — especially in an emotionally powerful art form like opera — can tell us much about its values and about *how* value is assigned in that particular culture.

Diseases and those who suffer from them have always taken on meanings well beyond their medical significance. Part of the reason is the force of certain representations that are repeated so often that they eventually create their own social reality. Think about the cultural associations of a disease like leprosy: despite the unlikelihood of its casual transmission, people suffering from it have been seen throughout the ages as dangerous to society as a whole and so have been isolated, even ostracized. Although few illnesses have led to such extreme social responses, cultures continue to give meaning to illness all the time and to make value judgments about it. These moral judgments establish a hierarchy of what we might call disease acceptability: it might well be more acceptable to get cirrhosis of the liver from hepatitis B than from alcohol consumption, or you might feel more comfortable being told you had heart disease than, say, syphilis — a serious but socially acceptable illness rather than a treatable but embarrassing one.

Such an understanding of the meanings and values attached to disease in the past is timely, even crucial, to us today: we are witnessing a struggle over the different meanings being given to a new disease — AIDS, or acquired immunodeficiency syndrome. With its arrival have appeared all the social, psychological, and cultural dimensions that have always *accompanied* but have also been *part of* a biomedical understanding of disease. Although this has usually been the case — from the very first recorded plagues — our focus is on the particular period since science began to understand that diseases might not be a matter of personal idiosyncrasy and predisposition. With the rise of pathologic anatomy, diseases came to be seen as entities that could be studied scientifically and categorized through observable, abnormal changes in body organs. This approach meant that they were understood to result not from some personal lack of balance or harmony of the "humors" within the self (or between the self and the environment) but from biological abnormalities with clinical signs manifested (and experienced) by individual sufferers.[2] With the advent of bacteriology in the mid-nineteenth century came knowledge of the causes of some of these pathologic entities. These revelations are all part of the legacy of "modern" medicine.

It has been claimed that the way any society responds to disease reveals "its deepest cultural, social and moral values"; that "these core values—patterns of judgment about what is good or bad—shape and guide human perception and action."[3] Our particular interest in this book is precisely these patterns of judgment and what they reveal about the interaction of cultural and medical knowledge. The time frame is from the mid-nineteenth century to the present. We have chosen to study those particular diseases that are portrayed (and the manner of their representation) in one art form: as public, staged musical drama, opera has the ability to offer to the human mind—and body—one of the most complex and powerful of intellectual, emotional, and visceral experiences.

Why Opera?

Though opera is often seen these days as an elitist, "highbrow" form of art, its long and continuous history in Europe is not as class bound as some would like to make it. Opera in seventeenth-century Venice, for instance, took on its particular eclectic mix of the comic and the serious because its audience included all classes—as did Shakespeare's.[4] In our own age of translated surtitles and with bold, irreverent directors busy updating even the most sacred of canonical operas (and doing so for television and movie audiences), opera may have a chance of escaping that elitist label.[5] With major advances in audio and video technology, opera can now enter the home with an ease only dreamed of by the first listeners to the Metropolitan's *Saturday Afternoon at the Opera* radio broadcasts. The history of opera, however, helps explain why that elitist label exists.

Because opera is, and was from the start, an expensive dramatic form, the economics of performance demanded the early patronage of nobility and royalty. The well-documented French extravagances of Louis XIV's court operas might well have justified Dr. Johnson's remarks about eighteenth-century opera in his dictionary: he called it "an exotic and irrational entertainment." Tellingly, however, during the French Revolution opera was not banned as aristocratic art: it was taken over and democratized. Indeed, more operas were produced in the years following the Revolution than before, as new subjects were freed from the control of the royal censor.[6]

In nineteenth-century Europe, where we begin this book, however, opera was the most popular form of bourgeois entertainment. The sumptuous and conspicuously situated opera houses of nineteenth-century Paris or Vienna "celebrated both the imperial power . . . and the participation of the urban middle-class in the imperial enterprise."[7] There have been many theories about why opera held this attraction for the bourgeoisie of Europe, theories that range from the social (a desire to ape their social betters) to the symbolic (the "sonorous fullness and choral masses" as both symbolic of and aimed at larger audiences, not small aristocratic courts).[8] In a place like Paris there would have been a choice of operas for the middle classes to attend on a given evening, not unlike our present choice of films, perhaps. There was no fixed canon of repeated operas such as we are familiar with today; instead, operas often were written, were performed, and closed, in some cases never to be revived—much like films in the days before infinite television and video repeats became possible.

In these same years opera played important roles in broader social domains, from the shaping of national identity to—we shall argue—the formation of concepts of illness and health, sexuality and morality.[9] In all such domains, opera both reflected social and cultural concerns and repeated and reinforced them. As an art form, opera cannot but be embedded in the social and intellectual contexts it comes out of. Literary and intellectual historians like Herbert Lindenberger and Paul Robinson have argued for the important role opera plays in cultural change: we know that it was crucial to the thinking of Kierkegaard and, of course,

Nietzsche. But in more general terms it both mirrored and helped shape a range of European society's intellectual concerns, from psychological concepts of love to abstract ideas of the relation between order and chaos.[10] Such arguments are typical of the move in the past decade and a half to treat music in general (and opera in particular) in a broader context of culture and its "social discourse."[11] As an activity, a cultural practice, music is now being seen as available to cultural (as well as strictly formal musical) analysis because of its dynamic relationship to what Lawrence Kramer calls a "network of social, intellectual, and material conditions that strongly, though often implicitly, affect meaning."[12] Collections of essays such as *Music and Society: The Politics of Composition, Performance and Reception*, edited by Richard Leppart and Susan McClary, are typical of this attempt to add to the discipline of musicology the study of the connections between music and social-cultural values.

This is one way to challenge the idea of music as "an autonomous sphere, separate and insulated from the outside world."[13] Another is to bring to the study of music analytical methods and techniques of interpretation from other disciplines such as literary criticism. With opera this particular strategy seems especially attractive and has, in fact, proved very productive in recent years—as shown by the work of Herbert Lindenberger, Catherine Clément, Peter Conrad, Wayne Koestenbaum, and some of the contributors to collections such as *Reading Opera* and *Opera through Other Eyes*, to name only a few.[14] As we mentioned in the prologue, we see this book too in the context of those interdisciplinary studies that aim for more comprehensive criticism of culture as well as of opera.[15]

Opera is such a complex art form that it cries out for more than one approach: after all, it brings together dramatic narrative, staged performance, a literary text, a certain subject matter, and complex music in a particularly forceful way. In artistic terms, the power of opera likely stems from what might be called this "overdetermination" of effect: the combination of the dramatic + the narrative + the thematic + the verbal + the visual + the auditory. There is no such thing as the single "text" of opera. Indeed, it is even reductive to talk, as many do, of its *two* texts, the libretto and the score.[16] The history of opera criticism reveals a disagreement about just what the libretto is: a split between the view that it consists of *words* (poetic text) and the idea of it as *drama*. And the history of opera itself has been marked from its earliest times by major debates about the relation of both words and drama to the music, as theorists and composers fought over which had (or should have) precedence. Here is one succinct sketch of that history:

> *Although at its beginnings opera sought to emulate and restore the conditions of Greek tragedy and although its first great composer, Monteverdi, respected the primacy of drama in opera, Monteverdi's followers lost sight of the dramatic ideal and allowed the medium to become dominated by the needs of singers and the desire of audiences for spectacle; not until Gluck's "reform" of the 1760s was the dramatic mode restored — but only temporarily, for the performative and purely musical values once again dominated until the next great "reform," that of Wagner, returned the dramatic element to the foreground, where, despite many changes in operatic style, it has remained to this day.*[17]

The idea that opera consists of a libretto text and a musical score gave us, with different balancing of the two parts, works like Gary Schmidgall's *Literature as Opera* and Joseph Kerman's *Opera as Drama*.[18] Without the music, the libretto would be a (strangely written) stage-play script; without the libretto, the score would be a long and oddly structured piece of music.[19] Both are clearly necessary to the identity of this very particular art form, though it would be hard to guess that from the history of opera criticism, which has consistently disparaged and even ignored the libretto — literally reduced in name to the "little book." Yet composers have for centuries talked of the importance of the text — both as words and as drama — to the inspiration and also the form of the music: echoing Monteverdi, Gluck, and Wagner, contemporary composer John Eaton says his operas always begin from "musical-dramatic" ideas.[20] Recent collections of essays, such as *Reading Opera*, attempt to take the implications of the secondary and the diminutive out of the very word lib*retto*.

For a long time it has been common for commentators of all kinds to conflate the separate dimensions of the words and the drama in discussions of librettos or to ignore the fact that the "text" sung is not simply words (often in a foreign language) but particular words that construct a dramatic plot.[21] What is usually forgotten is that the opera libretto is a *script*, and as such it is words, but words that make possible the dramatization on stage of a place, a time, a set of characters and dramatic action—all crucial to the *experience* of opera as a performed art form and therefore to the *meanings* given to it. Our discussion of opera will treat the libretto as a theatrical script designed to be set to music (just as the score was written specifically to a libretto text), and at least three separate components of that script will be considered: its verbal text, its dramatic narrative, and its directions for staged action. If opera librettos do "read badly," the problem is with the reader, not the text: the assumptions that guide the reading of a novel or even a play are simply inadequate for reading librettos, where the musical setting plus the conventions of the dramatic script are part of what must be "read" and understood.

The first component, the verbal text, is usually bypassed by plot-outlining operatic commentary, of course. Yet as Patrick J. Smith writes in *The Tenth Muse: A Historical Study of the Opera Libretto*, the history of the librettist is as a poet "to be judged by the musicality of his lines and the aptness of his rhythms, rhymes and similes."[22] In chapter 3 of our book the verbal texture of Wagner's *Parsifal* is the focus of part of the discussion, for it is through wordplay that Wagner (as his own librettist) embedded in language the major themes of his work. As such this chapter illustrates David Levin's argument that the ambiguities and complexities of the libretto's linguistic text cannot be ignored. But Levin seems to feel he must advocate a concern for the instabilities of language at the expense of the second component of the operatic text, its dramatic plot, for he refers to "the *bald* juxtaposition of situation, the *Manichaean* terms of character, and the *strained willfulness* of plot construction and resolution."[23] It is not that we necessarily disagree with the description; but one must understand the specific demands of opera narrative in order to contest the judgment it implies.

In *The Tenth Muse* Smith notes that, early on, the librettist had to become not only a poet but a dramatist capable of creating "the dramatic node around which the final work was constructed."[24] Composer Virgil Thomson calls opera "drama at its most serious and most complete."[25] Opera, in other words, is theater. And theater has never been able to do what, say, the novel could in terms of characterization: some of the subtler shadings get jettisoned, but we gain the intensity and immediacy of a character's physical presence on stage. Not having five or ten hours of reading time to develop a character or a situation, staged drama relies on different techniques to different ends; so too does opera. Yet many critics consider opera's dramatic narrative only in reductive terms such as the "lurid overstatement of understated narrative material" or "the conventionality, the freakishness, and the manifold silliness" of the stories.[26] What they often ignore is that the operas were frequently made from plays or novels that were very popular in their time, that were not considered particularly silly or freakish or lurid. Although librettists often had to move plot details around to suit opera's conventions (an aria should be followed by a trio, and so on), the basic narrative materials of the source texts persist in operas like *La Traviata* or *Carmen*, as we shall show in detail in later chapters. What makes operatic drama seem more extreme is likely a combination of two factors. The first is the music, though the critics often turn to it in relief when they have disposed of the libretto. But it is the music that is responsible for so much of the emotional power of opera, that allows passion to be "celebrated uncompromisingly" in a way it cannot be, without irony, in fiction.[27] The second reason for the apparent extravagant excess of operatic narrative is the necessary compression of the plot. There is no doubt that, if a story is to be told on the operatic stage, it has to be shortened and compressed: it simply takes longer to *sing* than to *deliver* a line of text. The result is that, on the level of plot, opera's bold strokes condense and, in a very complex way, unrefine.[28] But what might get lost in narrative complication and detail is made up for in the "concentrated and striking expressivity" achieved by excision and by reduction of narrative to its potent basics.[29]

If narrative is a specific mode of human understanding, as Peter Brooks has argued, if it is one of our ways of organizing experience, then the denigrating of it in opera criticism seems unwarranted and even misleading.[30] The stories count in opera because they cannot be separated from the music that was written specifically to and for them. But above all they are stories for the stage. Librettists as dramatists don't just write words to be put to music; they have to bring the singers of those words to life on stage through the most effective means possible. Critics have made much of Wagner's advanced sense of the technical possibilities of the stage, as seen in the visual and aural instructions written into his librettos.[31] It is no exaggeration to say that librettos contain directions for the singers, the director, and the production crew that are as significant to the effect and meaning of an opera as the directions in the score are for the conductor and musicians. As Carl Dahlhaus explains, it is the "visible plot" that counts most: "Unlike spoken drama, the only element of opera which is dramaturgically effective is . . . what we see on stage."[32] In chapter 6 we will discuss a particularly good example of the importance of this visibility of plot detail: the act of smoking, in operas as different from one another as *Il segreto di Susanna*, *La Fanciulla del West*, *Il tabarro*, and *Carmen*. Smoking is a wordless form of expression that is loaded with multiple and contradictory meanings, both in nineteenth-century Europe and today. One critic has claimed that "cigarettes are everywhere in Bizet's opera; *Carmen* may be said to define the principal motifs surrounding cigarettes for modernity."[33] If this is the case, then it does so without much help from words. As we shall see, the meanings of smoking are established largely in the setting of act 1 (outside the Seville tobacco factory) and the stage directions (often people on stage are said to smoke at particular times). All this is part of the libretto of the opera *as dramatic script* and part of the meaning of the opera as *staged theater*. Although few would argue that the score on paper *is* the music, too many are willing to consider the libretto on paper as the text. Performance is crucial to the identity of both.

As script, then, the opera libretto should be read for its combination of words, dramatic narrative (plot, characters), and stage directions and other mise-en-scène instructions. But the opera script is also written to be set to music, and with the help of musical analysts, that dynamic interaction of libretto and music will be considered throughout the chapters that follow. The distinctive theatricality of opera, we feel, is to be found in its hybrid nature, its integration of all these dimensions—not in any resolved harmony, but in tensions that give life and energy to the form of art we call opera.[34] To talk of "theatricality," though, implies an audience. For this reason the reception history of operas (and their source texts) will be part of the extended operatic "text" to be considered here. It has to be. One of the things music shares with the rest of the culture in which it is embedded is that it is *given meaning* by those who experience it. It is a matter not only of composer's intention and formal musical structures, but of the "acts of interpretation and perception" it gives rise to.[35] Reception is crucial, then, to the meaning of an opera—as it is to the meaning of what the opera is about. And it is to this that we now turn.

Music has always been used for its dramatic power, from ancient Greek plays to film sound tracks. But the complex music of opera is brought to life—literally incarnated—in singing bodies, bodies singing words and acting out their stories on stage. These are not words or stories as abstractions; these are corporeally real. We watch these bodies as they eat, drink, fight, make love, and of course suffer and die. Or at least such is the powerful illusion of the theater. As Marc A. Weiner argues at length in *Richard Wagner and the Anti-Semitic Imagination*, an opera can draw in a particularly direct and immediate way on an audience's associations with the human body, and it can do so in complex visual, acoustic, and other sensory ways: bodies and bodily images are understood as signs of sexual, racial, ethnic, and even national identity—and "otherness."[36] The body has received a lot of critical attention in recent years from anthropologists, historians, and literary theorists, not only as a physiological entity but as a cultural "construction" in which the values of a society are inscribed. Peter Brooks announces the focus of his *Body Work: Objects of Desire in Modern Narrative* as "the creation of fictions that address the body, that imbed it in narrative, and that therefore embody meanings: stories on the body, and the body in story."[37] As Brooks argues, the body is the point of intersection of nature and culture, and thus of the medical and the human sciences, because it is "at once the subject and object of pleasure, the uncontrollable agent of pain and the revolt against reason—and the vehicle of mortality." In this book our focus is on this particular nexus of the singing body as the representation of both pleasure and pain, as desired and desiring as well as sick and suffering, for in opera the two often go together.

The history of opera teaches that composers and librettists look for powerful subjects that will speak to their audiences. As Sander L. Gilman suggests in his important study *Disease and Representation*, they take into consideration "much more than aesthetic appropriateness. They are aware of the cultural implications, including images of disease, and of the force that cultural presuppositions will have in shaping the audience and drawing it both into the work, as well as, perhaps even more important than, into the theater."[38] They have to: opera is expensive to put on, and the economics of performance preclude taking too great a risk. Staged sung drama requires hiring often more than five hundred people: a conductor, an orchestra, a director, soloists, a chorus, a stage crew, designers and producers of sets and costumes, lighting designers and technicians, plus all the "house" personnel that go with any public performance. This all costs money, and lots of it. So before a company decides to produce an opera, it has to be convinced that the audience will respond. The effect of this economic reality principle on the composing of operas has been that by the time a story makes it to the operatic stage, chances are it is what could be called a "cultural cliché," a tried and true recipe for success. Composers aren't always good at guessing, however, though many initial failures have become successes with time. Much to our surprise today, such perennial favorites as *Madama Butterfly* and *Carmen* were not immediate hits. What interests us here is what we can learn about the obsessions and preoccupations of a certain time and place by studying the cultural clichés that make it onto the operatic stage for public consumption.

Why Disease and Opera?

Opera has always been an art form obsessed with death: Monteverdi's *La favola d'Orfeo* (1607) establishes a story pattern of love and loss that influences the staged representations of operatic death from the very start. In most nineteenth- and twentieth-century operas of the tragic variety, those obsessions and preoccupations with death continue to be associated with love, but the deaths are most frequently violent. There are stabbings: think of *Rigoletto, Pagliacci, Wozzeck, Tosca, Lucia di Lammermoor, Un ballo in maschera* (Boston setting). Then there are shootings: *Tosca* again, *Un ballo in maschera* (Stockholm setting), *Eugene Onegin*. Occasionally there are drownings: *Lady Macbeth of Mtsensk, Kátya Kabanová, Jenůfa*. Catherine Clément has suggested in *Opera, or The Undoing of Women*, that the victims are most frequently female.³⁹ Frequently they are, but by no means always, as the lists above suggest. In the name of love, women do often die at their own hands (Cio-Cio-San in *Madama Butterfly*), but so too do men (Edgar in *Lucia di Lammermoor*). In short, as we shall see, the gender question in opera is more complex than some people have suggested: it may be that for every Senta who leaps to her death (in *Der fliegende Holländer*) there is a Peter Grimes who rows out to sea to die. Indeed, as Michel Poizat notes in his "quick autopsy of the heaps of bodies strewn across the opera stage since the beginning," "male and female graves appear with equal frequency"—however "counterintuitive" that may seem.⁴⁰ Nevertheless, it is clear that opera has many ways of configuring death for both sexes in conjunction with love and desire, many of them violent.

Here we will look at what happens when an opera forgoes the obvious dramatic power of such sudden and violent final action in favor of a differently structured story of illness and suffering leading to death. As the testimony of works like *La Bohème* suggests, giving up the shock of violent death does not mean depriving the audience of tragic catharsis or emotional satisfaction. What is gained is the narrative power of an individual's struggle with illness. Recent medical thinking about suffering suggests that bodily pain is not the only element to be considered.⁴¹ Suffering is said to occur when one's personal identity is threatened or disrupted. Of all the art forms, perhaps only opera is so thoroughly dependent on suffering in general as a narrative and emotional staple. The *body*, the singing body, gives voice to the drama of the suffering *person*—in this case the sick person; in the process it also gives meaning to both the disease and the one who suffers from it, meaning that includes but *supplements* the medical understanding of bodily pain.

In *The Body in Pain*, Elaine Scarry has argued that physical pain resists language. It "has no voice," she claims, but adds: "When it at last finds a voice, it begins to tell a story."⁴² David B. Morris, in *The Culture of Pain*, specifies the form that story takes: for him it is in the action of staged tragedy that pain and the suffering it entails can be seen and heard. *King Lear* and *Oedipus the King* present "the ruined human body and the sound of suffering."⁴³ But imagine for a moment staged tragedy amplified by the emotional power of music—in other words, imagine opera—and you have an even more effective representation of the suffering person. It is also one that, through the music, would go a long way toward eliminating Lessing's famous nineteenth-century aesthetic worries about the negative effect of having someone scream on stage—that this sign of physical pain would offend the ears and eyes of the audience and arouse only pity or compassion.[44] But that may be the whole point, as chapter 3 will argue. Through the aural and visible staged manifestations of his physical pain and psychological suffering, the character of Amfortas, in Wagner's *Parsifal*, has to arouse precisely such compassion (and the word for compassion in German, *Mitleid*, literally and significantly means "with suffering")—both in his redeemer, Parsifal, and in the audience.

Bodies, however, are unavoidably gendered, and with gender enters sex: in opera, in fact, questions of gender turn out to be inseparable from representations of not only love and desire but also "sexuality," that shorthand term for the social organization of sexual relations. This is why gender is more complicated in opera than Clément and others have suggested. It is only relatively recently that sexuality has come to be thought of as an important part of our understanding of the dynamics between the individual and the social, both in the present and in the past, and especially where moral judgments are concerned.[45] At the point where we begin, in the nineteenth century, it has been argued that there was a major shift in how people in the West thought about sex and sexuality: Lawrence Kramer writes, "What had been physical became biological; what had been moral became physiological."[46] This was a shift to a medicalized focus on sexuality as potentially pathological or aberrant, and certainly in need of regulation. Because sexuality cannot be separated from desire—in theory or in practice—one of the consequences of this new psychobiological model was that sexual identity and desire became basic to how people thought of themselves as human. This complicated immensely that connection between disease (or pathology) and any aspects of sexuality that fell outside the narrow confines of nineteenth-century bourgeois societal norms.

Given the obvious importance of desire and death to opera plots, then, this book is a study of the operatic representations of disease in conjunction with sexuality and its increasing medicalization over the past two centuries. Such a focus offers a way to look at the historically different ways people have constructed notions of themselves and their societies, in part through the prevailing concepts of love and death, but also through those of disease and health — social as well as individual.[47] We were curious because there are no major operas we know of about yellow fever, typhus, or influenza; there seems to be little sung on stage about diphtheria or polio or cancer. When so many women died of childbirth in earlier years, why did this so rarely make it onto the stage? Debussy's Mélisande in *Pelléas et Mélisande* seems one of the few even to give birth, and her death as presented in the opera could well be the result more of her love than of childbirth. Wagner's Sieglinde dies offstage somewhere between *Die Walküre* and *Siegfried* (in *Der Ring des Nibelungen*), but we are hard pressed to think of others.

For a disease to appear as a significant thematic element or plot device in opera, it seems that it must have strong cultural associations beyond its medical meaning and physical signs. The cultural clichés it has to draw on seem all to involve desire — that much discussed but vaguely defined term in cultural theory today.[48] On the opera stage, however, desire (especially if linked to suffering and disease) always means specifically sexual desire, perhaps because that is a time-tested way "to score a direct hit at the spectator's sensibility."[49] But it almost always also means sexual anxiety. And so we find syphilis, not surprisingly, but also cholera and tuberculosis. Such a linking of sexuality and disease goes far back in Western culture, of course. *Oedipus the King* is the story of parricide, but also of incest and the resultant plague. As we shall see in the epilogue as well, "plague" is a word newly revived in discussions of AIDS. It is emotionally charged, for good historical reasons. Unlike a word like "epidemic," "plague" (be it in literature or in historical accounts) has always connoted moral blame. The idea of an incurable and devastating illness suddenly attacking an entire society has long been read as a divine scourge, a punishment for godlessness, evil, or sometimes a specific sin. This has always been seen as an affliction with a moral purpose, and so it has been available, from the Bible and before, as a metaphoric domain for matters of sexual transgression.[50]

Framed as it is by the Florentine plague of 1348 that killed over 100,000 people, Boccaccio's *Decameron* articulates forcefully the view that God sent the plague to punish evil ways and cleanse the city of filth. The clinical horrors of this scourge are rehearsed in gruesome detail; so too is its terrifying contagiousness — for this is what drives the seven young women and three men to flee the city for the safer countryside where they would tell their famous stories.[51] No doubt the panic of mass death, the sight of the plague cart passing through the streets hourly, and the physical horrors of the disease itself all made the city a place of personal as well as public terror — as they had done since the Athens of Thucydides and would continue to do through Pepys's London and Camus's Oran.[52] When religious or medical authorities failed to halt a plague, George Deux reports, societies "were tempted in their disillusionment and despair to find cause in the malevolence of men: witches and poisoners who, for whatever reason, were killing them."[53] They often blamed specific people, scapegoating the powerless (the poor, witches, Jews, and so on). Or they sought the phantom poisoner who was believed to be working among them.[54] As we shall see, this conjunction, in one form or another, of sexual worries with some sense of a pestilential divine scourge, scapegoating, and poisoning offers a particular configuration of plague that operatic narratives (like literary ones) have used to powerful ends in operas that vary from Wagner's *Parsifal* to Benjamin Britten/Myfanwy Piper's *Death in Venice*.

As European cultures learned from the Black Death, plagues have emotional and aesthetic power not only because of their moral or sexual associations but also because they are both "a personal affliction and a social calamity."[55] In a sense any disease can be seen as double: "as a *biological event* that infects our bodies and as a *social event* to which a variety of meanings are attached by the choices we make in response to disease."[56] Plagues seem to be dual, in this sense, in a particularly significant way. Though a disease that affects individual people, plague also affects the whole society: rich and poor, evil and good, all can die from it. Social hierarchies are ignored, transgressed, and then abolished; political and religious authority collapses. The physical breakdown of the body becomes the model for the pathological breakdown of the culture.[57] The plague's threat to the community and to the very existence of a communal social life is as terrifying as its power over individual death. It is these parallels between the social and the physical body that give the plague much of its dramatic potential and, as chapter 5 will explore, its metaphoric value in the political arena.

This is the terror of anarchy and social chaos that Stravinsky's opera *Oedipus Rex* (1927) explicitly draws on. The opera relies on the power of the familiar, ancient story and the associations of plague in conjunction with forbidden sexuality to better dramatize its composer's theory of the power of music's form. This is the power of form and order to restrain the imagination—or, in Greek mythic terms (as made popular by Nietzsche), to curb the riot of Dionysus with the control of Apollo. In Stravinsky's words: "Music is given to us to establish an order in things; to order the chaotic and the personal into something perfectly controlled, conscious and capable of lasting vitality."[58] Rejecting what he saw as the easy emotionalism of nineteenth-century psychological music drama but still wanting a plot with power, Stravinsky chose what he called a "universally known tragedy," the Oedipus story, with its focus on plague.[59] He asked Jean Cocteau to provide a French libretto of the Greek play, which he then had translated into Latin— a dead language he felt was devoid of triviality but dense with associations of artifice and control. He inserted a plot-narrating speaker between the audience and the stage action, such as it was: he made his characters stand like living statues in a kind of operatic still life.[60] The music of what he called this "opera-oratorio" was composed to stand aloof from the words and narrative action, not emotionally reinforcing either.

This is, in a way, "opera in a straightjacket."[61] But it is nonetheless a powerful opera, one whose subject—illicit sexuality and plague—represents the chaos to be restrained by that straitjacket. It opens violently, with the chorus and orchestra "attacking the downbeat together in a gesture of panic and despair."[62] The curtain rises on the chorus and Oedipus, both of whom obsessively, ritualistically repeat the word "plague." It appears six times in the first eight lines of the work, always in conjunction with the fate of the city, Thebes. The chorus begins

Caedit nos pestis,	*The* plague *falls on us,*
Theba peste *moritur.*	*Thebes is dying of* plague.
E peste *serva nos*	*From the* plague *preserve us*
qua Theba moritur.	*for Thebes is dying.*
Oedipus, adest pestis;	*Oedipus, the* plague *has come,*
e peste *libera urbem,*	*free our city from* plague,
urbem serva morientem.	*preserve our dying city.*

To this Oedipus responds, "Citizens, I shall free you from the *plague*" ("Liberi, vos liberabo a *peste*"). Throughout the opera, as in the play, the plague is directly linked to moral guilt, to one individual's murder and incest; but it is the city, the suffering society, that must be purged of its stain if the god who has infected it with plague is to be appeased.

George Enescu and Edmond Fleg's opera *Oedipe* (1936) focuses more on Oedipus as a tragic figure, for whom the plague is but the culmination of the horrors to be confronted. But act 3 opens with a funeral procession in the background and loud crowd lamentations about the deaths of the wealthy, the virtuous, the virginal, and the innocent. Three times the chorus begs Oedipus to heed their laments and moans ("nos pleurs et nos gémissements") and to deliver them from what the High Priest calls the plague with the fiery teeth that is devouring the city ("La Peste aux dents de feu dévore ta Cité"). In his tragically ironic innocence, Oedipus calls on the gods to find the cause, the scapegoat, on whom the physical horrors of the plague should be made to fall: "May the Plague, with its rotting teeth, devour his bones" ("Et que la Peste, aux dents de pourriture, dévore ses os"). Incest and parricide, as the opera makes clear, are sexual and social transgressions that carry a heavy price, for societies as well as individuals.

As these operas show, the meanings that have accrued to plague in Western culture go well beyond its medical meanings to include those notions of the attribution of divine wrath and punishment, scapegoating, and the threat of social chaos. As we shall see, all these elements recur in the representations of other diseases that are also made to involve sexuality in some way or other: syphilis, cholera, and most recently, AIDS. Even tuberculosis was dubbed the "white plague." The act of representing these diseases *on stage* in singing bodies is what so forcefully calls up and calls upon such a wealth of cultural associations. Our argument is that the act of paying critical attention to these diseases can bring into focus different aspects of the narrative and the text — and even the music. Details that previously went unnoticed now become significant. New perspectives allow new interpretations of operas.

But it is not only the interpretation of operas that can change. These same cultural concepts of disease work to help frame scientific theories. Sander Gilman and others argue for a two-way communication between culture and medicine.[63] Art creates images of disease based on history, popular belief, and medical science; these images in turn often provide the models for that same science to understand and articulate its own goals. Art's images of the sick, they argue, become images of the disease itself. Repeated representations can work to bring about social and scientific reality. These representations and the complex and dynamic interaction between medical and cultural meanings in European opera in the past two centuries form the core of this book.[64]

Why These Diseases and These Operas?

The chapters that follow are organized around the changing European attitudes toward disease as patterns of mortality and illness have shifted since the time of the bubonic plague — last seen in Europe about 1720. As the swift and massive killing power of plague and other epidemic diseases such as typhus and smallpox declined through the eighteenth century, the consequences of chronic and common endemic diseases became more evident. Thus at the turn of the nineteenth century it was clear that consumption was now the cause of death for 25 percent of the population in most European nations. Although not as significant by this time as a cause of mortality, syphilis had a greater social weight because it was openly associated with sexual transgression. Throughout the nineteenth century there was a stabilization of death rates, an increase in life expectancy, and a decrease in general worry about the fragility of life.[65] This new sense of security was interrupted by the arrival of cholera in Europe in 1832, when all those social and cultural associations of plague from earlier centuries resurfaced with the terror of a disease that William McNeill calls "both uniquely dreadful in itself and unparalleled in recent European experience."[66]

Over the nineteenth century, however, modern medical science defined and found the causes of tuberculosis, syphilis, and even cholera. In the twentieth century all have been brought under some measure of control in the West, at least, though the reasons have not been at all clear. It has likely been because of some combination of changes — new pharmaceutical discoveries, public health measures, alterations of diet, increased sex education. So from the age of pestilence through an age of receding pandemics, Europe and North America have moved into a new age of longer life spans when human-created and degenerative diseases predominate.[67] Cancers and cardiovascular disease are the new causes of death that have come with the more affluent lifestyles brought by economic and social development.[68] As the health effects of long-standing social habits (such as tobacco and alcohol consumption) became clearer, the habits themselves took on new meanings. With the appearance of AIDS in the early 1980s, however, has come the terror of an unknown and deadly disease, and the responses have been all too familiar: as the epilogue will show, in the social reactions to it as much as in its medical implications, AIDS recapitulates much of the history of infectious diseases in the West.

This, then, is the medical but also, inescapably, the social framework of this book. The diseases that are represented in opera — tuberculosis, syphilis, cholera — do not get there by accident, and they have been represented by European and North American society in ways that are particularly powerful in their conjunction of sexuality and death. Why? As Gilman has argued, "the social reality of disease is constructed on the basis of specific ideological needs and structured along the categories of representation accepted within that ideology."[69] If we are to understand the precise ideological needs of Western society in the nineteenth and twentieth centuries, however, we cannot ignore the history of its earlier representations of disease. For instance, the impact of the Black Death, with its combination of high mortality and sudden death, must be investigated because in many ways it provided the first and most lasting cultural and social model. One of the reasons was its devastating scale, of course: estimates of the number of dead at the time of the plague ranged as high as 31 percent of the population in the four years from to 1347 to 1351.[70] The recorded history of the bubonic plague may have begun in the fourteenth century, but evidence of sporadic local epidemics continued to be collected for four hundred years. As the Oedipus story shows, these plague times had earlier ones to draw on, and all in turn left their legacy in the association of human catastrophe with divine retribution, as well as in the selecting of certain individuals to bear the guilt. Another important inheritance of the plague years was a reminder not only of the general transience of life but of the specific fragility of the social order. Rupturing social ties and disrupting political hierarchies, the Black Death in Europe also undermined confidence in both personal relations and social institutions.[71] Since plagues have always forced fundamental questions about social values, about the individual's rights and responsibilities, it is not at all strange that powerful allusions to them would continue to recur in opera, as in literature, for centuries to come. But they did not recur only as metaphors or even as reminders of the power of disease in the larger social realm; they provided the very model according to which other diseases would be represented.

The nineteenth century saw not only a decline in the death rate from this kind of devastating epidemic disease but also the rise of what we have been referring to as "modern" clinical medicine. Up to this time the understanding of the body and its illnesses had been dominated by concepts generated by Hippocrates and Galen. The complex theory of humors described an individual's composition, his or her requirements for "balance" or "harmony," and the predispositions to illness each might face. Galenic thought and theory changed slowly with empirical evidence of their limitations or inaccuracies: concerning anatomy, with Vesalius in the sixteenth century, and in the early days of physiology, with Harvey's description of the circulation of the blood in his De *motu cordis* of 1628. In the eighteenth century this line of thought yielded the pathology studies of Morgagni that firmly established the anatomical basis of disease. Bringing together this knowledge of pathological change in the anatomical structure of an organ and the clinical signs of an illness formed what we now recognize as the modern clinical paradigm. It was most clearly seen in the methods and studies of the Parisian school of anatomical diagnosis, of which Corvisart and his students Laënnec and Bayle are perhaps the best known: "With these men the mere symptomatic method of describing and classifying a disease came to an end. A disease for Corvisart, and especially for Laënnec, is a situation in which the patient's condition is the result of pathologic alteration in structure, and it is the duty of the physician to elicit the objective signs of these pathologic changes in order that he may diagnose the disease, the postmortem pathology of which must agree with standards previously laid down."[72] It was in the following years that syphilis and tuberculosis gradually came to be understood as single biological entities.

Then as now, health and disease were general social concerns, not only medical ones. As Charles E. Rosenberg writes, "The discovery of the causes of cholera, tuberculosis, typhoid, and diphtheria were not esoteric events isolated in the pages of technical journals, but front-page news."[73] The chapters to follow will show that such news also made it into the art forms of the day, including the operas. As we learned while working on this book, the disease most commonly associated with opera in people's minds is tuberculosis. As a disease that affects the lungs, and thus involves (literally and metaphorically) both inspiration and expiration, it is also perhaps the archetypal operatic disease. But as chapter 2 explores, between *La Traviata* (by Giuseppe Verdi/Francesco Maria Piave), which premiered in 1853, and the 1896 opening of *La Bohème* (by Giacomo Puccini/Luigi Illica and Giuseppe Giacosa) came the medical discovery of the tubercle bacillus by Robert Koch in 1882, and with it the knowledge that tuberculosis was a matter not of heredity, but of contagion. We know today that tuberculosis is and always has been a "classic social disease"—an infectious illness transmitted from person to person.[74] Although Verdi could not have known that, Puccini could and very likely did. The two operas—like the Antonia story in *Les Contes d'Hoffmann* (1881)—reveal the continuing strength of the cultural stereotypes of the tubercular woman as desired, desiring, and desirable (so well documented by, among others, Susan Sontag in *Illness as Metaphor*).[75] But as we shall show, there are also significant if subtle changes in the meaning given to the febrile sexuality and pale beauty of the suffering heroine, as the knowledge of the infectious nature of the disease became widespread. The social difference — from the bourgeois world of the courtesan Violetta Valéry to the bohemian demimonde of the working woman Mimì — marks the changing awareness of the role of urban poverty and overcrowding in the spread of tuberculosis.

Both Italian operas are derived from French novels and plays of the mid-nineteenth century, a time when millions of people were dying from this disease.[76] The other worry, not to say obsession, of European society in these same years was syphilis: if it was talked about less (or less openly), it was because it was a secret disease, rendered shameful in a bourgeois world because of its moral implications and its known source of contagion: sex. In opera women, marked by their sexuality and beauty, may suffer from tuberculosis, but it is men who suffer from this secret disease. It is always seen as the direct consequence of their sexual transgression, their sin, and it is usually read as the sign of some moral failing, though the woman who infects them (but somehow never seems to suffer from the illness) must also be punished.[77] The history of syphilis in Europe from 1495 on has been a history of Christian interpretations of this disease based on the earlier plague model: as a divine scourge, but this time specifically against the sexually sinful.

In chapter 3 we revisit, in the light of precisely this history, the dominant and oddly persistent Christian interpretations of Wagner's *Parsifal* (1882) in order to offer a new way of reading Amfortas's shameful wound, received in a moment of sexual surrender: a wound that will not heal and that causes severe night pain, preventing Amfortas from carrying out his social and moral duty as leader of the Grail realm. Such an interpretation offers a way to explain why Kundry — consistently presented in the nineteenth-century cultural vocabulary of the syphilitic prostitute — must die at the end when Parsifal restores moral and social order. Placing the long composing time of *Parsifal* in a broader cultural and historical context, we noticed that it was Philippe Ricord's work in Paris in the 1830s — the same years when Wagner conceived the opera, while living in Paris — that led to the first clear understanding of the clinical manifestations of syphilis. The "syphilophobia" of the nineteenth century and of *Parsifal* was firmly rooted in general knowledge of the disease's mode of transmission as well as its consequences. Ricord himself felt that this disease "marked the transition from communal to individual patterns of contagion, with an impact as shattering in the domain of popular and medical consciousness as that of the French Revolution in political affairs."[78]

Chapter 4 continues the study of the drama of syphilis into the twentieth century. The two world wars (and the need for healthy troops) exacerbated the general fear of the debilitating consequences of infection. The guilty, the ones who spread the disease, were again deemed to be prostitutes—as in Alban Berg's opera *Lulu* (unfinished when he died in 1937). By the last act Lulu, now a London prostitute, has infected her husband, Alwa. In the twentieth century, research also proved conclusively that one of the common manifestations of tertiary syphilis was insanity. So when Igor Stravinsky and W. H. Auden, with Chester Kallman, worked together in the late 1940s to transpose William Hogarth's eighteenth-century set of paintings "The Rake's Progress" onto the operatic stage, despite their major plot additions, the "progress" of the rake from brothel to Bedlam is one that audiences would recognize as sadly familiar thanks to urgent public health warnings, in the United States in particular. With the discovery and then widespread dissemination of penicillin to treat the disease by the 1950s, syphilis suddenly became much less threatening; it could become a source of humor in Leonard Bernstein's *Candide* (1956), though even then it never lost its time-honored association with sexual transgression.

The disturbing arrival of cholera in Europe in the 1830s—reviving the fears of both sudden death and social anarchy inherited from the plague years—was not represented in opera until the next century. Chapter 5 explores how that appearance once again brought together sexuality and disease; but this time the sexuality in question was specifically between members of the same sex: Geschwitz and Lulu in Berg's *Lulu* and Aschenbach's love for the boy Tadzio in Benjamin Britten/Myfanwy Piper's *Death in Venice* (1974). In Greek myth, it has been argued, plagues were seen to disrupt all cultural and natural activities.[79] Here that notion of disruption is framed by an awareness of the increasing medicalization of homosexuality (as pathological) in the nineteenth and early twenti-eth centuries. The opera based on Thomas Mann's novella *Der Tod in Venedig* is structured on that opposition between control and abandon (or Apollonian and Dionysian impulses) that has been so important in Greek culture but also in Western culture at large. It is no accident that Stravinsky's *Oedipus Rex* also embodies this opposition, in direct associa-tion with the plague. But *Death in Venice* also draws on other aspects of the plague model of the representation of disease. It brings to the fore no-tions of social or moral order and chaos in openly linking homosexuality and cholera in a new but historically resonant way. The nineteenth-century growth of the medicalized discourses about sexuality and the movement to control sexual conduct through education, social mores, and legislation have been directly connected to the discussions about sexual immorality that grew up around the cholera epidemics, and the new surveillance of private life they allowed. When public health offi-cials visited the homes of the poor who were dying in large numbers from the disease, they discovered not only appalling sanitary conditions but severe overcrowding that led to sexual mores shocking to the bour-geoisie of Europe and North America. Along with the easily invoked plague model, the associations with syphilis as the scourge of God against the sexually sinful were called into service, but this time with a decided *class* bias as well.[80] The increasing powers of surveillance in the name of public health are another legacy of the nineteenth-century cholera epidemics, one that has raised new worries in the era of AIDS.

Despite a rich history of cultural construction to draw on, there are still obvious problems in putting cholera on the stage. Death from this disease is not pretty; it is hard to romanticize or eroticize death by diar-rhea and vomiting. But as with plague, any allusion to cholera, be it meta-phoric or clinical, can be an effective way to dramatize a character's sense of disintegration—both moral and physical. In Aschenbach's case in *Death in Venice* that dissolution is represented as a conscious but re-sisted violation of the bourgeois standards according to which he had always lived. Mann used the metaphorical linking of homosexuality and contagion in other stories as well. Harry Somers and Rod Ander-son's 1992 opera of *Mario and the Magician* moves from the realm of real infectious disease to the metaphorical spaces of what is called "acoustic contagion" but makes the connection between the spreading of fascism by powerful oratory and the model of contagious disease and its effect on both the society and the individual. The image of the "body politic" and its health has a long history.

As we mentioned earlier, with the scientific discovery of the microbiological causes of cholera, tuberculosis, and syphilis came greater understanding of the personal and social conditions of the spread of such diseases. Public health surveillance and pharmaceutical advances were among the reasons for the new sense that certain diseases, at least, were now under control. As deaths from these causes decreased, however, cancer and cardiovascular disease showed up as the new killers. With this knowledge came a change in attitudes regarding what we call "lifestyle" habits, such as smoking, that medical research connected directly to these new problems. From its first importation into Europe in the late fifteenth century and its diffusion into common social use in the sixteenth, tobacco has had a consistent history of being represented in a dual, even contradictory, fashion: as both curative and harmful, both relaxing and stimulating, both pleasurable and dangerous. Chapter 6 investigates the changing representations of smoking in opera, changes that cannot help conditioning how a director today chooses to put certain operas on the stage. For example, can one still rely in quite the same way on the associations of smoking with male bonding and friendship that could be drawn on in the 1910 premiere of *La Fanciulla del West* (by Puccini/Civinini and Zangarini)? Even that opera, of course, makes use of the doubleness of smoking's cultural associations: in opposition to the relaxing gold miners in Minni's saloon in act 1 stands the solitary smoker, the dangerous outsider, Jack Rance.

In operas like Ermanno Wolf-Ferrari/Enrico Golisciani's *Il segreto di Susanna* and, most obviously, Georges Bizet/Henry Meilhac and Ludovic Halévy's *Carmen*, it is not men but women who are associated with smoking, and therefore not only with (by now) familiar things like sexuality and desire but also with perhaps less familiar things like violence. *Carmen* is very much a late nineteenth-century *French* opera, deliberately framing sexual passion in Spanish smoke and smoking: it opens outside the favorite three-star attraction of (male) French tourists — the infamous cigar factory in Seville. Today, of course, smoking connotes different things: social unacceptability and the danger of disease. But in Bizet's time, especially when associated with gypsy women and Spain, its meanings were predominantly sexual and exotic but also dangerous, at least for women.

In the light of these various representations of disease in opera, our final chapter will look at the meanings that are being formed today — as we watch — around a new disease, terrifying in its fatality and incurability. AIDS has not yet made it onto the conventional operatic stage, but we think it is simply a matter of time: plays, musicals, films, and performance pieces on the subject have all appeared, and many of them are "operatic" in spirit. To use Herbert Lindenberger's terms, they show the same "verbal extravagance, an indifference or hostility to mimesis of the external world, and a tendency to the histrionic."[81] Although millions of heterosexuals are infected with this disease in Africa, Asia, and South America, not to mention intravenous drug users, their partners, hemophiliacs, and many others in Europe and North America as well, it is because of the importance of opera to gay culture that we suspect it is from there that the operas about AIDS will come: think of how Tom Hanks, in his role as a person living with AIDS, responds to Maria Callas singing in the film *Philadelphia*.

There is, however, a struggle going on today before our eyes (and ears) for the control of the cultural meanings assigned to AIDS. Knowingly, self-consciously, deliberately, and with wit and daring, artists from within the gay community — one of the groups (though not the only one) most "at risk" for this disease in the West — are contesting the dominant social construction of AIDS in the media and mainstream culture, a construction that can be described as a sum of all the representations of disease ever offered in opera, from the plague to tuberculosis, from sexually transmitted syphilis to contagious cholera. Gilman has argued that it is the internalization of such social constructions that gives them their power.[82] And it is precisely this process of internalization that is being challenged, from *within* the male homosexual AIDS context: in plays like Tony Kushner's *Angels in America*, among many others, there is a conscious rejection of the images of both the dangerous carrier (who must be under medical surveillance) and the victim of God's anger. To take on the many myths that have arisen around AIDS — again, myths that often have a long history of association with other diseases — what could be called a conscious "countermythology" is being developed in the works for the stage written from within the gay community, and this is the topic of our epilogue.

What makes the social construction of AIDS different from that of other diseases is its rapidity, its early politicization, and its self-consciousness. Thanks to our current awareness of the impact of advertising, television, and film images, everyone knows that the stakes are high; the power of giving meaning to a disease and the person who has it is a very important one to wield. AIDS has brought to the fore and forced into the arena of public debate the same issues that earlier diseases raised, but it has done this much more quickly and with the even stronger pressures that come from the push to find a cure (through medical science) and the fear of control (through social regulation). In the late twentieth-century cultural response to a new life-threatening infectious disease of possibly epidemic proportions, the search for explanatory models from the past is understandable, to be sure, but also decidedly suspect.[83] Rosenberg notes that as a disease "that combines sexual transmission with a terrifyingly high mortality, AIDS was bound to attract extraordinary social concern."[84] When it first comes to the operatic stage, however, it will likely look more familiar than we think, but a little (read important, countermythological) bit different. Its way has been prepared.

Chapter 2

Famous Last Breaths:
The Tubercular
Heroine

Believe me that I felt for her a sombre elegiac attachment, which, without her knowing it, put me in the vein of poetry and music. — Franz
Liszt, letter to Marie d'Agoult on the death of Marie Duplessis, the model
for the consumptive heroine of *La Dame aux camélias* and *La Traviata*

In the popular imagination tuberculosis has a range of historical associations that includes everything from romantic poets to romantic lovers.
Given her status as a virtual cultural cliché, it is hard to believe that the
consumptive heroine of opera had, to our knowledge, very few important
nineteenth-century models: the best known are Antonia (in *Les Contes
d'Hoffmann* by Jacques Offenbach/Jules Barbier), Violetta Valéry (in *La Traviata* by Giuseppe Verdi/Francesco Maria Piave), and Mimì (in *La Bohéme* by
Giacomo Puccini/Giuseppe Giacosa-Luigi Illica). But such is the considerable power of these gendered representations of disease and death. The
rekindled interest in tuberculosis in the West today — as seen in the media's increased reporting of its reappearance — is the result of both new
concerns and old ones. This disease, which many people in Europe and
North America assumed had disappeared, has continued to be responsible
for the death of no fewer than three million people a year throughout the
world. But whatever our (mistaken) beliefs before this new attention to
tuberculosis, it would be no exaggeration to say that a century ago it was
a major medical — and cultural — obsession, not unlike AIDS in our present
world. The representations of tuberculosis therefore might well, by analogy, help us understand how the scientific realities of medicine and aesthetic representations work together to construct meanings — in this case
gendered meanings — within a specific historical context.

There wasn't always general agreement about the existence of some-thing called "tuberculosis," of course. Until the end of the nineteenth century it would more commonly have been known as "consumption" or "phthisis." The term with the longest history is phthisis: in ancient times, it was part of a classification of diseases linked to emaciation. Consumption is a later term, also describing illnesses with weight loss. Both terms gradually became specifically associated with pulmonary dis-ease. The dawn of the nineteenth century saw both increasing mortality from this disease and, as noted in chapter 1, the beginnings of what we have been calling modern medicine—in the form of clinical description along with pathologic anatomy. Working in Paris in the early years of the century, Gaspar Laurent Bayle brought together patients' histories and physical findings with the postmortem anatomic abnormalities and thereby set the foundations for the study of phthisis. It remained for René-Théophile-Hyacinthe Laënnec to take such clinical-pathological correlations and hypothesize from them a unitary model of the disease: phthisis now could be considered as a single disease with different man-ifestations. It was seen as systemic in nature, able to involve the entire body, but the most important organs affected were the lungs.[1] One sig-nificant result was to make consumption into an "entity"—a disease process that could be identified, classified, and studied. Another effect was that individuals could now suffer *from* something and be seen as its "victims."

Diagnosis Despite Mystery: Antonia

Antonia—the young heroine of one of the tales in the opera *Les Contes d'Hoffmann* (1881)—is doomed precisely because she is a "victim" of this disease, even if it is not named as such in either the original literary text or the opera libretto. She is also a singer and therefore offers a kind of ideal model for the *operatically* ill. The source text, a story called "Rat Kres-pel" by E. T. A. Hoffmann, describes her as young, beautiful, mysteri-ously unwell—and therefore very attractive. She has a pale face, rose-red lips, and cheeks that flush at certain times. Her voice is said to be unique and is described in metaphors of the breath of an aeolian harp and the warbling of a nightingale. More ominously, we are also told it seems impossible that the human breast could ever have room to contain such a voice.[2]

Her father, Krespel, notices that when she sings a red flush appears on her pale cheeks (in the German text, "auf den blassen Wangen") as two dark red blotches ("zwei dunkelrote Flecke") (81). He immediately makes a connection with the physical appearance of the girl's late mother, also a famous opera singer. The family likeness here is presented in terms of disease, and the doctor to whom Krespel has told this concurs: Antonie (as her name appears in the German text) appears to suffer from some organic defect in her chest and will die within six months if she continues to sing. This defect, however, is precisely what gives her voice its wonderful power and strange, unearthly tone. In an attempt to save his daughter, Krespel demands that she stop singing, break off her engagement to a promising young composer, and live a simple, sheltered life alone with him. One night Krespel has a dream in which the former fiancé is playing the piano and Antonie is singing, first quietly and then rising to a shattering fortissimo. He then has a vision of Antonie and her beloved in each other's arms. On awakening he finds his daughter dead, with a blissful expression on her face.

The conjunction of desire, disease, and death in a story about singing is what likely made this an attractive subject for opera. The adaptation of this and two other Hoffmann stories in the form of a play (*Les Contes fantastiques d'Hoffmann*) in 1851 by Jules Barbier and Michel Carré had been a great success. Offenbach had conducted the stage music for it and had shown interest in it as the subject for an operetta.[3] In fact the play became the basis of Barbier's later libretto for Offenbach's final (and unfinished) work, *Les Contes d'Hoffmann*. Both play and opera present Hoffmann himself as the protagonist and thus as the linking thread of the three love stories in three acts that (in one popular ordering, at least) culminate in the tale of another artist figure, Antonia.[4]

In the libretto this particular act opens with Antonia accompanying herself and singing what has been described as the only sad song Offenbach ever wrote.[5] She then collapses, exhausted. Her father (in the French of the operatic text spelled Crespel) rushes in to beg her to stop—as she had promised him she would—because her voice reminds him too painfully of her dead mother, the famous singer. In a "restored" version of the libretto, he openly tells her that she has inherited her mother's fatal chest condition and risks her fate should she continue to sing.[6] Driven by a father's "jealous tenderness," he begs her, if she loves him, never to sing again. Antonia resists momentarily, complaining that he is asking her to give up all her dreams, dreams that he himself had fostered. But she finally gives in. When she leaves the room, Crespel remarks again on the frightening family resemblance, for in the daughter he sees the mother's symptoms as well as her talent: specifically that "feverish coloring" that announced her death by making her even more beautiful than before: "Il me semble toujours voir monter à sa joue cette coloration fiévreuse qui annonçait la mort de sa mère en la rendant plus belle." He explicitly says that six months of life as an artist would kill her, so he has hidden her away from her musical fiancé, represented in the opera version by Hoffmann himself.

Hoffmann's secret reunion with his beloved Antonia is the scene for his own announcement that he is a little jealous of her love of music: "La musique m'inspire un peu de jalousie; tu l'aime trop!" The repetition of the paternal note of jealousy over her music is curious, if not yet ominous. Much less ambiguous is the song of love they then sing, part of which speaks of the rose greeting the spring with a smile, if only for a brief time: "Las! Combien de temps vivra-t-elle?" ("How much more time will it have to live?") In the French the feminine pronoun "elle" means "it" and refers to "la rose," but of course it cannot help suggesting "elle" as "she" who also may not have much time left. Hoffmann's subsequent address to Antonia as the flower of his soul ("fleur de l'âme") is thus foreboding, and indeed, at the end of the song Antonia raises her hand to her heart and seems about to collapse. Hoffmann's worried question about the cause of her suffering elicits no helpful reply. Of what does she suffer? Her denial — "Non, ce n'est rien" — does not undo her father's opening warning about the conjunction of singing, illness, and death.

The demonic Dr. Miracle enters the opera shortly after this scene. He informs Crespel that despite his attempts to keep his daughter's presence secret, the doctor knows that Antonia is present and that she is ill, re-

1. The demonic Dr. Miracle
(Christopher Coyea) in the 1988 production
of *Les Contes d'Hoffmann* by the Canadian
Opera Company.

minding the father of the dire presage of how her cheeks flush when the "demon of music" possesses her: "Ces taches roses de fâcheux augure, qui montaient aux joues d'Antonia toutes les fois que le démon de la musique s'emparait d'elle." Crespel responds with a despairing acknowledgment of the truth of his observation. By quasi-magical means, Miracle then displays his unearthly talent by showing he knows a lot about the hidden Antonia: that she is twenty years old, in the spring of her life, as he puts it, but that her pulse is uneven and fast — a bad sign ("mauvais symptôme!"). And when she sings, he says, her eyes glitter and she brings her hand to her agitated heart.

Having overheard this ominous conversation, Hoffmann then adds his voice to her father's, begging Antonia never to sing again. She agrees out of love for him. Dr. Miracle then appears, after her fiancé leaves, and whispers in her ear admonitions about the sacrifice she is about to make, giving up beauty and talent — her sacred gift — and allowing them to be buried in a bourgeois marriage. He persuades her to sing again by magically making the painting of her dead mother come to life and sing. This dramatic scene is one of steadily increasing tension that ends with Antonia gasping for breath but giving in to the transport of song, in full knowledge of its deadly consequences. The scene ends with her death in her father's arms and Hoffmann's cry of despair.[7]

The changes from the source text are many, but the original story, the play, and the opera share the representation of Antonia as a beautiful young woman suffering from some mysterious illness that is connected with her chest and thus with her singing — which in turn is connected with love, both familial and sexual.[8] But what could this mysterious disease be? In the nineteenth century it might have been difficult to tell with precision — medically, that is, if not culturally. But today what a physician would call the "differential diagnosis" might include such widely varying entities as functional illness,[9] hysteria,[10] cardiac disease,[11] or tuberculosis. That Antonia brings her hand to her heart would not necessarily have meant — in the last century — that it was specifically her *heart* that caused the pain or discomfort. The understanding of (and therefore differentiation between) cardiac and pulmonary diseases happened slowly over the course of the nineteenth century. In fact, in the middle

2. Antonia (Kathleen Brett), singing
just before her death, in the 1988 production
of *Les Contes d'Hoffmann* by the Canadian
Opera Company.

of the century Austrian and German physiologists were asserting that tuberculosis was due to "the failure of small weak hearts to circulate the blood forcefully enough to prevent the deposit of tubercles."[12] But even more important is that the major cultural—and medical—association with that clinical sign of red cheeks at this time would have been consumption. In Thomas Bartlett's 1855 book on the disease, for instance, we find: "As evening approaches, there comes on each cheek a red flush, which is accurately defined, the surrounding skin being of an ashy paleness, the more remarkable for its close propinquity to a heightened colour: this is the hectic flush."[13]

The "Phthisic Beauty" and the Tubercle Bacillus

In the short story Antonie, of course, is described as being pale, as well as having red cheeks. Consumption has a long history of being understood as "a disease of extreme contrasts: white pallor and red flush."[14] In addition, in the opera the emphasis is on Antonia's inheriting her fatal chest complaint from her mother.[15] In the nineteenth century heredity was certainly considered an important factor in the predisposition to consumption.[16] The disease was therefore seen as having social dimensions, first of all within the family. In the words of Thomas Bartlett, once again, "When . . . it is remembered that, passing with the blood from parent to child, it is transmitted from generation to generation, it must in truth be considered as a disorder of appalling importance."[17] In addition, of course, Antonia's youth is itself a sign of her possible consumptive condition. Bartlett describes the typical tubercular as a "delicate young lady": "Even in the bloom of her young beauty does she waste away." That the disease should be associated with love (and even called *tuberculosis amatoria*) is therefore not surprising: the age of first love becomes also the age of death.[18]

To her youth, her consumptive appearance, and her family history must be added that Antonia is presented as an artist, a singer of great talent. Our first glimpse of her is as she sings a tellingly sensitive song of longing and love. Interpretations that see a conflict between art and love in Antonia's life do not explain why in the beginning Antonia herself sees no conflict: it is her lover and her father who establish the separation and forbid her to sing. What she sees as unnatural—like forbidding birds to sing—they see as lifesaving, as keeping her from an early death like her mother's. In the nineteenth century it was also commonly believed that those "in whom the hereditary tendency is apt to betray itself, are those characterized by refinement of feeling, and delicacy of sentiment."[19] The cultural association of the artist and the genius with this particular disease is familiar. Among the well-known tubercular artists were John Keats, Percy Bysshe Shelley, the Brontë family, Friedrich Schiller, Carl Maria von Weber, Frederic Chopin—the list could go on and on. Although this relationship between consumption and artistic genius has been questioned in the twentieth century, it was widely held that "mental activity is greatly stimulated by certain substances, designated as toxins, produced by the infecting organism."[20] Thus to focus on Antonia as a singer, as the story does, is to point to yet another sign of consumption.

Siegfried Kracauer claimed that Offenbach felt a particular affinity for this tale, one of the three stories in the work he hoped would change public evaluation of him as only a composer of light operetta: "He was deeply affected by the story of Antonia, who, if she sang, was bound to die."[21] Given his own long-standing bad cough and his appearance at this time—"like a transparent, pale sadly smiling ghost"—Offenbach may well have suffered from tuberculosis himself.[22] However, he had even more reason for being attracted to this story of a father and a condemned child. His musically talented (and only) young son, Auguste, to whom *Les Contes d'Hoffmann* is dedicated, suffered from consumption and in fact died from it in 1883, two years after his father's death.[23]

Even without this biographical context, the sum of Antonia's pale skin, red cheeks, and shining eyes, her youthful death, her inherited debility, her talent and sensitivity, and her love would most likely suggest to a nineteenth-century opera audience a diagnosis of tuberculosis, however mysterious or nonspecific the disease may appear in the operatic and literary texts themselves.[24] As we noted in chapter 1, tuberculosis is perhaps the perfect operatic disease: it involves the breath—as both inspiration and expiration, as both site of song and locus of disease. Antonia's younger and older operatic sisters are those even more often cited consumptive heroines, Mimì and Violetta. *La Bohème* premiered in 1896, *La Traviata* in 1853. Both, however, are based on tremendously successful French plays and novels of the midcentury. Unlike *Les Contes d'Hoffmann*, both are operas about *overtly* tubercular women whose living, loving, and dying are inseparable not only from their disease but from their sexuality.

An 1853 medical text on consumption put this connection most vividly: "Of all vices, however, none are so apt to lead on to consumption as the unnatural or unrestrained indulgence of the sensual passions."[25] Though one was thought to inherit a predisposition to the disease (called "consumptive diathesis"), it could be brought out under certain conditions. In 1861 Dr. James Copland outlined fourteen causes of consumption, most of which were "moral inferences drawn from the belief that tubercular illnesses were culpable deviations from a normal moral, healthy state."[26] Among the fourteen were many features that became part of the "code" or meaning of the disease itself: nostalgia, disappointed hopes and affections, depressing mental emotions, and premature or excessive sexual indulgence.

It was not only as a possible cause of tuberculosis, however, that the erotic dimension entered both the medical and aesthetic pictures. As Susan Sontag pointed out in her study *Illness as Metaphor*, "TB was — still is — thought to produce spells of euphoria, increased appetite, exacerbated sexual desire. . . . Having TB was imagined to be an aphrodisiac, and to confer extraordinary powers of seduction."[27] These powers had a lot to do with the erotic appeal of what was called "phthisic beauty" by the French and Germans: extreme thinness, long neck and hands, shining eyes, pale skin, and red cheeks. Although this describes Antonia and Mimì, its first and perhaps most famous operatic embodiment was Violetta Valéry, and indeed the Italian expression "tipo Traviata" came to be a code word for the tubercular beauty. This physical type became not only fashionable but sexy. This romanticization (and sensationalization) is, we must remember, that of a disease that was the single most common cause of death at the time, that was found in 40 percent of autopsies in Paris in the early part of the century, that afflicted almost 100 percent of the children examined in a workhouse in Kent in 1844.[28] When a society does not understand — and cannot control — a disease, ground seems to open up for mythologizing and mystifying it. The need to attribute positive values to it is perhaps more than understandable in this context.[29]

As Sontag noted, "Like all really successful metaphors, the metaphor of TB was rich enough to provide for two contradictory applications." She then specifies, "It was both a way of describing sensuality and promoting the claims of passion and a way of describing repression . . . and a suffusion of higher feelings."[30] The febrile sexual intensity of Violetta in act 1 and the more spiritualized wasting away of Mimì (and Violetta in act 3) represent these two extremes as vividly as their pale skin and flushed cheeks point to their shared disease. The romanticizing of consumption as somehow transcending the physicality of the disease can be seen in Charles Dickens's description of the "dread disease, in which the struggle between soul and body is so gradual, quiet, and solemn, and the result so sure, that day by day, and grain by grain, the mortal part wastes and withers away, so that the spirit grows light and sanguine with its lightening load."[31]

What separates *La Traviata* (and *Les Contes d'Hoffmann*) from *La Bohème* is Robert Koch's famous lecture on 24 March 1882 announcing the discovery of *Mycobacterium tuberculosis* — the cause of the illness.[32] With this new knowledge came the confirmation of earlier medical theories that this was an infectious disease, passed from person to person. We know that the new awareness of this discovery produced "a phenomenal sensation among the lay public and in medical circles."[33] Koch's discovery in Berlin quickly became big news around the world, thanks not only to medical discussions but also to popular press coverage. Both the English medical journal *Lancet* and the *London Times* carried descriptions of Koch's announcement a month later, on 22 April. The *New York Times* covered it on 3 May.[34] By 1883 a British report could refer to the "now famous research of Koch."[35] The concept of the infectious nature of tuberculosis was reinforced by Koch's announcement in August 1890 of a possible treatment ("tuberculin"). A contemporary described the effect of this news: "Medical men are flocking to Berlin from all parts of Europe; at the present about 1,500 have arrived, and it will easily be believed that consumptive patients of all classes clamour for treatment."[36] In fact, within a year 2,172 patients had been treated, as thousands flocked to Berlin hoping to be cured. (Unfortunately this did not prove to be an effective intervention; that came only with the discovery of streptomycin in 1943 and its use to treat tuberculosis after 1946, and then the development of para-aminosalicylic acid (PAS), isoniazid (INH), and rifampin shortly after that.)

In Italy too, the years from the discovery of the bacillus through the tuberculin excitement were marked by much scientific and popular attention focused on tuberculosis.[37] Italy was not the center of research in the field at this time, according to one theory, because the political turmoil around national unification "rendered discussions impossible, obstructed the life of the universities and arrested for a definite period the progress of scientific research."[38] This did not prevent Koch's work from being translated quickly and influencing Italian research to the point that it too was soon considered part of the scientific "patrimony" of the nation.[39] This intense interest was due to the large number of cases of tuberculosis, especially in the northern urban, industralized areas. We know that newspapers in these cities published medical statistics at the time. This practice not only offers researchers today some valuable information about causes of death but also reflects the kind and amount of public discussion generated by the prevalence of this disease at the time and place *La Bohème* was conceived and produced.[40]

The Consumptive Model: The "Tipo Traviata"

Like *Les Contes d'Hoffmann*, however, *La Traviata* was written on the other side of that medical fault line, before Koch's discovery. As we mentioned earlier, at this time a predisposition, often hereditary and frequently provoked by certain personal characteristics or living habits (including sexual activity), was believed to cause someone to fall into a consumptive "decline." Precisely these beliefs provide the building blocks of the story of the Verdi/Piave opera. From the opening music's intimations of tragedy onward, *La Traviata* is permeated with the mood of death and what one might call dis-ease as well as a particular disease: "The prelude is a musical picture of the heroine. Eight first and eight second violins portray the frail consumptive."[41] Although the curtain goes up on a party scene, the libretto stresses that the hostess, Violetta, is seen talking to her doctor. First described as a pale, beautiful woman, she is recovering from a long illness and announces to her guests that she now wants to enjoy life fully, for it is fleeting like a flower. Parties will be the drug to kill her pain, she insists. She is introduced to Alfredo Germont, a young man who saw her only once in the street but was so taken with her that he has called every day during her illness. The toast he then sings at her request (the famous "Libiamo ne' lieti calici") is (not surprisingly) a song to love. When Violetta joins in she, in contrast, describes love as a frail flower that is born and dies and advocates more intense passion instead—what the libretto calls "un fervido / Accento lusinghier." The Italian word "fervido," meaning burning or impassioned, also has connotations of "feverish." And as if to signal her incomplete recovery from her illness, Violetta suddenly collapses. This brings out Alfredo's protectiveness and his passion—neither can be separated from her consuming illness, her dangerous lifestyle, and her powerful sexual attractiveness. We are in Paris in the 1840s, and Violetta is a famous young courtesan and the very image of the romantic heroine.

When Alfredo comes to declare his love for her, it is in terms of mystery and paradox: it is both a cross and a delight ("croce e delizia")—not unlike the illness that both disturbs and attracts him. Indeed, musicologists talk of the "broken consumptive melody" of their love.[42] And to her surprise, Alfredo's passion attracts the woman who usually "loves" only for money, partly because she is also alone and feeling abandoned in what she calls the populated "desert" of Paris. After he leaves she ponders his devotion during her illness and begins to feel what she significantly describes as a new "fever" taking over ("nuova febbre accese"): this is love, and love that might actually last. Simultaneously, however, its association with fevers and therefore with her consumptive condition is both ironic and ominous.

In act 2 Violetta and Alfredo have moved to a house in what the contemporary audience would have recognized as the health-bestowing countryside, far from those debilitating Parisian parties.[43] They are deeply in love, but also deeply in debt. The arrival of Alfredo's father, accusing Violetta of ruining his son financially, allows the libretto to underline her sacrifices for love: he—and we—learn that, on the contrary, it is she who is selling all her possessions to support them. Germont senior describes her effect on his son by saying he is "ammaliato"—bewitched by her. Hidden (only barely) in "ammaliato" is the word "ammalato"—made sick. Perhaps in the good bourgeois father's mind is the popular view at the time that courtesans, who used their bodies as capital, more than likely were dangerously syphilitic. (Of course had he known of the contagious nature of tuberculosis, he would have had yet another reason to be afraid.) Alexandre Parent-Duchâtelet's famous 1836 report *De la Prostitution dans la ville de Paris* had stated that such women ("femmes galantes" and "femmes à parties") could destroy one's fortune as well as one's health.[44] Their danger lay in how closely they resembled "honest" women, in how they could be clever and refined: "Their duplicitous exteriors, deliberately constructed, undermine the organic connection between appearance and personal history that renders women openly readable to the informed male gaze; this duplicity erodes the moral and sexual code of the bourgeoisie from within, installing prostitution in its midst as a *contresens* that subverts naturalized ethical and class distinctions."[45] Indeed, the bourgeois Germont is surprised at Violetta's fine manners and unexpected sense of honor.

The reason he gives, however, for demanding further sacrifices of Violetta is the honor of his bourgeois family and its "name": for Alfredo's sister's happiness and marriage prospects, Violetta is asked to renounce her love. She pleads her illness and short life expectancy: "Non sapete che colpita / D'atro morbo è la mia vita? / Che già presso il fin ne vedo?" Without Alfredo, she would prefer to die. Nevertheless she does eventually agree, but she makes Germont promise to tell Alfredo later of her renunciation. He should someday know the sacrifice she has made out of love: "Conosca il sacrifizio / Ch'io consumai d'amor." The verb "consumare" here, with its added connotations in Italian of consume (waste, wear out) and consummate (fulfill), brings to the forefront of the very language of the text the cost for her in terms of desire as well as health. Violetta returns to Paris and her debilitating life, followed closely by Alfredo. The next scene finds her at a party, as in the opening scene of the opera, yet here she is not loved but insulted in public by her lover—all the while under oath not to tell him the reason for leaving him.

The final act opens in Violetta's sickroom; the doctor makes another appearance, but in keeping with the medical knowledge (or lack thereof) of consumption at the time, he is helpless against the disease, reduced simply to comforting its victim.[46] In music whose cadence has been said to betray "a dreadful finality,"[47] he tells her maidservant that her death from phthisis is not far off: "La tisi non le accorda che poche ore." Outside the window can be heard a carnival song about the killing of the sacrificial Dionysian ox, crowned with vine leaves. The life Violetta had led—parties, sensual experience—not only was Dionysian in some people's eyes, but literally predisposed her to consumption. Although it may be true that "Violetta, the true candidate for the sacrificial altar, wastes away with none of this gross and overfed enthusiasm"[48] of the fatted ox, the association with her sacrifice is nonetheless evident. As noted earlier, tuberculosis was a disease of multiple, even contradictory, connotations—an affliction of the sensual decadent as much as of the disembodied, spiritualized woman. Violetta, like Mimì, manages to be sinner and saint in one. Her very name, seemingly innocent in its suggestion of a common flower, embodies this dual identity of transgressor and victim: in it is contained the root of the verb *violare,* which in Italian means both to transgress or profane and to violate sexually.

Clear-eyed about her fate and knowing that with this disease all hope is dead ("con tal morbo ogni speranza è morta"), Violetta can pray to God to forgive "la traviata," the fallen women, the one who has literally left the path ("via") of virtue and is now paying the price. Her misery, of course, is caused as much by her self-sacrifice in the service of the bourgeois family order that has left her alone, without even Alfredo's love: "L'amore d'Alfredo pur esso mi manca." It is no accident, then, that Violetta's solitary, desperate aria here ("Addio, del passato") should echo in its poetic and musical form Germont senior's reminder to his son of bourgeois homelife ("Di Provenza il mar") in act 2.[49] In this moving aria, the music has been interpreted as charting Violetta's physical decline—her heavy, irregular breathing, her shortness of breath. When her "melodic continuity fails," "the plangent oboe serves as a temporary substitute during a pause for recovery."[50] But not even the return of Alfredo can save her. A thunderous chord announces her realization that, after all her suffering ("Io che penato ho tanto!"), she is going to die young: "Gran Dio! morir si giovine!" As they sing together of their love, "the fragility of their future prospects is underlined by a curious chromatic figure which keeps recurring" in the music.[51]

The music climaxes with a burst of energy, as she hopes beyond hope to live and love. At the time such an experience was held to be clinically accurate. A typical description of what was called "spes phthisica" notes that those who suffer from consumption "are filled at times with vain and delusive hopes — seduced by fancies that change of some kind would effect a cure, and yet, in most cases . . . [under ideal circumstances] they fade and weaken, and at last drop into untimely graves."[52] Even the opera's music here "uncannily depicts the cruel delusion of the consumptive."[53] Alfredo calls her his "sospiro" — his longed-for "desire"; but the Italian word in this context cannot avoid strong connotations of its other meanings of "breath" and "gasp" as well. And the weaker Violetta becomes, the more "diaphanous" is Verdi's scoring.[54] Suddenly, however, Violetta claims that the pain has stopped, that her strength is reborn: "Cessarono / Gli spasmi del dolore. / In me rinasce . . . m'agita / Insolito vigore!" She then dies, singing joyfully with tragic irony: "Oh gio . . . ia" on high B♭. The doctor announces her demise: "È spenta!" and all lament, "Oh mio dolor!" Pain (though not hers) has the last word.

This opera is based on an 1848 novel by Alexandre Dumas fils called *La Dame aux camélias*, a novel whose subject was judged indelicate on publication but that has never been out of print.[55] The 1852 play based on the novel was a big hit, especially after it was banned by the censors. People certainly were not used to such familiar characters being portrayed so sympathetically on stage.[56] The opera, first seen the next year, was equally new and shocking in its sexual explicitness and presentation of contemporary mores. In addition, it was known to be based on Dumas's real-life relationship with an infamous courtesan who died of consumption at the age of twenty-three — though without her former love, Dumas, at her side. Rose Alphonsine Plessis had come to Paris at age fourteen; within two years she had become the mistress of a powerful minister of state

3. Violetta (Nancy Gustafson), singing "O gioia" in a moment of tubercular "spes phthisica" preceding her death, in the 1991 production of *La Traviata* by the Canadian Opera Company.

(among others, as the epigraph from Liszt shows) and had changed her name to Marie Duplessis. Contemporary accounts confirm Dumas's own description (in the preface to the 1867 edition of his play) of her "phthisic beauty": "She was tall, very thin, dark-haired and with a pink and white complexion. Her head was small, her eyes long and slanting like those of a Japanese woman but lively and alert. Her lips were the colour of cherries and she had the most beautiful teeth in the world."[57]

The portrayal of her as Marguerite Gautier in Dumas's novel is entirely presented through what a contemporary audience would have recognized as the overt signs of tuberculosis, even without the text's explicit discussions of her illness. There are significant details, such as the information that her only legacy from her dead mother is the disease they share: consumption. This malady is said to give her those feverish desires that follow almost invariably on consumptive disorders. In addition to being described as a classic phthisic beauty, Marguerite coughs red blood onto her white handkerchief or napkin. This color contrast recalls as well the white and red camellias that encode and signal her sexual availability at various times of the month.

What is particularly striking in the novel, however, is the unromanticized and clinical description of her death. However painless and beautiful the consumptive's death was thought to be, the reality was often anything but. As Sheila Rothman describes the nineteenth-century clinical situation: "The incessant coughs made talking and eating almost impossible and breathing, painful; the swelling of joints and the loss of weight precluded walking; and the dying often subsisted on opium and whiskey. By the time death was at hand, emaciation was so complete that it appeared as if a cadaver had already replaced the human form."[58] Dumas's description is not so very different. A friend recounts that Marguerite's voice goes and she loses the use of her limbs. Delirious most of the time, she seems unable to see anyone. Though bled by the doctor, she cries out that she can speak, but cannot get her breath when she does: "J'étouffe! de l'air!" (293). We are told that no martyr ever suffered such torment as she did in her mortal agony, to judge by the screams she uttered. Two or three times she sat bolt upright in her bed, as though she wanted to grab at the life that was making its way back to God: "Comme si elle eût voulu ressaisir sa vie qui remontait vers Dieu" (294). She uttered her lover's name, then all went silent and she slumped back on the bed, exhausted. Weeping silently, she died. One of the narrator's final remarks makes the connection between desire and disease through death by noting that Marguerite was a woman who, once in her life, experienced a love so deep that she was willing to suffer for it and even die of it.

In the play as in the opera, Marguerite's death is sanitized and romanticized for the stage. She experiences "spes phthisica," feeling that her health is restored when her lover returns to her: "la santé que renaît sous ton amour."[59] Pale and weak, she trembles and stumbles. Assuring him of her happiness and the return of life, she suddenly dies. The play ends with a female friend drawing the sentimental moral that, because she has loved so much, she will be pardoned: "Dors en paix, Marguerite! il te sera beaucoup pardonné, parce que tu as beaucoup aimé!" (136). As we have already seen, the opera follows the romantic play more closely than the clinical novel in the final scene, but it does keep the focus on "dolore" — pain.

In all three texts, however, there is more of that (explicit and implicit) play on the various meanings of the word "consumption." Most obviously it is the name of the disease. But in the novel we are also told by the heroine — who describes herself as a woman who spits blood and spends a hundred thousand a year, that little by little she is using up her heart, her body, her beauty: "On use peu à peu son coeur, son corps, sa beauté" (118). The consumption of the resources of the courtesan is in fact what makes the situation of being loved by one all the more potent: in such women, we are told, "le corps a usé l'âme, les sens ont brûlé le coeur" (126) — the body has consumed the soul, the senses have burned up the heart. Our English translation here picks up on the synonyms for "user" in French: "brûler" and, of course, "consumer." Not irrelevant to this play on "consuming" is the notion of the beginnings of a consumer society: the heroine tells us it is the vanity that comes with the idea of having gowns, carriages, and diamonds that lures courtesans on (118). As Sontag has noted, "Early capitalism assumes the necessity of regulated spending, saving, accounting, discipline — an economy that depends on the rational limitation of desire. TB is described in images that sum up the negative behavior of nineteenth-century *homo economicus*: consumption; wasting; squandering of vitality."[60] Catherine Clément, in *Opera, or The Undoing of Women*, calls *La Traviata* the "exemplary history of a woman crushed by the bourgeois family," citing Engels's writings on the family. Consumption thus becomes, for her, the "bodily corruption inherited by those who are not part of the family."[61] Others have noted that as the "ultimately diseased, sexual woman living outside of marriage," Violetta must be defeated, for she has "no place on a familial chain."[62]

The bourgeois ethic that subtends the opera and the source texts is part of their social realism, of course. Critics have made much of the references in Dumas's novel to l'abbé Prévost's *Histoire du Chevalier des Grieux et de Manon Lescaut*. The hero gives his beloved a copy of the novel, which is subsequently purchased by the narrator after her death. It is the hero's grief and desire to have the book back that launch the story we read. Throughout the novel, the protagonists are constantly compared to those in Prévost's story. Both novels, of course, are stories about women, told by men to men. And both link sexual activity to money and, in the end, to early death.[63] The other opera—and source text—that makes this same connection and, like *La Traviata*, adds consumption into the equation is *La Bohème*.

Poverty and Contagion: Mimì

As the nineteenth century went on it became clear that tuberculosis was a disease of poverty, poor nutrition, and inadequate housing. With Koch's confirmation of the transmissibility of tuberculosis, this connection made increasing medical sense. Nevertheless, what persists in Puccini's 1896 opera, despite this new knowledge, is the predominant representation of Mimì as conventionally consumptive—that is, as sexually attractive in part because of her particular physical appearance.

If audiences had perhaps found *La Traviata* a little too familiar and realistic in its subject matter, they found *La Bohème* even more so. Its story of contemporary urban poverty, illness, and rather loose morals was different fare for audiences learning about Wagnerian mythic dwarfs, giants, and gods. Our invoking Wagner here is not merely rhetorical: Toscanini, who conducted the premiere of *La Bohème* at the Teatro Regio in Turin, had just opened the season there with the first Italian performance of Wagner's *Götterdämmerung*. Nevertheless, it seems that the public enjoyed the opera; the critics were the ones who had problems with it. Edouard Hanslick's reaction against its narrative realism and its new operatic language (of colloquial diction and freer verse forms) is emblematic: "The few earlier operas that deal seriously with affairs between wanton courtesans and weak youths ('Traviata,' 'Carmen,' and lately 'Manon') have at least dressed them in picturesque national or historic garb, or set them in romantic surroundings and thus raised them out of the lowest regions of everyday wretchedness."[64] Reacting against what he called "the naked prosaic dissoluteness of our time," Hanslick saw that this opera, however, represented something new: "a sensational break with the last romantic and artistic traditions of opera." The "verismo" of the late nineteenth century in Italy had indeed brought new subjects into literature and onto the stage. In this case, as Hanslick saw, it included a "long, painful death, quite horribly drawn out and endowed with every pathological misery, to which is added the naked poverty and helplessness of the surrounding artist-proletarians." As a French critic put it (inured by Zola's naturalism, perhaps), those final brass chords arrest the audience "brutally before the reality of the corpse much more than before the mystery of death."[65]

La Bohème's mixture of tragedy and comedy further baffled aesthetic purists, but part of the mix came from the literary source texts. Drawing from the Henry Murger sketches that appeared in *Le Corsair* between 1845 and 1849, from the play he then wrote with Théodore Barrière in 1849, but mostly from his novel of 1851, *Scènes de la vie de bohème*, the opera once again offers a more condensed, more dramatic, but also more romanticized and sanitized story of illness and death from tuberculosis.[66] But the setting has changed slightly from that of *La Traviata*. We are still in Paris, but we have moved from the demimonde to bohemia. The time has been set back to 1830, a more peaceful time in France, before the 1848 rebellions and the subsequent social and political changes.

Murger had described the bohemian artist's life — one he knew from experience — as the preface to the academy, the hospital, or the morgue (6) and as lying between the two gulfs of want and anxiety (11). Gradually losing its original association with gypsies, Jerrold Siegel writes, bohemia continued to resist bourgeois respectability: "Bohemia enacted the polarities of wealth and poverty, work and indulgence, duty and liberation, and thus acquired its theatrical quality of being half life and half symbol."[67] Although the opera clearly draws on the free-spirited and utopian aspects associated with what Murger too saw as a temporary stage of life, one should not forget that the real Parisian bohemia was also a scene of poverty where Murger's friends — the models for his characters — died of consumption and even starvation.[68]

For the librettists, Giacosa and Illica, and for Puccini (whose involvement — not to say interference — in the libretto preparation was notorious), the material consequences of increased urban poverty were clearly visible in the newly industrialized cities of northern Italy. The ominous combination of bad working conditions, especially for women in the silk textile industry (Mimì, as we shall see, embroiders flowers on silk), general poverty, poor nutrition, and crowded housing had led to a dramatic rise in the mortality from tuberculosis. To the earlier morbid fascination with the disease could be added worries about its epidemic spread. The poverty of Murger's bohemian artists and scholars likely would have had particular resonance in this social context.[69]

Certainly, when the opera opens, the cold that the writer Rodolfo and the painter Marcello complain of — and that frames the entire narrative — is a realistic detail in the representation of a cheap Parisian flat rented by poor artists; it also quickly takes on other associations, however, both with love and with disease. In 1855, not long after the publication of Murger's source text, Thomas Bartlett had stated that the "causes of pulmonary Consumption are, hereditary predisposition, . . . the breathing a vitiated atmosphere especially if it be cold and damp, deficient clothing, damp residence, want of cleanliness, sedentary habits, . . . improper diet. . . . Any one of these conditions will produce Consumption; while the advent of the disease is the more imminent in proportion to the number of them which co-exist."[70] In the opera all of these are portrayed in the opening scenes, and the link between love and the conditions that foster illness is firmly established. Marcello complains that his fingers are as cold as if he had been touching the great frozen mass of the heart of his former lover, Musetta. Despite the joking tone of the conversation among these young men and their friends, Colline and Schaunard, the topic is still cold and poverty. When Mimì enters, coughing and weak, to ask for a light for her extinguished candle, it is her cold hand ("Che gelida manina"), that cements Rodolfo's affection for her. He had been attracted first by her frailty and her pallor ("Impallidisce!"). To the "phthisic beauty" here is added the "femme fragile" that Antonia also embodies.[71] Mimì can barely get out her complaint about the stairs and her shortness of breath ("E il respir . . . Quelle scale . . .") before she collapses. The smitten Rodolfo ponders the beauty of her face, a beauty inseparable from her illness: "Che visa d'ammalata!" His subsequent declaration of love in the aria "O soave fanciulla" is interestingly sung to her as a "girl," a "fanciulla" who is somehow innocent even in her sexual appeal, and as a moonlit figure who is the object of his "intense aesthetic contemplation."[72]

4. Rodolfo (Keith Olsen) falls in love with the
ill Mimì (Yoko Watanabe) in the 1992 production of
La Bohème by the Canadian Opera Company.

Mimì tells Rodolfo that she embroiders flowers on silk, inauspiciously adding that she enjoys fashioning "gigli e rose"—lilies and roses. The consumptive extremes of coloring are here associated not with the real camellias of Dumas's courtesan but with a working woman's manufacturing artificial ones. The entire social context reminds us that by 1896 tuberculosis was understood to be the disease of the poor and victimized. This did not stop the earlier associations with passion and sexual seductiveness, however. The presentation of Mimì in the opera combines at least two of Murger's characters (Mimi and Francine).[73] This accounts for what some see as a central ambiguity or confusion about her character in the opera. There is some evidence that she is the materialistic and even promiscuous flirt of the novel, described there as pale and fragile with a delicate, sickly beauty ("beauté maladive" [165]) that attracts Rodolphe. She is also ill tempered, cruel, ambitious, a gossip and a flirt. His jealousy and her insolence make for a tempestuous relationship. In the opera, however, Mimì appears overall to be more a virtuous and faithful lover, as befits the simplicity and innocence of the "fanciulla" we first see on stage. In act 2, however, there is a moment where the other Mimi of Murger's novel seems to be revealed, even if briefly. The bohemians have gone to celebrate Christmas Eve at the Café Momus. En route, Rodolfo buys Mimì a pink bonnet, which he says suits her coloring. She would like a necklace too, but Rodolfo tells her that his millionaire uncle hasn't died yet! When Mimì notices a group of students nearby, Rodolfo is suddenly jealous. But enter Musetta, the real foil for Mimì, a flirt with materialistic desires that she satisfies by less orthodox means that provoke rightful jealousy in her former lover, Marcello. Clément has called Musetta "one of the few women in all of Puccini's works who does not die of dependence," but Mimì herself finds Musetta "sad" because, though she loves Marcello, poverty means she is willing to live with another man in order to have a better life.[74] The jealous Rodolfo firmly informs his new love that he would never forgive her if she acted that way.

This statement appears at first to be relevant to the action of the next act. The time is winter; the setting is the Barrière d'Enfer, the tollgate at the edge of Paris, which still marked the transition from the city to the countryside in 1830, when the opera takes place. That the Barrière area might also have been associated with the more healthful rural location is not irrelevant to Rodolfo's arrival here. Having left Mimì, Rodolfo has come to the inn where Musetta and Marcello are working. Mimì enters coughing, looking for Marcello. That "anxious" clarinet phrase that had accompanied her first arrival in Rodolfo's room is recalled in the "poignant" flutes and clarinet that can be heard as she tells Marcello that Rodolfo has left her, seemingly out of jealousy, even though he loves her.[75] Watching her as she pretends to sleep at night, he had finally told her to take another lover, for she would not do for him. After she had been coughing badly for a day or so ("Da ieri ho l'ossa rotte"), he finally left, saying "È finita." The Italian here is ambiguous because there is no subject to the sentence, but the adjectival form of "finished" — "finita" — has a feminine ending. Therefore Rodolfo may not simply be saying "it is over," but may be suggesting something more foreboding, perhaps (literally) "she is finished."

What is particularly interesting here is the temporal conjunction of her coughing spell and his departure. This is a detail rarely given significance by commentators, but it stands out when considered from a medical-historical perspective and in the context of Rodolfo's subsequent remarks. Mimì hides; Rodolfo approaches and proceeds to tell Marcello that he has decided to leave Mimì once and for all. His reasons include boredom and irritation but especially jealousy, he admits, recalling his warning to her in act 2. When he asserts that she is a flirt, what music critics call the "languid Puccini octaves" and the "unusual harmonic simplicity and uncharacteristically low tessitura" of the theme might alert us to his insincerity, as it does Marcello.[76] Rodolfo then admits that the real "torture" is that he loves Mimì but, as he repeats twice, is afraid: "ma ho paura, ma ho paura." But precisely what he is afraid of is not yet clear. As he relates to his friend — within Mimì's hearing — that she is in fact dying, the musical theme becomes dark and solemn. He says she declines daily and is "condemned": "Mimì è tanto malata! / Ogni dì più declina. / La povera piccina / è condannata!" He then describes with clinical accuracy her consumptive cough, her wasted frame, her pale cheeks with their red flush ("Una terribil tosse / l'esil petto le scuote, / già le smunte gote / di sangue rosse") to music with a "distinctive rhythm in parallel triads that graphically evokes the spasms of Mimì's cough."[77]

Ostensibly, then, Rodolfo is afraid for Mimì, but there is more than a suggestion that it might be his own health he fears for. By the time this opera was written, Koch's discovery had proved that tuberculosis was an infectious disease, and he had suggested that it could be transmitted from the sick person to others by a wide range of "infective" material such as sputum and contaminated bedding and clothing. (More recent information narrows the modes of transmission.) This concept of contagion combined with nineteenth-century theories of treatment eventually led to the isolation of the ill in sanatoriums. But this news might have been less surprising to Italians in the nineteenth century than to those in more northern European countries. The ancient worries (beginning with Aristotle and Galen) about consumptives as infectious were formally articulated in 1546 by Fracastorius in his early theory of contagion.[78] This theory had been dismissed in northern Europe but had continued to have significant power in the (then) kingdom of Naples, where an ordinance of 1782 required (under severe penalty) notification of cases of the disease, disinfection of the premises, and destruction of the belongings of consumptives. Although such ordinances had been proclaimed in the eighteenth century in Barcelona, Florence, Rome, and Venice, the first decree was in 1699 in the Republic of Lucca—Puccini's birthplace.[79]

Rodolfo's fear and his flight from the room he shared with the coughing Mimì, therefore, might have older associations, all the stronger because reinforced by recent medical discoveries. The newer knowledge is evident in his feeling responsible for her fatal illness ("Me cagion del fatal / mal che l'uccide!") because he is poor and his room is squalid and, once again, cold. Marcello's exclamation, "*Povera Mimì!*" ("*Poor Mimì!*") thus has more than one meaning. Yet Rodolfo calls Mimì a "hothouse flower," recalling the associations with luxury and fragility in *La Dame aux camélias* or perhaps Théophile Gautier's contemporaneous poem "Camélias et pâquerette," which compares such flowers to beautiful courtesans. But there are differences too: this is a flower that poverty has wasted away ("Povertà l'ha sfiorita") and that love alone will not bring back to life. A reprise of the "cough" theme of his narrative, merging with a variation on her leitmotif, announces Mimì's presence. The audience has already heard her interpretation of Rodolfo's earlier "È finita" in an anguished aside: she thinks it is her life that is finished ("O mia vita! È finita!"). Rodolfo, realizing she has overheard his remarks, tries to downplay their seriousness, telling her he is too easily frightened: "Facile alla paura." The lovers agree to stay together through the lonely winter and to separate in the spring. But Rodolfo's association of spring with the company not only of the sun but of those consumptively coded lilies and roses, mentioned earlier, is all too accurate in its connotations of the pale face and red cheeks of the tubercular heroine.

This omen sets the tone for the rest of the opera. The jealousy motif returns in act 4, but briefly. It is spring and the lovers have indeed separated, with Mimì having found a "viscontino" who dresses her like a queen. Rodolfo laments the death of their love. An earlier draft of the libretto had inserted an act here (one that Leoncavallo's contemporaneous version of *La Bohème* retained) in which Rodolfo would confront Mimì and her viscontino, calling her a flighty, vain creature who shamelessly deceives. The materialistic and flirtatious Mimi from Murger's novel resurfaces in this scene as we hear her chatter to her conquest about new clothes. In despair, Rodolfo gets drunk. He then picks up the glass Mimì has just drunk from and empties it, with a grand speech about putting his mouth where her divine lips — "the implacable undertakers of love" — have been. He goes on to proclaim that he will raise his voice to sing his final song, and the odd image he chooses to express this is: as if on the cross of a white funeral monument. In this version he says not simply that he is frightened, but that her cough literally creates terror in him. This melodramatic confrontation makes the connection between love, illness, and death, but its major focus is Rodolfo's jealousy and Mimì's flirtatious infidelity. Perhaps because Puccini was most interested in having the death of Mimì as tubercular victim be the focus of the opera, the final version restricts itself to a mere mention of the viscontino, almost in passing, and cuts this scene entirely. Here it is not only Murger's consumptive, flirtatious Mimi but also his equally consumptive and more sympathetic Francine who provide the models.[80]

In the last act of the opera, then, Musetta enters the squalid attic room where the friends have been joking around, to announce that she has a very sick Mimì with her. Mimì is so ill, in fact, that this time she cannot make it up the staircase at all. As if to signal her physical decline from act 1 in the music itself, the version of her leitmotif that accompanies her entry, supported by Rodolfo, is said to be "painfully intense, chromatically inflected."[81] Musetta tells the others that Mimì has left her other lover because she knows she is at the end of her life ("era in fin di vita") and wants to die with Rodolfo. Musetta has found her in the street, exhausted, and brought her to Rodolfo's room, where, as is typical of "spes phthisica," she feels herself coming to life again: "Si rinasce . . . Ancor sento la vita!" With understatement (or irony), she admits that she still has a bit of a cough: "Ho un po' di tosse!" But though it is spring, Mimì's hands are once again cold. Just as this detail had signaled the beginning of their love in act 1, it now stands for her impending death. She wishes she had a muff to keep them warm, and, though Rodolfo once again offers to warm them in his, he should recall his own earlier statement that love alone would not save Mimì.

When the lovers are left alone, Mimì sings one of the most powerful melodies of the opera. This "Sono andati?" aria is uncharacteristically eloquent for a young woman who, thus far, has been rather inarticulate and simple in her expression:

Ho tante cose che ti voglio dire . . .	*I have so many things I want to tell you . . .*
o una sola, ma grande come il mare,	*or only one, but one vast as the sea,*
come il mare profonda ed infinita . . .	*as the deep and infinite sea . . .*
Sei il mio amor e tutta la mia vita.	*You are my love and my entire life.*

It is as if her disease has rendered her poetic — as it had those romantic poets before her. The music here works to undermine any last hopes Rodolfo might have: "By preceding it [the melody] with a statement of the opening of the Act I love-theme, Puccini uses one of the simplest musical means of shattering Rodolfo's hope, namely, a continuation in C *minor* of a phrase that the listener will have expected to proceed in the major."[82] One source of the power of the music here is that only two themes in the entire opera are given new meaning through this kind of transformation, and both occur in this act: Mimì's motif and the love theme. The new harmonic setting at this point of the love theme—that is, different from that in act 1—suggests that their happiness will not last: "The harmony, instead of opening out from the tonic to the dominant, now closes up towards the tonic."[83]

Musetta and Marcello return with a "cordiale" and a promise that the doctor will come shortly. The muff they bring Mimì delights her, and she appears to drift off muttering about love, warm hands, and sleep ("Qui . . . amor . . . sempre con te! . . . / Le mani . . . al caldo . . . e . . . dormire"). A harp suggests her slackening heartbeat. The music shifts suddenly to the minor key, accompanied by "the intrusive sound of brass instruments" and "a sinister motif in the bass" as the others realize she has died.[84] The Italian—"è spirata"—with its associations of breathing as well as expiration, recalls Violetta's "io spiro."

This is, once again, an operatically romanticized and somewhat sanitized death made fit for the stage, but it is nevertheless a rather different one from Violetta's dramatic collapse in her lover's arms, singing "O gioia." The librettist and composer Arrigo Boito once remarked about the end of *La Traviata* that "to describe someone who dies of consumption we say *muore di mal sottile* [dies of the subtle disease]. The prelude [to act 3 of Verdi's opera] appears to say this with sounds, with elevated, sad, frail sounds, almost without body, ethereal, sick, with death imminent . . . the soul of a dying woman tied to her body by the most subtle thread of breath!"[85] Although Puccini's music does not suggest this at all, the physical, corporeal moment of death of his heroine on stage does, but with none of the transcendence suggested by Boito's romantic rhetoric. Despite its sentimentalizing, this is still a somewhat more realistic portrayal of death by consumption, the disease of the poor. Clément has said that, given current political sensibilities, we can no longer see *La Traviata* as the story "of an unhappy love between a prostitute and a slightly crazy young man" but must recognize "the cruel conflict between family, its property interests, and the parallel world of prostitution."[86] To this we would add that it is also the related story of the cultural construction of both a disease and the woman who suffered from it. Clément likewise asserts that we cannot separate La Bohème from "a romantic Paris, its wretched poverty and the icy cobblestones where the barricades were born; look, beyond the conventional poetry of youth that adapts to everything, at a life destroyed by the lack of food and warmth."[87] But we also cannot separate that opera from its heroine and her particular disease, which was very much a result of that "life destroyed by the lack of food and warmth."

Although the Leoncavallo version of La Bohème mentioned earlier is focused primarily on Musette and Marcello rather than on Mimì and Rodolfo, its final act also recalls Murger's notion of the poverty of the bohemian life as a preface to the hospital or the morgue: Mimì returns, sick and homeless, to die near Rodolfo. Kicked out by her wealthy viscontino for visiting Rodolfo earlier, she had tried to return to work but ended up in the hospital, related in specific detail, complete with ward name and bed number — "a San Luigi, salla Vittoria, Letto numero venti." The cold room, her coughing, her "spes phthisica" are constants that accompany her stage demise too, to the sound of Rodolfo's desperate cry.

It has been suggested that "at first glance, death by consumption or pulmonary tuberculosis seems to present limited narrative options. The victim's lungs gradually cease to function, and — in literary portrayals at least — the decline is so regular that its course can be predicted with accuracy."[88] Tuberculosis has often been presented as a disease that, despite its uneven progression, allows mental integrity and physical autonomy to remain intact to the end — which may explain why so many writers were able to write of their own decline.[89] But the romanticizing of the disease that was possible before Koch's discovery of its pathogenesis and that had led to the mythologizing of the spiritual yet sexual, sick yet seductive, dying yet desired consumptive heroine slowly began to give way, with this new medical knowledge, at the end of the nineteenth century and start of the twentieth, when the fears voiced by Rodolfo blossomed into full "phthisis-phobia."[90] With the knowledge of infection came new attention to the concept of contagion. From the back cover of the 1900 *Annual Report of the Free Hospital for Poor Consumptives* in Philadelphia came this warning: "A consumptive letter carrier brings contagion in your mail; a consumptive car conductor hands it to you in your change; a consumptive saleswoman ties it up in your package; a consumptive cook contaminates your food; a consumptive maid implants the disease in your children; a consumptive mechanic contaminates your house."[91] With such fears came an intensified stigmatizing of the tubercular person as a source of disease, and this contributed in part to the subsequent rise of the sanatorium movement.[92] But the association between desire and disease that had earlier made for moving operatic narratives never quite disappeared. As one poet noted about the malady he called "malignant, repellant, appalling," "white death lurks in the kisses / That lovers exchange on the stair."[93]

The presentation of Antonie in the Hoffmann source text, from the early years of the nineteenth century, predates the medical conceptualization of tuberculosis as a single disease entity. As we have seen, at this time in northern Europe especially, consumption was believed to be hereditary and was indeed a very common cause of mortality, particularly among the young: the time of love coincided all too often with the time of death. In 1881, when the opera *Les Contes d'Hoffmann* was first performed, Koch's discovery was still a year away. In fact this was the time of the height of the mythologizing of the disease, and *La Traviata*'s Violetta was its operatic epitome: the tubercular "look" had become both aestheticized and eroticized. By the time of *La Bohème* (1895), however, Mimì could be represented as the victim of a specific disease process and of a set of circumstances, including poverty. But she was still beautiful and desirable in her illness and—now—all the more dangerous for that: she was the *femme fragile* as literally the femme fatale that Rodolfo's jealousy had made her seem to be.[94] The medical modelings and the aesthetic representations of art come together in the nineteenth century in this potent construction of the social meaning of gendered desire, disease, and death. Today, with the advent of multiple-drug-resistant tuberculosis, those who suffer from the disease are once again considered a social danger, but now the way of coding the sick person as "other" is different, this time in terms of HIV positivity. Clearly, then, sexuality and life habits (such as intravenous drug use) still figure in the cultural construction of this particular disease.[95]

Plus ça change . . .

Chapter 3

Syphilis, Suffering, and the Social Order: Richard Wagner's *Parsifal*

Hatred, strife, and combat make men forget this God.
Passion clothed in filth lifts up its noisome head.
Thus [are] man and mother church trodden in the sod,
and honest men forget their holy nuptial word
and seek in darkest night the harlot's golden bed.
— Francisco Lopez de Villalobos (from his
1498 poem on syphilis)

In the age of AIDS, few would be suprised to find sexuality associated with suffering and disease; in the age of syphilis—that is, from its first documented cases in Europe in 1495 to today, when it is on the rise once again—the connection between sex and suffering is equally strong, though many of us may have forgotten that history. The brief respite offered by the discovery of a cure for syphilis (with penicillin) in the 1940s ended with the appearance of HIV. Over the past five hundred years the Christian interpretation of syphilis suggested in the epigraph—as the scourge of God directed against the sexually sinful—has merged with sexual anxieties about the effects of syphilis on the general social fabric and, in the nineteenth and twentieth centuries, on the family in particular. The perhaps unexpected focus of this chapter's discussion of suffering and sexually transmitted disease is Richard Wagner's last music drama, *Parsifal*. This is the one he finally completed in 1882 and called a "Stage Consecration Festival Play" for his northern Bavarian theater at Bayreuth. As with all his works, Wagner acted as both poet-librettist and composer.

Suffering and Sin

Parsifal tells the familiar story of the simple and pure young Parsifal's eventual redeeming of the (sexual) sin of Amfortas, keeper of the Holy Grail. Though it has many forms in different myths, here the Grail is the cup consecrated by Christ at the Last Supper and then used, as he hung on the cross, to catch his blood as it poured from the wound in his side made by the spear of Longinus. Among Wagner's obvious sources were the romances of Chrétien de Troyes and, in particular, Wolfram von Eschenbach. These were both connected to the stories of the worship of nature and the rites of godly death and rebirth that reverberate through those early myths of Adonis to the Celtic legends of the maimed Fisher King ruling over the "Waste Land" and on into Christian doctrine.[1] His equally obvious inspirations were his own earlier works, as he himself noted in his letters and other writings: the simple Parsifal is a more passive version of his earlier Siegfried, just as the suffering Amfortas is an intensified version of his Tristan, unable to die despite his physical wound.[2]

Amfortas too has a wound that, like Christ's, is in his side in Wagner's final libretto text; in the sources it is not. Wagner's transposition of the wound from the genital area to the chest, while obviously offering a gain in Christian symbolism, also serves to distract attention; it displaces but does not, we would argue, obliterate in the spectator's mind the sexual associations of the positioning of the injury. In Chrétien's text the Fisher King's incurable wound, euphemistically placed simply between his legs—"parmi les hanches ambedeus"—is made by a javelin.[3] In Wolfram's version it is explicitly caused by a poisoned lance in his scrotum—and by the "pursuit of love beyond the restraints of wedlock," which in turn "brought harm to the world."[4] As more than one critic has noted, Wolfram makes the punishment fit the crime: a poisoned, festering wound in the genitals is an apt punishment for riding out alone "to seek adventure under Love's compulsion." That nothing could cure the wound with the gangrened look is interpreted here as a sign from God himself.

Though placed in his side and not lower, Amfortas's wound in Wagner's tale was indeed inflicted as he sank into the arms of the beautiful Kundry. It is also significant that it is made by his own spear—that is, by the sacred Spear of Longinus that had been given by the angels to his father, Titurel, along with the Holy Grail.[5] In other words, God's scourge here is literalized in the form of the Holy Spear. The Christian and the sexual, the sacred and the profane are ineluctably intertwined in the all-important moment of Amfortas's wounding.[6] In the history of the interpretation of *Parsifal*, however, it is the Christian reading that has dominated—leading to either adulation or rejection.[7] Friedrich Nietzsche's infamous outbursts of irritation at the opera's Christian context are complicated in origin and arguably based as much on personal resentment against Wagner as on philosophical disagreement. Nevertheless, in *Ecce Homo* he decried Wagner's pious decline; in *On the Genealogy of Morals* he attacked not only the religious dimension but what he saw accompanying it—asceticism and chastity—and lamented that Wagner had betrayed his own ideal of the *"highest spiritualization and sensualization of his art."*[8] The "healthy sensuality" he saw Wagner once espousing had disappeared, argued Nietzsche. He was obviously responding to the manifest Christian context and the apparent attack on sexuality through the associations with wounding and suffering. Although the issue of the relation of art to religion is a general one that Wagner himself raised in his essays, the attention devoted over the past century to only one half of the "sexuality = sin" equation is as striking as it is suggestive.[9] Our reading is an attempt to bring the other, the sexual half, back into the discussion by pointing out that, in *Parsifal*, the (undeniable) Christian elements consistently merge with the sexual in ways that are medically significant and culturally resonant.

This is not to deny the Christian context: though Christ is never explicitly named in the text, his sacrificial suffering and death on the cross are never far from the surface of Wagner's text. Indeed, the last act takes place on Good Friday, the day of greatest pain ("höchsten Schmerzentags").[10] Christ's suffering and redemption of humankind provide the narrative model for Parsifal's redeeming of the Grail realm and of the suffering of Amfortas in particular: Parsifal's moment of identity with Amfortas—when he too is kissed by Kundry—is in fact at the physical center of the opera. But it is equally evident that there are significant differences in the kind of sin that must explicitly be redeemed through suffering in Parsifal and in Christ's story. In the years from his first thoughts about Parsifal in 1845 to its completion in 1882, Wagner had been reading the work of Schopenhauer and had found his own views confirmed and strengthened by that philosopher's connection of desire, pain, suffering, and Mitleid — compassion. Not surprisingly, perhaps, the plot of the opera joins together specifically *sexual* desire, wounding, suffering, and the eventual renunciation of desire to achieve release and redemption.[11]

Before the curtain goes up, Titurel has given over his holy office of protector of the Grail and Spear to his son Amfortas. As the new leader of the knights of the Grail, Amfortas has taken the Spear and gone out to subdue a great moral and physical danger to the Grail realm and its knights: the sexual lure of the Flower Maidens ("Blumenmädchen") who reside in a luxuriant garden in the desert created by the evil Klingsor. We are told by the Grail knight, Gurnemanz (the major narrator of the plot details), that Klingsor had committed some unknown sin somewhere in the heathen lands and sought atonement by becoming a chaste Grail knight. Unable to control his physical lust by force of will, however, he resorted to castrating himself. With this act he simultaneously disqualified himself from knighthood and gained evil powers. In his envious attempt to get control of the Grail, he has created that magic desert garden with its alluring Flower Maidens, who have already brought down many a Grail knight before the opera even opens. It is this threat that Amfortas sought to end but himself fell prey to. He lost his virtue to Kundry and his Spear to her master, Klingsor, who wounded him with it. This is only fitting, perhaps, since both men have fallen victim to the very force (sensuality) they have tried to fight.[12]

Amfortas was then sent a message through the Grail that a "simple fool" would redeem him through "Mitleid" — sympathy, compassion. Meanwhile, as he awaits redemption, he has experienced both unbearable pain from his wound and unendurable psychic and spiritual suffering from the knowledge of his sin. Current medical thinking on the nature of suffering offers us a way to read this state of affairs in a more complex way than simply as the result of physical pain. As we mentioned in chapter 1, Eric Cassell, in *The Nature of Suffering and the Goals of Med-*

5. Amfortas (Thomas Stewart) suffers, as Gurnemanz
(Cesare Siepi) looks on, in the 1970–71 production of *Parsifal*
at the Metropolitan Opera, New York.

icine, argues that *bodies* do not suffer; it is *persons* who suffer.[13] Personhood,
for Cassell, is the complex of physical, spiritual, psychological, and social
aspects that make up an individual life. Suffering occurs when the integrity of the person is threatened on one or more of these levels. In
Wagner's text, then, Amfortas suffers *physically* from the kind of pain Cassell describes as uncontrolled, uncontrollable, and continuing into the
future — and therein lies its power over the person (even more so than
over the body alone). *Psychologically*, Amfortas has failed his own ideals
and goals as protector of the Spear and Grail and suffers too from this
knowledge, rendered incapable of any kind of self-love or even self-
respect. *Socially*, his inability or unwillingness to carry out his role — to do
the office of the Holy Grail — leads to the distress and decline of the Grail
knights' society and, eventually, the death of his own father. Amfortas
says that the pain of the wound is nothing compared with the agony, the
"Höllenpein" (hellish pain) of doing his office and unveiling the Grail.

From being the leader of a victorious order of men, he has become the slave of his illness ("seines Siechtums Knecht"). This is a religious failing as well, for he has caused the loss of the Holy Spear, the very one that was used against him. If Amfortas's wound in his side is meant to recall Christ's, then, it can only be what one critic has called a perverse imitation of it.[14] The suffering of Christ, described by the Grail youths' song as redeeming the sinful world with "tausend Schmerzen" (a thousand pains), is clearly not unrelated to Amfortas's suffering—but as we shall see, only as it is reexperienced through the redeeming Parsifal.

Although this is the suffering that is at the literal center of the opera, there is hardly a character in it whose identity is not marked by the physical, psychological, and social dimensions of suffering. The focus of act 2 moves from Amfortas to Klingsor—another male body transformed through sexual wounding into a person who suffers. Taunted by Kundry about his self-castration, he cries out in pain about the untamed longing and "hellish lust" that created such "fearful need" that he stifled them at great spiritual and physical cost. His lamenting is answered by Kundry's own as she tries to resist her own curse and its seeming enforcer: for laughing at Christ, she has been condemned to wander forever and, it appears, to seduce men and, laughing, bring their souls to perdition. When Kundry tries to seduce Parsifal, she does so initially by what can only be called a kind of bizarre erotics of suffering, telling him how much his mother, Herzeleide, suffered because of his leaving her. Her long and sensual kiss causes Parsifal to start in fear and put his hand to his heart as if to subdue a rending pain. At this moment he first identifies with Amfortas through the wound: "Die Wunde!—Die Wunde! / Sie brennt in meinem Herzen!" But he then corrects himself, saying the pain is not from the wound but from a fearful longing: "Nicht die Wunde ist es . . . im Herzen der Brand! Das Sehnen, das furchtbare Sehnen." It is the agony of loving ("Qual der Liebe") or, more explicitly, the agony of sinful desire ("in sündigen Verlangen"). As one critic described this scene rather less reverentially: "Wagner's power to yoke opposites in powerful symbiosis is never more daring than in his hero's substitution of a burning in his side after such build-up to a burning somewhere else."[15]

Parsifal then goes into a kind of trance and relives the Grail ceremony he had witnessed earlier, linking the holy sacrificial blood of Christ in the Grail to the sinful blood of Amfortas and, now, himself. Kundry caresses him as he describes her caressing of Amfortas, but this time in terms of pain and agony, not pleasure. Rejected by him, Kundry then tries to win his compassion for *her* suffering too, telling the story of her accursed existence and yearning for death. As Kundry's tactics suggest, there is a direct Schopenhauerian connection between the fact of suffering — in German, *Leid* — and compassion — *Mitleid* (literally, "suffering with"). As Adolph Appia once put it: "Only suffering can evoke compassion, but there are a thousand kinds of suffering."[16] It is only after resisting Kundry's seduction and subsequently wandering the paths of suffering ("der Leiden Pfade") for many years that Parsifal can return to the Grail realm on Good Friday, the day Christ suffered for humankind, in order to redeem Amfortas, the sinful keeper of the Grail: Gurnemanz calls him a "Mitleidsvoll Duldender" — a sufferer full of compassion. The voices of suffering — Klingsor's, Kundry's, and even Amfortas's — are silenced in the end as Parsifal takes over the holy office and unveils the Grail, now reunited with the paradoxically "wounding" but "wondrous" spear ("O wunden wundervoller heiliger Speer!") that he has reclaimed from Klingsor and used to heal Amfortas's wound.[17]

In Hans-Jürgen Syberberg's controversial film version of *Parsifal*, the role of Amfortas was acted (though not sung) by the conductor of the music, Armin Jordan. In one critic's view, this is appropriate because Amfortas is the character closest to Wagner, "from whose lesions the musical blood and suffering pour."[18] Whether or not this autobiographical argument is convincing, the linking of Amfortas's suffering to the music of the opera is obviously important. Lucy Beckett writes about the opening moments that set up the prelude's disquieting "atmosphere of strangeness and unease."[19] She argues that a double mood is invoked, between a "sense of grieving aspiration" established through unresolved harmonies, on the one hand, and the familiar and consolingly diatonic notes of what was known as the "Dresden Amen," on the other — though the first one prevails, "insistent and darkening." Motifs to be associated with pain and suffering are constantly played off against the healing tones of the Grail music.[20] In musical terms, the diatonic music associated throughout the opera with social order and spiritual salvation is consistently interrupted by the chromaticism associated with Amfortas, Kundry, Klingsor, and Parsifal (when he is identifying with Amfortas or distressed about his mother's suffering and death). In Beckett's terms, there are moments of "troubled" and even "tearing dissonance" even within the diatonic music representing the ideal (if no longer real) order of the Grail realm — moments of pain and distress such as, when the knights try to force Amfortas to uncover the Grail in acts 1 and 3 or when Kundry reappears in the last scene. Musicologists have frequently linked Amfortas's music to his suffering with arguments such as "Amfortas comes very close to the healing purity of a calm, cadentially confirmed B flat major, and the orchestration, with its lulling ostinati in the four horns, seems on the verge of a paradisal release, but this ultimate resolution is denied him. He must continue to suffer."[21] But exactly what does he suffer from?

Syphilis: The Medical Signs of the "Scourge of God"

Though far from explicit, the libretto text does describe four main characteristics of Amfortas's wound. The first is that it will not heal. Gurnemanz repeats twice and (Beckett notes this is unusual in Wagner) to different music the line "die Wunde ist's, die nie sich schliessen will," doubly underlining that this wound will never close. Indeed, we watch it bleed afresh with what Amfortas calls his sinful ("sündigen") blood during the Grail ceremony. Second, the pain gets worse at night, leaving the sleepless leader exhausted in the morning: "nach wilder Schmerzensnacht." Third, the text offers two kinds of "Lindrung" or means of soothing the pain: taking baths in the holy lake ("heil'gen See") and using balsams from faraway lands, including Arabia. The final element repeatedly insisted on by the text is the injury's sexual association. Mike Ashman has argued that Amfortas's wound

> *has rather less to do with Christ's wound than with the Celtic myths of an infertile (Grail) king, and hence an infertile kingdom awaiting a saviour. In other words, Amfortas is wounded in the genitals, not in the side — a fact hinted at in Wagner's first prose draft of the drama and seemingly confirmed by rehearsal ac-*

counts of the Wagner family. . . . It is hard to say whether prudish conventions or
a deliberate desire for ambiguity stopped Wagner from establishing this fact. Ei-
ther way, there is a profitable gain in suggestive imagery and the parallel between
Klingsor and Amfortas . . . becomes even clearer: both have been effectively "un-
manned" by sexual lust.[22]

Although Klingsor may indeed have inflicted the wound, it is Kundry's
seduction that rendered Amfortas helpless in her arms. Woman is not
to be absolved from her role in this sexual injury, as the text keeps
reminding us.

What might these four elements add up to for a nineteenth-century
audience with a basic cultural and medical mathematics? A nonhealing
lesion associated with pain, especially night pain, and acquired through
sexual contact would be suggestive then, as now, of syphilitic infection—though today penicillin has given many of us the luxury of not
having to recognize it.[23] We know now that syphilis is an infectious disease caused by the organism known as the "pale spirochete," or *Treponema
pallidum*, which is transmitted venereally. It initially appears as a hard ulcer, or chancre, usually found on the genitalia, that spontaneously clears.
The disease reappears in a secondary stage some weeks later, often involving skin and mucous membrane. This too may clear, only to be replaced by signs of the tertiary stage: cardiovascular disease, neurological
symptoms, paralytic dementia, or chronic inflammatory lesions or "gummas." To get technical about it, Amfortas's wound in the side could be
seen as a gumma involving a rib and ulcerating through skin.

In the nineteenth century earlier theories about syphilis were given
new attention, as physicians and social commentators alike sought to understand the complex meanings that had been given to such physical
symptoms over time. That syphilitic gummas can involve bone pain was
noted by Wagner's contemporary Zeissl in his 1875 *Lehrbuch der Syphilis*,
where he also noted that these dreadfully strong radiating pains from
the depths of the bones worsened at night and so were named "dolores
nocturni."[24] German physicians were reexamining the findings of people like Jean Fernel, the famous sixteenth-century French physician
known as the modern Galen, who had noted early on that the worst

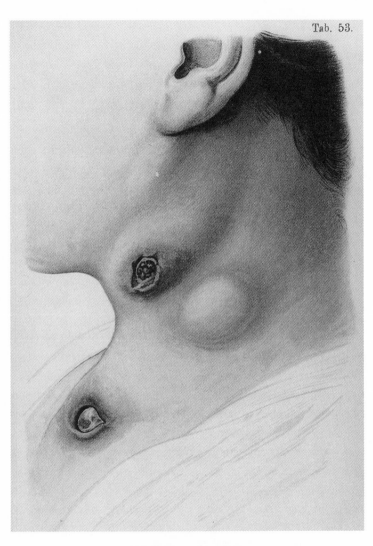

Tab. 53.

6. Syphilitic gumma, from
Prof. Dr. Franz Mracek, *Atlas of
Syphilis and the Venereal Diseases.*

pains of syphilis came from its attack on the periosteum, the membrane that covers the bones, causing terrible pains that increase in ferocity at night.[25] A similar clinical description of syphilitic gumma can be found in the same century in the famous work of Fracastorius, the man whose poem gave syphilis its name: "For, as soon as the kindly beams of departing day usher in the sad shades of dusk . . . the arms, the shoulder-blades and the calves of the legs are racked with pain."[26]

This particular conjunction of symptoms had actually been remarked upon since the disease's first appearance in the 1490s. Alfred Fournier, an eminent nineteenth-century syphilologist, stated that the noctural character of syphilitic pain had been noted from earliest times: "All authors of that period have described it insistently and considered it a special attribute of the sufferings peculiar to this disease."[27] For instance, in 1497 a Venetian doctor painted this picture of the venereal disease that he believed had arrived in Europe from the Americas only a few years before: "Through sexual contact, an ailment which is new, or at least unknown to previous doctors, the French sickness, has worked its way in from the West to this spot as I write. The entire body is so repulsive to look at and the suffering is so great, especially at night, that this sickness is even more horrifying than incurable leprosy or elephantiasis, and it can be fatal."[28] When gummas involve skin, as Sir William Osler noted in his landmark medical textbook of 1892, they tend to break down and ulcerate, leaving ugly sores that heal with great difficulty, and that often, like Amfortas's wound, flow "copiously with corrupted blood and matter."[29] In the nineteenth century, when Wagner was writing *Parsifal*, this kind of knowledge, already almost four hundred years old, had likely made its way in various forms into common medical lore, for this was an age obsessed with the "hidden decay of syphilis" and "its mythic relationship to sexuality."[30]

Also well known were the suggested means of alleviating its symptoms, though no treatment was especially efficacious. Though it may surprise us today, mercury was still the major means that was tried. Two other remedies of interest here did exist—baths and balsams—the same ones Amfortas turns to in the opera. We first see him being carried to the holy lake to bathe because it soothes the pain. Although the use of baths as a syphilis treatment was recorded as early as Fracastorius, it was never really accepted as very therapeutic, though there were clearly other Christian associations with baptismal purification that would remain useful for Wagner. And of course the entire discourse surrounding cleanliness in the eighteenth and nineteenth centuries, it has been argued, was both medical and religious.[31] Amfortas's use of soothing balsams is also suggestive in light of medical historical evidence that they were commonly used in treating syphilitic ulcers. That the balsam Kundry brings to him comes from "Arabia" recalls the Arab origins of mercury ointments used for other skin diseases, a practice adopted by Europeans as early as 1496 to treat syphilitic dermatologic problems.[32]

Although it is still being debated today, as it certainly was in Wagner's time, one theory of the origin of syphilis is that it came to Europe with the sailors returning from Columbus's voyage to the Americas in 1492.[33] The first European descriptions of the disease appear to date from the battle of Fornovo (July 1495) between the Venetians and the French troops of Charles VIII. It was first called the "French disease" in Italy because it was rampant in Charles's army, whence it traveled to Naples and from there—rapidly—to the rest of Europe. In 1495 a Danish commentator noted its subsequent killing of thousands of Germans and Danes: "Because of our sins it wormed its way surreptitiously into all countries, with the result that nowadays there is no other sickness which is more common." A few years later Ulrich von Hutten (who was himself syphilitic) wrote: "It pleased God to send us in these times maladies which, as we are well aware, were unknown to our ancestors. Those entrusted with the Holy Scriptures said that the pox was the result of divine wrath."[34]

It was not long, however, before God's vengeance was seen to be directed against certain *specific* sinners: those guilty of sexual license. The connection between sexual intercourse and syphilis was canonized, in a sense, in 1527 when Jacques de Béthencourt named the disease "mal vénérien" and described it as "originating in sexual relations and contagion." He asserted that this venereal sickness was the consequence of debauchery and was therefore an offense against God.[35] Amfortas's suffering, as we have seen, comes as much from having offended God and the

¶ Tractatus de peſtilentiali Scorra ſiue mala de Franzos.
Originem. Remediaꝗ eiuſdem continens.cõpilatus a vene
rabili viro Magiſtro Joſeph Grunpeck de Burckhauſen.
ſup Carmina quedam Sebaſtiani Brant vtriuſꝗ iuris pro
feſſoris.

7. Syphilis as the scourge of God against the sinful.

Grail as from the physical pain of the wound inflicted during his sexual transgression with Kundry. This is not to downplay the physical pain or its source, however. According to one early and particularly vivid description, "The searing droplets of this cruel sickness fall on those who are hot with love and dirtied with lust; it is a punishment for their misdeeds and their shameful desires."[36] But it is a punishment specifically sent by God. Indeed, as early as 1634 Ambroise Paré claimed there were two "efficient causes" of syphilis: one sent by God "as by whose command this hath assailed mankind, as a scourge or punishment to restraine the too wanton lascivious lusts of unpure whoremongers" and the other "an impure touch or contagion, and principally, that which happeneth in copulation."[37] This connection of the Christian and the sexual meant that as early as the sixteenth century the belief was that "having contracted the disease clearly indicated that one was physically and morally 'tainted.'"[38] The culmination of this view is perhaps that of Pope Leo XII, who in 1826 banned the use of the condom as a protection against syphilis because it "defied the intentions of divine Providence, namely, to punish sinners by striking them in the member with which they had sinned."[39] That Amfortas was punished in the same way is striking, even if Wagner's displacement of the wound to his side might divert our attention.

Literary, cultural, and medical historians alike have noted that the nineteenth century—and *Parsifal* was conceived and written from 1845 to 1882—was marked both by a general obsession with syphilis and by a change in its general social meaning.[40] One of the reasons for both these phenomena was the rise of the middle class in the previous century. Although the "attitude of the upper classes toward syphilis became decidedly frivolous in the *siècle galant*," the middle class "condemned sexual licentiousness and emphasized the sanctity of the family. Virtue, or at least the appearance of it, was demanded from its members. By adopting such an attitude the bourgeoisie claimed to be better than the nobility and therefore entitled to power."[41] Flaunting their resistance to this bourgeois ideology in Paris, for instance, were those decadent artists whose writings challenged the social order and whose bodies were syphilitic: Baudelaire, Maupassant, Huysmans, the Goncourt brothers. One commentator has noted that there was hardly any part of the cultural domain that was not tainted by the scourge of syphilis in nineteenth-century Paris — whether the disease was seen as socially menacing (the naturalist view) or decadently spiritualized (the symbolist version).[42]

Medically, too, Paris became the center for research on venereal disease, beginning with Philippe Ricord's work at the Hôpital du Midi. In 1838 he published his "practical treatise on venereal disease," which for the first time definitively separated syphilis from gonorrhea; this work also founded the modern clinical knowledge of syphilis, including the differentiation of its primary, secondary, and tertiary stages. In 1842 the French Academy of Sciences recognized the value of this work by granting it the Gold Medal. We know that Wagner spent many years in Paris at various points in his life, including the years just before he began to work on *Parsifal*, between 1839 and 1842, and it is likely he would have heard about this work. Ricord's fame was such that even the lay public might well have known of his research, disseminated as it was through such media as popular magazines. His caricature appeared, for instance, on the cover of *Les Hommes d'Aujourd'hui*. We know from J. K. Proksch's 1885 study of the history of syphilis that many well-known contemporaries were followers of Ricord in Germany and elsewhere in the mid-nineteenth century, thus testifying to considerable public and professional interest at the time around the issues of syphilis.[43]

It is not only in France, then, that syphilis had a rather high profile in the nineteenth century. In England it appears that lay knowledge about the disease had been extensive since the sixteenth century. Because syphilis was so pervasive and its symptoms so obvious, it was perhaps hard to ignore. In addition, many books were written about it, not only in Latin but in the European vernaculars, including German and English, so the literate lay public, at least, could be informed. As Elaine Showalter has argued, in Victorian England the visible signs of the disease made it "a powerful deterrent in the theological and moral reform campaigns to control male sexuality," and these symptoms were well known thanks to the proliferation of books of popular medicine and to rather graphic and explicit advertisements for medicinal "cures."[44] We are suggesting, in other words, that it would be much easier for a nineteenth-century audience than for us today to perceive that the signs of and associations with Amfortas's wounding (and its consequences) were compatible with syphilis. Indeed Edouard Hanslick's review in the *Neue Freie Presse* (Vienna) of the 1882 premiere of the opera focused on Amfortas's suffering: his bloody wounds, his baths and medications were so much the topic of discussion, he claimed, that the audience felt more a "clinical-pathological" than a tragic sympathy for him.[45] The intertwining of syphilis and sexuality in the nineteenth century made a reading of events of sexual transgression in terms of disease (and specifically *this* disease) more than likely. If to this is added the extensive historical context created by the Christian interpretation of syphilis as the scourge of God against the licentious sinner, then both the libretto and the music of *Parsifal* might profitably be reread against this background landscape of sexuality, sin, and suffering, even without postulating any conscious intent on Wagner's part. As we shall show, details once problematic or unnoticed can suddenly take on new meaning.

Soldiers and Prostitutes

When we first enter the realm of the Grail knights, we meet Gurnemanz, an older man who knows the entire story behind the afflictions of both the leader and the society. However, we also discover that he is curiously reticent—as parents or those in loco parentis often are about things sexual—when it comes to explaining the current situation and its cause to the younger squires. The boys ask him the name of the only one who can cure Amfortas, and Gurnemanz distracts them "ausweichend," evasively, by calling attention (ironically) to Kundry. When they press him for more details about Klingsor, he turns to others on stage and asks about Amfortas's bath to avoid replying. This evasion might well be, as has indeed been argued, a deliberate fragmentation and distortion in order to create tension; but it could also reflect shame and embarrassment about the sexual nature of this entire episode—especially for a celibate Grail knight. Wagner was not likely to be so realistic as to make it an example of "an old man's dogged slowness that gets around to everything eventually, but in its own good time."[46] Whatever his penchant for repetition in *Der Ring des Nibelungen*, here it is first-time information, and it is being overtly presented in an evasive manner. Considering that in some countries there was a long history of those accused of syphilis (or leprosy or the plague) being legally removed from society, there might be any number of good reasons for reticence and evasion.[47]

The fact is that between Amfortas's mention of his worry that another knight, Gawan, might fall into Klingsor's "snares" and Gurnemanz's explanation of what these dangers are, many minutes and many exchanges pass. We finally learn that in Klingsor's magic garden grow (and that is the verb used, "wachsen") "devilishly" beautiful women who wait to lure the Grail knights to what the libretto calls shameful pleasure and hell's defilement. We eventually learn from Klingsor himself in the next act that many have already fallen.

It is said that Baudelaire is responsible for the quip that "faire l'amour, c'est faire le mal"—to make love is to make (what can be translated as) pain—but "mal" also means both "evil" and "sick." His infamous "fleurs du mal" linked flowers and syphilis in the nineteenth-century literary imagination in a way that *Parsifal* too evokes. Of course Baudelaire was admired not only by Wagner, but by Huysman's Des Esseintes in A *Rebours*—perhaps *the* nineteenth-century text most openly linking syphilis and flowers.[48] Wagner's Flower Maidens taunt Parsifal for his apparent lack of interest in them, asking whether he is afraid of women or does not trust himself. They call him fainthearted and cold, and indeed they might simply be issuing a seductive challenge. They might, on the other hand, be describing what they see. Their banter—sung to "an archly sweet waltz tune" with "a sickly chromatic lilt"—also strongly suggests prostitutes trying to chat up a new and wary customer.[49] We know that enough of the Grail knights have already succumbed to this lure to worry Amfortas and to delight Klingsor.

Theodor Adorno is one of the very few commentators on Wagner that we have found to make a direct connection between this magic flower garden and "dreamland brothels . . . simultaneously calumniated as places that no one could leave unscathed." As he explicitly remarks, "In a regression familiar from the process of bourgeois education and known to psychoanalysis as 'syphilophobia,' sex and sexual disease become identical."[50] Though Adorno never really takes the next step, for those Grail knights and Amfortas, and potentially for Parsifal, that con-

nection between sex and disease was a probable reality. Wagner underlines the links between the knights and the Maidens by using the key
of A♭ major for both. Although a more formalist-oriented musicologist
might see this as structurally significant, "without necessarily suggesting
that the two groups of individuals are meant to be seen as symbolically
or actually related," we would argue that they are indeed related—and
in many ways.[51] Most obviously, the Flower Maidens (and Kundry) are
the explicit causes of the disorder within the Grail realm. As Carolyn Abbate has suggested, the Flower Maidens and the knights are "in a perverse way musically analogous": both are presented in choral passages, in
the same key, in basically diatonic music, with chromatic moments of tension (the Maidens' seduction of Parsifal; the knights' pressuring of Amfortas).[52] But is this connection really so very mysterious or "perverse"?

For five hundred years prostitutes have been considered a veritable
reservoir of syphilitic infection—and syphilis has been seen as a "soldier's disease" from the beginning.[53] According to popular lore if not historical fact, Indian women brought back by Columbus in the 1490s were
thought to have ended up as prostitutes in Naples at the time when
Charles VIII and his troops besieged the city. In the words of a seventeenth-century medical commentator, "The soldiers (of whom there
were as many French, German and Spanish ones wandering around as
Italians) who mixed with these shameless and unchaste Indian women
and behaved lewdly with them were struck down with this deplorable
sickness."[54] Another version of this seige has the Neapolitans driving
their prostitutes out of the citadel precisely so that they could then infect the enemy troops.[55] Whichever version might be closer to reality, it
does seem that wars make venereal diseases more visible by moving
them from the private to the public sphere.[56] In the twentieth century
too, the German imperial army is said to have been infected by the
French women of Lille and Roubaix as a result of enemy intelligence
planning: "Syphilis is not simply something one *has*. It is either a condition deliberately *given*, or a function of enemy intelligence."[57]

Already in the nineteenth century, military physicians were concerned about the general effect of this disease upon their forces, and
with good reason. Guy de Maupassant's tale *Le Lit 29* is set in Rouen dur-

ing Wagner's lifetime, that is, during the Franco-Prussian War. It is the tale of the revenge of a French courtesan who was raped and infected by the Prussians. She refuses treatment and uses her syphilis as an instrument of vengeance by infecting as many Prussians as possible. This is the sort of thing an army doctor had in mind a while later when he called prostitutes deadly "treponema machine guns": the chief surgeon of the navy at Brest had estimated that 2,144 of 6,294 able seamen contracted syphilis from 1850 to 1855. In England, within a seven-year period, 8,032 soldiers out of 44,611 were found to have venereal disease.[58]

Even earlier than this in seventeenth-century Germany, Hans von Grimmelshausen, in *Simplicius Simplicissimus*, had one of the camp followers of the armed forces in the Thirty Years' War describe her, shall we say, fee-for-service work in these strong and suggestive terms: "When, for great craving for the money thereby gained and because of my own insatiable nature, I went too far and went indiscriminately with almost any one who wished, behold I got what by rights I should have got twelve or fifteen years before, namely the dear French pox did me the favor! It broke out and began to adorn me with rubies, as the gay and merry spring garnished the whole ground, decorating it with all manner of beautiful flowers."[59] The Flower Maidens ("Blumenmädchen") are called early fading blossoms by Kundry ("früh welkende Blumen"), and thanks to those works by Baudelaire and Huysmans, nineteenth-century audiences would very likely have made the association here between flowers and syphilis.[60]

Soldiers and prostitutes, Grail knights and Flower Maidens — these are the dualities that structure the relationship between Amfortas (and potentially Parsifal) and Kundry. When Robert Gutman calls Kundry a "vampire who draws her nourishment from a destructive kind of sexual intercourse," we recall Elaine Showalter's reading of Bram Stoker's *Dracula* in terms of nineteenth-century "syphilophobia."[61] When Gutman then labels Kundry a "demonic prostitute, a true Art Nouveau *femme fatale*," what comes to mind is Showalter's description of how male writers constructed women as the enemy, "as the femmes fatales who lure men into sexual temptation only to destroy them."[62] The "demonic" prostitute was specifically the syphilitic prostitute, and in nineteenth-century bourgeois society, with its anxieties about waste, excess, and disease, the prostitute was seen as a threat to the "bourgeois economy of thrift and moderation," as Mary Ann Doane has argued and as the previous chapter explored in another context.[63] As a diseased woman, however, she also posed a very direct threat to the bourgeois family (through the dissolute male): the threat of infection and thus of hereditary syphilis. *Ghosts*, Ibsen's play about the ravages of syphilis, opened the same year as *Parsifal*, and the reason it was found so offensive, as Peter Gay has pointed out, was that so many in his audience knew precisely what he was talking about and that its plot involved the inheritance of money along with disease.[64] Doane's economic argument would dovetail with our medical one here, since the prostitute's "intolerable and dangerous sexuality" meant it was not only money but also disease that was in "free and unanchored circulation."[65]

Doane also calls on Sander Gilman's thesis, developed in his essay "Black Bodies, White Bodies: Toward an Iconography of Female Sexuality in Late Nineteenth-Century Art, Medicine, and Literature."[66] Gilman argues that in the past century prostitutes and black women were seen as highly sexual and therefore pathological. The nonwhite, non-European, non-Christian woman was made into the erotic "other." This process was of course not unfamiliar in opera: as we will see in chapter 6, the bourgeois audience at the Paris Opéra-Comique was shocked at Bizet's portrayal of the sexually aggressive gypsy Carmen. Kundry is another such dangerous alien: in the text she is called a heathen and a sorceress. She is described as wildly dressed, with black hair flowing in loose locks and piercing black eyes, sometimes wild and blazing, sometimes fixed and unmoving. Yet in act 2 this strange and accursed woman ("eine Verwünschte") is transformed into a "fearfully" beautiful temptress. She is also consistently associated with Arabia: she brings Amfortas's balsam from there; her dress when she tries to seduce Parsifal is said to be in Arab style; she is the one who tells Parsifal that his father, Gamuret, has died in Arab lands.

A number of critics have read Kundry's beauty as specifically Semitic, indeed Jewish.[67] Cursed by Christ for laughing at his suffering, she is explicitly linked in the text to the Wandering Jew and to Herodias in her double identity as both irresistible evil seductress and saint, suffering the anguish of humanity.[68] One doesn't even have to get into the debates over Wagner's anti-Semitism to argue the likely recognition of Kundry as "other" by a nineteenth-century German audience. Nor does one necessarily have to read *Parsifal* in particular as a story of the "Aryan dilemma" of racial impurity, though the Jewish subtext here might well be yet another way to explain the insistence and persistence of the explicitly Christian readings of the opera.[69] The Jewishness or Arabness of Kundry might instead work for Wagner's contemporaries to construct Kundry as different and dangerous on many levels. As Marc A. Weiner has convincingly argued at length, Wagner used body images — understood as signs of racial, sexual, and national identity — that were part of his nineteenth-century German audience's cultural and ideological baggage (even if not necessarily part of our own today).[70]

The year 1492 marked not only the encounter of Columbus with the New World (and thus perhaps with syphilis) but also the expulsion of the Jews from Spain. That both should come to be associated with the contemporaneous appearance and spread of syphilis in Europe is not historically surprising. Jews, like prostitutes (or even Jews as prostitutes), have commonly been associated with venereal disease and pollution — from Paracelsus to Hitler.[71] The panic-stricken rhetoric of nineteenth-century manifestos and debates about syphilis and sexual education or public health often betrays what has been called "an ominous obsession with racial purity."[72] Syphilis has always been a disease named after the "other," the enemy: the "mal de Naples" for the French, the "French disease" for the Germans and Italians, and so on. For some Germans it also later became the "Judenpest."[73]

In *Wagner: Race and Revolution*, Paul Rose argues in this vein that Amfortas's wound "is obviously a sexual wound, symbolic of racial sexual contamination."[74] But perhaps the real threat here is the *sexual* contamination itself. "Blood" is certainly at issue, but not only in the sense of racially inferior blood; it may also be a matter of infected, syphilitic blood. Therefore if Amfortas's music is indeed related to Klingsor's, it may be because Klingsor's sexual danger to others operates through his (contaminated)

Flower Maidens and Kundry: his castration would therefore be not only a sign of his Jewishness, as many have argued, but also a symbol of his own contagious and debilitating venereal disease.[75] In act 2 his slave, the seductive Kundry, appears amid those Flower Maidens, reclining on a couch—linking her visually to the always reclining, sick Amfortas, her earlier victim on that same couch. It was Wagner's innovative and suggestive changes in the source texts' portrayal of Kundry that made her into a beautiful and dangerous woman. In Wolfram's romance, Cundrie la surziere (the sorceress) is indeed also the Grail messenger and does, like Wagner's Kundry, know much about salves and medicine, but she is an ugly woman with yellow eyes, a blue mouth, and animal-like fangs. But tellingly, both have dark skin and long, dark hair. Wagner merged a number of female characters from Wolfram's text and others into a single dramatically powerful one who is terrifying because of both her sexuality and her concomitant radical otherness.[76] Thomas Mann once described Kundry as being "portrayed with an unsparing clinical accuracy, an audacious naturalism in the exploration and representation of a hideously diseased emotional existence."[77] But perhaps it was not only her emotional existence that we are meant to read as "diseased" or as "clinically" portrayed.

Sander Gilman has argued that in the nineteenth century, the "female is seen as the source of pollution, but also as the outsider, the prostitute, the socially deviant individual."[78] The desirable but physically corrupt body of the prostitute as source of infection fits precisely the presentation of Kundry in Wagner's text. A hundred years after the opera's premiere, a French critic could still construct syphilis in the nineteenth century as a female-carried, indeed feminized, disease that caresses before it condemns.[79] While both men and women obviously got the disease, from the late fifteenth century on much of the moral outrage seems to have been directed specifically against women as carriers, the descendants of the sinning Eve, who was blamed for introducing sex and even sexuality into the world. The nineteenth-century bourgeois representations of sexuality tended to be in terms of extremes: on the one hand, "personified in the figure of the syphilitic prostitute, sexuality can typify an abyss of contamination"; on the other hand, there was an "ideal of a regenerate sexuality."[80] But how was that ideal to be achieved when syphilis was as common as it clearly was—except, perhaps, through abstinence before marriage and fidelity after?

Sexuality and Social Decline

It is important, given that syphilis is a "soldier's disease," to note that the group of men who are so closely linked musically and narratively to the Flower Maidens—the Grail knights—have traditionally been discussed in terms that are simultaneously monastic and militaristic. But they also come to stand for the larger society that Amfortas's sin has troubled. Wolfram's source text has been read as presenting a world shaken by erotic passion: "In the figure of Anfortas, the Grail world, too, suffers the burden of sexual disorder. Anfortas's hideous wound in the groin was inflicted as he undertook a *minne* adventure unacceptable to the Grail."[81] If images of passion and unruly sexual desire connected to social decline do abound in the early romance, then so too, in a more subtle form, do they appear in the nineteenth-century music drama based on its narrative outlines. And as Thomas Laqueur has argued, "Serious talk about sexuality is . . . inevitably about the social order that it both represents and legitimates."[82] The linking of general social decline to sexual transgression by way of syphilis has been with us at least since the Renaissance.[83] However, a modern medical historian has placed the date of the culmination of this view closer to the time when Parsifal was created and performed:

> *Since the late nineteenth century, venereal disease has been used as a symbol for a society characterized by a corrupt sexuality. Venereal disease has typically been used as a symbol of pollution and contamination, and cited as a sign of deep-seated sexual disorder, a literalization of what was perceived to be a decaying social order. . . .*
>
> *Within the social constructions of venereal disease in the last century a number of important values have been expressed; themes that reflect longstanding historical traditions regarding sexual behavior. In particular, venereal disease came to be seen as an affliction of those who willfully violated the moral code, a punishment for sexual irresponsibility.*[84]

Amfortas's sexual transgression is one such violation. As Parsifal sees in act 2, even on his first visit, the Grail realm was experiencing the effects of this sexual disorder: he recalls the knights' desperate, physically tormented desire for the grace of the Grail, denied them by the sinful Amfortas. By act 3 a now aged Gurnemanz, bowed by grief and necessity, describes the decline of the Grail knights almost to an animal state. When Parsifal enters, having finally found the Grail realm again, he discovers major changes. The sorrow he had witnessed before, as Gurnemanz tells him, has been exacerbated to "greatest need" by Amfortas's persistent refusal, despite their pain and their pleas, to perform his office. Dejected, lost, lacking both courage and a leader, the Grail knights now represent a degenerate and degenerating society.

The music would also support such a reading of a world where disorder has gradually come to prevail. As Arnold Whittall points out, in the midst of generalized stable diatonic progressions of the opening can be heard shifting complexes of chromatic chords with the entry of Kundry and then Amfortas in act 1.[85] What Whittall calls the "dramatic appropriateness of the diatonic/chromatic interaction" becomes evident when the diatonic music of the knights' procession can be heard to form the strikingly contrasting background to Amfortas's anguished lament. Act 2's persistent chromaticism—we are now in the realm of Klingsor and his magic brothel-garden—is most intense during Kundry's kiss and Parsifal's response, where the young man (appropriately) recapitulates the music of both Amfortas and Kundry from the previous act.[86] But it cannot be "relatively incidental," as Whittal claims it is, that Kundry, Klingsor, and Amfortas should be linked through the most dissonant passages of the opera; nor is it likely in the least incidental that in act 3 chromaticism noticeably reappears with Parsifal's guilty anguish at being the inadvertent (because tardy) cause of the Grail realm's disorder and Titurel's death. In the Grail temple we witness two processions of knights, one carrying Amfortas on a litter and the other carrying the dead body of Titurel. They sing alternate passages of question and answer, leading up to the accusation that Amfortas is responsible for the death of his father. The music moves from despondency to menace as they turn on their leader, demanding that he perform his office ("Du musst! Du musst!"). Amfortas, "tormented by his own knights like a sick animal rounded on by the pack," begs them to kill him instead.[87] Into this brutal scene enters Parsifal to silence both the dissonance and the chromaticism by the diatonic resolution that accompanies his redeeming healing of Amfortas's wound and his acceptance of the role of Grail protector.

The issue of the redemptive role of Parsifal the character and of *Parsifal* the opera is one that has exercised critics for over a century, prompted no doubt by Wagner's own writings on religion and art and by the Bayreuth Circle's reading of the redemption of the Grail world in terms of the contemporary situation and of the function of art, *this* art, in the regeneration of an ailing society.[88] The merging of Christian redemption and Schopenhauerian negation of will (and desire) returns us to the sexual and even to the syphilitic, for in Germany, as early as the Diet of Worms (1495) and Maximilian's imperial edict, syphilis was not separable from sinful sexual immorality. But how does one redeem a sexually disordered or diseased society?

Redemption and the Sanctified Heterosexual Ideal

Parsifal's solution is as mythic as it is medical. One way to read it is as a moral lesson about the necessity for the legitimated—and thus non-diseased—union of male and female. One does not even have to invoke Freud to see that the end of the opera brings together, once again, the symbolically male spear and the equally obviously symbolically female Grail. This is the Grail—often associated with the womb of Mary in Christian legend—that Amfortas's sexual sin had offended and that he cannot bear to uncover; he has failed as its (her?) protector and can no longer do his office. A sexual reading of this situation might recall the nineteenth-century construction of the syphilitic male as "an arch-villain . . . a carrier of contamination and madness, and a threat to the spiritual evolution of the human race" through the threat to his wife and children, and through them (because of congenital syphilis), to the society at large."[89] In the Fisher King myths too, the king's potency was directly related to the reproductive force of the land as well as the society.[90] There is also a long mythic tradition that a sacred spear was used to pierce the side of a public scapegoat figure—of which Christ is one variant. But as with the portrayal of Kundry, Wagner's innovation is that he took what in Wolfram's romance are three different spears (the Grail processional spear, the one that wounded Anfortas, the one given to Parsifal for battle) and condensed them into one, which he set in its "rightful" place alongside the Holy Grail. It is Amfortas, in Wagner's libretto, who has separated the male Spear from the female Grail, profaning it by taking it into battle against Klingsor's deadly magic lure (in the form of the Flower Maidens). He falls prey to Kundry and loses the Spear at the moment of his sexual impropriety; its recovery and sanctified reunion with the Grail are at the center of the final healing and redemption.

Another of Wagner's innovations was his clear sexualization of Parsifal's quest. In both source texts and libretto, Kundry provokes Parsifal's realization that it is he who can redeem Amfortas; but in Wolfram she does this by an angry tirade against inaction, and in Wagner she does it explicitly with a passionate kiss: "So war es mein Kuss, / der welthellsichtig dich machte?" In the medieval romance version, Parsifal must ask the healing question to demonstrate his compassion; in Wagner's text, he must experience the sexual excitation of Kundry's kiss and then resist. Only then can he reclaim the Spear and eventually reunite it with the Grail, telling Amfortas that his suffering has thus been blessed: "Gesegnet sei dein Leiden." This act of giving the leader's ordeal significance is in itself redemptive: "Suffering ceases to be suffering at the moment it finds a meaning."[91]

Nietzsche's irritation at seeing *Parsifal* as advocating chastity and abstinence is certainly a possible reading.[92] It has to be admitted that, of the various unions of men and women portrayed in the opera, none can be called unproblematic in their final consequences or even in the immediate context in which they are presented. We know that Titurel had a son—Amfortas—who fails him in the end (literally); Gamuret and Herzeleide—Parsifal's parents—are evoked by Kundry, with powerful textual irony, to seduce him into unlawful union. All other sexual contacts are destructive—the Grail knights and the Flower Maidens, Amfortas and Kundry. But this does not necessarily mean that Wagner was advocating chastity as the only possible answer, for his audience would have known that Parsifal was later to marry and have a child—that is, Lohen-grin—since the opera of that name, with its protagonist's famous decla-ration of his lineage ("In fernem Land"), predates this one by over thirty years. They might even have known that in the Wolfram source text, once the ailing king is healed, Parsifal's wife (for he has one—called Con-diwiramurs), can finally go to her husband in Munsalvalsche because at last (as the translation puts it) "her sad state of deprivation was over."

Neither Gurnemanz nor the critics deny that Amfortas's is a story about the "venereal" consequences of sexual transgression.[93] Whether the interpretations are psychological or philosophical ones, they all sug-gest, in their very different ways, a kind of sexual anxiety pervading *Par-sifal*, even if not one that to our knowledge explicitly makes any con-nection to the major source of sexual anxiety in the nineteenth century: syphilis.[94] As we mentioned at the start, the Christian interpretation of the opera has dominated for a century, despite attempts of people like Theodor Adorno and Thomas Mann to redirect emphasis onto the sex-ual component that is so consistently linked with the Christian. *Parsifal* might indeed look like a denial of the sexual in the name of a "eucharis-tic philosophy of sanctification through abstinence from 'fleshly enjoy-ment.'"[95] But what we have been arguing here is that this seeming denial should be regarded anew in the light of that other dimension of the nine-teenth-century imagination—its identification of sexuality and disease. This reading is based on a series of textual details that become cumula-tively suggestive: Amfortas's particular kind of wound; his worries that his soldiers, the Grail knights, will fall prey to the dangers of the demonic and ominously named Flower Maidens; Gurnemanz's reticence; Kundry's con-struction as "other" in her perilous sexuality; the restoration of social order through the legitimating of rightful, sanctified male-female union. As we said at the beginning of this chapter, to argue the addition of such a read-ing is not at all to deny the Christian one: syphilis, from the very start, has been seen as the scourge of God upon the sexually promiscuous sinner.

The "Polyphony" of Wagner's Language

That we should be prepared to keep such multiple readings of *Parsifal* going at the same time is suggested by the libretto's resolute multiplying of meaning on every level, from the individual word to larger narrative structures. If this is "polyphony," it is without its musical associations of harmony: here different meanings are kept in tension with one another. Critics have often noted a series of dualities (or what some read as contradictions) in the opera. Mann, for instance, saw Wagner as having mastered "the trick of embodying the most sophisticated intellectual ideas in an orgy of sensual intoxication and making it 'popular,' the ability to clothe the profoundly grotesque in eucharistic solemnity and the tinkling mysteries of trans-substantiation, to couple art and religion in a sexual opera of supreme audacity."[96] Others have read the dualities in terms of "a religion of racism under the cover of Christian legend" or in terms of two "rival fields of energy": those of the Christian Grail world versus the pagan Fisher King myths.[97] Interpreters of the music have opposed the chromaticism of Klingsor's kingdom and Amfortas's anguish with the diatonicism of Parsifal's simplicity and the Grail's sublimity.[98] At the level of characterization, we have already seen that Amfortas has been compared to Klingsor (as both "unmanned by lust") and contrasted with Parsifal. As Mann put it, Amfortas is quite literally a "love-sick" high priest "who awaits redemption at the hands of a chaste boy."[99] The "reiner Tor" — the pure fool — who will cure his wound is "pure" in the sense of being holy and free from sin, but he is also "pure" in the sense of being free from disease, for he has resisted Kundry's dangerous charms.

The spiritual and the physical, the Christian and the sexual can never be separated in this text, even on this level of the individual word, for it is on this microcosmic level that characters are linked as well as set apart. Amfortas is described by Gurnemanz as one who is "Allzukühner" — all too brave — as he set out to rid the Grail realm of the danger of the enchanted garden and its beautiful women; the Flower Maidens call Parsifal, the man who has just defeated their lovers in that same garden, "Kühner" — not too brave this time, but obviously just brave enough. To be *too* brave is to court the hubris of Kundry's power. Amfortas and Parsifal are also both called "stolz" or proud — a designation that always precedes a fall, or the threat/hope of one. It was when Amfortas was in his proud manhood ("in seiner Mannheit stolzer Blute") that he had fallen prey to Kundry; in that light both Klingsor, when he sees Parsifal arriving in his garden ("Wie stolz er nun steht"), and the Flower Maidens, addressing him once he has entered ("du Stolzer"), verbally attempt to project Amfortas's fate onto Parsifal—who, however, turns out to be more pure than proud.

It is Kundry who is the literal connection between the two men, and she too is a doubled or even contradictory figure: both temptress and penitent, corruptor and balsam-bringing healer "with cataleptic transitions between these two states of being."[100] She is consistently linked, in the text's language and structure, to the man she is condemned to try to seduce but who can save her only if he resists. When, at the start of act 2, Klingsor taunts Kundry with her many names—original she-devil, rose of hell, Herodias, Gundryggia—we may well recall the boy (Parsifal) telling Gurnemanz in act 1 that he once had many names, but he no longer knows what he is called.[101] When Kundry calls out "Par-si-fal" in the garden, he asks if she is calling him, the nameless one ("Namenlosen"). In response she offers her (faulty) Persian derivation of his name as "Fal parsi," meaning pure fool. The text refers to both characters as wrongdoers or culprits ("Frevler" and the feminine "Frevlerin"); both too are said to be cursed ("verwünscht")—Kundry by Christ and Parsifal by Kundry herself.[102] In act 3, when the end of their sufferings is near at hand, both return to the Grail realm, and both are resolutely silent at first—much to the consternation of the poor talkative Gurnemanz.

That the former Grail *messenger* should be silent here points up the wordplay on Kundry's name that Wagner the librettist establishes early in the opera and consistently plays on. In associating Kundry with the German word "Kunde"—news, information, knowledge—the text, on one level, reminds us of her role as Grail messenger: to enable the Grail knights to send news to far-off lands ("*Kunde . . . entsenden*"). The noun reappears in the text in association with the Grail, when the young Parsifal asks what the "Grail" is and is told that he will find out that information ("bleibt dir die *Kunde* unverloren") only if he is pure. It is not accidental that Kundry has just that moment left the stage, for she has much information (about Parsifal's parents, among other things). But in accordance with another meaning of "Kunde" in German, she also has "customers"—or victims—as we will find out in the next act when Parsifal comes to Klingsor's castle and garden. His adventure there was motivated by what Kundry calls a desire for knowledge ("der K*unde* Wunsch"—not far from "der Kundry Wunsch," desire of Kundry).

The complex punning here that links knowledge and desire, and even messengers (carriers?) and customers, is not in the least atypical. Wagner the librettist often used doubling of meaning to echo doubling of structure in his narratives, doubling that his listeners' *ears* will catch. In other words, the links are not strictly etymological, but aural. The entire opera is, in a way, based on an aural wordplay on the German root "heil" that links health to holiness (and thus disease to sin). We are told early on, and in a noticeably poetically playful way, that Titurel built the Grail sanctuary after the angels gave him the Spear and Grail: "Dem H*eiltum* baute er das H*eiligtum*" (our emphasis). "Heil" is the root of "heilig" (holy), but "heil" also means unhurt, whole. Though not etymologically linked, "Heiltum" is thus aurally as well as thematically connected in *Parsifal* to "Heilung," the healing of Amfortas's wound. The listener's ear hears that the savior ("Heiland") is the one who can cure ("heilen"). And he does so, as we have seen, with compassion, "Mitleid," or literally, "mit Leid," by "suffering with" Amfortas.

Wagner's sensitivity to the plot value of the possible polyphony of language is never more acute than in this opera, and it often brings together, in the very words of the libretto, the Christian and the sexual, the redemptive and the healing. That Christ's passion should have taken place in a garden finds its ironic echo in Amfortas's different kind of passion in a different kind of garden. But both are equally scenes of suffering: Christ's and Amfortas's (and Parsifal's).[103] That verbal connection of the French "pécheur" (sinner) and "pêcheur" (fisherman) may well be a faulty derivation, but it was a popular pun and was used in Chrétien de Troyes's version of the Parsifal story to link, in effect, the pagan Fisher King, Christ, and Amfortas.[104] In Wagner's libretto there is a related punning in act 3, which takes place on Good Friday, the day commemorating Christ's atonement for the sins of the world ("der *sündigen* Welt zur S*ühne*"), but this time the aural connection is between the notions of sin ("Sünden") and atonement ("Sühne"). The similarity of the sounds—when sung—emphasizes the two terms and their relationship in Parsifal's lament at Titurel's untimely death. In the next scene Amfortas says that death would be a mild "Sühne" for his own great "Sünde."[105]

Wagner changed the name of the wounded king from Wolfram's Anfortas to Amfortas, and a possible reason might be to embed within his very name his (failed) social role, his "Amt." This reading is suggested by Titurel's asking, in act 1, if Amfortas is up to his job of uncovering the Grail: "Mein Sohn Amfortas, bis du *am Amt*" (our emphasis). The suffering son begs his father to resume the post he once held—"verrichte du das Amt"—but he knows he himself is condemned to do it. The rhyming language in which this knowledge is expressed underlines the connection between the task and the pain to which he is condemned: "zu diesem *Amt* ver*damm*t zu sein." And this suffering can be alleviated only by the same weapon that inflicted it: fittingly, in a kind of visual pun, Wagner has Parsifal enter at the end with both the Spear and Kundry, for both have been responsible for the wounding. Parsifal heals Amfortas's "Wunde" with the "Wunder" of the Spear, now reunited with the Grail. He thus verbally recalls the early description by Gurnemanz in act 1 of the Holy Spear as paradoxically wounding and wonderful: "wunden wundervoller heiliger Speer." Again the polyphony of meaning is embedded in the very texture of the language.

Wagner as librettist always manages to milk words for all their connotative and denotative significance. However, one more example, a telling one, must suffice: his repeated use of the verb "verfallen." As the German novelist Christa Wolf once remarked, this is a complex and contentious verb. In *Kindheitsmuster* (translated as *Patterns of Childhood*), her fictionalized narrative of growing up under Nazi rule, Wolf recounts her later coming to terms with its meanings:

> Verfallen—*a German word.*
>
> *A look into foreign-language dictionaries: nowhere else these four, five different meanings. German youth is addicted*—verfallen—*to its* Führer. *The bill drawn on the future is forfeited*—verfallen. *Their roofs are dilapidated*—verfallen. *But you must have known that she's a wreck*—verfallen.
>
> *No other language knows* verfallen *in the sense of "irretrievably lost, because enslaved by one's own, deep-down consent."*[106]

Wagner's usage of the verb also invokes this same notion of falling by "one's own deep-down consent," for it is Amfortas who fell to Kundry's charms—"der festest fällt . . . / und so verfällt er dem Speer"—and so forfeited the spear and his health ("verfiel"), wrecked because of his sexual enslavement to the accursed Kundry: "meinem Fluche mit mir alle *verfallen*." For *verfallen*, as Wolf noted, means to forfeit, to enslave, to go to ruin.[107] She does not mention that it also means to fall into sin and, not surprisingly, to decline in health. In none of these senses of the word does the idea of doing so by one's own consent disappear: it is not accidental that Kundry describes Amfortas to Parsifal as the "Verfall'nen," in other words. Even a simple verb like this can open out to a plethora of meanings that render the text dense with allusions and multiple possibilities.

There is no denying the almost rigidly balanced structuring of Wagner's opera—with its paralleled characters and its fiercely symmetrical scenes (two transformation scenes; two Grail ceremonies; a described [Amfortas's] and an actual [Parsifal's] seduction by Kundry)—though the repetition is always with significant differences. But equally there is no denying the dynamic ambiguities that are set in motion against this static structure by the kind of wordplay just examined. Commentators on the music of the opera have arrived at similar conclusions and have related these directly to the thematic tension we have been suggesting between order and disorder, redemption and sin, health and disease. Robin Holloway claims that the musical materials set up the plot's oppositions between "purity and impurity, innocence (or 'foolishness') and guilt, chastity and carnality, spiritual health and spiritual sickness, selfless compassionate suffering for others and suffering that indulges its torment in remorse and self-pity," but that in the end these are not oppositions at all but are "deeply interfused and interdependent, utterly ambiguous."[108] Where Carl Dahlhaus once read the music of *Parsifal* in terms of the opposition of chromaticism and diatonicism, Pierre Boulez has claimed instead that Wagner's music "places the emphasis for the first time on uncertainty, on indetermination, an aversion to definitiveness."[109] Adorno once said that Wagner was the first for whom ambiguity had been "elevated to a principle of style."[110] However, another interpretation could be that the tight balancing of scenes and character on the level of plot is an attempt to impose aesthetic order on a dramatic *and* musical narrative of (not ambiguity but) disorder — moral, political, and sexual disorder. But that ordering impulse is articulated in musical as well as verbal language that constantly undermines it by exploding into multiple rather than simply ambiguous meanings.[111]

Almost in passing, Peter Conrad once mentioned that music in *Parsifal* was what one might call both "salvation and venereal perdition."[112] In a sense this chapter has been a long explanatory footnote to precisely that complex duality — with its echoes of Christian redemption and syphilitic damnation, of healing and suffering. Wagner obviously made significant changes in the basic plot of Wolfram's text, but he did retain a core of Amfortas's pain and suffering, Parsifal's role as redeemer, and the theme of *Mitleid* or compassion. Wolfram's medieval concerns about faith and belief and about the relation between the human and the divine were obviously not Wagner's nineteenth-century concerns about sexual morality, as Marianne Wynn has argued.[113] But that plot core is one that in fact can be read as *both* Christian and sexual — in the context of the history of the meanings that have been associated with syphilis. It is as if Wagner "syphilized" a well-known story, recoding its poisoned wound in terms his contemporaries would react to.[114] Against the prevailing one-sided Christian readings of *Parsifal*, then, we offer the possibility that the spiritual and the sexual are permanently linked throughout the opera — indeed even before it begins, in Amfortas's sinning and wounding and in the social decline of the Grail realm. Such an interpretation of Wagner's opera — set against the backdrop of both the nineteenth-century obsession with syphilis and also the constant linking, throughout the past five hundred years, of the disease with God's punishment for sexual transgression — might at least begin to account for Thomas Mann's strikingly paradoxical descriptions of "Wagner's healthy brand of sickness, his diseased brand of heroism."[115]

Chapter 4

The Pox Revisited:
The "Pale Spirochete" in
Twentieth-Century
Opera

"Lovely! Seductive! Sensual! Poisonous! Something to burn the brain and blood!" — The Devil, pondering the siring of his daughter, Syphilis, in Oskar Panizza's 1895 *The Council of Love*

In his *History of Syphilis*, Claude Quétel points out that "nothing is more revealing of a society than the history of its diseases, particularly the 'social' diseases (as they were still called in the fifties): alcoholism, tuberculosis, insanity, syphilis, and so on."[1] Although in sheer numbers more people may have died of tuberculosis, the specter of syphilis managed to terrorize even more people even more effectively in the nineteenth century and well into the twentieth, as this chapter will examine further. Part of the obvious reason for the psychological power of this disease was its naming. Called "venereal," it was designated by its means of transmission and therefore had built-in connotations that were not only medical but moral, not only personal but social: William Blake, in his poem "London," wrote of "the youthful harlot's curse / . . . [that] blights with plagues the marriage hearse." Syphilis appears to be a disease that can't avoid getting tangled up in complex ways with our social and ethical notions about sexuality, notions that usually prove culturally specific rather than universal.

The Femme Fatale as *Femme Malade: Lulu*

As we saw in the previous chapter, in nineteenth-century Europe this moral-social-medical entanglement brought to the fore issues of race, class, and gender that a music drama like Wagner's *Parsifal* incarnated in singing, suffering bodies. In the ironic and critical terms of twentieth-century feminism, syphilis can today be read as "a true equalizer of men at this time, as the prostitute transmitted the pollution of the underclass depravity to those seeking to impose their privilege on her body."[2] But as even that contemporary position suggests, when it comes to talking about syphilis, male and female bodies continue to be represented differently: as exemplified by Kundry and Amfortas, women pollute, while men are polluted. In Sander Gilman's terms, by the eighteenth-century the male was seen as the "primary victim of the disease, rather than its harbinger . . . victim of the sexual pollution of the female."[3] The female, as only passive sufferer, was represented not as being in pain but solely as the contaminated source of the disease, its "seductive cause." Her beauty became the very image of "the potential for disease."

As our epigraph suggests, in Oskar Panizza's 1895 play about syphilis, *The Council of Love*, a literalized version of this potential appears on stage in the form of Syphilis. Called "The Woman" — the offspring of the Devil and Salome — she is described as "a young blooming creature with black hair and deep black eyes in which a smouldering sensuality, as yet only half awakened, is apparent." She is said to speak only the language "that every woman speaks! The burning language of seduction."[4] Panizza was able to activate that long European history of association of syphilis with prostitutes, a history Wagner too could draw on in his portrayal of Kundry. In the nineteenth century this seductive syphilophobic specter of disease did indeed say much about European social preoccupations, not to say obsessions, surrounding sexual matters. The twentieth century inherited these concerns, and medical science gave it new ones to worry about. New theatrical and literary conventions of realism (theoretically) allowed more open presentation of those worries (though the censors of various countries didn't always agree). Gradually, the need to refer by means of symbolic association to prostitutes as Flower Maidens disappeared; by the end of Alban Berg's opera *Lulu*, written in the 1930s, the protagonist is openly a prostitute in London. She is also the infecting agent of syphilis, and her latest husband, Alwa, is the very portrait of the male sufferer.

By the turn of the century it was known that, after a long latency, syphilis could once again reappear, and in a more dangerous form than the skin and bone conditions already noted: in cardiovascular and neurologic syndromes—including insanity—often leading to death. After Alfred Fournier's *Syphilis and Marriage* in the late nineteenth century, there were increasing concerns about the integrity of the family—and by extension the entire society—threatened by syphilis and its possible hereditary transmission.[5] These fears were made all the more immediate by new medical discoveries, but less by the identification of the *Treponema pallidum*, the "pale spirochete," by Schaudinn and Hoffmann in 1905 than by Wasserman's description in the next year of a blood test that could identify individuals with syphilitic infection. This allowed frighteningly high estimates of infection to be tested, estimates such as Fournier's that 15 percent of Parisians had syphilis in 1900 and a comparable German one suggesting that 10 to 12 percent of all Germans were infected. By means of the Wasserman test, the Germans were able to determine that indeed 12 percent of the adult population of Berlin did have the disease, and therefore to speculate that 22 percent of all Prussian men would have syphilis at some time in their lives.[6]

By the time Berg died in 1935, this was common knowledge in Europe. Berg never finished the orchestration of this, his second opera, which he had based closely on Frank Wedekind's two scandalous plays, *Erdgeist* (*Earth Spirit*) and *Büchse der Pandora* (*Pandora's Box*), both written between 1892 and 1894—in other words, immediately preceding Panizza's *Council of Love*. The opera and play are both explicit in their depiction of disease. In the last act Alwa cannot work because he has been cast, as he puts it, on a bed of sickness and torment ("das Krankenlager") by Lulu. The now classic configuration of gender and syphilis is invoked: Lulu, though infected by an earlier lover, is herself seemingly immune to the usual symptoms: "Sie hat es mir von ihrem Marquis übermacht, sie selbst ist längst nicht mehr dafür erreichbar." The prostitute pollutes but does not suffer. The plays are set in various parts of Europe in the 1890s, at a time when the fin-de-siècle panic over what was seen as the sexual epidemic of syphilis was once again translated into a public furor over prostitution.[7] The same terror of the seductive dangers of Wagner's magic garden brothel and the same need to contain and indeed punish the infecting agents determine that Lulu, like Kundry, must die. Whether she dies for her sins or in order to free men from anxiety is never made clear.

Our links to Parsifal here are not meant simply to remind readers of the previous chapter. Berg himself saw the music drama at Bayreuth and wrote to his fiancée that the event was "immensely invigorating and at the same time shattering." He begged her to help him "bear this great, this greatest experience."[8] The impact of seeing the opera has led commentators to suggest that Berg was attracted to Wedekind's plays because they were in a sense an anti-Parsifal.[9] The Lulu of Earth Spirit could be read as a parody of the character of Parsifal, the simple fool who does not have a single name and appears to know nothing. And indeed, his repeated proclamation of ignorance ("Ich weiss es nicht") is echoed exactly by Lulu early in the play. But the same interpretation cannot avoid noting the even more striking parallels between Lulu and Kundry. Both are femmes fatales with multiple and mythic names attached to them: Lulu is called Eve, Nelly, Mignon; Kundry, as we have seen, is called Herodias, Gundryggia, "Urteufelin" (original she-devil), and "Höllenrose" (rose of hell). Both women personify a demonic sexual drive, at least in the eyes of men — demonic because autonomous and non-productive, and therefore by definition deviant.[10] According to dominant ideology, if male sexual urges were natural and necessary, women (assumed to be asexual or at least without sexual desire) were deemed unnatural if they were promiscuous or became prostitutes. Although Lulu and Kundry are also different in some ways, to the list of their similarities should be added their Pandora-like power to seduce and to bring sickness and disease into the world.

Unlike Wagner's careful symbolic displacement of Kundry's diseased identity, however, Wedekind's strangely unmotivated and bizarre Lulu shocked both the general public and the religious, literary, and political establishment of his time — for a number of reasons. The plays were more or less constantly banned during his lifetime as an outrage to moral decorum. For some people, though, he became a kind of hero who dared to confront issues of sexuality and the hypocrisy surrounding it at the end of the nineteenth century. When Berg chose these very issues as his subject material in the late 1920s, he made a controversial and provocative decision. As one recent critic put it, "With a plot the subject-matter of which includes prostitution, blackmail, homosexuality, white-slave traffic, suicide, sex murder and a variety of other unsavoury topics, *Lulu* has a libretto that is undeniably sordid and that many people find distasteful and offensive."[11] Of course Berg's music itself was soon proscribed by the Third Reich. As a student of the Jewish Schoenberg, he too was labeled a decadent "Jewish Internationalist" whose twelve-tone music exemplified "musical communism" in its flouting of order, hierarchy, and priorities characteristic of "natural," organic tonality.[12]

It is probably the personality of Lulu the character, however, that has provoked the most profound disagreements in the subsequent criticism of both the plays and the opera.[13] Neither offers any motivation for Lulu's actions: she is seen only from the outside, by men. Many men die because of this woman on whom they have projected their needs and fears of Woman. Critics have associated Lulu with Lilith, who in Talmudic tradition was Adam's sensual and demonic first wife; given the title of Wedekind's play, she has been connected to Goethe's "Erdgeist" and even seen as an inversion of his Eternal Feminine ("Ewig-Weibliche").[14] The opera's prologue certainly invokes a rich web of related associations, introducing her as the dangerous—because beautiful—serpent who is the root of all evil and suffering:

Sie war geschaffen Unheil anzustiften,	*She was created to bring disaster,*
Zu locken, zu verführen, zu vergiften—	*to allure, to seduce, to poison—*
Und zu morden—ohne dass es einer spürt.	*and to murder—without a trace.*

In the German, the associations to the rhetoric of syphilis are clear: "Unheil" may mean "disaster," but its negation of "heil" (unhurt) and its association with "unheilbar"—"incurable"—in the context of a mission to allure, seduce, and especially poison act as syphilophobic reminders. Defined in this way, from the start, through the gaze of men, it is not surprising that Lulu becomes the projection of "an aggressiveness and destructiveness whose subjective correlative is guilt and self-punishment: for transgression, for violation, perhaps for desire itself."[15] As was the case with Amfortas, however, these men also project onto her the fear of infection that desire entails: in Wedekind's *Pandora's Box*, Dr. Schön calls Lulu the incurable disease for which he seeks a cure.[16] This is a woman who has been seen both as destructive lust personified and as a victim of social circumstances.[17] But no matter which interpretation you choose, the facts remain at the end of both opera and plays: Lulu does infect Alwa with syphilis; she does end up as a prostitute in London; she is murdered by Jack the Ripper. Like Kundry, Lulu, it seems, must die; the feminine source of pollution cannot be granted any rightful place in the social order.

That Berg's twentieth-century opera can draw on the same syphilophobia and the same cultural representations of disease, even after the identification of the "pale spirochete," is not surprising: from the start its sexual transmission was evident, and the identification only confirmed its infectious nature. Although the Nobel Prize had gone to Paul Ehrlich in 1910 for his discovery of Salvarsan, a treatment for syphilis, no true cure had yet been found for a disease whose epidemic proportions could now be quantified. In addition, with the new understanding of the ravages of tertiary syphilis came new fears that amplified existing ones, specifically fears about madness.

The Terrors of Bedlam: "The Rake's Progress"

Pierre Boulez once called *Lulu* a "morality play, a sort of *Rake's Progress*" with the familiar plot of its protagonist's rise and fall.[18] This comparison to the 1951 opera composed by Igor Stravinsky from the libretto written by W. H. Auden and Chester Kallman has been made often, usually in terms of parallels that involve both the story and the moral. Certainly *The Rake's Progress* offers characters who are as unrealistically portrayed, yet at times as tragically moving, as any in *Lulu*.[19] What both operas also share, however, is the venereal disease that determines the particular form — narrative as well as ethical — of their endings. In the last act of *Lulu* there is an overt connection made between promiscuity and syphilis, with a reassertion of order in the form of the retributive punishment meted out to the offending and infecting woman; in the last act of *The Rake's Progress*, it is those new fears about the particular fate of the infected that are called on as the context of the final moral.

Unlike *Lulu*'s setting in "decadent" fin-de-siècle Europe, *The Rake's Progress* moves both forward and backward, on both sides of the Atlantic. Written in the United States in the 1940s but with a plot set in eighteenth-century England, *The Rake's Progress* sits temporally and geographically on both sides of the operas of Wagner and Berg. That its references to syphilis are indirect—as in *Parsifal*—should not be surprising, given the long association of the disease with sin and shame. For the middle classes of both Europe and North America, even in the twentieth century, the most common response to this most common disease was denial. It goes without saying that this *pudeur* hampered medical research: even in the previous century syphilis had been seen as "an elusive disease which persisted not only as a complex medical challenge but also as a social dilemma. Those who studied the disease confronted many obstacles—ethical controversies and frequent refusals among patients to cooperate, as well as doctrinal biases among colleagues and confusion as to the proper application of the scientific method in medicine."[20] In the twentieth century some of these "doctrinal biases" fell away, but the refusal of patients to admit to the disease did not. The evasion and embarrassment Wagner's Gurnemanz betrays when questioned about Amfortas's wound and its source are typical of the silence and shame surrounding venereal disease right through to the middle of the twentieth century.

Just as Wagner had adapted and recoded a well-known medieval poem, Stravinsky's librettists, Auden and Kallman, gave both voice and motion, so to speak, to William Hogarth's famous set of eighteenth-century paintings and engravings called "The Rake's Progress." It was on the advice of Aldous Huxley that Stravinsky first made contact with Auden in 1947 after seeing the Hogarth paintings at the Art Institute of Chicago. It seems he had been struck by how suggestive they were when considered as operatic scenes.[21] This was to be Stravinsky's first (and only) full-length opera and the last of his neoclassical works. It was written for chamber orchestra, complete with arias, recitatives (to harpsichord), chorus, and a Mozartian finale. The eighteenth-century visual inspiration appears to have provoked an eighteenth-century parody on the level of the music as well, though critics are divided on the success of the latter.[22] Although the music and the libretto's plot, milieu, and atmosphere may well recall that earlier period, this is still very much a work of the first half of the twentieth century, and not only in formal terms: there is a strong thematic subtext concerning the social and medical anxieties about the public as well as private consequences of venereal disease, anxieties shared by both Europeans and North Americans until that mid-century discovery and use of penicillin as a cure for syphilis.

In the eighteenth century too, as Hogarth's art shows so clearly, the intersection of sexuality, morality, and disease was a major concern. In 1732 Hogarth produced a series of engravings entitled "The Harlot's Progress." These tell the tale of a fresh-faced country girl, Moll Hackabout, who comes to the city and meets a well-known bawd, Elizabeth Needham—shown sporting those facial "beauty marks" that could hide the ravages of various sorts of pox. By the second engraving Moll too bears such a mark; by the third, her woman servant is shown with the flattened nose of a syphilitic, and her window ledge houses medicine bottles and a pot of ointment.[23] In the fifth are figured a variety of contemporary attempts to treat syphilis: Moll, whose teeth have all fallen out, is wrapped in blankets so that she will sweat and salivate (from taking her mercury pills); an "Anodyne Necklace"—a well-advertised and popular panacea of the day—can be seen; two doctors are shown arguing over whether pills or liquid could cure best, a debate that was carried on daily in every newspaper. The two men were easily identified at the time as Dr. Jean Misaubin and Dr. Richard Rock, whose "incomparable Electuary" was touted as "the only VENEREAL ANTIDOTE."[24]

"The Rake's Progress," Hogarth's subsequent series, was executed both in the form of paintings (1733–34) and as engravings (1735). As its title suggests, it is a kind of male parallel to Moll's story. The first image presents a young man, Tom Rakewell, who inherits a fortune on the death of his father. He then proceeds, as Ronald Paulson explains, to act as a stereotypical rake "who would get a young girl pregnant and buy her off; ape all the latest London fashions;[25] wench and gamble; be arrested for debt; recoup through a loveless marriage with a rich old hag; lose it all at gambling; go to debtors' prison; and die of chagrin and tertiary syphilis in Bedlam."[26] Paulson's effortless move here to "tertiary syphilis" is, however, a specifically twentieth-century interpretation. In Hogarth's day, as we shall see shortly, no one had yet talked explicitly in medical terms about any cause-and-effect relation between syphilis and madness, although the pox, debt, and insanity were often seen as the logical outcomes of a life of dissolution.

Stravinsky had been particularly impressed with the operatic possibilities of what he called the "Asylum finale."[27] Significantly, although his librettists made liberal changes to the plot suggested by Hogarth's images, it was this scene and the one that takes place in a brothel, the other that can be directly connected thematically to venereal disease, that they did choose to retain. Auden and Kallman later often remarked that they had found Hogarth's figures generally to be too passive, too "acted upon," to bear the weight of operatic action and so had had to find ways to enhance the drama of "the basic line—here is a young man who comes in for a lot of money and goes to the bad and ends in Bedlam."[28] In an attempt to add dramatic force to Hogarth's basic narrative, they first decided to invent what on one level can only be called a stock nineteenth-century melodramatic villain figure: Nick Shadow. But his very "obviousness" as a creature of melodrama works in conjunction with the double echoes in his name of the devil—Nick—and of Jung's concept of the "shadow" to give him more a symbolic than a real identity in the opera. The libretto's plot introduces him mysteriously: he suddenly appears to offer his services to Tom Rakewell for a year and a day; at the end, in return for granting Tom his three wishes (for money, happiness, and success), he demands his life and soul in payment. Tom's life is saved only by the voice of Anne Trulove, his innocent beloved; enraged, Nick curses Tom into madness.

With the introduction of this new plot agent, Auden and Kallman appear to have broken the narrative chain that exists in the Hogarth works between the brothel and Bedlam, between sexual dissipation and madness. In the third of Hogarth's images, set in the Rose Tavern, the young rake is surrounded by what commentators love to call the "votaries of Venus," complete with their beauty marks. Tom appears to be infected already: in the foreground of the work, his sword points to a box of mercury pills that seems to have fallen out of his pocket onto the floor.[29] In

8. Tom Rakewell in the brothel, from William Hogarth, "The Rake's Progress."

the background, one of the women appears to be either illuminating or, more likely, setting fire to a map of the world. As the famous commentary of that eighteenth-century German Anglophile Georg Christoph Lichtenberg put it, she does so at the spot "just in front of the East Coast of America, whence, as is well known, the Spaniards brought a certain product to Europe with which girls of that type carry on a sort of smugglers' trade, up to this day."[30] This is the part of the world "where the former American Company first started a conflagration *in natura*," he continues. Others have therefore seen this incendiary act as a symbolic prefiguring of "the Rake's being consumed not only by lust but by infection as well—part of the rake syndrome, and an obsessive consequence in Hogarth's works."[31]

The specific consequence Hogarth suggests is to be found in the final work of the series: insane, Tom is in an asylum on the point of death. Paulson has argued that Hogarth is "too physically oriented to have sent the Rake to Bedlam only on the basis of his mounting troubles" of a finan-

9. Tom Rakewell in Bedlam, from William Hogarth, "The Rake's Progress."

cial nature.³² And certainly it is not only "The Rake's Progress" that reveals Hogarth's physical orientation and his awareness of the medical as well as social impact of venereal disease: besides "The Harlot's Progress," there is his 1745 series "Marriage à la Mode," in which both a money-hungry aristocrat and the alderman's daughter are represented as having the physical signs of the syphilitic. But the portrayal of Tom Rakewell goes one step beyond even this medical realism: he appears to die of his madness. Today we know much more about syphilis than Hogarth could have, of course. And one of the things we know is that few causes of insanity are actually fatal other than "dementia paralytica," the mental disorder associated with syphilis. But, this was not medically proved until 1913.

In the eighteenth century, madness was the cause of both terror and morbid fascination: the young women pictured in the background of that final image of "The Rake's Progress" are visiting Bedlam for entertainment and titillation. Toward the end of that century, a clinical discourse developed around a particular form of madness characterized by grandiose and expansive delusions, accompanied by neurological symptoms of a general paralysis, not infrequently leading to death. "Dementia paralytica," as a clinical entity, was named by Jean Etienne Dominique Esquirol at the beginning of the nineteenth century; by 1857 it had been described as a manifestation of tertiary syphilis.[33] The syphilitic origin of "general paresis of the insane," as it was known, however, was the topic of a famous debate, carried on in part between Jean Martin Charcot and Alfred Fournier in the late 1890s. The debate was not really settled until 1913 when Hideyo Noguchi and J. W. Moore demonstrated the existence of *Treponema pallidum* in the brains of patients with general paresis.[34]

This clinical condition was one of the first psychiatric diseases shown to have a known etiology. It quickly became apparent that this was a frequent cause of irreversible madness in young individuals; indeed, by the 1930s it accounted for between 10 and 20 percent of admissions to asylums.[35] Its classic psychiatric features included delusions of grandeur, disturbances of body image and identification, and also self-mutilation. In Hogarth's image of Bedlam, Tom appears to have stabbed himself in the chest and has perhaps been placed in irons for his own protection. There may be other "coded" hints meant for a contemporary, eighteenth-century audience who may have intuited or observed that (not yet proved) connection between the asylum and things venereal: on the bannister of the stairs is carved the name of "Charming Betty Careless," a well-known courtesan of the time and perhaps the cause of the problems of more than one of the inmates. In the engraving Tom appears to be bald, another sign of syphilitic infection.[36] Although in Hogarth's day the accepted sequence of decline went "love–sexual attraction–abandonment–insanity," there was also an implied relationship among "venereal excess–venereal disease–nervous disease–insanity" that came to make medical sense only in the twentieth century.[37]

The Rake's Progress: Made in the U.S.A.

We suggested earlier that, for all its eighteenth-century inspiration, *The Rake's Progress* was very much a twentieth-century opera, and its composer and librettists were very much twentieth-century men.[38] Stravinsky spent the years between the two world wars in France, primarily in

Paris. And according to Quétel's *History of Syphilis*, in France "the whole inter-war generation was literally obsessed with the fear of syphilis."[39] Among the most likely reasons for this obsession and this terror was the prevalence, even before the First World War, of a widely used and socially powerful public discourse that renewed old fears about the disease that had been confirmed by new medical evidence. Building on existing associations in the history of the disease—associations such as those that *Parsifal* too manifested with the sanctified and legitimated male-female union and with general social decline—this revival of earlier meanings given to syphilis was in part the work of the European and American "social hygiene" movements, such as Fournier's revealingly named "Société Française de Prophylaxie Sanitaire et Morale." The many articles on these topics that appeared in the popular press kept these newly reawakened associations in the forefront of the public's attention.

The outbreak of war in 1914 had focused worries about venereal disease on the familiar combination of prostitutes and fighting men. As Dr. Walter Clarke, a prominent American social hygienist, put it: "The army and navy which is the least syphilized will, other things being equal, win."[40] In the years after the war these concerns did not go away; they were simply transferred to the civilian population. In one year, 1926, over fifteen thousand articles on the subject appeared in the popular French press and, in Paris, five thousand metal plaques were put up in municipal urinals and factory washrooms to warn of the dangers of this "social" disease and to explain the facilities available for treatment.[41] Our reason for concentrating on Paris here is probably obvious: in the city where Stravinsky lived during these years, it would have been difficult to avoid coming into contact with this new public discourse of venereal disease on a more or less daily (and rather familiar) basis.

When Stravinsky emigrated to the United States in 1939, he moved into a social context that was equally obsessed with syphilis. The then surgeon general of the United States, Thomas Parran, had already identified venereal disease as the most pressing of all the country's public health problems. His strongly held views were disseminated widely through such popular magazines as the *Ladies' Home Journal*, *Reader's Digest*, and *Time*, on whose cover he appeared in 1936. In 1937 he published a book on the topic, ominously titled *Shadow on the Land*. His public health measures — including aggressive case finding and contact tracing — led to widespread screening for syphilis. The Wasserman test, in fact, became a premarital requirement in many states. This obsessive public concern actively promoted in America the same kind of syphilophobia as had flourished in Europe in earlier decades, with the same social results: social stigmatizing, fear, and denial. With the onset of the Second World War came, once again, almost a panic response to the possibility of prostitutes' infecting the armed forces: by 1941, when the United States entered the war, a public debate raged about the insufficiency of military venereal disease programs to protect the troops.[42] Although the cure for syphilis — penicillin — came to be generally available after the war and worries and fears gradually receded, the social stigma often remained. And since tertiary syphilis appears only many years after the primary infection, general paresis of the insane (dementia paralytica) remained an important clinical entity well into the 1950s.

Parran had been provoked to take his strong public stand against the disease by findings suggesting that by 1937 there were more than six million syphilitics in the United States, constituting about 10 percent of the adult population. As we noted earlier, other reports suggested that as many as 20 percent of all the inmates in American mental institutions suffered from the direct consequences of tertiary syphilis. Today we may also need to be reminded of the intensity of both the shame and the despair felt about psychiatric disturbances of all kinds in an age before the development of major tranquilizers and before the neurochemical explanations of some conditions. In the 1930s in the United States, mental illness from syphilitic infection carried multiple stigmas. This was the social climate when Stravinsky emigrated in 1939. It might well have been the strong similarities of concern between his own and Hogarth's time that suggested to him, in 1947, the dramatic possibilities of the asylum scene in particular. Also living in the United States at this time, Auden and Kallman may have perceived the similarities as well, retaining only the Bedlam and the brothel scenes in a libretto that otherwise departs greatly from the outlines of the Hogarth plot.

In fact, both the music and the text of the opera structurally relate and even parallel the two scenes. Both are also connected to the opening scene, set in a garden in the country where Tom Rakewell and his inno-cent and pure beloved, Anne Trulove, sing of spring, nature, and "the Cyprian Queen"—also known as Venus, of course. In their duettino, the music introduces a minor-major appoggiatura that is repeated in both the brothel and the Bedlam scenes, thereby musically linking the three scenes in a progression of innocence, its loss, and subsequent insanity and death. In a similar way the pastoral world of Anne's garden is paro-died in Mother Goose's brothel in act 1, scene 2, where the innocence of Anne's opening line—"The woods are green"—is transmuted into the "Lanterloo" song ("The sun is bright, the grass is green") sung by the cho-rus of the "Whores" and "Roaring Boys" accompanying Mother Goose and Tom to bed. Here what musicologists call the "country reed ensem-ble" has expanded into "an urban serenade band of oboes, clarinets, bas-soons and horns in pairs, sounding a ritornello, and the innocence of the opera's beginning is quite gone."[43] Indeed, if anything this is more the fallen garden in which the shepherd Syphilis once roamed—in the six-teenth-century poem by Fracastorius that gave the disease its name in the first place.

The C major of one of the main choruses sung by the Roaring Boys and Whores in the brothel scene does not appear again in the opera, ev-idently, until the music accompanying the chorus of madmen mocking Tom in Bedlam: "The atmosphere is of course very different, flat where the earlier number was thoroughly dynamic, but this is again a chorus of statement on behalf of a particular section aside from normal society."[44] But perhaps the repetition of the C major is meant to suggest that they represent the *same* group of outsiders, who are simply, like Tom, shown at different moments in their lives. And perhaps the shift in atmosphere from dynamic to flat reflects the progression from cause to effect, from the energy of dissipation to its devastating consequences. After all, in the brothel the Roaring Boys sing to Mars and the Whores sing to Venus in a way that recalls that familiar conjunction of the military and prosti-tution that fueled syphilophobia throughout the centuries. The women also echo, with sinister overtones, Tom's opening evocation of the goddess of love who gave venereal disease its name. In what on the surface are utterly conventional terms, Tom sings of

> *the season when the Cyprian Queen*
> *With genial charm translates our mortal scene,*
> *When swains their nymphs in fervent arms enfold*
> *And with a kiss restore the Age of Gold.*

The classical decorum and distance of "swains" enfolding "nymphs" in "fervent arms" disappear in the brothel scene, which follows directly. Here military metaphors explicitly frame both desire and disease (with its ironically named "trophies"), as the Whores sing:

> *In triumph glorious with trophies curious*
> *We return victorious from Love's campaigns;*
> *No troops more practiced in Cupid's tactics*
> *By feint and ambush the day to gain.*

These women—who claim to "open fire upon young and old"— join with the Roaring Boys to toast both Venus and Mars and to urge Tom on to "reckless enjoyment / For too soon the noiseless night will come."

In this scene, however, Tom's initiatory song is sung to love, not pleasure, and in it he sets up the imagery that will take on its full meaning at the end of the opera:

> *Love, my sorrow and my shame,*
> *Though thou daily be forgot,*
> *Goddess, O forget me not.*
> *Lest I perish, O be nigh*
> *In my darkest hour that I,*
> > *Dying, dying,*
> *May call upon thy sacred name.*

Indeed, in his darkest hour in Bedlam, Tom does call upon the goddess of love, Venus. From the first moments of his madness, he believes himself to be her Adonis:

10. Tom Rakewell (Eugene Conley) with Mother Goose
(Martha Lipton) in the brothel scene in the 1952–53 production
of *The Rake's Progress* at the Metropolitan Opera, New York.

> *With roses crowned, I sit on ground;*
> *Adonis is my name,*
> *The only dear of Venus fair:*
> *Methinks it is no shame.*

Some productions of the opera have also visually linked the brothel and
Bedlam scenes: that of John Cox at Glyndbourne in 1975, designed by
David Hockney, made Tom's straw pallet here recall Mother Goose's
large throne-bed and repeated visually in the madmen's cells (as in the
Hogarth) the doors and rooms of the prostitutes' chambers.[45]

In the next scene the libretto shows Tom awaiting the arrival of Venus among the "heroic shades": "Come quickly, Venus, or I die!" This is
the point at which the chorus of madmen echoes both the musical key
and the admonition (enjoy life before the arrival of "noiseless night") of
the Roaring Boys and the Whores of the brothel scene: "Banker, beggar,

whore and wit / In a common darkness sit," in the "night that never ends." Anne Trulove arrives and plays into Tom's delusion, assuring him that "the wild boar is vanquished." One obvious echo here is of John Blow's seventeenth-century opera *Venus and Adonis*, itself a satire on the liberal sexual mores of the court of Charles II.[46] In that work Adonis, mortally wounded by a mighty boar, sings to Venus: "Let me on your soft bosom lie / There did I wish to live, and there I beg to die." At this point Auden and Kallman choose to have Tom stagger, perhaps to signal the ironic presence of Venus in yet another form: he could well stagger from Tabes, a neurological feature of tertiary syphilis sometimes coexisting with general paresis. Anne helps him to the ground, laying his head on her breast. After she has left, singing "Every wearied body must / Late or soon return to dust," Tom starts to his feet searching for her and betraying what would, in psychiatric terms, be his grandiose and paranoid ideation: "Where is my Venus? Why have you stolen her while I slept?" He begs the madmen around him to "weep for Adonis whom Venus loved"—which they do, as he falls back on his pallet.

The opera keeps the name of Venus in our ears through crucial interconnected scenes from beginning to end, from that opening clichéd euphemism ("Cyprian Queen") through the brothel to the Bedlam scenes: the venereal haunts the opera's language as it does its protagonist. The librettists added that song to Venus by the Whores and Roaring Boys at a later stage, as if in recognition of the structural and thematic connections.[47] The hortatory epilogue, in part a parody of Mozart's in *Don Giovanni*, opens with an echo of the introductory bars of the brothel scene. Given the moral and even medical links between the warnings voiced in the epilogue and the action that took place in the Rose Tavern, this is hardly the "frivolous" echo some commentators have suggested.[48] These warnings are sung with the houselights up and wigs off. Anne's is the first: "Not every rake is rescued"—as the opera had shown and as the high numbers in United States asylums were making abundantly clear. Tom's warning then underlines what are in fact some of the delusional characteristics of syphilitic dementia:

11. Tom Rakewell (Eugene Conley) in Bedlam in
the final act of the 1952–53 production of *The Rake's Progress*
at the Metropolitan Opera, New York.

Beware, young men who fancy
You are Vergil or Julius Caesar,
Lest when you wake
You be only a rake.

Even before his imagining himself to be Adonis, Tom had arguably suffered what could be read as delusions of grandeur. In act 2, scene 3, he
awakens from a dream in which he has imagined a machine that could
convert stones to bread: "I saw all want abolished by my skill / And earth
become an Eden of good will." Nick Shadow then enters with what the
audience can see to be a crude false-bottomed trick apparatus that Tom
truly believes is the materialization of his dream:

Thanks to this excellent device
Man shall re-enter Paradise
From which he once was driven.

Tom believes that he will now be able to secure humanity from need, "the cause of crime," and thereby reduce all "toil, hunger, poverty and grief." To the audience, Nick ironically mocks these delusions:

> *Omnipotent when armed with this,*
> *In secular abundant bliss*
> *He shall ascend the Chain*
> *Of Being to its top to win*
> *The throne of Nature and begin*
> *His everlasting reign.*

It is from experience, then, that Tom can warn the audience not to imagine themselves a "Vergil or Julius Caesar."

In that same epilogue, Nick sings that "poor Shadow / Must do as he is bidden." As mentioned earlier, Nick is an addition of the librettists and is a stock villain, as melodramatically demonic (in name and deed) as Anne Trulove is melodramatically pure and noble. (She too is their invention, or at least their adaptation of Hogarth's long-suffering Sarah Young figure, once seduced and later abandoned, but somehow always managing to be present to help Tom.) The familiar black-and-white moral dualities of melodrama evoked by the libretto demand that Tom be torn between the devil and the angel, evil and good. With echoes of Goethe's (and Gounod's) *Faust* as well, the damning demonic ("Nick") and the redemptive pure ("Trulove") do indeed meet in the graveyard scene of act 3, scene 2, in which Nick demands his wages for his services of the last year and a day: Tom's life and therefore his soul.[49] Nick appears to agree to give Tom three chances to save himself: he must guess the identity of three cards he will pull from a pack. It is only through the subconscious associations of the cards with Anne, his true love, that Tom miraculously manages to guess all three. The first, the queen of hearts, he guesses simply by thinking of her. When a spade falls forward with a great crash, Tom exclaims, "The deuce!" and then looks at the spade and sings: "She lights the shades / And shows—the two of spades"—the correct identification of the second card. For his third card, Nick has stealthily reinserted the queen of hearts into the pack to guarantee Tom's failure and his own victory. But Tom hears, as we do, the offstage Anne sing a line from the first act — "A love / That is sworn before thee can plunder hell / Of its prey" — and we see her love do precisely that, as Tom once again recalls his "queen of hearts." Tom may win, but in the libretto version of this story, Nick is left with one final weapon:

> *Thy sins, my foe, before I go*
> *Give me some power to pain:*
> *To Reason blind shall be thy mind:*
> *Henceforth be thou insane!*

But it is Tom's own "sins" that give Nick the "power to pain": this condemnation to madness is not so much an external plot action as the consequence of Tom's own life choices and their medical consequences. As Nick reminds him: "The sins you did may not be hid."

In fact, throughout the opera there have been hints — from Nick's surname of Shadow on — that he is but a part of Tom himself, perhaps his Jungian "shadow," the "dark aspects of the personality" of which one can become conscious only through "considerable moral effort."[50] When Tom awakens from that delusional dream in act 2, scene 3, he calls out, "Who's there?" Nick puns in reply: "Your shadow, master." And once again it is Nick who, in the graveyard, hands Tom a bag containing "steel, halter, poison, gun" — the means to suicide. From its first firm medical identification, syphilitic dementia was shown to be characterized by such suicidal impulses.[51] If Tom's residency in Bedlam had indeed been brought on himself through his dissolute life, then "poor Shadow" must indeed "do as he is bidden," for he has no separate identity.

Nick's descent into hell at the end of the graveyard scene may well recall musically the descent of Mozart's Don Giovanni. But neither Tom nor his shadow has the demonic don's arrogance or power, cynicism or resolve.[52] Both operas may be moral fables, with moralizing epilogues, but their protagonists have been interpreted very differently. For instance, Arnold Whittall has suggested that Tom "deserves his fate" for different reasons than the don might: because of weakness of character.[53] In the context of our interpretation here, such a remark recalls the long history of condemnation of the syphilitic: in the 1960s a medical historian could still comment on the belief that "holds until this day that he who contracts syphilis deserves no sympathy. He is only receiving his just due."[54] In his 1954 review of the opera, Joseph Kerman saw the ending as proof that the "life of pleasure involves grave responsibilities" but claimed that Tom dies unredeemed and "without understanding" because he has lost his mind.[55] But in the context of general paresis of the insane, that is precisely the point: syphilis is among the consequences of the life of pleasure.

The opera's structural connections, both musical and textual, between the brothel and Bedlam make this same point and faithfully translate the moral ethos and medical message of Hogarth's images, with their obsession with the physical and, indeed, the pathological. Written and composed as it was in the United States in the late 1940s and early 1950s, however, the opera *The Rake's Progress* can be read as another addition to the well-documented archive of America's obsession with syphilitic dementia. The classic clinical signs of general paresis are there: Tom's delusions of grandeur and identity (Adonis), his suicidal tendency, his paranoia, his staggering gait, and ultimately his death resulting from his "sins." No wonder, then, that Venus so ominously presides over the major scenes of the opera.

It has been said that *The Rake's Progress* can be read as everything from "a moral tract to a razor-edged satire, . . . from a series of musical tableaux to a symbolic music drama."[56] If so, then it can also be read as yet another moral tale of the venereal peril, a successor to Wagner's *Parsifal* or Ibsen's *Ghosts*, or even to riches-to-poverty stories of real-life experience such as that told by that nineteenth-century syphilologist, Alfred Fournier:

> A *manufacturer married in despite of an insufficiently-treated syphilis. Thanks to his intelligence in business matters and to his wife's fortune, he established a large manufactory, which prospered wonderfully. Some years later he was affected by gummatous periostoses and exostosis of the skull. There followed gradually cerebral symptoms of various kinds; intellectual disturbances, vertigo, epileptic fits, hemiplegia. At last he dissipated all his fortune, and compromised his commercial honour, in great and adventurous undertakings which he had become incapable of directing; or, to speak more plainly, which he would never have undertaken had his*

mind been clear. He was ruined. Finally, he fell into a state of dementia and died,
leaving his wife and four children in a state bordering on poverty.[57]

Tom's delusions about his dream machine and his subsequent financial
ruin do more than recall, therefore, Hogarth's familiar middle-class moral
parable in which drink, women, and gambling lead to wasted money.
They suggest as well an awareness—which Hogarth also shared—of the
medical consequences of the common syphilitic parable in which prostitutes are the seductive causes of disease that can end in madness as
well as physical pain.

Syphilis continued to be a terrifying disease, with good reason, until
the discovery of a cure in the middle of the twentieth century. Although
mercury continued to be used in its treatment into that century, there
had been uncertainty about its efficacy. Therefore there was great excitement in 1909 when Paul Ehrlich developed the first true antimi-
crobial, arsphenamine or Salvarsan—the "magic bullet" he had been
seeking. However, a truly effective treatment awaited the discovery of
penicillin by Fleming in 1929 and the later investigations by Florey and
Chain from 1939 to 1941 that allowed the manufacture of enough for clinical treatment. The first actual use of it to treat syphilis was in 1943. In
the postwar period it was shown to be effective in all stages of syphilis,
and by 1950 it became the standard treatment.[58] It was not until its more
widespread use in the early 1950s, however, that the public panic around
venereal disease—especially involving congenital syphilis and general
paresis—began to abate. The sense of liberation this abatement brought
can be seen in yet another opera of the 1950s, once again one written in
the United States but about eighteenth-century Europe: Leonard Bernstein's *Candide*. Only after a danger is over can you make fun of your own
anxieties.

From the Top, This Time with Humor: *Candide*

Critics have noted that Auden and Kallman appear to have looked for inspiration to another eighteenth-century work, John Gay's *The Beggar's
Opera* (1728), when writing the brothel scene.[59] In the world of this "ballad opera," also populated by "whores and rogues," syphilis is very much

present, embedded in the very clichés of the language, sometimes in the form of the familiar curse ("Pox take the tailors for making the fobs so deep and narrow!"), sometimes in equally familiar gender-coded terms: "A fox may steal your hens, sir, / A whore your health and pence, sir."[60] In other words, here syphilis forms part of the background of the work, almost taken for granted as the inescapable scourge. Thirty years later Voltaire's *Candide*—Bernstein's source text—brings the disease into the forefront, for it contains a meditation on the subject of syphilis, its causes and effects, all in the context of a satire on the meaning of suffering. The protagonist, Candide, meets a diseased beggar on the road who turns out to be his former tutor, Pangloss. The description of the beggar would have offered Voltaire's contemporaries a familiar picture of the syphilitic: "His eyes were lifeless, the end of his nose had rotted away, his mouth was all askew and his teeth were black. His voice was sepulchral, and a violent cough tormented him, at every bout of which he spat out a tooth."[61] But this is a satire, and in a parodic version of (the popular view of) Leibniz's philosophy, Pangloss—who always believes all is for the best—explains the ironic cause of his physical decline: "Love, the comforter of humanity, the preserver of the universe, the soul of all living beings."[62]

In 1956 Leonard Bernstein put Voltaire's text to music, working from a libretto prepared by Richard Wilbur, with John La Touche, Dorothy Parker, Lillian Hellman, Stephen Sondheim, and Bernstein himself. Perhaps because of the need to provide dramatic logic for stage action, this *Candide* shows the cause of the disease before offering its dire effects: we see Pangloss in the bushes giving "very intensive private tuition" to a young woman named Paquette. Then comes the scene of Candide's recognition of him: the diseased Pangloss is described in the stage directions as "an old man with a tin nose . . . : syphilis has rotted away several of his fingers, and left him cruelly disfigured." The opera too is a satire, however, and this equally optimistic Pangloss is just as clear about the amatory cause of his disease:

> Dear boy, you will not hear me speak
> With sorrow or with rancor
> Of what has shrivelled up my cheek

And blasted it with canker;
'Twas Love, great Love, that did the deed,
Through Nature's gentle laws,
And how should ill effects proceed
From so divine a cause?

For Pangloss, "Whatever pains disease may bring / Are but the tangy seasoning" of "Love's delicious fare."

The effect of the philosophical parody offered here—either of the notion of cause and effect or of the value of suffering—is different in the context of Voltaire's eighteenth-century text and Bernstein's twentieth-century opera. But even more surprising, clearly something had happened in the twenty years since *Lulu* or even in the five years between *The Rake's Progress* and *Candide* that allowed Bernstein to joke about something that Stravinsky, Auden, and Kallman still had to take so very seriously. For the North American audience of 1956, syphilis had come close enough to being under control that humor might be possible, even if only to laugh at one's former worries: thanks to increasingly widespread treatment with penicillin, the disease no longer produced the terrifying physical results described here with such levity or new cases of the general paresis of the insane that had sent Tom to Bedlam. Social attitudes to the disease were changing too: in Quétel's perhaps too strong terms, there was "an instantaneous shift from a frenzy of fear to a complete lack of concern."[63]

This is why *Candide* the opera could draw on but nevertheless alter, through humor, the long history of meanings that had collected around the causes and consequences of venereal disease. Voltaire's Pangloss had typically blamed Paquette for being the immediate source of his infection, but he also provided a comic genealogy of the disease that went back to Columbus.[64] As we mentioned in the previous chapter, there have continued to be fierce debates over the origins of the syphilis epidemic that struck Europe at the end of the fifteenth century. Pangloss articulates one of these: that it arrived in Europe either with Columbus's sailors or with the aboriginal people they brought back from the Americas and then spread across the European continent with the movement of various (infected) armies.[65] As the ever ironic (or perhaps ever cynical) Voltaire writes, syphilis made "remarkable progress" among the Europeans, "most of all in these huge armies of honest well-trained mercenaries, who decide the destiny of nations."[66] He then adds that when thirty thousand men face thirty thousand men on the field of battle, twenty thousand on each side will have the pox.

The operatic Pangloss, at a different point in medical (and military) history, can put it rather more lightly:

> *Columbus and his men, they say,*
> *Conveyed the virus hither,*
> *Whereby my features rot away*
> *And vital powers wither.*

Ever the optimist, however, this Pangloss can decide that this is a small price to pay for what Europeans also managed to acquire along with the disease: tobacco and chocolate. Where in earlier centuries syphilis was the divine scourge that castigated sinners, by the age of penicillin it is possible to joke about what was a grim reality for Voltaire's earlier readership: "Nothing can prevent the spread / Of Love's divine disease."

In *Parsifal*, the conjunction of prostitutes and soldiers—Flower Maidens and Grail knights—drew on familiar cultural and social associations with syphilis that the Whores and Roaring Boys of *The Rake's Progress* repeat. The venereal transmission of the disease and the military context are brought together by *Candide* as well, but once again as a source of humor rather than anxiety:

> *Men worship Venus everywhere,*
> *As may be plainly seen;*
> *Her decorations which I bear*
> *Are nobler than the* croix de guerre,
> *And gained in service of our fair*
> *And universal Queen.*

It seems that for a few brief decades in the late twentieth century in the West, this morally and physically disfiguring venereal disease (to which Venus lent her name) changed drastically in its social as well as medical meanings. In both realms this was thanks to the intervention of penicillin. Today, since the appearance of AIDS, that has changed once again, and as the epilogue to this book will explore, it is as if we have moved back to an earlier set of cultural associations that this 1956 opera appeared to have left behind. For over five hundred years, the representations of syphilis as a "social" disease intimately connected with sexuality and morality have continued to tell us much about the society that creates them.

Chapter 5

"Acoustic Contagion": Sexuality, Surveillance, and Epidemics

Whenever any person of substance died of cholera, it was an immediate cause of consternation, a consternation invariably allayed by reports that this ordinarily praiseworthy man either had some secret vice or else had indulged in some unwonted excess.

—Charles E. Rosenberg, *The Cholera Years*

Plagues have always had a certain power over the human imagination because of the part they play in history as the cause of both individual suffering and general social distress. Randolph Starn writes: "How can anyone presume to do justice either to the immensity or to the immediacy of so much suffering? Or, for that matter, to the numbing capacity of people to resist or to tolerate tremendous losses? The plague is one of the classic subjects of historical writing in part because it forces such fundamental questions and elicits answers in which the purpose and intelligibility of history are at stake."[1] As discussed in the opening chapter of this book, the plague, given its inevitable effect on social, moral, intellectual, and imaginative life, has always raised questions about suffering and tolerance; it has always created situations of stress that test social structures and the more general habits of thought and behavior that usually work to hold a society together.[2] And as such it has normally provided rich grounds for literary and artistic treatment. Or at least the bubonic plague, the major European epidemic of the Middle Ages, did.[3] One of its successors—cholera, the scourge of the nineteenth century—did not, despite the fact that it killed roughly half of those who succumbed to it and did so in a very rapid and dramatic fashion, focusing popular and professional fears with a force that nothing had repeated since the Black Death.[4]

Cholera: Danger, Shame, Social Unrest

Possible reasons for the relative paucity of artistic representations of cholera have been advanced by Richard J. Evans in his *Death in Hamburg: Society and Politics in the Cholera Years, 1830–1910*. For one thing, death from cholera was different from at least the conventional view of the consumptive death, which could be spiritualized or beautified: the massive loss of body fluids from vomiting and diarrhea was seen as "horrifying and deeply disgusting in an age which, more than any other, sought to conceal bodily functions from itself. . . . Cholera broke through the precarious barriers erected against physicality in the name of civilization."[5] In psychological terms, Evans goes on to argue, "This was a disease which had no mitigating features, there was no means of coming to terms with the degrading violence it inflicted on the human body, and no consolation in the event of it gaining the victory over life."

According to this view, one result of seeing this disease as vulgar and demeaning was that cholera came to share with syphilis a limited "metaphorical power." Yet as the previous two chapters of this book have argued, syphilis has, on the contrary, been rich in associative power, even if its "coding" is more or less covert—like so much to do with sexuality and the body in the past two centuries. Likewise, although references to cholera may be relatively infrequent in opera, as in other art forms, when they do appear they are powerful enough not to allow the disease to be reduced, as Evans suggests, to "a synonym for pestilential horror, nothing more."[6] As this chapter explores, the richness of connotations around this disease in opera comes in part from its sexual association. This may seem surprising in a way that, certainly, the associations of sex with syphilis and even tuberculosis might not; but cholera and sexuality have just as long a connection, though a somewhat different one. Indeed, it has been claimed that the very notion of "sexuality" was constructed in medical and social (governmental) terms in the early nineteenth century precisely *by* the discussions about sexual immorality that grew up around the cholera epidemics from 1831 on.[7]

The theory that pestilence was sent as a punishment for sin has a long history in the Greek, Roman, and Hebrew traditions, a history early modern Europe drew on to explain syphilis, as we have seen. But cholera, although known in India earlier, did not arrive in Western Europe in epidemic proportions until 1831, and so its social meanings *there* cannot be separated from the century in which it was first experienced. The first pandemic, from 1816 to 1823, stopped before it reached Europe, but it was sufficiently terrifying that European medical authorities were already concerned, as well they might have been. The next five pandemics did sweep across Western Europe between 1831 and 1923. Although cholera now seems to have (more or less) disappeared in these countries, we should not forget that it is still endemic in much of the world. The World Health Organization was notified in 1991 of 400,000 cases of the disease, but a review panel of experts has estimated that up to 5.5 million cases occur annually in parts of Asia and Africa.[8]

What is cholera? In clinical terms it involves an "acute endemic or epidemic diarrhea, often with vomiting and muscle cramps, but with little or no abdominal pain, and accompanied by loss of water and electrolytes but not of protein, leading to dehydration and shock if untreated."[9] What made it so frightening to those medical authorities in the nineteenth century was its rapidity and virulence:

> *The speed with which cholera killed was profoundly alarming, since perfectly healthy people could never feel safe from sudden death when the infection was anywhere near. In addition, the symptoms were particularly horrible: radical dehydration meant that a victim shrank into a wizened caricature of his former self within a few hours, while ruptured capillaries discolored the skin, turning it black and blue. The effect was to make mortality uniquely visible: patterns of bodily decay were exacerbated and accelerated, as in a time-lapse motion picture, to remind all who saw it of death's ugly horror and utter inevitability.*[10]

Today we know that this swift and terrifying disease is caused by a microscopic bacillus called *Vibrio cholerae*, which is transmitted through water contaminated with human feces. Cholera does not manifest itself until it enters the human digestive tract — by means of tainted water or fruit or vegetables washed in it.[11] The importance of the water supply was most convincingly demonstrated by Dr. John Snow in London when he localized an outbreak of cholera to the Bow Street pump in 1849, and again in

1854 when he described the radically different rates of cholera between users of two different water suppliers, one of which drew its supply from a region of the Thames contaminated by sewage. Definitive proof, however, awaited the descripton of *Vibrio cholerae* by an international team of scientists (headed by Robert Koch), which investigated outbreaks of the disease in Egypt and India in 1883. Before this time (and considerably after it as well), theories proliferated about cholera's causation — often confusingly contradictory.

Like tuberculosis and syphilis, cholera generated familiar concerns about personal (and, as we shall see, sexual) habits; but it also took on broader social dimensions, raising worries about contact with others and also about the habits of the poor or working classes. As with venereal disease, both the cultural and medical discourses of cholera in the nineteenth century also recalled those earlier representations of mass death from the bubonic plague. Finding analogies with the most devastating European epidemic to that date was perhaps an understandable early stage in coming to terms with the frightening new disease: like syphilis, cholera was said to have its source in divine punishment, and it too seemed to require scapegoats to carry the blame. It appears that it was only the *rationale* of punishment and blame that changed with fashion, the availability of medical information, or simply new theories.[12]

In other words, people explained epidemic diseases differently in different periods, but the cultural representations retained striking similarities. In the case of cholera, however, to the usual moral metaphors that circulated around the concept of plague were added two other sets of related associations with disease in general that have equally long medical histories. From the writings of Aristotle and, later, Galen on the causation of disease, concepts had evolved linking external factors to the presence of what now might be called "host factors" (such as a predisposition of the person or the state of a particular organ or body part) in the development of the disease.[13] To explain an epidemic disease by which many were affected at the same time, a powerful external cause seemed necessary. From the time of Hippocrates this cause was usually assigned to atmospheric changes that would affect many people simultaneously, most particularly those with "appropriately weakened constitutions."[14]

Contamination of the atmosphere and environment might arise from a "miasma" associated with ideas of decay, putrefaction, and stench and connected to stagnant water, marshes, and poorly drained land. At other times astrological conjunction might similarly be thought to produce hazardous atmospheric conditions. The logical implication of this theory was an attempt to clear the environment by cleaning the streets, bettering ventilation, and improving the air—even with cannon shots and burning tar.

A second hypothesis, that a disease could be passed from person to person, also had a long history from Greek times but was perhaps most clearly stated by Aretaeus in the second century. Contagion was most closely associated with skin diseases and conditions resulting from direct contact with sick individuals. The logical extension of this thought led to the isolation of those with leprosy in Europe in the Middle Ages. Quarantine was a regulation first put in place in Venice in the thirteenth century. By the Renaissance, then, these were among the various theories used to explain epidemic diseases. That is to say, atmospheric disturbances and environmental conditions were believed to cause internal changes in large numbers of people. But in the sixteenth century Fracastorius, in his *De contagione*, formalized the contagion theory—that disease could be passed on by direct contact, by contact with the effects of sick people, and even by contact at a distance—postulating the presence of invisible living matter that was capable of causing disease. One of the historical ironies here is that over the next three centuries the theory of contagion gradually lost way and was eventually considered obsolete in comparison with the medical science of the nineteenth century—at least until the 1880s, when the discoveries of medical bacteriology proved that diseases like tuberculosis and cholera were infectious.

Whatever the fate of the contagion theory over the centuries, however, what continued and even strengthened was the belief that epidemic diseases could be brought on by impurities in the air and atmosphere. Putrefaction, decay, and filth were felt to create these negative changes in the atmosphere; lack of ventilation and light was considered detrimental to health. The theory was that exposure to this unhealthful atmosphere might cause disease, especially where the exposure was greater—that is, either around dirt and decay or where a personal pre-disposition (moral or physical, perhaps through diet or drink) weakened the body's resistance. What came to be known as the "miasma" theory took its name from the Greek word meaning pollution, staining, or defiling. In this very naming begins the particular social construction of the meaning of epidemic disease for both societies and individual suf-ferers that is the topic of this chapter. To fall victim to cholera took on a significance well beyond the physical. As our epigraph suggests, it was the sign of some secret vice, some dishonorable and "polluting" per-sonal habit that might not be known but manifestly existed: "To die of cholera was to die in suspicious circumstances."[15] This secrecy and suspi-cion are crucial to the the representation of cholera in both Thomas Mann's *Der Tod in Venedig* (1911) and the opera based on it by Benjamin Britten and Myfanwy Piper—*Death in Venice* (1973).

It was through major commercial seaports like Venice that cholera did in fact enter Europe from the East in the 1830s.[16] As can be seen in *La Traviata* and *La Bohème*, the view that cities were unhealthful places to live gained currency through the century as the link between urban poverty and tuberculosis became clearer. In the case of cholera, though, there was no doubt from the start: it appeared first (and most impressively) in ports and then spread to other urban centers. The mortality rate in Eu-ropean cities was soon higher than the birthrate. It was only in the latter part of the century that cities finally became capable of maintaining their population numbers without depending on migration from the countryside.[17] But industrialization concentrated people in cities in a way that rapidly outstripped available housing and sanitary facilities meant to serve a much smaller population. Notoriously unhealthful con-ditions in the new industrial towns intensified encounters with what we now know to be infectious diseases. Those who could afford to flee a city afflicted with cholera did so, leaving for the country and "purer atmo-sphere."[18] Those who could not—the poor—stayed to face disease and death: "Cholera followed the lines of poverty, and death cut a swath through the slums."[19] The miasma theory, in which dirt and decay poi-soned the atmosphere, offered both the reasoning behind the need for cleanliness, ventilation, and light and the rationale for new state powers of search, surveillance, and regulation of the poor: "The priviliged exercised control on the underprivileged (who were seen as a dangerous source of infection) through a system consisting of charity offices, teams of constable-observers, and aid stations staffed by physicians."[20] The middle classes' suspicion of the poor was reversed as well: all over Europe, the poor rioted in protest against what they saw as class-related oppression and, even worse, in the belief that cholera was a form of poisoning being used by the privileged and by the civic authorities as a eugenic solution to population growth—a quick way to reduce the numbers of the poor.[21]

In the wake of the political disturbances of 1848, people were not long in making the analogy between the European capitals infected by cholera and those swept by "the contagion of democratic ideas."[22] That familiar Old Testament rhetoric of pestilence and pollution—and thus of abomination and depravity—created what has been called a "language of moral frisson" that permeated the political, ethical, and medical representations of cholera. Disease, filth, and material squalor came to be associated with both moral degeneracy and political sedition through this kind of targeting of the human agents of infection. And clearly the miasma theory promoted this connection, for it was elastic and capable of infinite variation, able to cover everything from unsanitary housing conditions to immoral sexual practices.[23] The availability of the powerful (taboo) imagery of excretion—made possible by cholera's clinical symptoms—did not in the least limit the disease's "metaphorical power," as Evans claims; on the contrary, it helped reinforce miasmic connections to pollution and decay. Such rhetoric was seen to be corroborated, in fact, by the new empirical evidence of the deplorable sanitary conditions in the crowded hovels of the poor. But the associations were not limited to toilet facilities: the discovery of facts such as what one report called the "promiscuous mixture of the sexes in sleeping-rooms" upset the nineteenth-century European and North American bourgeoisie even more. It was only with such new surveillance powers that home visits revealed what the authorities saw as the moral as well as physical realities of urban poverty.[24] As mentioned earlier, the exposure of this physical squalor led to the articulation of sanitary standards and subsequent so-

cial hygiene movements. In England, for instance, this meant the successful demand for adequate housing, roads, piped water, and efficient
sewers. Although still based on a medical concept of protection against miasma, such measures were ultimately effective against the actual cause
of the disease: transmission of an infected organism through contaminated water. But beyond the issue of sanitary conditions—though connected directly with it—was the sexual and the moral dimension; and
even with better hygiene, that worry did not go away.

Lulu: Lesbian Love and Death

In Alban Berg's opera *Lulu*, based (as noted in the previous chapter) on
Wedekind's late nineteeth-century plays, yet another piece of new medical evidence about cholera is used as a plot device in a manner that is
both historically accurate and symbolically loaded: the only way person-
to-person transmission of cholera can occur is indirectly through infection of food or clothing. This fact becomes the pivotal detail in a plan to
get Lulu out of jail, where she has been sent for the murder of Dr. Schön.
Indeed, in an operatic "first," cholera bacilli make their appearance on
stage in person, so to speak. In the "interlude" between Lulu's crime and
her rescue, a silent film shows her arrest, detention, trial, and imprison-
ment. But it also shows a slide of cholera bacilli. This is Berg's way of introducing the disease's entry into the plot: the Countess Geschwitz has
gone to Hamburg during a cholera epidemic and taken an emergency
course on nursing. One day, while taking care of the sick, she has put on
the underwear of a dead cholera victim. She then visits Lulu in prison,
and they in turn exchange underclothes. Both come down with the disease on the same day and end up in the isolation ward of the hospital.
Geschwitz does what she can to make herself look like Lulu during this
time. Once discharged from the hospital she returns, pretending to look
for a forgotten item; she and Lulu quickly change places, and Lulu walks
out a free woman. With echoes of the syphilitic prostitute (which she
is about to become) who never seems to suffer from the disease she
spreads, Lulu is said to draw health and strength from the illness that
has laid others low ("Was uns unter die Erde bringt, gibt ihr Kraft und
Gesundheit wieder"); others, however, do note her extreme thinness.

Lulu's husband, Alwa, remarks to the countess that he is impressed with her sacrifice and her superhuman contempt for death ("Ihre über-menschliche Todesverachtung"). In the source text, Frank Wedekind's play, though not in the opera, he goes on to remark that no man ever risked so much for a woman.

The gender of this comment is pertinent: Geschwitz, as a lesbian, has been in love with Lulu for some time. That, according to her, passionate declarations of affection have taken place in the hospital suggests that the text is making some sort of connection between the cholera they share and same-sex affection. Nineteenth-century medical and moral discourses around cholera certainly did construct a "distinct repertoire of representations of the sexual around the linked themes of ill-health and immorality."[25] Among these linked themes were what even the sympathetic Wedekind called the "terrible curse of sexual abnormal-ity"—a theme that he felt had not been dealt with on the stage but that deserved to be considered with more sympathy and less of the ridi-cule and outrage typical of middle-class morality.[26] As many critics have noted, however, unlike the men in the opera and plays—who may love Lulu but also possessively use her—Geschwitz is the one character por-trayed as capable of self-sacrificing love. Lulu cannot understand this and can see her only as a monster, as crazy, as neither man nor woman: "Du bist kein Menschenkind wie die andern. Für einen Mann war der Stoff nicht ausreichend. Und zum Weib hast du zu viel Hirn in deinen Schädel bekommen. Darum bist du verrückt." Geschwitz calls herself an outcast; Dr. Schön calls her the devil. And Lulu is not above manipulating her by promising her a night together if Geschwitz does as she asks.[27] Jack the Ripper, just before he kills both women, calls her a "poor animal" for being in love with Lulu and strokes her hair as he would a dog's. She has followed Lulu to London, even into the streets where Lulu is soliciting, and now she follows her to her death. The final words of the opera are her *Liebestod* to Lulu as her angel whom she wants to be with for ever-more: "Lulu! Mein Engel! Lass dich noch einmal sehn! Ich bin dir nah! Bleibe dir nah! In Ewigkeit!"[28]

The ironic echoing of Wagner's heterosexual *Tristan und Isolde* that critics talk of here rebounds not only onto the lesbian Geschwitz but

12. Lulu (Rebecca Caine) promising
herself to the Countess Geschwitz (Felicity Palmer)
in the 1991 production of *Lulu* by the
Canadian Opera Company.

onto Lulu's final spouse, Alwa. Both die in the last act, along with the woman they have loved; both suffer throughout because of their attraction to her, but also from infectious diseases directly related to her. As we saw in the previous chapter, to Alwa she gives syphilis (at this point, largely seen as a heterosexual disease), but Geschwitz and Lulu are linked through cholera. Critics have noted other parallels between Alwa and Geschwitz: both are treated somewhat sentimentally, and in their relationships with Lulu, both reveal themselves as masochistic.[29] If, as Wedekind believed, the flesh has its own nature, its own spirit and knowledge ("Das Fleisch hat seinen eigenen Geist"), then he seems to imply that something went awry with the flesh in these two instances, in terms of both disease and sexuality.[30] One commentator goes so far as to argue that Geschwitz is in fact more like Jack the Ripper: "two human beings condemned by fate to an obsessive deviation from normal sexuality that isolates them from their fellow creatures."[31] This is said to be why Jack pets her like a dog. But because the rhetoric and the narratives that connect sexuality and concepts of "normality" are closely allied with those of bodily health and illness, it is with Lulu that Geschwitz is most directly associated in the end. Lulu, as the sexualized—and syphilitic—prostitute, dies with Geschwitz the lesbian, for both would be marked as sharing what Sander Gilman calls "an inherent pattern of degeneracy," according to the European fin-de-siècle imagination. Geschwitz, like Zola's earlier bisexual Nana, is a threat to the patriarchal order's biological model of reproductive sexuality.[32] The Berlin Royal District Court that banned Wedekind's play on the grounds of its outrage to morals and decorum focused on Geschwitz's "sexual perversions," among other signs of depravity.[33]

Bourgeois Un-ease and Homosexual Dis-ease: *Death in Venice*

The association of "miasmic" cholera with the many things that bourgeois nineteenth-century European culture thought of as immorality, sexual excess, degradation, or even animality was obviously not limited to the medical or religious domains. Wedekind's turn-of-century German plays—like Berg's later opera—drew on an existing tradition of associations with cholera and were able to do so even well after the actual mode of transmission of the disease was known. Once again, as with the operas written before and after the discovery of the tubercle bacillus, the cultural continuities may surprise us more than differences. Both Thomas Mann's *Der Tod in Venedig* (1911) and *Death in Venice* (1973), the opera made from it by Benjamin Britten and Myfanwy Piper, invoke the almost century-long history of belief that for respectable bourgeois people death from cholera was "death with a hint of dishonor."[34] The sexualized connection seen in *Lulu* between this disease and same-sex affection is in fact repeated in the story of the aging writer Gustav von Aschenbach's love for the young Polish boy Tadzio. The portrayal of cholera in the second act of the opera, as in the novella, is complex: it is at the same time medically accurate and richly metaphoric.

As with *Lulu*, here too the disease is a significant plot device that is discussed openly by characters on stage, so that there is little danger of missing its presence or, for that matter, its multiple meanings. Aschenbach smells what he calls a "sweetish medicinal cleanliness, / overlaying the smell of still canals" of Venice. He comes across people in the streets reading notices about taking precautions against infection: they are warned to avoid using canal water and eating shellfish. Indeed, the citizens repeat the word "warned" a number of times to reinforce the danger. In the opera as in the novella, a clerk in a travel bureau (in scene 11) offers a long, detailed, and accurate description of the situation that bears quoting in full:

> In these last years, Asiatic cholera has spread from the delta of the Ganges: to Hindustan, to China, Afghanistan and thence to Persia. They thought it would travel westwards by land, but it came by sea, to the southern ports — Malaga, Palermo. . . . Last May, two dead bodies were discovered here in Venice with signs of the plague. It was hushed up. In a week there were ten more — twenty — thirty. A guest from Austria went home and died; hence, the reports in the German newspapers. The authorities denied it — the city had never been healthier, they said. Sir, death is at work, the plague is with us. It flourishes, redoubles its powers. It is violent, convulsive, suffocating, few who contract it recover. The Ospedale Civico is full. The traffic to San Michele is continuous. And Sir, the authorities are not moved by scruples, or by international agreements. They fear for their pockets — if

there should be panic or blockade. . . . Meanwhile the city is demoralised. Crime,
drunkenness, murder, organised vice — evil forces are rife.

In addition to such historical and medical accuracy of detail, the opera
(like its source text) simultaneously draws on current medical knowledge and also upon that set of nineteenth-century associations between
cholera and miasma, that is, between the disease and the foul-smelling,
stagnant lagoons of Venice, its oppressive, hot summer atmosphere,
its faintly rotten smell of swamp. In miasma theories, cholera was related
to climate changes, fogs, and damp as well as strong stenches.[35] But both
Mann and Piper knew that cholera was a waterborne disease — and that
made Venice doubly attractive as the site of this new urban plague: the
city's atmosphere of moral and physical decay could be connected both
to the actual source of the contagion and to the earlier associations of
infection with environmental conditions.

What is also curious, however, is that both texts quite deliberately recall the cultural representations of some other diseases we have seen.
This is aided by Mann's (wise) decision to make explicit the *kind* of cholera his protagonist is threatened with: it is what is known as the "dry" variety, *cholera sicca*. This is the most malignant kind, but also the most dis-
creet and least bodily embarrassing. Instead of diarrhea and vomiting,
we are told by the novella, victims lose the ability to excrete water,
shrivel up, and then die of suffocation in a few hours, after falling into a
deep coma. Perhaps it is this "easier" death that allows the calling up of
the associations of that paradoxically sexualized and spiritualized disease the nineteenth century thought of as consumption. Although tuberculosis was a chronic, not acute, condition, Mann (and Piper) could
still draw on the associations of that disease to aestheticize — but also implicitly to sexualize — their protagonist's condition. Its signs and symptoms are scattered through the opera. Aschenbach considers leaving
Venice because the "foul exhalations . . . oppress [his] breathing." When
he falls in love with Tadzio, he sings of the fevers he suffers in his passion. In the novella, where the constraints of compression are not as
strong, there are still other examples of imagery suggestive of consumption's clinical signs (paleness with fevers) and its cultural associations (of

burning more brightly, both sexually and artistically). Aschenbach is a writer, after all, and his earlier work, we learn, had contrasted the "pallid" languors of the flesh with the "fiery" ardors of the spirit. Art, he once believed, heightens life, gives deeper joy, but consumes quickly. References to Aschenbach's growing physical unease in Venice are frequently in terms of his own "feverishness," and he fears that the pale young man he loves may also be sickly from what he calls an oppression in the chest. Indeed, at the end of the novella, when defeated in his games with his friends, the boy is described as very pale—and he finally becomes the pale and lovely summoner who beckons Aschenbach to his death.

Echoes of consumption combine with both modern scientific information about cholera's etiology and earlier miasma theories to offer a complex and historically rich ground for the representation of a disease and of the person suffering from it. In the background of this story of love and death in Venice, however, is that the East is the source of more than cholera: it was also, as we shall see in more detail shortly, the place of origin of the ecstatic Dionysian rites that figure as the opposite of Apollonian control in a crucial dream Aschenbach has and in the structure of the novella and opera.[36] And for the *German* writer, walking in the North Cemetery of Munich, at the beginning of Mann's narrative, Venice is in a way almost half-way to India. The "Traveller" Aschenbach sees on his walk inspires in him restlessness and a desire for distant places. In the words of the translation that the English libretto is based on:

> *Desire projected itself visually: his fancy . . . imaged the marvels and terrors of the manifold earth. He saw. He beheld a landscape, a tropical marshland, beneath a reeking sky, steaming, monstrous, rank—a kind of primeval wilderness-world of islands, morasses, alluvial channels. Hairy palm-trunks rose near and far out of lush brakes of fern, out of bottoms of crass vegetation, fat, swollen, thick with incredible bloom. There were trees, mis-shapen as a dream, that dropped their naked roots straight through the air into the ground or into water that was stagnant and shadowy and glassy-green.[37]*

In this lush thicket he imagines a tiger lurking and feels both terror and inexplicable longing. Even though Aschenbach has always thought of travel as something one endures for one's health, the opposite of the enervating daily struggle of work, this desire that overcomes him, this need for "freedom, release, forgetfulness," is expressed from the start in suspect language: as an "unexpected contagion" (6). In the light of this expression, the passage cited above suddenly reveals itself as rife with associations of the cholera that would be so important to the story and to his life: the miasmic, reeking, steaming, rank, stagnant swamplands where tigers lurk suggest the landscape of the Ganges whence came the epidemic. It does not help that Aschenbach decides to go only as far as Venice—that is, not to go "all the way to the tigers" (7). The disease will travel *to him* in Venice—the city of the lion (of Saint Mark), if not the tiger.

Literally built on the water, Venice is historically, geographically, medically, and metaphorically an appropriate setting for a cholera epidemic. As a port city at the heart of a busy mercantile society, it was badly hit by the bubonic plague in the sixteenth and seventeenth centuries.[38] Equally appropriately for Britten and Piper, Venice has a long association with music and especially, since the seventeenth century, with opera: Wagner had written the love music of act 2 of *Tristan und Isolde* there in 1858 and had died in the Palazzo Vendramin in 1883.[39] The cultural associations of passion with death and of both with music are, then, part of the city's cultural heritage. And Britten's operatic portrayal of Venice is self-consciously musical: we hear its bells and its gondoliers' cries, boats full of singers and the songs of strolling players.

However, Venice also has other historical associations that both opera and novella draw on. The infamous secrecy of the doges' deliberations in earlier times is echoed in the secrecy of Aschenbach's love. The mercantile history of the city continues in debased form in the Venetians' denial of the cholera epidemic for commercial reasons. The fabled beauty of the city cannot be separated, in the imagination of non-Italian writers in particular, from associations with decadence and moral corruption.[40] This connection is not inappropriate in a novella where beautiful Venice is feminized as "*die* Schöne" and made to sit in juxtaposition to both the neuter "*das* Schöne" (abstract Beauty) and, even more important, the male "*der* Schöne" (the beautiful boy, Tadzio).[41] Venice, as the operatic Aschenbach sings in scene 3, is "ambiguous." Its position and image blur boundaries of all kinds — geographical, historical, sexual: it is the "timeless, legendary world / of dark, lawless errands / in the watery night." It is also the historical bridge between East and West: "Metaphorically, Venice both represents the Western achievement and reveals its darker underside, deeper roots, and foreign face."[42] In fact the disturbance of Aschenbach's Apollonian calm and control by his experiences of love and disease in Venice has been read as an allegory of the crisis of modernist culture as it encountered "a resurgent challenge from the Other, the Other not as inert object but as intrusive presence from outside the dominant metropolis."[43]

The "other" here, however, not only is represented by Asiatic cholera, it is also literally embodied in Tadzio, the young boy Aschenbach falls in love with. A pattern of dualities, modeled on this self/"other" opposition, emerges early in both opera and novella: the Germanic north is opposed to the Italian south; age is set in contrast to youth; the writer's family heritage is that of both paternal "dry, conscientious officialdom" and maternal "ardent, obscure impulse" (8). Not surprisingly, out of this mix of the *bürgerlich* and the Bohemian came not only an artist, but a profoundly divided person who used his art to control his "sympathy with the abyss" (13). Through detachment and austerity of style, Aschenbach has managed to write of passion and, tellingly, of biological decline with "ordered force" and "antithetical eloquence" (8). With the same antithetical eloquence and elegance, Mann constructs a novella that balances oppositions on a number of levels: mythic (Apollonian devotion to reason versus Dionysian surrender to passion); religious (Christian versus pagan); psychic (attraction versus repulsion or emotion versus intellect); psychoanalytic (id versus ego and superego); social (individual desire versus public mores); existential (life versus death); aesthetic (form versus content or control versus passion).[44] All of Mann's early work has been said to exhibit a fascination with the dualities of aesthetic refinement and nonrationality, so perhaps an opera composer's attraction to *Der Tod in Venedig* is not surprising: after all, music has often been read as the paradigm of the aesthetic duality of order and form versus excess in affect (and effect).

The music Britten wrote for this opera, however, is not what anyone would ever call excessive. Nevertheless, the descriptions of it are often interestingly dual or paradoxical in themselves: Theodor Adorno wrote of its "triumphant meagerness"; Arnold Whittall calls its effect one of "intensity and restraint" and its formal features an "economical blend" of twelve-tone and tonal harmony.[45] Because of precisely this economy and restraint, as well as the intricate motivic structure, the music is utterly appropriate to the story of the artist of will and self-discipline; however, because of its intensity of effect it can also convey the disintegration of Aschenbach's control under the influence of passion. Britten chose to give his protagonist — who sees himself as the observer, the abstainer — a free vocal line that has, in the score, pitch but not rhythmic notations. Aschenbach's formal aesthetic, his rationalism, and his psychic obsessiveness take on aural form in the "quasi parlando" recitative; his isolation is marked by the accompaniment of his sustained monologues by piano only.[46] Mann had been able to give his Aschenbach a rich inner life by focusing the narrative through his mind; Piper's invention of monologues (heard only by the audience) works in much the same way. The decision to unite seven roles and have them sung by the same baritone was both economical (conveying the novella's sense of both unity and fatality) and psychically revealing, for they all play similar parts in Aschenbach's disintegration: the enticing Traveller, the Charon figure of the Gondolier who rows him to the Lido, and the Leader of the Strolling Players all share a physical description and a designation as foreign; they also share with the Elderly Fop, the Hotel Manager, and the Hotel Barber a similar five-note musical motif that finds its culmination in the music of Dionysus (also sung by the same singer) in Aschenbach's dream. The structure of the music of *Death in Venice* cannot, in fact, be separated from the structure of the narrative about passion, disease, and death.

The intricacy of this interweaving can be seen in the musical development of one four-note cell (D–C–E–D$\sharp$). This has variously been called the "fate" motive, the "canker" motive, the "plague" motive.[47] The reason for all these related designations is its first appearance as the Traveller begins the passage that will arouse in Aschenbach the restless desire, the inexplicable longing to travel. On the first words — "Marvels unfold!"—the motive is heard. These seemingly innocent words—redolent of travel brochures of the tritest variety—quickly take on more ominous connotations, as does the motive itself:

> A *wilderness, swollen,*
> *with fearful growth,*
> *monstrous and thick,*
> *and heady flowers*
> *crowd in the steaming marsh.*

With echoes of Huysman's decadent, syphilitic flowers and Mann's cholera-infested "primeval wilderness-world," Piper's libretto economically evokes both the repulsion and the attraction in its parenthetical "(O terror and delight)."

As the labeling of the motive suggests, critics have not been shy about associating this music with both the psychic or emotional life of the protagonist and the disease that is the physical cause of his death. Christopher Palmer writes:

> Britten builds this sense of the inevitable, the uncontrollable, the all-possessive, all-obsessive, into the foundations of the opera. The entire edifice is permeated by—or to put it more emotively, infected by, corrupted by, finally consumed by—the tiny motif first heard in Act One, scene 1, in the first line of the Traveller's solo "Marvels unfold.". . . Here the major third falls to the minor, light turns to darkness. It is an archetypal musical symbol for the transforming of good into evil, and to chart its progress through the opera and its multifariously noxious thematic activities would keep (has kept) analytical music-chemists happy for weeks.[48]

This passage seems worth citing at length for its detail and its choice of images: infection, corruption, noxiousness. Other critics have used similar language to describe this motive: the "'natural' third of sweetness and serenity is poisoned by its 'dissonant' minor inflection," thereby creating a "major/minor ambiguity."[49] As we shall see, what others have called the protean nature and the diabolical ambivalence of the motive allow it to come to be associated with all the forces that work to bring about Aschenbach's fall.

As Palmer has shown, the orchestration also works to corroborate this cumulative effect of inevitability and doom. The "sacrificial drums"—the untuned percussion of timpani and tomtoms, heard in the Traveller's music—suggest the "dark side of passion, the swamp, the black beast" and act as an aural danger signal Aschenbach does not heed. The woodwinds heard here as well become powerful and consistent symbols of both primordial chaos and illness. The woodwind arabesques in the Traveller's music offer the first hint of the threat that will be repeated in both the sirocco motive (a two-part woodwind trill) and the travel bureau clerk's description of the sources of Asiatic cholera. The increasing presence of the tuba, often at unexpected moments, suggests the lurking beast of prey that both terrifies and delights Aschenbach—and sends him off to Venice.[50]

Everything about Mann's description of the departure is more menacing than enticing and is presented in what, for the protagonist, is a disturbingly sexualized way: a dirty, hunchbacked, smirkingly polite sailor leads the prim and proper Aschenbach to a goat-bearded man from whom he buys a ticket on a boat. On board he meets what the translation dubs an "elderly coxcomb," complete with wig and makeup, who provokes great disgust in the restrained and repressed writer. The dreamlike distortion of perspective, the floating sensation Aschenbach experiences on board, is given musical form in Britten's haunting "Serenissima" melody, which appropriately and menacingly adapts part of the plague motive from the previous scene. The leering "Elderly Fop" sings in falsetto; his sexual ambiguity reinforces his grotesque mix of youth and age. He makes sexually suggestive remarks to the writer: "You'll find everything you're wanting" in Venice, he says, and then adds: "Our love to the pretty little darling." All this contributes to Aschenbach's unease as he approaches Venice, the city where he feels "passion confuses the senses." In the novella a new dimension is added: the boat must wait over an hour for the sanitary inspector to approve their landing.

The lyrical arioso sung while Aschenbach is transported—unwillingly—by a surly and mysterious Charon-like gondolier to his hotel on the Lido also introduces a dirge which will be heard again at various moments of foreboding: when he first watches Tadzio on the beach; when he tries to leave Venice the first time; when he finally faces his love for the boy at the opening of act 2. That the dirge should first appear in conjunction with the description of the "black, coffin black" gondola is, of course, most appropriate and conveys the connection between death and the feeling of indolence that the ride in the warm sirocco air is said to induce in Aschenbach, according to Mann's text.

Once settled in his hotel, the writer reminisces (in *recitativo secco*) about his youthful Bohemianism and his now mature devotion to "simplicity, beauty, form." These thematic dualisms (youth/age; passion/form) prepare us for the appearance of the figure who will both provoke new contradictory oppositions and also destroy any hope of balancing them. Piper's libretto here is very close to Mann's text: Aschenbach describes the beautiful Polish boy he sees at dinner as "the soul of Greece," as "perfection of form," and as a "mortal child with more than mortal grace." The subtle sexualization of this seemingly innocent description is one Mann conveyed through suggestions of what we have seen to be "phthisic beauty": Aschenbach wonders if Tadzio might be "delicate" because his complexion was so ivory white. Britten manages the same effect musically by associating the boy with Balinese gamelan-style tuned percussion—a musical device he had previously associated with sexual seduction (Quint) in *The Turn of the Screw*. The simple and sinuous motif played on the vibraphone suggests a tone world utterly different from the piano-accompanied "dry recitative" of Aschenbach.[51] Tadzio's music becomes increasingly rich and exotic as the opera progresses, as xylophone, marimba, glockenspiel, and other percussion instruments are added. But what remains constant is the "foreignness" of the music associated with the young Polish boy, a foreignness that is not Polish, but oriental. And the Orient turns out to be the source of both Asiatic cholera and, as we shall see shortly, the libidinous cult of Dionysus. In other words, Aschenbach is made vulnerable to more than aesthetic beauty by his attraction to the boy. Echoing H. T. Lowe-Porter's translation of the Mann text, the libretto acknowledges this danger in its paradoxical imagery: "There is indeed in every artist's nature a wanton and treacherous proneness to side with beauty."

The language the two texts use to describe both the weather and the effects of the atmosphere on Aschenbach's health recalls the miasma theories of disease that held sway in Europe for so long. As he sits on the beach beneath what is called a colorless, overcast sky and smells a stagnant odor from the lagoons, Aschenbach suddenly feels out of sorts; he finds he cannot write and determines that he must leave—as indeed, it seems, he has had to do once before. The ambiguous suggestiveness of this incident in the past is conveyed in Mann's description of it in terms of secrecy and flight: once before the "wind had found him out" and forced him "to flee from the city like a fugitive" because of what the novella calls "actual bodily surrender" (37). Whether the surrender is to desire or to disease is left ambiguous, as is the description of this "physical defeat" as "a shameful thing." That the very next incident in the story—one that makes him change his mind about leaving—should be the arrival of Tadzio is enough to suggest that this is perhaps not the first time the writer has been vulnerable to youthful beauty, and that it might *not* be a "father's pleasure, a father's warmth" that he feels.

Aschenbach had decided that the atmosphere of Venice, the "fallen queen of the seas" (35), with its faintly rotten scent of swamp and sea, could not be good for his health. The details underlined by Piper's libretto—the waiter luring him to try the seafood, the beggar woman telling about the illness of her children's father ("Il padre is sick"), and the rubbish everywhere—all these add up to a portrait of cholera, even before we are told that every doorway "harbours feverish fears" that make Aschenbach yearn for "fresh mountain air." This miasmic association is emphasized by the music, with its quotations and harmonic conflations of the major and minor third of the plague motive. Despite the "unfriendly lagoon / horrible, evil, nauseous," Aschenbach does not leave Venice: instead he returns to dedicate himself to "the sun / and Apollo himself."

Scene 7 of the opera, the "Games of Apollo" on the beach, provides the staged enactment of what in the novella is an extended development of the association of the sun with Tadzio and also with the Greek tradition linked to both Apollo and Socrates (though given a specific Germanic context by Nietzsche's *Birth of Tragedy from the Spirit of Music*). The scene consists of choral commentary on danced athletic action—

for Tadzio is played by a silent dancer in the opera.[52] Following on Apollo's pronouncement that "He who loves beauty / Worships me," the Chorus's twice-repeated description of Tadzio as "No boy, but Phoebus of the golden hair" and the homoerotic association of the boy with Hyacinthus "basking in Apollo's rays" prepare us for the discussion, initiated by the Chorus, of Phaedrus and Socrates, of youth and age, and of beauty of the body and the spirit. There is a clear tension between, on the one hand, the philosophical position that beauty is but the outer image and mirror of spirit and, on the other, the real pain and longing that Aschenbach feels. This is a tension that cannot be completely sublimated (and repressed) despite his hope that, as he puts it, "Eros is in the word."[53] Even in translation, Mann's text reveals the tension—and contradiction: "Strangely fruitful intercourse this, between one body and another mind!" (46). Aschenbach's desire to talk to the boy—for nothing, he convinces himself, would be "more natural"—is offered to suspiciously dissonant or "unnatural" orchestral tones, however. When he panics ("this is frenzy, absurd") and cannot bring himself to address Tadzio, he blames the heat of the sun for making him ill, and the orchestral bass sounds the plague motive to underline the connection between disease and passion and to symbolize the presence of the plague in Aschenbach's emotional world.[54] But it is at this moment that he also faces the truth and utters "I—love you." The opera's music allows him to sing this secret declaration to an E major triad—his own "natural" key.[55]

This "I—love you" ends the first act; the recitative that opens the second articulates the aging lover's sense of degradation. He says that he feels as if he has "taken part in an orgy." This sexualization of a love that he experiences as both "ridiculous and sacred" is followed immediately by the first actual mention of what the miasmic imagery and atmospheric details have already hinted at very strongly: the "sickness" whose motive can be heard looming up on the tuba. The next scene presents Aschenbach with proof positive that cholera has reached Venice, but he refuses to believe it: "The city's secret, growing darker every day" is likened to the secret in his heart. There is considerable economy in the opera's presentation of the lover pursuing the young man through the sick city ("O voluptuous days, / O the joy I suffer: / feverish chase") to music in which the ground of the plague motive is conflated with Tadzio's theme to create what has been called a "yearning" theme.[56] This musical device replaces the more overt discussion in the novella in which are brought together associations of the plague, of social disorder, and of homoeroticism:"Passion is like crime: it does not thrive on the established order and the common round; it welcomes every blow dealt the bourgeois structure, every weakening of the social fabric, because therein it feels a sure hope of its own advantage. These things that were going on in the unclean alleys of Venice, under cover of an official hushing-up policy—they gave Aschenbach a dark satisfaction" (52–53). As the odor of the "sickening city" increases, Mann's Aschenbach gets bolder in his need to see Tadzio; "drunk with passion," he is led on by "daemonic power" (54) through the heavy, foul air of a crumbling but voluptuous city of "fair frailty that fawned and that betrayed, half fairytale, half snare" (54). He compares the "exotic excesses of feeling" (55) he experiences with the "decent manliness" of his bourgeois forefathers and ends up vindicating, in the name of his art, the "unwholesome secret" of both Venice and his heart. Eager to have the rumors and his suspicions of the contagion confirmed, Aschenbach goes to the British travel bureau.[57] There, as we have already seen, the clerk tells him the truth, accompanied by "the strident or slithery woodwinds and the tuba with its oily malevolence [that] are primarily carriers of pestilence, bringers of chaos."[58] The orchestral bass of the Munich Traveller's solo (and its associations with the swampy exotic landscape where "marvels unfold") here at last takes on its full significance.

In a dream that Mann's text describes as leaving "the whole cultural structure of a lifetime trampled on, ravaged, and destroyed" (65), Apollo and Dionysus battle for Aschenbach's devotion in such a way that the association of cholera with homoerotic affection is confirmed. In the opera the power of Dionysus, the "stranger god" of nature and the "abyss," is pitted against the "beauty, reason, form" urged by the countertenor voice of Apollo. The latter leaves in defeat. The ecstatic orgiastic climax of Dionysus's victory—which in Britten's music is marked by the violent distortion of Tadzio's theme by the plague motive—is described by Mann in terms of the sexual stench of goats mingling with the odor of stagnant waters and of "wounds, uncleanness, and disease" (66). On awakening and feeling himself utterly degraded ("I can fall no further"), Piper's Aschenbach surrenders: "Let the gods do what they will with me." He repeats the sentiment in the next scene as well: "Do what you will with me!" This passivity, this renunciation of control and agency, takes many forms, including his lovesick refusal to curb his "passion and folly" to see the boy and his surrender to the Barber's urging to make himself look younger by dying his hair and using cosmetics that make his lips the color of ripe strawberries.

The irony of this fruit image haunts the next scene in which the frantic lover looks for the boy in the city streets: "His head burned, his body was wet with clammy sweat, he was plagued by intolerable thirst" (69). His response is to buy what the libretto calls "soft, musty, over-ripe" strawberries. Not surprisingly, given the role of fruit in the spread of cholera, the next line is "Chaos, chaos and sickness."[59] The plague motive has entered not on the tuba (as we have come to expect), but on the solo double bass. In the novella Aschenbach's physical condition is never separated from his emotional state: his spells of giddiness are said to be only "half physical" in nature. As is realistic in medical terms, this is a short illness. He sits on the beach watching Tadzio play. Suddenly the tuba can be heard playing the plague motive with "unprecedented savagery" and, to an ascending version of the boy's theme, combined with an earlier melody associated with Aschenbach's own phrase about the "indissoluble fusion of feeling and thought," he loses consciousness as he imagines Tadzio beckoning him to follow him out to sea.[60] As one critic notes, with perhaps appropriate understatement, Aschenbach dies "of more than Asian cholera."[61]

Homoerotic desire is marked in terms of disease throughout Mann's novella, from Aschenbach's very first remark about the boy Jaschiu, who also appears to be smitten with Tadzio's beauty: he imagines that the lad will need at least a year for a "complete recovery" (32). In the background of all this imagery of eroticized pestilence is, as many have noted, Nietzsche's *The Birth of Tragedy* — a work dedicated to explaining the double heritage of Attic tragedy as "an Apollonian embodiment of Dionysiac insights and powers."[62] Whereas in ancient Greek culture Apollo stood for

13. The dying Aschenbach (Kenneth Riegel), being summoned
to death by Tadzio (Jeffrey Edwards), in the 1984 production of *Death
in Venice* by the Canadian Opera Company.

self-control, contemplation, temperate beauty and what he calls *"princi-
pium individuationis,"* Dionysus represented rapture, passion, violent com-
motion and the "un-selving" (39) of the individual in a bond with others
and with nature. But Nietzsche argued that with the lyric poet, who creates images and words under the influence of music, these two can balance and enhance one another.[63] When Aschenbach allows Dionysus
to rout Apollo in his dream, he loses the balance that both Mann and
Britten succeeded in maintaining.

Nietzsche believed Plato was responsible for destroying the balance
in Greek tragedy. The enemy of the Dionysiac spirit, his Socrates replaced Apollonian contemplation with "cold paradoxical ideas" and
described Dionysian transports as "fiery emotions" in order to denigrate
them (78–79). "Esthetic Socratism"—"whatever is to be beautiful must
also be sensible" (79)—is what Nietzsche saw as the death of tragedy, the
defeat of the instinctual life by the intellect. Mann's recalling the *Phae-*

drus in *Der Tod in Venedig* brings to the fore the problems of the intellect trying to deal with the physical reality of (young male) beauty. Socrates' resolution — that truth can work through the senses, through beauty — is not quite Aschenbach's: the warning of the abyss (to which Plato knew excess could lead) is not in fact really heeded by the aging writer in his attempt to justify his Dionysiac passion with what Kenneth Burke once appropriately called his "diseased reworking of the Platonic dialogue."[64]

Nietzsche had begun his study with the assertion that art owed its continuous evolution to that Apollonian/Dionysiac duality, and the analogy he then drew is perhaps not irrelevant to *Death in Venice* either: "even as the propagation of the species depends on the duality of the sexes" (19). The explicitly heterosexual nature of this procreative comparison casts an interesting light on the connections between homoerotic passion and the victory of Dionysus over Apollo, and between both these and the necessary death of Aschenbach as artist (and man), once the balance or duality is lost.[65] The familiar Greek connection of Apollo with the staying of pestilence — in Homer and Sophocles (and Stravinsky/Cocteau) — is significant here, for there is a tight interweaving, in Britten's music as in the libretto and novella texts, of the various strands of meaning associated with plague, homoerotic desire, and death.[66] In other words, Susan Sontag's claim that Aschenbach becomes "just another cholera victim" is not quite accurate, for this is a very particularized and eroticized death suffered by a very individualized person.[67]

And "suffered" is an important word here. From the start, Mann presents Aschenbach as not at all robust and also as attracted to notions of fortitude under suffering. Within the German romantic tradition, suffering was the fate of the artist, but usually the antibourgeois artist, not a resolutely *bürgerlich* Munich writer like this.[68] In *the Birth of Tragedy* Nietzsche had argued that the Greek attitude toward pain could not be separated from the Dionysiac spirit. The Greeks, he felt, were a "race so hypersensitive, so emotionally intense, so equipped for suffering" (30) that they needed the "esthetic mirror" to be able to deal with it. So art was "that sorceress expert in healing" (52). But if Dionysiac suffering is to appear on stage — as it does in the masks of Prometheus or Oedipus, "in the likeness of a striving and suffering individual" (65) — it needs the clarity and precision of the Apollonian impulse, an impulse that Aschenbach rejects in the end. So he suffers. As Eric Cassell's work, discussed earlier in this book, would put it, he suffers not only from the physical pain of his cholera but from the psychological distress caused by the loss of his individual personality in (homoerotic) Dionysian abandon and also by the loss of his professional role as artist capable of balancing the Apollonian and the Dionysian.

Cholera has historically been seen as a disease of society, one that "exposed relentlessly political, social and moral shortcomings."[69] At the time Mann was writing, there were newly medicalized and pathologized discourses that presented homosexuality as a disease threatening the body politic as well.[70] For this reason, we would argue, *Der Tod in Venedig* cannot really be read entirely as an exploration of romantic alienation, Schopenhauerian pessimism, or "Wagnerian morbidity"—though elements of all certainly can be found in the novella.[71] The move that critics have seen in Mann's work—from this German romantic tradition to a greater integration of social and political concerns following the First World War—is perhaps more one of degree than kind, for the close connection of sexuality and disease in the 1911 work in fact gave it social dimensions that went well beyond the life of one fictional character. Mann's concerns about illness and death within a decadent, even sick, society did not disappear when he moved to more overtly political themes: they simply changed form.

Mario and the Magician: Fascism and the "Paralysis of Will"

In 1929 Mann wrote another story about Germans in an Italian resort hotel, also based on his own experience. It too has been made into an opera: *Mario und der Zauberer* became Harry Somers and Rod Anderson's *Mario and the Magician* (1992).[72] A political allegory of the dangerous power of fascism, this novella (like its opera) is hard *not* to read politically. But *Der Tod in Venedig* and *Death in Venice* also have been interpreted in similar terms. The repression of nature-emotion by German *bürgerlich* duty and discipline has been seen as causing an attraction to its extreme opposite. Some have argued that the end of Bismarck's Germany can be seen in Mann's allegorical depiction of "the self-love of European régimes in the age of empire" through his exploration of male narcissism and homosexuality.[73] And certainly the general relationship among nationality, sexuality, and aesthetics has been the focus of much of the critical work on the novella. In *Mario und der Zauberer* and even more so in the opera based on it, this relationship is in the forefront, and once again it is the metaphor of disease that brings them together.

René Girard's connection of the notion of plague not only to social images of contagion but to violence is particularly apt in this context: "The plague is a transparent metaphor for a certain reciprocal violence that spreads, literally, like the plague. The appropriateness of the metaphor comes, obviously, from this contagious character. The idea of contagiousness implies the presence of something harmful, which loses none of its virulence as it is rapidly transmitted from individual to individual. Such, of course, are bacteria in an epidemic; so is violence when it is *imitated*."[74] Like Sontag writing about cholera, however, Girard argues that plague *un*differentiates and destroys specificities. But though the final fate of all its victims is indeed the same, the individual responses to that fate are what make literature — and opera — about epidemic disease particularly interesting.

The Somers/Anderson opera *Mario and the Magician* creates a new narrative frame to stage Mann's story of a German family's trip to Torre di Venere in Italy in August 1928. In this frame the novella's narrator is given an individualizing name — Stefan — and is shown lecturing, in spoken voice, to an audience in Munich. His topic is "our disease." "Disease?" he repeats, as he deals with possible objections to what some in his audience obviously feel to be his exaggerated term to describe what seem like times of economic prosperity in Germany. The irony is that the lecture is being given in 1929, months before the October stock market crash. Stefan claims, however, that "there is a disease infecting our world" that he calls "paralysis of will." To illustrate its ubiquity, he proposes to tell the audience — in the room and in the theater, of course — the story of his Italian holiday the year before. The retrospective irony of a German using Italy as the site of a cautionary tale about nationalism and fascism is one we can savor today, though Mann (writing in 1929) obviously could not . . . or at least not yet.

Stefan's first words about the time spent in Italy echo directly the opening of Mann's novella, that begins with a discussion of the atmosphere of Torre di Venere, an atmosphere that remains unpleasant in the narrator's memory: "From the first moment the air of the place made us uneasy."[75] For anyone familiar with *Death in Venice*, the references to the stifling sirocco air and the sultry atmosphere may well call up those miasma theories of cholera that haunt the other work. This is an atmosphere presented as "southern" in both works: the German protagonists, who define themselves in terms of the "northern" soul, see themselves as utterly different from the Italians. And like Venice in the 1911 story, Torre di Venere here is fundamentally ambiguous: it is a place where "African" heat weighs one down, yet it also represents the "western cradle of the art of song" (139). Mann's narrator also refers to the "emotionalism of the sense-loving south" (141), a trait that quickly takes on a political dimension. The Italian pleasure in and respect for speaking well—the mother tongue is "national cement" (151)—makes them particularly vulnerable to those whose oratory plays to their nationalistic pride, those like the story's hypnotist Cipolla and, of course, the country's leader, Mussolini.[76]

Both the nationalism-xenophobia of the Italians and their auditory sensitivity or vulnerability are made the focus of the first major episode of conflict in the opera, as in the novella. Stefan's child coughs during a meal in the hotel dining room, and an Italian Principessa quickly has her baby taken away, commenting disparagingly on people who travel with "diseased" children. When the Hotel Manager insists that the family change rooms—for theirs adjoin the Principessa's—he is assured by Stefan that the German doctors have said she is no longer ill with whooping cough and thus is no longer at all infectious. The Principessa, however, is afraid her baby will be infected by the *sound* of her coughing, through what the Manager calls "acoustic contagion"—a phrase repeated by a number of characters on stage and therefore fixed firmly in the audience's collective ear and memory. Although surprised by this concept, Stefan admits that doctors "are not in agreement on the exact nature of the disease—so some people imagine anything they want." But when the Hotel Doctor—described by Mann as acting "like a faithful and

honest servant of science" (136)—pronounces the child no longer contagious, the Manager is still not satisfied: "It is not the medical facts alone,
which I have to consider. But the sensibilities of our clients." Fracastorius's sixteenth-century concept of contagion at a distance lives on.

Echoing the "disease" metaphor that frames the opera, this concept
of "acoustic contagion" sets up an allegorical force field that structures
the rest of the work. Just as Mann has his narrator return obsessively
to this "stupid business of the whooping-cough" to explain his unease
in the town, so the opera libretto returns again and again to the idea of
aural contagion, always associated with nationalism and control. For instance, on the beach the German children are harassed because they are
foreigners and, they are informed, should not be playing with Italian
flags. Stefan makes the connection to "acoustic contagion" overt: "These
flags. This stiff sense of dignity. This heat. The hotel. The veranda. The
fear of coughing. . . . Fear and pride. . . . Symptoms of an illness we all
might catch."

When his young child washes out her sandy bathing suit in the water
and is momentarily naked on the beach, there is a general outcry, and
Stefan is taken to the municipio, where he is lectured about "Roman discipline" and "cultural purity" in relation to Il Duce's laws protecting
Italian civilization from "the excesses of foreign licentiousness." In fact,
Anderson includes part of one of Mussolini's speeches in this tirade,
making ironic the Hotel Manager's admiring remark: "Parlate benissimo.
Il Duce himself could not turn a phrase more eloquently." But the joke
serves only to underline the dangers of "acoustic contagion" in the form
of manipulative oratory. Mann too had brought the metaphor of disease
to bear on the Italians' newfound nationalism by having the narrator explain to his children, "These people . . . were just passing through a certain stage, something rather like an illness, perhaps; not pleasant, but
probably unavoidable" (141). The message here was as much for the German reader of 1930 as for the children.[77]

The playing out of these oral nationalist dangers is the topic of the
rest of the narrative. In the opera, a band of Blackshirts arrives with
posters announcing the visit of the Cavaliere Cipolla. The name—Sir
Onion might be a literal translation—comes from Boccaccio's *Decamerone*,

whose tales, as we have seen, are told as entertainment by a group of Italians who have fled the city of Florence to protect themselves from the plague.[78] The Cipolla of the novella and opera is described as "Forzatore, Illusionista, Prestidigitatore." The last two terms are the same in English—illusionist, prestidigitator—but the first is problematic: a "forzatore" is usually a strongman in a circus. As the opera progresses, the notion of *forzare*—to compel or force—is central to the identity of this manipulative and frightening performer. His first mention in the opera is followed by a chorus of an actual fascist anthem, "Giovinezza, giovinezza," with its call to youth to realize that in fascism lies the salvation of liberty ("Nel fascismo è la salvezza della nostra libertà"). At this point Somers inserts quite recognizably diatonic, melodic music into a basically atonal score in order to represent (and elicit) patriotic mass emotion (in the stage listeners). However, the theater audience's manifest delight in hearing comfortably tonal music for almost the first time in the opera cannot help implicating it in subtle and historically interesting ways. What does it mean that "Giovinezza, giovinezza"—a fascist song—is the only tune being whistled on the way out of the theater?

Acts 2 and 3 of the opera place the theater audience in the same (physical and psychic) position as the characters who attend Cipolla's performance: as potential victims of his compelling power. The description of his appearance in the novella is made alternately estranging and familiar. He is decidedly odd looking, with a "sharp, ravaged face, piercing eyes, compressed lips, small black waxed moustache, and a so-called imperial in the curve between mouth and chin" (147). His dress, however, marks him as less odd than typical—of an eighteenth-century "charlatan and mountebank type" (147). This archetypal nature of his appearance is commented on repeatedly: he is "the historic type," "the traditional type" (147), even an "outmoded personal type" (152). Yet for all this typicality, there is also "something not quite in order about his figure" (147), for he is physically malformed, and this is emphasized from the start.

Cipolla's oratory is a curious and contradictory mix of what is called "thin-skinnedness and animosity" and "self-confidence" (151). He constantly calls attention to his own malformation, his ill health, and his difficult life—but usually in the context of a comparison with sexually attractive young men in the audience—or rather, with young men he *constructs* as sexually attractive to women: such as the "lady killer—of Torre di Venere" who is "spoiled by the favours of the fair sex." To compensate for what he presents as his own lack of such spoiling, he boasts of his successes on stage, of the praise of even Il Duce's brother. To this the crowd respectfully mutters, "Il Duce!"—thus reinforcing the Hotel Manager's earlier connection between Mussolini and fine speaking, but here specifically in the context of Cipolla: "Parla benissimo!" "Che ispirato oratore." Cipolla's patter constantly calls up nationalistic sentiments. A woman is said to follow "the honorable profession of Roman matron—giving our country its glorious sons!" Italy is said to have "brought the flower of culture to the world." At the end of act 2, just before it breaks into song (singing the "Garibaldi hymn"), the crowd cries—in a significant overlapping—"Viva la cultura italiana!" "Viva la civiltà Romana!" and "Viva Cipolla!"

Lest we forget the force field of that "acoustic contagion," act 3 opens with Stefan's remarks about the miasmic atmosphere of the town— "queer, uncomfortable, troublesome, tense, oppressive"—that seemed to be personified in the person of Cipolla that night. The original meaning of miasmic (polluting, defiling) is here transferred from a theory of physical contagion to an allegory of political and thus acoustically transmitted infection, as Cipolla reveals his true identity (and with it a rich web of associations): he turns out to be a hypnotist as well as an effective orator. It is the display of his hypnotic powers that brings the political allegory to the fore, for these are powers that play to the will and instinct and silence reason and virtue. The opera, like the novella, illustrates the vulnerability of human reason and logic, because of the equally strong human attraction to what Nietzsche would have recognized as the Dionysian, the "instinctual frenzy and barbaric, primitive power" that fascism fed into.[79] Each of the demeaning demonstrations of his power to which Cipolla subjects the people of Torre di Venere involves the confrontation of their will with his; in each, Cipolla's is victorious. The "claw-handled" riding whip that he cracks becomes the sadistic, the "insulting symbol of his domination" (167). From his first manifestation of his power to his last, he manages to persuade his victims that they should, as he puts it, "divide up the willing and the doing" and abdicate the responsibility, "the burden of voluntary choice" (170) to him. Implicitly reducing all human relationships to that of the master-slave, Cipolla also proves not only that resistance is futile but that people happily fall under the spell of his "attacks upon the will-power, the loss or compulsion of volition" (166). Librettist Rod Anderson has said that Cipolla, for him, was the "symbol of the fascist leader, of the hypnotic domination of fascism over the masses, and of its expropriation of individual liberty in the name of service to a nationalistic hysteria."[80] But as he cracks his whip and everyone — except the isolated and resisting Stefan — is forced to dance on stage, Cipolla goes too far.

In the opera as in the novella, Mario, a quiet young waiter, is brought on stage by the hypnotist, who declares his name to be a "classic," "one of those which preserve the heroic traditions of the Fatherland" (174). Twice Cipolla does the "Roman salute" — further encoding this as a scene of political import; twice, however, he also calls Mario "Ganymede" — after the beautiful boy loved by Zeus. This scene thereby becomes the culmination not only of the nationalist-fascist network of associations with "acoustic contagion," but of another set that — as in *Death in Venice* — is organized around homoerotic desire. From the start of the novella, the resort town's name has been rendered both sexual and ironic, for Torre de Venere — the tower of Venus — no longer has the phallic tower that once gave it its name. The narrator's seemingly innocent description of the audience at Cipolla's performance therefore becomes a loaded one: "There stood the manhood of Torre di Venere," he remarks (145). After a confrontation with the youth he mockingly dubs the "lady-killer of Torre di Venere," Cipolla calls attention to his own ill health and his malformation in a nationalist context: "I have a little physical defect which prevented me from doing my bit in the war for the greater glory of the Fatherland" (151). Immediately after, he again complains about the youth "spoilt by the favours of the fair sex."

This youth, whom Cipolla has constructed as heterosexual — as "questo torregiano di Venere" — is one for whom he feels a genuine antagonism. We are told by Mann's narrator: "No one looking at the physical parts of the two men need have been at a loss for the explanation, even if the deformed man had not constantly played on the other's supposed success with the fair sex" (151). The operatic association of physical malformation with moral deformation has a long history, and includes Verdi/Piave's Rigoletto and Wagner's Alberich in *Der Ring des Nibelungen*. But Mann calls special attention to the *kind* of deformity given to Cipolla: though "the chest was too high . . . the corresponding malformation of the back did not sit beween the shoulders, it took the form of a sort of hips or buttocks hump" (152). The moving of the deformity to the general area of the pelvis may well be intended to call attention to Cipolla's sexuality. And the descriptions of his relations to various young men upon whom he exercises his hypnotic powers appears to code that sexual dimension as specifically homosexual. For instance, he induces a trance "by stroking and breathing upon a certain young man who had offered himself as a subject and already proved himself a particularly susceptible one" (167).

But it is with Mario that the homoerotic suggestions take on a certain ominous character. Cipolla teases Mario about his love for — and suffering over — a young woman named Silvestra. As has by now become a familiar rhetorical pattern in both opera and novella, this remark is followed up by a reminder of his own physical form: "I know what you are thinking: what does this Cipolla, with his little physical defect, know about love? Wrong, all wrong, he knows a lot" (176). Hypnotizing the young man, he begins with the hypothetical — "If I were to put myself in her place" — and then convinces Mario that he actually sees Silvestra, not himself. But he does this in decidedly ambiguous terms, saying to him: "It is time that you see me and *recognize* me, Mario, my beloved!" (177; our italics). The narrator of the novella notes with horror how the hypnotist made himself "irresistible, wreathed and coquetted with his crooked shoulder" (177). Mario believes him, and the audience is shown "a public exposure of timid and deluded passion and rapture" (177).

In the opera, Cipolla sings in falsetto: "Mario, my beloved! Tell me, who am I?" When the young man replies, "Silvestra," Cipolla responds with "Kiss me! Trust me, I love you. Kiss me here" — on the lips. Mario does so — as all watch in silence. Cipolla breaks the spell with "Ah, mio

14. Cipolla (David Rampy) hypnotizing Mario
(Benoit Boutet, seated) to convince him that Sylvestra loves
him, in the 1992 production of *Mario and the Magician*
by the Canadian Opera Company.

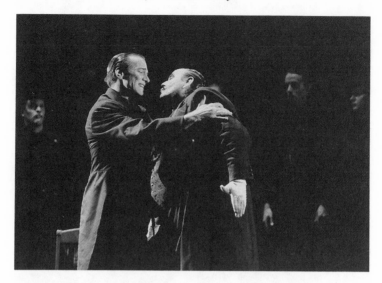

15. Mario (Benoit Boutet, on the left) preparing
to kiss Cipolla (David Rampy), convinced that he is Sylvestra,
in the 1992 production of *Mario and the Magician*
by the Canadian Opera Company.

amore! I need breath," followed by loud, mocking laughter. Mario awakens, shocked at what he has just been made to do by such "acoustic contagion," and runs away. But at the crack of Cipolla's whip, he turns and
shoots the hypnotist-orator dead. The deceptive seductive charm of fascism meets its end through the violence engendered by its own irra-
tionalist power. Demagogic oratory and chauvinistic hypnotic power, in
the novella as in the libretto, release repression and "libidinize" both authority and submission to it, suggesting the theory of fascism as compensatory satisfaction for the repressed.[81] Although a reading of Mann's
novella in these terms would be in terms of sexual jealousy and homophobia, the notions of physical malformation and contagion that link the
fascist discourse and the homoerotic attraction through verbal (and musical) power suggest a more complex interaction of sexuality, nationalism, and disease.

George L. Mosse, in *Nationalism and Sexuality: Respectability and Abnormal*

Sexuality in Modern Europe, claims that European nationalism developed and maintained nineteenth- and twentieth-century concepts of "respectability" in such a way that certain fixed notions of the abnormal and the diseased—in terms of sexuality—could then inform ethics, aesthetics, religion, and politics. In this context Cipolla would be physically marked from the start as *not* fitting the ideal of "manliness" that came to symbolize the nation's spiritual and material vitality and its standard in physical beauty.[82] His malformed body would likely have been read by Mann's readership as the outward sign of the abnormal and the degenerate. This would have aligned him (even if there were no other textual evidence) with the homosexual, the very antithesis of bourgeois respectability. Given that Gabriele D'Annunzio had been so important in articulating the opposite of the degenerate—the cult of physical beauty—for Mussolini's fascist Italy, there may be other ways to explain Cipolla's aggressive behavior toward Signora Angiolieri—a woman whose identity as the former wardrobe mistress of the actress Eleonora Duse (whose "fame has long been bound up with the Fatherland's" [164]), is emphasized by both texts. Mann implies that this patriotic association may well have been as much the result of her affair with D'Annunzio, the famous artist (and orator), as the product of her theatrical talent. The connection between fascism and disease that the "acoustic contagion" metaphor has established recalls in interesting ways Gramsci's remark that D'Annunzio was the Italian people's "last bout of illness."[83]

Although Cipolla dies a violent death very different from Aschenbach's quiet drift into unconsciousness preceding his demise (from the dry form of cholera), there are continuities in these two Mann-inspired operas that are related to the social dimensions of epidemic disease, stemming from the terror of contagion. In the operas as in the novellas, disease is associated with social tension and the fear of disorder and panic—be it from a cholera epidemic or from the allegorical plague of fascism, spread by "acoustic contagion." As we noted earlier, Sontag has argued that cholera, unlike tuberculosis, "is the kind of faculty that, in retrospect, has simplified a complex self, reducing it to a sick environment."[84] But from a broader historical point of view, it was cholera that in fact allowed public health authorities into the private lives of the urban poor, thereby making possible that nineteenth- and twentieth-century middle-class distinction between sexual respectability and various kinds of "abnormalities." And it was *that* construction in turn that made extremely complex the "self" deemed "different." That epidemic disease came to be associated with same-sex affection and with fascism is a sign of the power it has wielded over the bourgeois public — which has constituted, of course, the very audience for opera. And after all, if there ever was an art form whose power could be described in terms of "acoustic contagion," it is opera.

Chapter 6

Where There's Smoke,
There's . . .

Smoking cigarettes is both a source of visible sensual pleasure and an em-
blem of women's erotic life. At least that is how it appears to men, for
whom the sight of women smoking is both threatening and intensely,
voyeuristically exciting. — Richard Klein, *Cigarettes Are Sublime*

Those public notices about the dangers of syphilis that Stravinsky would
have seen in the *pissoirs* of Paris in the 1920s have been replaced in some
cities today by posters warning of the dangers not only of AIDS, but of
something even more familiar and ubiquitous: smoking. Although smoking is not in itself a disease, of course, medical research in the last half
century has provided ample justification for the old image of cigarettes
as "coffin nails." As we saw in the introduction, a demographic model
of mortality in Western countries over the past two hundred years suggests a shift from epidemic to endemic, chronic diseases (in the nineteenth century), and then to our current stable and relatively low death
rate.[1] The diseases now responsible for death are degenerative disorders
and human-made illnesses. This shift came about through a decrease in
deaths related to airborne microorganisms (particularly tuberculosis),
followed by waterborne and food-borne organisms (such as cholera), to
which one could add the decline in other infections (such as syphilis).[2]
This allowed the negative health effects of tobacco use to be unmasked
in the 1950s and 1960s with the description of its relation to lung cancer, emphysema, cardiovascular disease, and chronic bronchitis. Some
have claimed that tobacco is responsible for "the greatest epidemic of the
twentieth century."[3] The reasons are threefold: the late effects of tobacco use on health can simply be seen more clearly when people live
longer; as these disease processes have emerged as more prominent health
concerns, medical research has focused on their etiologies as subjects of

study; and tobacco use increased dramatically in the twentieth century, in part because the technology that allowed the manufacturing of cigarettes in the nineteenth century permitted the diffusion of inexpensive smoking materials. To this should be added that during times of social stress—especially wars—tobacco consumption appears to rise sharply.[4]

Tobacco: A History of Double(d) Talk

Although the debates about the New World origin of syphilis may still rage, there is no doubt that tobacco was brought to Europe at the end of the fifteenth century from what was later called the Americas, where Europeans found natives smoking both in their religious rites and for their personal pleasure.[5] In the early sixteenth century it was mostly Spaniards living in the colonies (and sailors) who were known to smoke pipes and take snuff, largely because Spain's empire included most of the colonies where tobacco was grown.[6] But by 1560 the plant had been taken to Portugal and from there, as we shall see shortly, to the French court. At the same time, pipe smoking was introduced into England, and by the end of the reign of Elizabeth I, we know that it was particularly popular with young men of fashion. Throughout the first half of the seventeenth century, tobacco use in this form continued in Britain and became common throughout northern Europe. By the next century snuff had become more fashionable, however, supplanting smoking in France and England—except for people in the middle and lower classes. This led Dr. Johnson to proclaim in 1773 that from what he could see, smoking had "gone out."[7]

The practice of smoking tobacco packed in a rolled leaf was known from aboriginal use. Although there is early evidence of cigars being smoked by well-to-do Spaniards, it is not until the late eighteenth century that cigars begin to appear in Europe from Havana and then to be produced in Spain. Only then does cigar smoking become more widespread. With the Napoleonic conflicts taking place in Spain from 1807 to 1814, cigar smoking was subsequently introduced to France and England by returning troops.[8] By 1831 a commentator could remark that "the taste for smoking . . . has revived, probably from the military habits of Europe during the French wars; but instead of the sober sedentary pipe, the ambulatory cigar is chiefly used."[9] Using a roll of paper as a holder for tobacco leaves was also a relatively early practice (Seville beggars recycled cigar butts for this purpose). The cigarette as we know it, however, does not seem to have become respectable until the eighteenth century: Casanova (who may not have been respectable in other ways) mentions smoking what we would recognize as a cigarette in 1766.[10] This mode of smoking spread to Portugal, to Italy, and by the 1840s, to France. With the manufacture of the cigarette came the real spread of tobacco use among all socioeconomic groups. The (fortunate or unfortunate) conjunction of a number of things made this possible: the discovery of new ways of curing tobacco, the automated production of cigarettes, and the invention of safe and practical friction matches.[11]

It is interesting that, before twentieth-century medical proof of the deleterious health effects of smoking, the negative cultural associations with tobacco have less to do with physical disease than with what we might call its social consequences. But it is precisely this earlier social judgment that has determined both the continuities and the changes in how smoking is represented, as we have learned more about its effects on health. The most striking common factor, over the years and despite the changes in knowledge, is the existence from the start of a curious and complex doubled discourse or way of talking about tobacco and its use. The first example can be found in the early and seemingly paradoxical claims that tobacco is both harmful and healing. The Spanish had noticed this in the aboriginal use of tobacco: it was both ritualistic (and used to mark war *and* peace) and medicinal (where it could act as either poison or remedy).[12] Jean Nicot, the French ambassador to Portugal in 1559, used the leaves of the plant (which was later to bear his name) as a poultice for a cut on his cook's thumb. When he noticed how quickly the wound healed, he recommended tobacco to Catherine de Medici for her migraines, and soon most of the French court was using what became known as the "herbe médicée" in various powder forms.[13] Not surprisingly, the plant began to be cultivated in botanical gardens for medicinal purposes. Nicoló Monardes, in his *Historia medicinal de las cosas que sirven al uso de medicina*, published in Seville in 1565, claimed that tobacco was helpful in the treatment of coughs, asthma, headache, stomach cramps, gout, and diseases of women.[14] The widespread impact of the theory of tobacco's multiple medical uses (and its usefulness) can be seen in the quick translation of this book into Latin, French, English, and Italian and in the appearance of other publications, such as Everartus's *De herba panacea* (1587). Tobacco use for medical purposes continued up until the nineteenth century for problems as diverse as constipation and drowning.[15]

In stark contrast to the current view of smoking as causing an epidemic, in earlier centuries tobacco was believed to have protective value during various visitations of the Black Plague. Samuel Pepys found himself "obliged to buy some roll tobacco to smell and chew" on seeing some plague houses in London.[16] In addition, it was firmly held at the time that tobacco had disinfectant properties useful against miasma and thus was "one of the wholesomest sents [sic] that is against all contagious airs, for it overmasters all other smells."[17] Even as late as 1831, during a cholera epidemic, Berlin repealed its edicts forbidding smoking in public — and did so for health reasons. In England at the same time, a house where cholera victims had died was fumigated with tobacco, and people everywhere could be seen smoking as a "preventive."[18]

The positive medicinal use represents, however, only one side of the doubled discourse that developed around tobacco. In England, James I's "Counterblaste to Tobacco" at the beginning of the seventeenth century is perhaps the best-known statement of the negative view at this time. Tobacco was seen as a "custom loathsome to the eye, hatefull to the nose, harmful to the braine, dangerous to the lungs, and in the black stinking fume thereof, neerest resembling the horrible Stigian smoke of the pit that is bottomless."[19] That the Crown profited from taxes and from the royal monopoly on tobacco might have had some effect on its refusal to ban smoking entirely — there as everywhere and then as now — for this discourse of harmfulness continues to the present day, of course. From the seventeenth century on, there has been this curious double, even hypocritical message, the result of the conflict between authorities who forbade it on principle and merchants and governments that saw its immense economic potential. Although there is now firm medical evidence to support the warning about the dangers to health, this was not

16. An English tobacco advertisement during the 1832 cholera epidemic.

always the case. H.-A. Depierris's 1880 screed against tobacco abuse in France was called La Vérité sur le tabac, le plus violent des poisons, la nicotine, and it blamed the plant for the physical and moral degeneration of the nation: it destroyed beauty and longevity; its effects on the intelligence led to madness, moral breakdown, and crime; it degraded men in particular by depleting their "generative" forces.[20] A nineteenth-century French antitobacco activist might well have to assert this as strongly as he did in order to position himself in opposition to the powerful and dominant associations of smoking with sexual attraction, as our discussion of Carmen will soon show.[21]

A number of other dualities characterize the discourse that developed around smoking throughout the centuries and, indeed, continue to this day. An obvious one would be that it is considered pleasurable—appealing as it does to all the senses—as well as transgressive and dangerous. It is a relaxant, yet a stimulant as well. It is the occasion for companionship and good fellowship. But at the same time it is the sign of the solitary rebel. Perhaps the most striking duality in which tobacco use is coded from the start is the one involving gender. From early on women were known to smoke only in South America and in Spain, which

17. An early negative view of smoking, from
J. Balde, *Die Truckene Trunckenheit*, 1658.

controlled most New World tobacco production before the Virginia colonies thrived.[22] In sixteenth-century France, because of Catherine de Medici's advocacy of the plant, the exchange and sharing of tobacco became the basis of social rituals between both men and women of the upper classes, an echo of the habits of aboriginal peoples in the Americas.[23] Although women as well as men seem to have smoked in England and Holland in the seventeenth century, it fell out of fashion for women to the point that the pleasures of tobacco became strictly masculine and remained that way at least until 1840: "Respectable folk in the middle and upper classes would have been horrified at the idea of a pipe or a cigar between feminine lips; and cigarettes had been used by men for a long time before it began to be whispered that here and there a lady — who was usually considered dreadfully 'fast' for her pains — was accustomed to venture upon a cigarette."[24] By the nineteenth century, in France as well, the gender division was firmly established: the cigar was for men only. Indeed, in Jules Sandeau's terms in 1865, it was what made a man a complete man: "Tout homme qui ne fume pas est un homme incomplet."[25] In France, women who smoked were seen as either immoral — prostitutes advertised their profession by smoking, and courtesans were imagined to smoke with their lovers — or unconventional and therefore threatening in their bravado.[26] Think of George Sand — wearing trousers, smoking a cigar, writing novels — that is, arrogating to herself all the privileges of masculinity. As the anonymous *Les Fumeurs de Paris* put it, women risked being the equal of men if they could smoke.[27] Fairholt, in his 1859 history of tobacco, may sound a little less judgmental than some of his French contemporaries, but even he, by association, links the unconventional and the sexual in his description of the novelist as "Madame Dudevant, better known by her soubriquet George Sand, who often indulges in a cigar between the intervals of literary labour, as the ladies of Spain and Mexico delight in doing at all other intervals."[28]

There is yet another dimension to this gendered history of association with tobacco, however. In the second half of the reign of Louis XV there was a fashion for what were called secret snuff boxes (*tabatières*), which under certain conditions would reveal a hidden picture of either a woman or some sexual subject.[29] Another variant of this connection of woman and smoking can be seen in the eroticizing of smoking in French nineteenth-century poetry written by men. Théophile Gautier's erotic sonnet "La Fumée," written for Marie Mattei in 1852, offers the image of a couple behind a protective veil of smoke that enables them to make love in public. A clever and deliberate use of ambiguous syntax and well-placed line endings suggestively allows the poet to "light up" both his cigar and his beloved: "J'allume un cigare et ma bien-aimée / Un papelito roulé par ses doigts."[30] As we shall see in more detail later in the chapter, the French literary imagination consistently associated smoking with the voluptuous, the languorous, the exotic.

Because of the persistent doubled coding throughout the centuries, however, although tobacco clearly did come to be associated in men's minds with things pleasurable, it also took on connotations of possible danger or destruction: once again smoking came to be associated with women, but this time with vice as both excitement and dissipation. As the title of Richard Klein's recent study would have it, "cigarettes are sublime" — sublime in the sense of a "darkly beautiful, inevitably painful pleasure that arises from some intimation of eternity."[31] Though it wasn't until the twentieth century that the definitive link between smoking and lung cancer would be made, the idea that tobacco was as dangerous to the health as it was pleasurable to the senses has a long history.

Male Bonding versus the Lone Rebel: *Les Contes d'Hoffmann* and *La Fanciulla del West*

Paradoxically, it is the male connection between women and smoking that makes possible another very strong cultural association, between tobacco and male bonding, that lasts to this day. Cigarette advertising still plays on connotations of conviviality, companionship, and hospitality that have a long history. As early as *The Beggar's Opera* (1728), the musical stage also drew on these same associations. Act 2, scene 1, takes place in a tavern near Newgate where highwaymen gather. The table, we are told, bears "wine, brandy, and tobacco."[32] By this date snuff was the fashion among the English upper classes, but here in the public house smoking made for genial company.

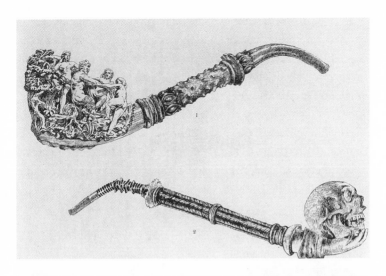

18. Pipes as reminders of the sensual and
the deadly pleasures of smoking.

19. Male bonding over a smoke.

In fact, the tavern scene became a kind of operatic staple and always signaled male companionship.[33] In the prologue of Offenbach/Barbier's *Les Contes d'Hoffmann* (1881), Luther's Nuremberg tavern is the setting for Hoffmann's call for a drink and a pipe, seconded by his companion (and disguised Muse) Nicklausse: "Je bois, fume et m'assieds comme vous." The French librettist and playwright who reworked E. T. A. Hoffmann's tales might well have known, as English novelists apparently did, that the German characters "would be expected to smoke hard"—like their real-life counterparts.[34] Hoffmann's Muse opens the opera with a celebration of taverns like this:

C'est là que, parmi la fumée	It is there that, amid the smoke
et le vin vieux des noirs celliers,	and old wines of dark cellars,
naissent les rêves par milliers;	are born dreams by the thousands;
là que d'Hoffmann je fus aimée!	there that by Hoffmann I was loved.

The students to whom Hoffmann agrees to tell his stories sing about the pleasure of listening to such mad tales while following the smoke of the pipes in the air: "en suivant le nuage clair / que la pipe jette dans l'air."

Perhaps the most famous of these tavern scenes, however, is the one that opens the Puccini/Civinini-Zangarini opera, *La Fanciulla del West* (1911). For audiences today, the connection between the western and smoking may well be a cultural given, thanks to advertising. When Marlboro men travel in packs, like their cigarettes, they would be perfectly at home among this opera's tough gold miners, complaining in the saloon about their hard day's work and seeking the consolations of whiskey and cigars. When one of them thinks the beautiful saloon owner, Minnie, has finally agreed to be his bride, he calls for cigars for one and all: "Sigari a tutti!"[35] In so doing, he draws on the connotations of smoking not only with celebration and male bonding but simultaneously with women and sexuality. Although Minnie is accepted and admired by the men, she is also separated from them: as an honorable woman, she does not smoke, but is directly implicated in the phallic connotations of the cigars sold in her saloon. When she offers one to the Wells Fargo agent, he replies that she should choose the brand for him because, whichever she selects, it will be perfumed by her hand: "Se le scegliete voi, / la qualità non conta

nulla. / Ognuno avrà per me il profumo / della man che li tocca!" This remark prefigures the act 2 conversation between Minnie and the man she
does love, Dick Johnson. Alone in her cabin, they speak of the gendered
differences in love, with Minnie expressing incredulity that, if you love
someone, you would want her only for an hour. Johnson's reply is that
there are women whom men would be happy to have for that one hour
and then die. When Minnie then offers him a Havana cigar, asking him,
in practically the same sentence, how many times he has died ("quante
volte siete morto? / Uno dei nostri avana?"), it is hard to resist correcting
Freud's famous remark to note that sometimes a cigar is *not* only a cigar.

It isn't at all surprising, then, that Johnson's unsuccessful rival for
Minnie's love, Jack Rance, also smokes. Typical of that doubled coding of
tobacco throughout its history, smoking not only is a marker of male companionship, but can also signal the presence of the outsider, the rebel —
as those Humphrey Bogart, James Dean, or Clint Eastwood roles in films
over the years have shown. Their somewhat more sinister forefather
is the man whose solitary lit cigar is the first thing the stage directions
tell us that we see gleaming on a darkened stage set as the opera begins.
As discussed in the introduction, along with opera's many other dimensions (musical, textual, narrative, and so on), the *staged* nature of its
drama cannot be ignored, and the importance of smoking to the plots of
many operas is, as we shall see, often a matter of visual, material detail.
Rance's cigar is one such detail, for its very presence calls up a set of cultural associations even without overt commentary. Later we do learn, of
course, that despite being the sheriff, Jack Rance is known to be a gam-
bler who (though he already seems to have a wife elsewhere) wants to
marry Minnie. When Minnie's real love, Johnson (alias the bandit Ra-
merrez), is turned over to him as sheriff, Rance insolently blows smoke
in his face as the final insult and, at the same time, as the final proof for
the audience of his villainy. In David Bellasco's American play *The Girl of
the Golden West*, the source text for the opera, Rance strikes Johnson in
the face; as a European, Puccini knew he could get the same effect with
a simple puff of smoke.

20. Jack Rance (Pasquale Amato) with his
cigar, in the 1910 premiere of La Fanciulla del West
at the Metropolitan Opera, New York.

Sensual Pleasures and Their Dangers: Il *Segreto di Susanna* and Il *Tabarro*

There are still other, related double associations besides those of sexual attraction and repulsion or of male bonding and solitary alienation. Over the years, the sensual pleasures of smoking have been paradoxically described: tobacco has been considered both a stimulant and a relaxant. This complexity can be seen in the different functions served by the cigarettes provided free to American soldiers in the First World War: "The cigarette is every soldier's best friend, for the solace it brings, for the relief from hunger and fatigue it provides, for the relaxation it encourages, for the courage it summons when the fighting gets thick and hard."[36] There are good physiological reasons for the paradox of tobacco as both exciting and calming: it has recently been proved that, for those addicted to nicotine, small doses excite and larger ones sedate. As a stimulant, tobacco has been shown to improve reaction time and increase concentration.[37] In a letter from prison, Antonio Gramsci wrote of the impact of the enforced reduction in his tobacco consumption: he found that he could not concentrate as well as usual and that he was reading and thinking less.[38] In the Somers/Anderson opera *Mario and the Magician* (1992), the hypnotist and illusionist Cipolla lights a cigarette each time he needs to "fortify" his powers of concentration. In the source text — Thomas Mann's *Mario und der Zauberer* — the narrator explains that when Cipolla looked exhausted, he would have a smoke and a drink of cognac to replenish his energy. He speculates that the hard life, of which the deformed performer constantly reminds his audience, was the cause of his evident need for the "stimulant" of tobacco.[39]

Smoking, however, is also seen as a relaxant. In *Lavengro*, George Borrow wrote that "smoking has a sedative effect upon the nerves, and enables a man to bear the sorrows of this life (of which everyone has his share) not only decently, but dignifiedly."[40] Closely related to this association is that of the sensual pleasure smoking offers. Ermanno Wolf-Ferrari and Enrico Golisciani's 1909 opera Il *segreto di Susanna* offers an extended hymn of praise to the charms of smoking. We learn of its sensual, caressing sweetness, its delicate spirals that inspire dreams:

O gioia la nube leggera	Oh what joy to follow
cogli occhi socchiusi seguire	with half-closed eyes the fine cloud
che ascende con cerule spire,	that rises in blue spirals,
ascende più tenue, più tenue d'un vel	rises more delicately than a veil
e sembra dorata chimera	and seems like a golden illusion
vanente nel limpido ciel!	vanishing into the clear sky!
Sottile vapor mi carezza,	The fine smoke caresses me,
mi culla, sognar mi fa;	rocks me, makes me dream;
libare con lenta dolcezza	I wish to taste your delight
io vo' la tua voluttà.	with a slow sweetness.

That a *woman* should experience this sensual pleasure adds a new element to the gendered coding of tobacco. But the association of smoking with women's sexuality is here given yet another twist, a transgressive dimension made dramatically visible through a husband's suspicion that his wife of only a month already has a lover. Why? Because he smells tobacco smoke in the house. He even rhymes seducer with smoker: in Italian, "seduttore" with "fumatore"—to which he adds the requisite operatic horrific "orrore."

This is where yet another association is added, one that also has a long history in the musical representations of smoking: that of men's violent jealousy and a need to control their women's lives at all costs. Gil, the husband in question here, is haunted, even obsessed by horrifying suspicions of his wife's infidelity. Though he believes she looks innocent enough ("E volto quello di chi un marito inganna?"), he has nevertheless forbidden her to go out alone. When not consumed by his jealousy, he sees in his Susanna the most virtuous, the most beautiful of women—to be compared to a lily or a limpid crystal mirror—and he knows his suspicions risk contaminating his love as well as his metaphors.

Gil claims to have no vices himself: he doesn't drink, gamble, philander, or smoke. But when he embraces his beloved, all he can smell on her clothes is "l'odor fatal" of smoke. His visceral outrage forces Susanna to admit to what she unfortunately too demurely calls a secret, a vice, a desire ("Un vizio . . . una voglia")—an admission Gil can read only in sexual terms. Therefore he responds with anger, threats, and name calling:

she is a model of falsehood ("model di falsità"), a witch ("Sciagurata"). She protests—to no avail—that he is maltreating her for no cause ("maltrattarmi . . . per nulla"). In a scene of potentially funny—but also potentially tragic—misunderstanding over Susanna's claim that many women "do it," Gil explodes. She means that many women *smoke*—for that is her secret vice and desire; he thinks she means that many women are unfaithful. While Susanna calls him a tyrant, he threatens her with more than shouting and foul language: he begins to smash everything in sight, overturning furniture and finally breaking a chair. When she runs off to hide in another room, he sits and sings of his obsession with catching her in flagrante delicto.

Unaware that Gil has misunderstood her indirect confession, Susanna returns with apologies and promises to give up her wrongdoing to please him. He leaves the house but plans to return to surprise her with her lover. At his exit Susanna—who clearly has no intention of giving up smoking—plans only to be more careful from then on. The subsequent scene of blissful pleasure when she indulges in her little perfumed vice, as she calls it ("vizietto profumato"), is interrupted by her frantic husband's reentry. Susanna still fails to understand that his furious search is for her (smoking) lover and so feels he is overreacting, to say the least. Once again he departs in a rage, brandishing a broken umbrella. Undaunted, Susanna returns to her favorite pastime and sings that song of praise cited above to the pleasures of smoking. Tellingly, one of the dreams the smoke produces is of her husband, but a more tender and charming version of him ("Ma più gentil, più tenera, / leggiadra"). When the not very tender Gil again suddenly surprises her, she hides the cigarette behind her back. When he grabs her hand roughly ("con forza"), he burns himself. Only now does he finally catch on that it is she who has been smoking. She begs his forgiveness again, but this now comic Othello finally has the decency to admit that it is she who should forgive him his jealousy.[41] She offers to give up smoking for him, but he responds by saying that he will take it up instead: they will smoke together. She lights his cigarette from hers—mouth to mouth, and they sing together:

Tutto è fumo a questo mondo	*All is smoke in this world*
che col vento, si dilegua . . . ,	*that with the wind, vanishes . . . ,*
ma l'amor, l'amor sincer, profondo	*but love, sincere, deep love*
fuma, fuma senza tregua.	*smokes, smokes without rest.*

Not surprisingly—as the cliché recalled in our chapter title is meant to suggest—this is a prelude to their departure to the bedroom, after relighting their cigarettes, this time with a candle. No doubt they shared one *after*, as well—another association of sex with smoking in our culture.

This work was written as an intermezzo, a short comic entertainment, and its often humorous rhyming and light music guarantee its genre. As the entry in *The New Grove Dictionary of Opera* puts it: "Its justly famous little overture establishes a zestfully comic atmosphere by almost literally imitating the manner and spirit of 18th-century *opera buffa.*"[42] But for all the happy resolution and comic misunderstanding, *Il segreto di Susanna* also makes a disturbing connection between smoking and male jealousy (and violence) that is not alone, as we shall see, in either Western society at large or the operatic repertoire. The obvious metaphoric connection here lies in the suspicion suggested by that very cliché: "Where there's smoke there's fire." But in French at least, there is a complementary expression that suggests that there's no fire without smoke: "Il n'y a point de feu sans fumée." The familiar idea that jealousy—like passion itself—can smolder, flare up, or ignite takes on narrative and dramatic form in the means by which a cigarette or pipe is lit. When the married couple Gil and Susanna light their first cigarettes mouth to mouth, the passion is a directly communicated and legitimated one; when they relight them from a domestic candle, the natural move is to their conjugal bedroom. But the invention of the friction match in the latter half of the nineteenth century not only made smoking easier and therefore promoted the use of tobacco, but also brought with it new dramatic stage possibilities with its inevitable metaphoric associations of sudden flaring—at any time or place.

An opera that made much of precisely these dramatic possibilities is Giacomo Puccini/Giuseppe Adami's *Il tabarro* (1918; from the trilogy *Il trittico*), based on Didier Gold's naturalistic proletarian melodrama about a *crime passionel* and overworked stevedores on the Seine.[43] The opera opens with what might seem like an odd — or subtle — nonaction: the barge-man Michele's pipe, we are told in the stage directions, has gone out. His wife Giorgetta calls attention to this significant detail right away, however: "Dalla tua pipa / il fiume bianco non sbuffa più." The implied connection between smoking and sexuality is made quickly. Approaching his cool wife, Michele tells her that his pipe may be out but his passion is not: "Se la pipa è spenta, / non è spento il mio ardor." Getting no response from her, he goes into the barge's cabin. In the next scene, by contrast, Giorgetta dances happily with Luigi, a young stevedore from her hometown. Shortly thereafter an ominous song is heard from the shore, sung by a Vendor of Songs. It warns not to bother looking for lovers in the evening shadows; by spring they will be gone. In context this is doubly foreboding: the time of the opera is only autumn, and the story told in the song is that of Mimì from *La Bohème*, the story of those who live for love — and die for it: "Chi ha vissuto per amore, / per amore si morì."

Luigi and Giorgetta find a moment of privacy to confess their mutual love, all the while terrified that Michele will find — and kill — them: "Se ci scopri è la morte." Their passion is all the stronger for being forbidden and secret. They make plans for a tryst that evening. The signal will be the same as the night before: he will come on board at the sight of a lit match ("fiammifero acceso"). The metaphor of passion flaring up is developed by Giorgetta, who says the flame may be a small one ("la piccola fiammella"), but it could set alight a star, for it is the fire of their love ("fiamma del nostro amore"). There is something foreboding in the music here, however, in the sustained piccolo note and the roll of the bass drum.[44] The *desire* she feels she calls mad ("folle il desiderio"); the *jealousy* Luigi feels he too calls mad ("folle di gelosia!"). And so, in a way, it seems to be, for it takes the form of possessiveness (to Luigi she is "come cosa mia") and extreme sexual jealousy: he cannot bear the thought of anyone's touching her body but him. He even goes so far as to threaten *her* with violent death should that happen. This admission of jealousy (and threat of violence) and the match as both plot device and metaphor recall the behavior of Gil (provoked by smoking) in *Il segreto di Susanna*.

When Luigi leaves there is an equally disturbing scene between husband and wife, in which Michele explains that he can excuse one of his men for drinking too much because, if he did not, he would kill his tramp of a wife. Recalling that Michele has given up wine, we may share Giorgetta's anxiety. Michele then tries to get her to explain why things have changed between them, why she no longer sleeps with him. He reminds her of happier times, when their baby was alive and he would wrap her in his cloak (the "tabarro" of the title) for warmth and protection. Recalling that opening conversation about his pipe's having gone out, he wonders if she finds his age repellent. She denies this, while admitting that they are indeed both older now. She also points out that he has changed, that he is always suspicious of her.

As she goes into the cabin, Michele calls her a slut ("Sgualdrina") under his breath. Once again the music heard on shore comments on the action on board: lovers sing of the moon spying on their love as Michele tries to figure out whom he should spy on to discover the identity of her lover. Intent on murder, he wants someone else to share his pain and suffering in what he calls a hell of jealousy. At this moment he strikes a match to light his pipe—and Luigi leaps on board. In the ensuing fight Michele strangles Luigi, forcing him to confess that he loves Giorgetta. The young man dies, admitting "L'amo—ah!" Moments later Giorgetta nervously emerges from the cabin; Michele quickly hides the body in his cloak. Looking about anxiously, his wife apologizes for making him suffer and moves closer to him, offering to let him wrap her in his cloak once more. She repeats his saying that sometimes the cloak hides happiness, sometimes pain: "Qualche volta una gioia, / qualche volta un dolore." And Michele dramatically adds, sometimes a crime: "Qualche volta un delitto." Uncovering the body, he presses her face against that of her dead lover as the curtain falls.

Sex, Smoking, and Violence: *Carmen*

Il *tabarro*'s perhaps melodramatic but certainly powerful conjunction of jealousy, violence, and female sexual independence tied to metaphors (and stage action) associated with smoking is the tragic reverse of the lighter but still menacing connection made in Wolf-Ferrari's opera. But both, of course, had a famous antecedent in Bizet/Meilhac-Halévy's *Car-*

men (1875)—an opera that frames sexuality and violence in smoke and smoking. It is hard to watch this opera today without seeing its heroine as the victim of violence to women, an important concern in our culture. As Catherine Clément wrote in *Opera, or The Undoing of Women*, "I have always heard permanent ridicule heaped on this opera; no music has been more mockingly misappropriated. Toreadors, blaring music, and a gaudy Spain. . . . They always forget the death."[45] Carmen's final no to Don José means no—but he doesn't listen. In other words, *Carmen* is one of those operas (and there are many) that probably will be watched differently in our social and cultural environment today, when sexuality, desire, and violence have different associations and even different meanings than in the Paris of 1875. Yet if there *are* continuities in the representation of any of these—and unfortunately there are—it is less because they constitute "universals" or reveal themselves part of "human nature" than because certain social and cultural attitudes, including those around ideas of "femininity" and "masculinity," have not changed all that much—despite major interventions by feminists and others—over the past 150 years.

Although *Carmen* clearly has contributed mightily to making Spain and gypsies exotic, not to say clichéd, it is important to keep in mind that both the opera (1875) and its source text, the novella by Prosper Mérimée (1845), are products of nineteenth-century *French* culture.[46] As we shall see, this aesthetic representation of a place, a race, and a woman is a culturally specific one that is quite literally framed by its strong associations with tobacco. The long European history that we have traced, linking women to smoking—as desirable yet possibly dangerous—was as strong in France as anywhere else.[47] By the nineteenth century women who smoked—as the outraged response to George Sand's cigars showed—were decidedly transgressive: their act signaled either dangerous rebellion or . . . sexual availability. This is no doubt why Carmen tells the narrator in Mérimée's novella, when they first meet, that she smokes. Indeed, part of the scandal that attended the first performance of *Carmen* involved the presence of a less than docile chorus of women who both smoked and fought on stage.[48]

The tobacco frame of this narrative begins with its setting: Carmen,

21. The smoking chorus of cigarette
makers, in the 1952 production of *Carmen* at
the Metropolitan Opera, New York.

in both the opera and novella, works in the cigar factory in Seville.[49] For a
French audience this famous place would suggest much more than just
picturesque local color. An immense building—larger than the cathe-
dral—on the outskirts of the city, guarded by armed men, the Seville factory housed hundreds of women: cigar making required small, agile hands
and lots of them.[50] Entry to the building was forbidden to men without a
permit because the women often partially undressed to be cooler in the
summer heat. This simple fact evidently made the factory a necessary stop
on any Frenchman's trip to Spain in the nineteenth century. As one critic
put it, the place carried a particularly strong erotic charge for the French.[51]
Recounting his visit at midcentury, Théophile Gautier registered his surprise that many of the women smoked—a most unfeminine thing. They
did so, he said, "avec l'aplomb d'un officier de hussards." He also wrote
about the extreme negligence of the workingwomen's dress: it allowed
him to appreciate their charms in full liberty.[52]

The voyeuristic erotic language of French visitors in the nineteenth century contrasts with the realistic description of contemporaneous Spanish visitors, who were more likely to stress the hard work, the smells, the noise, and the poor working conditions.[53] But French writers leaned toward the language of eroticism—most often that of a harem of stripped-down women rolling phallic cigars—and described what they saw in loving detail.[54] Even the coldest of men were said to "warm" to the Seville factory, and most seem to have deliberately planned their trips to take advantage of the hot summer weather and thus of the seminakedness of the cigar workers.[55] Their individual responses varied, of course. Pierre Louÿs wrote, in his fictionalized account, of the "monstrousness" of this harem of women who made rude and impudent gestures that embarrassed the narrator by suggesting that their hands were making "little lovers" ("petits amants") out of tobacco leaves.[56] Maurice Barrès' reaction was different: to the same scene of "les fameuses *cigarreras* sevillanes" he responds with real appreciation of their feminine beauty and sincere, if strange, sadness that the charms of these jewels, these lovely animals ("ces jolies bêtes"), as he calls them, are wasted.[57] They are condemned, he laments, to be what they are—to work in what he calls "étables d'amour"—cowsheds of love—and thus to be handled by unworthy hands. Although made to be appreciated by finer (read French) sensibilities, they will end up satisfying simpler sensual demands, cast like pearls before . . . Whatever the individual evaluation of the experience, there seems to have been a shared French association of the Seville cigar factory with half-naked women, heat, sensuality, and even overt sexuality. So neither the decision by Henri Meilhac and Ludovic Halévy to have their libretto's heroine work here nor the decision by Mérimée before them was an innocent one.

It is, of course, in front of this building that Carmen first makes her appearance in the opera. Outside the factory, the soldiers on guard have been smoking to kill time: "On fume, on jase, l'on regarde / Passer les passants." The tobacco workers (all women) appear—smoking—and the voyeuristic men sing

Voyez-les! regards impudents,	*Look at them! Impudent looks,*
Mine coquette!	*Coquettish expressions!*
Fumant toutes, du bout des dents,	*All smoking, held in their teeth,*
La cigarette.	*A cigarette.*

In a song that reminded Nietzsche of a breath from the garden of Epicurus, the women then sing of smoke as the analogue of the sweet talk of lovers. As Susanna would later sing equally rapturously in Wolf-Ferrari's opera, all love is like smoke—pleasurable—but, they imply, perhaps of short duration: "Le doux parler des amants, / C'est fumée! / Leurs transports et leurs serments, / C'est fumée!" This song brings together women smoking, love, and not a little cynicism with a certain seductively languorous melody that has been said to echo the tobacco smoke's psychological effects as well as its visual imagery.[58] The young men sing of their adoration of all the cigarette-smoking workers—but also of one in particular: La Carmencita.

This is the literal frame for the entry of Carmen, heralded by these male desiring voices asking when she will love them: "Carmen! . . . dis-nous quel jour tu nous aimeras!" In the novella she is said to move swaying her hips (as one English translation would have it) "like a filly in a stud-farm."[59] The narrator adds: in his country (France), a woman dressed as provocatively as Carmen would have obliged viewers to make the sign of the cross; in Seville men merely complimented her on her scandalous dress. In the opera, Carmen's famous habanera is preceded by her response to the men's asking when she will love them: maybe never, maybe tomorrow, but certainly not today: "Peut-être jamais! . . . peut-être demain! . . . / Mais pas aujourd'hui . . . c'est certain." The habanera then develops this theme of female control and feminine capriciousness, calling love a rebellious bird that can't be tamed or lured if it isn't ready. But love, adds the best-loved of the cigarette girls, is also a lawless gypsy child: "enfant de Bohème, / Il n'a jamais connu de loi." This image simultaneously introduces issues of race and legitimation, themes that are central to the opera.

Smoking, then, already frames more than Carmen's sexuality. It also isn't long before we learn that the cigar factory has been the scene of a knife fight between Carmen and another woman, a fight that contemporaneous records show was all too realistic.[60] Although smoking and tobacco are never again the major focus of action after act 1, both are present, ensured as always by those insistent stage directions. Act 2 opens with both officers and gypsies smoking; street vendors sell cigarettes in the opening scene of the final act. These stage reminders function to keep in the audience's eye and memory cigarettes and the tobacco factory setting and their associations with many things, including sexuality, race, and violence.

Mérimée's novella had drawn on still other connotations of smoking, most of them also operative to some extent to this day. In a classic scene of the kind of male bonding we saw earlier in other operas as well, the narrator offers a cigar to José, the fierce stranger he meets on the road, knowing that in Spain, as he says, a cigar given and received establishes relations of hospitality: one has nothing to fear from a man with whom one has eaten and smoked (75–76).[61] The same narrator makes the acquaintance of the gypsy Carmen too when he is smoking and throws away his cigar as "une politesse toute française"—likely reflecting Frenchwomen's distaste for tobacco at this time.[62] But Carmen tells him that she loves the smell of smoke and even smokes cigarettes herself. That they smoke together might well recall both the end of Il *segreto di Susanna* and that Parisian prostitutes often signaled their trade by smoking.

The same narrator later brings cigars to José, who is in prison awaiting execution for his murder of Carmen, so that he can enjoy that traditional last smoke.[63] While he is doing so, José tells the narrator the story of being a guard at the tobacco factory in Seville with those five hundred half-naked women workers—all willing prey to the interested male.[64] When José breaks up the fight between Carmen and the other woman, takes her into custody, and then allows her to flee—already entranced by her sexual promises—he is punished by a month in jail. On his release he visits Carmen, who always pays her debts; as she says, it's the gypsy way. As José later tells the story to the narrator, when he remembers that wonderful first day with her, he almost forgets about the next, when he will die for her murder. What is of particular interest to us in this scene is its mixing together of smoking, desire, and death in what follows this statement. José relights his cigar, then says that they passed the day together "mangeant, buvant, et le reste"—eating, drinking, and the rest (110). The silenced sexual activity is signaled here by the relit cigar, his last. Smoking has long been part of the ritual of execution, and perhaps by association it frames Carmen's final fate too in its operatic ritual of death.

Because of this time with her and because of his jealousy, José deserts his regiment and becomes a smuggler in order to be with Carmen, the gypsy "devil," as he calls her, who has bewitched him. In doing so he also reneges on his promise of respectability to his aged mother and to Micaëla, the sweet young woman she wants him to marry (or so the opera libretto by Meilhac and Halévy would have it). When Carmen tires of his love—and his frantic jealousy—and turns to a new love (in the opera, the flashy toreador Escamillo), José cannot contain his fury and ends up killing her when she defiantly refuses to return to him. Resorting to violence is not new for José: in fact Mérimée tells us that it was his history of violent crime that made him leave his home in the north of Spain and come to Seville in the first place. Bizet's opera ends with Carmen's fatal stabbing, as we simultaneously hear Escamillo kill his bull in the adjoining bullring. The novella has her die, instead, in an isolated mountain gorge—after José has a mass said for her soul and before he turns himself in. In other words, there is a moral context explicitly established in the novella through the ending—José is punished, as is Carmen, though the gypsies are blamed for having raised her as they did. This is missing from the opera, where the stark conjunction of defiance, desire, and death dominates the stage. Without the moral frame tale of the narrator and in its concentrated and condensed dramatic form, the opera version of *Carmen* was perhaps even more transgressive and disturbing than the novella.

Neither form of the story, of course, was a great success at first, though both have lived on in their respective canons. For the opera, the problem seems to have been that it was written for the Opéra-Comique in Paris, a place meant for family entertainment. Librettist Halévy recounted the response of Camille Du Locle, codirector at the Opéra-Comique at the time: "Gypsies, cigarette girls—at the Opéra-Comique, the theater of families, of wedding parties?"[65] What's more, never before had a woman died on that stage. For this and other obvious reasons, as the reviews made clear, *Carmen* was considered too vulgar — and too realistic.[66] Its subject — seduction, jealousy, murder — was seen as indecent, even obscene, though obviously not so much so that it was banned by the censor of Paris.[67] It seems that its characters, however, were deemed repulsive and uninteresting. With today's steady diet of sex and violence on television and in film, it takes some historical imagination — though not too much — to understand the response to the transgressive conjunction of smoking, violence, and sexuality that *Carmen* brought to the Paris opera stage in 1875.

Whereas the novella was written around a single named female character — Carmen — the opera added a character (Micaëla) as a musical and moral foil to the gypsy vamp. It thus set up a familiar European cultural opposition between the two extreme constructions of female sexuality — the virgin and the whore or, perhaps more accurately, the sexless and the sexy, the chaste and the sexually active.[68] Feminist musicologist Susan McClary has described the musical consequences of this addition: Micaëla's very proper, modest behavior (that of a typical Opéra-Comique heroine) comes to us in diatonic melody lines that sound normal to Western ears. This is what is played off against Carmen's slippery chromatic music — which signals her identity as the "dissonant Other" who is consistently associated in the opera with sexuality and the body.[69] After all, even Carmen's arias are known by the names of popular dances — dances associated with the cafés and brothels of Paris: the habanera, the seguidilla. It is as if she is always on display, always performing — or choosing to perform — for men.[70] Such is the French construction of the sexy Spanish woman; and such is the French musical idea of what Spanish "otherness" sounded like.[71] It took over a hundred years to get the Spanish version of this: Carlos Saura made a film in the mid-1980s that self-consciously translated the Carmen story into the sensual and popular-cultural language of real Spanish flamenco dance.

For the Paris Opéra-Comique audience, though, it may have been this very familiarity with the particularly *French* (and low-life) connotations of the music and the scene that made the opera disturbing; it didn't help that they were also presented with a rather different and thought-provoking kind of female protagonist—almost a villain and a heroine all in one. This particular audience was more used to seeing women of what Winton Dean once called "the spotless and suffering soprano school" who "tended to suffer rather than act," exemplifying at all times their undoubtedly scrupulous moral rectitude.[72] It had been shocking enough when Verdi's Violetta in *La Traviata* was a courtesan, but as he went on to say, "at least we had not seen her exercising her trade. Carmen on the other hand not only seduced José, but set about it on the stage, and only too successfully." In the opera as in the novella, Carmen's physical, bodily, sensual presence remains obsessively central. One way for French culture at the time to deal with such a social threat—which included her taking upon herself the male initiative in love (she throws a flower at the uninterested José)—was to make Carmen and her like into demonic creatures.

As we saw in chapter 3 in the context of Wagner's *Parsifal*, in the nineteenth century female resistance and ambitions, when read as a threat to male culture, were often rendered pathological: hence the monstrous, castrating, vampiric, preying woman.[73] In this opera and novella Carmen refers to herself and is referred to by others as a devil. In both texts she is the demonic woman as gypsy witch, diabolical in her powers of seduction and in her passion.[74] José begs Carmen, before he kills her, to save him and to let him save her as well. He claims he has lost the "health" ("le salut") of his soul to this female incarnation of the devil. In other words *his* passion, *his* jealousy, *his* desire are not to blame: in his mind, *she* is.

In this way Don José becomes recognizable to a late twentieth-century audience, sensitized to the question of abusive behavior toward women. José—even more than Gil in *Il segreto di Susanna* and both Michele and Luigi in *Il tabarro*—fits the psychological pattern of men who physically abuse their women.[75] Constantly self-justifying—it is never his fault—he is possessive, sexually jealous, and controlling of his partner. His is a dominating personality that paradoxically is also a dependent one. The need to assert his authority over Carmen, to keep her to himself, even if he has to hurt her, is tied up with stereotypical models of masculine behavior in a macho culture. His greatest anguish comes from his fear that Carmen will leave him. Gender roles and social conditioning prevent him from conceiving of her as an independent woman. Certainly he has a history of what psychologists call "poor impulse control" and of being violent with others: he has left his home for some reason associated with violence, and in the opera itself he fights both his lieutenant Zuniga and his rival Escamillo over Carmen's affections.

As Susan McClary points out, the "kind of desire-dread-purge mechanism" José displays is also a common one in operas where a relatively passive and weak male encounters a strong, not to say sexually aggressive, female character: it is as if the "victimized male" (who has been tempted) has to kill off the source of the temptation if social order is to be restored.[76] Musically this is all suggested, McClary argues, by the chromatic excesses of Carmen's teasing and taunting melodic lines, making them slippery, unpredictable, and finally maddening — until we, like José, may end up desiring her death by the final scene, when in her words "the harmonic bassline turns into a maddeningly slippery chromatic floor" that our Western-trained ears demand be stopped.[77] Although not everyone will agree with such a strong position, she does point out that Bizet ends the opera with a major triad — the sign of finality, resolving dissonance, and a conventional "happy" ending — but that the triad is not in the key the opera began with: instead, the F$\sharp$ ending does not unambiguously establish closure. It does, however, stop the chromaticism and allow a return to the diatonic. In other words, musically Carmen may die but the opera's contradictions remain and the stop is equivocal.[78]

On the level of the literary text too — in both novella and libretto — Carmen's sexuality is linked to her demonic powers. But once again, despite what the critics say, there is nothing "universal" or eternal about this view of the woman as devil, any more than there is about smoking as sexy: both are constructions of a certain culture.[79] As Stephen Heath argued in *The Sexual Fix*, our notion of sexuality is something we construct "through a set of representations — images, discourses, ways of picturing and describing."[80] For the French audience of the nineteenth century, certain sexual stereotypes were circulating in the culture at large — ones still operative years later in advertising for those French cigarettes associated by name with gypsy women: Gitanes. The Andalusian woman of the south of Spain (where Seville is) was also thought by the French to be particularly passionate—as signaled by her dark hair and eyes. Add gypsy blood (which, as we shall see, Mérimée's narrator first takes to be Jewish) and that Seville cigar factory, and you have a heavily overdetermined representation of exotic sexuality in the imaginary erotic geography of nineteenth-century France.[81] As a northern Basque or "Navarrais," with whom the French spectators (as northern Europeans) might well identify more easily, José is presented as doomed when faced with such seductive southern passion.

A review in the *Revue des Deux Mondes* of the 1875 premiere of *Carmen* at the Opéra-Comique is revealing of these culturally specific associations. On the one hand, the reviewer tells his readers that if they see the opera they will feel as if the picaresque civilization of modern Spain is emerging from its "Judaic, Arab, Egyptian" origins: "ses origines judaïques, arabes, égyptiennes, que sais-je?"[82] Alluding in that list to the roots of specifically gypsy culture, however, he also goes on to announce that *all* Spanish women, whether "grande dame" or peasant, share certain of this Carmen's sexy physical movements and habits.[83] The description here of what is called the "abominable" role of Carmen in the opera is entirely in animalistic terms, recalling Maurice Barrès' image of "jolie bêtes" mentioned earlier: Carmen is called a wild animal or creature ("bête fauve," "créature inculte"), and she was evidently played on stage all too realistically (that is, too close to the Mérimée original) by the singer Celestine Galli-Marié. The reviewer's sympathies are clearly with the "victim" of this ferocious creature; he feels for the despair and pain of the "pauvre homme" Don José. Claiming such repulsive subject matter generally uninteresting and inappropriate for the stage, he nevertheless allows that the creation of Micaëla, the angel to balance the demonic gypsy Carmen, goes far to make the opera acceptable to most people.[84]

Clearly there is a certain element of misogyny involved in this "Orientalist" northern European view of the south and its peoples, and Spain had been seen by the French (at least since Victor Hugo's 1829 *Les Orientales*) as that part of Europe halfway between Africa and the Orient.[85] In fact the epigraph to Mérimée's novella is shockingly misogynistic. It is from the fifth-century aphorist Palladas and appeared only in Greek. Thus, given French education at the time, it likely was understandable only to male readers. In translation it reads: "Women are bitter. But they have two good times: in bed and in death."[86] Tellingly, perhaps, the negative criticism at the time of the novella's publication in France was directed against the use of the Greek language, not against the sentiments expressed in it.[87] The startling conjunction of sexuality and death here continues into the opera libretto, but the misogyny is less obvious. Meilhac and Halévy's Carmen—despite or because of her sexual appeal—has a kind of integrity and dignity that the thieving, lying, promiscuous, and often downright nasty Carmen of the novella certainly does not. Susan McClary argues that the opera domesticates the novella and reduces Carmen to a follower of men and a femme fatale, ignoring her identity as "a healer who risked her own well-being to save others."[88] But we still have to deal with the fact that, even given that the point of view of the novella is that of a French male narrator, Carmen seems to be the one who urges José to kill the narrator and engages in other such acts of violence and deception that McClary's reading cannot easily account for. Both texts do indeed refer to her as demonic, as does Bizet's music itself, with its echoes of the instrumentation of Weber's *Die Freischütz*.[89] She is said to share her gypsy race's occult powers and magic arts. But the novella goes further in aligning Carmen with the antisocial, indeed the nonhuman, in much the same way as those other French visitors to the Seville cigar factory presented the women they saw. Her beauty is described as strange and savage; the expression in her eyes is at once voluptuous and fierce, an expression the narrator says he has never seen in a human. He then cites a Spanish proverb as relevant to this "pretty witch" that could be translated as "Eye of a gypsy; eye of a wolf" (90). The novella's wild, capricious, charming, clever—but also dishonest and even vicious—woman is indeed, in a way, tamed in the opera, no doubt in part because of the sensitivities of the bourgeois Paris audience, but she retains her integrity to the end. She is, however, in both a femme fatale—though here that cliché has a meaning beyond the obvious, for it is also Carmen who is made *fatally* to pay for being a *femme*. True, she still lures José away from his post, his family, his fiancée; but it is *his* jealousy as much as *her* seductive power that causes her death.

The Carmen figure in both texts remains a defiant woman who chooses her own life and death, no matter how much her gypsy fatalism may make her accept it as her destiny to die at José's hand.[90] In the novella she reads her fate "dans du marc de café"; in the libretto, in the cards. Facing her murderer, she refuses to give in to him and his jealousy: throwing away the ring he gave her, she loudly proclaims her freedom and her love for Escamillo—knowing (and suffering) the consequences. But from the start Carmen has not played the game by society's rules, or at least not by French nineteenth-century society's rules. Whereas Micaëla's love for José is structured on what might be called a traditional bourgeois social economy of straightforward exchange, Carmen's economic model of desire (even more than love) has always radically contradicted the accepted norm: in other words, Micaëla brings a message and a kiss from José's mother and returns with one of each in exchange; but Carmen perversely sings that if you do *not* love her, then she *will* love you—"si tu m'aimes pas, je t'aime"—and vice versa.

In that habanera love is called an "enfant de Bohème"—a gypsy child. As we have already suggested, that racial connection is presented as central to the economy of Carmen's sexuality and desire. In nineteenth-century French culture, the chain of associations with gypsy women included sensuality, lasciviousness, and charm—but also manipulativeness, deception, and a certain sexual and social autonomy. In short, they stood for all that was not bourgeois and domestic—hence their attraction and their danger. "Les gitanes" also smoked, of course.[91] Mérimée makes a further connection, this time between gypsies and Jews, when his narrator takes Carmen for one of the latter, though he dare not say the word. The opera libretto leaves out this scene, but it has been argued that Bizet incorporated the sense of it by linking Carmen musically with the augmented second, that "illicit" interval in traditional counterpoint that has connotations in European music both of the exotic—oriental or Jewish—and also of sensuality and/or anguish.[92]

As we saw in the earlier discussion of Wagner's Kundry, in Europe Jews, like gypsies, were particularly suspect because, though marked as alien, they lived on the home turf.[93] Familiar yet radically different, gypsies were seen as nomadic, seemingly free from organized European social constraints. Yet we also know historically that they have been highly organized socially, with their own language, history, and ethic. Persecuted in various countries over the centuries, gypsies were seen as satanic (Mérimée's narrator calls her a "servante du diable") as well as superstitious, dangerous as well as exotic.[94] That Carmen should lure José into a life of *smuggling* underlines the French bourgeois view of the gypsy position on the fringes of the legal economy as well as correct society. As Clément puts this, Carmen is "somewhat whore, somewhat Jewess, somewhat Arab, entirely illegal, always on the margins of life."[95] The issue of race, like that of gender, is brought to the fore from the start of both the opera libretto and the novella. Race and gender appear not to be easily separated from sexuality in the European imagination. As Klaus Theweleit has suggested in *Male Fantasies,* "Can we not then trace a straight line from the witch to the seductive Jewish woman? Is the persecution of the sensuous woman not a permanent reality . . . which derives from the specific social organization of gender relations in patriarchal Europe?"[96]

In the background too is the notion of class, for Carmen is a working-class cigar maker.[97] She is occasionally referred to by the diminutive, "la Carmen*cita,*" and D*on* José is given a title of noble class status not perhaps warranted by much besides the sensibilities of the Opéra-Comique's audience.[98] But though she can sing in the "high art language" of Don José's well-bred diatonic music, she is also fluent in the lower-class vernacular—the French cabaret version of that popular dance music of Spain and Latin America.[99] As we mentioned earlier, this music connoted not just a class context, but "Spanishness" (and "otherness") to a French audience, even if it was no more ethnographically accurate than it was operatically conventional. Promiscuous in her music as in her sexuality, the singing Carmen is transgressive because everything about her—from her sensuality to her racial, class, and musical "otherness"—comes to life in her physical body. Therein lies her danger and her appeal.

The recent feminist interpretations of *Carmen* have stressed the obvious gender (as well as race and class) fantasies that its heroine's representation played into. The opera has been seen as participating in that exoticizing of sexuality by nineteenth-century imperialist and patriarchal Europe, that projecting onto the "other" of emotions that varied from desire to contempt, from envy to terror.[100] In conflating gender, race, and class identities in its single protagonist, *Carmen* brazenly brought to the stage a number of very familiar tensions within Western culture—tensions we saw in *Parsifal* and still, to some extent, see today. This is despite the work of feminist theory, despite the new theorizing of sexuality not as a "universal" but as something socially constructed by precisely such cultural discourses as music and literature: the stereotypes that exist in *Carmen*—and the chain of associations with things like smoking, violence, and sexuality—are still with us in films and in advertising. In the nineteenth century, and even into the twentieth, opera was one of the main cultural forms through which gender and sexuality were articulated and defined—and that performers such as Madonna, among others, have also used this particular image of Carmen suggests that those definitions have not lost their power. At a time when violence toward women is as much a social issue as it is today, how we read *Carmen* may say a lot about how we feel about the social construction of women . . . and of men.

"No Smoking": Medical Knowledge and Social Change

Directors of productions of *Carmen* these days face a special challenge then. How are they to present an opera whose portayal of women and of violent male-female relations is framed in the context of smoking—that is, of a complex nineteenth-century French code of transgression that involves gender, race, nationality, ethnicity, and class? What smoking meant in the Paris of 1875 is, however, radically different from what it means today in North America, especially, where it is associated not so much with sex as with disease. In the past hundred years the consumption of tobacco certainly increased rapidly. The plot of *Il segreto di Susanna* pointed ahead to a new social reality: more and more women, as well as men, began to smoke. Smoking has continued to retain its sexualized associations—from Marlene Dietrich and Lauren Bacall through to current tobacco advertising. But as is the case throughout its history, the meanings given to smoking still remain double or doubly coded. In North America, most obviously, the emphasis has shifted toward the negative with the realization that serious diseases of the respiratory and cardiac system are associated with long-term smoking.

The initial evidence began to mount in the 1950s that smoking was a risk factor for lung cancer, chronic bronchitis, and emphysema. This led to the United States surgeon general's health warning in 1964, at the peak of cigarette consumption. Subsequent years have seen a decrease in tobacco use, along with a much clearer linking of cigarette smoking and illness, and there has been a gradual change in the representation of smoking behavior itself in all but perhaps some European films and, of course, the cigarette companies' own advertising. Beyond the concern for individual, personal disease, there has now developed a social discourse that bears considerable resemblance to the one that flourished around tuberculosis in the twentieth century: the smoker, like the infective tubercular, is no longer seen as the unfortunate victim of a disease but is considered a hazard to others ("secondhand smoke") and therefore is socially stigmatized.[101] The representation of the smoking Cipolla in the 1992 premiere of the Somers/Anderson opera *Mario and the Magician* represented this change most vividly. The director (Robert Carsen) and the designer (Michael Levine) of the Canadian Opera Company production set up a subtle but effective context for this negative stigmatization. The opera opened with Stefan lecturing in a room in Munich on whose wall was printed, in large letters, "Nicht Rauchen" — No Smoking. In the Cipolla performance scenes, in Italy, the theater wall bore the same message in Italian, "Vietato di Fumare." When Cipolla entered — smoking ostentatiously — the audience in Toronto (where smoking is forbidden in public places) could and generally did read this as doubly negative: this man cared neither about public safety nor about public health. The smoker as purveyor of disease to others (through secondhand smoke) here becomes the allegorical purveyor of fascist dis-ease, as we saw in more detail in the previous chapter. The cigarette use and the evil character of Cipolla become one and the same as he impudently blows smoke both at the characters on stage and at the audience. The personal and the political, the individual and the social, come together and are amplified by a long cultural history concerned with the social (race, class, gender) dimensions of smoking.

So productions of *Carmen* today have a choice: given the consistent double coding of tobacco through the years, they can choose to draw on the continuing strength of its connotations of sexiness and exoticism; or they can deconstruct those very stereotypes and reveal their social and cultural roots. Francesco Rosi's 1984 film version tried to make a French opera into a Spanish movie, with its realistic on-location filming and equally realistic casting. In contrast, Romanian director Lucien Pintilie's production (for the Welsh National Opera and for Expo '86 in Vancouver) chose instead to self-reflexively address the meaning of *Carmen* today — at a time when it is one of the infamous ABCs of opera (with *Aida* and *Bohème* as the A and B). *Carmen* cannot mean today what it meant in 1875: so, when his Carmen sings her habanera or Escamillo his toreador song, the on-stage audience responds with loud fans' cheers and, in the case of the habanera, actually forces Carmen to begin again. How Pintilie deals with the smoking frame is equally reflexive and equally parodic: the cigarette workers enter accompanied by comically immense volumes of smoke, as if to underline the inescapability of the association. They all smoke; they are all sexy; but some of them here are transvestites. Sexual transgressiveness may mean something different in the late twentieth century, but it is still real, and sexual jealousy and violence have rarely been portrayed on stage more powerfully than in this production.

It has been said that "those who wish to project an image or signal something about themselves to the outside world have a great communication device in the cigarette."[102] If that is the case, then what they choose to communicate will depend to a large extent on the particular social context at that moment. And inseparable from that context today will be the knowledge of the medical effects of smoking that cigarette. This is not to say that the long history of dual coding, of positive and negative associations, will not be at work; it likely will, for the continuities of meaning are also real. But even *they* become more problematic in the face of the now inescapable knowledge of tobacco's role in creating what has been called one of the new epidemics of the twentieth century. Not too surprisingly, in Hollywood movies today it is usually only Jack Rance–like villains who smoke.

Epilogue

"Life-and-Death Passions": AIDS and the Stage

Opera is about us, our life-and-death passions — we all love, we're all going to die. — from Terrence McNally, *The Lisbon "Traviata"*

With these words one gay male tries to explain to another both opera and its appeal. The speaker, Stephen, like his friend Mendy, is an "opera queen" much like those described with such insight in Wayne Koestenbaum's recent book *The Queen's Throat: Opera, Homosexuality, and the Mystery of Desire*.[1] In this play, *The Lisbon "Traviata,"* Terrence McNally not only presents the learned, even obsessively informed character of these particular opera lovers but also reveals the important role opera and its divas have come to play within gay culture in general. In McNally's particular representation of this world, the stories of opera turn out to be ones lives are lived by. It begins innocently enough: Stephen cannot help using analogies from opera when he speaks of falling in love with Mike, his current lover. For him it was destiny "like the first act of *Carmen*."[2] Mendy's caustic response ("I love your choice of role models. Carmen and Don José. They were a fun couple") and his subsequent speculation about "who might be who" seem to be answered by Stephen's repetition of Carmen's last spoken line, daring José to kill her or let her be free: "Frappe-moi donc ou laisse-moi passer!" But in the second act, when Mike says he is going to leave Stephen, the roles reverse; in fact Stephen recites José's jealous, despairing lines and all but forces Mike to speak Carmen's. He stops short of plunging the scissors he is holding into his lover's breast, but nevertheless he manages to enact both Mike's complaint that he lives in opera, rather than life, and his own contention — the epigraph to this chapter — that opera is about "our life-and-death passions."

Giving AIDS Meaning(s)

Haunting this play, however, is another opera, one about disease and the different results of another kind of "life-and-death passion": La Traviata and AIDS (acquired immunodeficiency syndrome). Verdi's opera appears first as the production in the play's title, one sung by Maria Callas in Lisbon on 27 March 1958—a recording of which Mendy desperately wants to hear. Like Violetta, Mendy laments, Callas's "time was so brief" (34). In Mendy's description of Violetta's "profession," however, it is Stephen who is placed in her position: "Traviata's about a courtesan dying of consumption. A courtesan: what Stephen was before he became the youngest senior editor at Knopf and an avocation to which he will soon be returning if he doesn't come up with another best seller" (34). Stephen isn't dying of consumption — or AIDS — as far as the audience knows, but he is terrified of the possibility, were he to venture out of his current relationship: "Those are dark, mean, and extremely dangerous streets, right now" (85). Playing the prelude to Traviata as his relationship with Mike comes to an end, however, he points out: "You're leaving me at a wonderful moment in our long, happy history of queerness to seek a new mate to snuggle up with right at the height of our very own Bubonic Plague" (85).

Stephen's comparison of AIDS to the plague is a common enough one in both art and the media, as we shall see, but it is not the only analogy to other known and (by now, to the reader of this book) more familiar diseases: cholera, tuberculosis, and syphilis all turn out to share something with AIDS, both medically and socially. It will come as no surprise that the associations that have developed around the new disease have drawn on those of the others examined in earlier chapters: any illness that involves (or can be made to involve) both sex and death has powerful stage possibilities. At this time there does not seem to have been a fully staged, mainstream opera on the direct topic of AIDS, though there have been some that have it in the background.[3] Various productions of other operas have also used AIDS as part of their updating to the present, as we will discuss later. However, there have appeared numerous performance pieces and musicals, and these, along with stage plays on HIV infection and AIDS, will be the focus of this chapter, as we examine how

the history of the representation of AIDS within the homosexual population, at least thus far, has recapitulated (with interesting variations) the
history of the other diseases we have already studied. The AIDS operas—
soon to appear, without a doubt—may well feel quite familiar in some
ways, if disconcertingly different in others.

As we mentioned in the introduction, acquired immunodeficiency
syndrome is the disease that all of us have watched—and are still watching—take on meanings. On 10 December 1981 the first medical article
related to it appeared in the *New England Journal of Medicine*, with an accompanying editorial; the Centers for Disease Control's *Morbidity and Mortality
Weekly Report* had reported the outbreak of *Pneumocystis* (an unusual form
of pneumonia) on 5 June 1981; by the next July the disease had its current
acronym, AIDS. From this point on it began acquiring other meanings,
many of which drew on past associations with other diseases, either epidemic or sexually transmitted (or both). Of course one of the reasons
it could do this so very easily is that, with the immune system's inability
to resist infection, many of these other diseases have actually reap-
peared as part of the condition labeled AIDS. Some may want to argue
that AIDS, with its connections to sex, drugs, and blood, "expresses our
era."[4] But on the contrary, it is more likely that our era is giving its specific meanings to AIDS and to those who contract it. This is not new by
any means, but what *is* new is our ability, in the West today, both to ob-
serve (and monitor) the process of construction itself and to understand
the power it wields. Almost as much has been written about the discourses *on* AIDS and its meanings as about the disease itself. With this self-
consciousness comes new responsibility, however. In Susan Sontag's
words: "With this illness, one that elicits so much guilt and shame, the
effort to detach it from these meanings, these metaphors, seems particularly liberating, even consoling. But the metaphors cannot be distanced
just by abstaining from them. They have to be exposed, criticized, bela-
bored, used up."[5] They also need to be "historicized"—placed in the
context of their past use—and that is another of the purposes of this
final chapter.

As a disease named and investigated in the 1980s and 1990s, AIDS has
been a disease defined *by* and *in* the world of the media and of electronic

information technology. If it has always been true that "biological mechanisms define and constrain social response" to disease, then it may be even more obviously so today in North America and Europe, when medical information is more available to a general lay public than ever before—partly thanks to the AIDS activism of such groups as ACT UP (AIDS Coalition to Unleash Power) in the United States, OutRage in the United Kingdom and AIDS ACTION NOW in Canada.[6] It is also true that "AIDS has ushered in a further development of sexual speech which cannot but partake of the larger twentieth-century 'obsession' with sexuality and its colonization by the professions, the media, and the state," so that now the question is "Who controls whose bodies?"[7] In other words, the stakes are high. The interaction of biomedical discourses with a range of cultural ones is perhaps easier to trace today than it has ever been. That there has been an explosion in both is clear, and people write about the "epidemic of signification" and the "plague of discourse" that attend AIDS and HIV infection.[8] This is a disease whose naming we have watched, whose identity we have observed being formed, whose cultural representations we have all, however indirectly or unconsciously, participated in creating. The point is not that other diseases did not go through exactly the same process: tuberculosis also went from being unnamed (or rather multinamed) and multiform in its manifestations to being recognized as a single disease entity, and its complex cultural representations changed with the changing knowledge of the disease process. As earlier chapters have shown, diseases have always taken on plural and often even contradictory meanings and associations; but this time—thanks to the relative speed of both research and communication of information—we can watch it all as it happens.

Unlike syphilis or tuberculosis, AIDS as a known disease has had a short history that has seen major changes. Within little more than a decade, we have recognized that what we call AIDS, that devastating and rapidly fatal disease—believed, in the early 1980s, to be of sudden onset—is in fact the late stage of a much more prolonged viral infection, a chronic progressive illness. From being of unknown origin AIDS has come to be understood as a disease transmitted through body fluids, a retroviral infection (caused by the human immunodeficiency virus). The various cultural images of AIDS and the person living with AIDS (PLWA) over the past fourteen years need to be understood within these changing configurations. But they also need to be placed in an even larger historical and cultural context. When North American or European commentators want to limit certain metaphors of contamination and pollution to the particular cultural discourse of the 1980s, they in fact fail to take into account the five hundred year history of syphilis and its associations that such a discourse can draw on for a good deal of its emotional power. When they speak of AIDS as an "unprecedented sexual threat" or as creating a crisis on "an unparalleled scale" in terms of sexual pleasure in relation to medical knowledge, they are not necessarily wrong, but they do appear to forget that history.[9] Syphilis too is a disease that has linked sexuality and death in ways that were seen as threatening—and not so very long ago.

In 1990 a review of Susan Sontag's *AIDS and Its Metaphors* in the *New England Journal of Medicine* confidently claimed: "Certainly no disease in history has involved as many metaphors as AIDS, from military metaphors and the metaphorical innocence or guilt of the victims to metaphors of divine retribution."[10] But the history of medicine suggests that many other diseases—starting with the plague—have in fact involved precisely these metaphors. But in the West, so far, many have remained at the level of metaphors and have not yet become exact analogies. Prior Walter, the protagonist of Tony Kushner's two recent plays, *Angels in America: A Gay Fantasia on National Themes*, may lament in *Part Two: Perestroika* that "it's 1986 and there's a *plague*, half my friends are dead and I'm only thirty-one," but that remark has to be read in the context of *Part One: Millennium Approaches*, in which his "thirteenth-century" British ancestor appeared to him saying he had died of the "spotty monster." Prior's remark of "Pestilence. . . . You too what?" is greeted with the historicizing line: "The pestilence in my time was much worse than now. Whole villages of empty houses."[11] Though the analogy may not be precise, as the ancestor implies, its power remains. The cultural construction of AIDS/HIV infection in North America and Europe, as in what is called the Third World, is "framed, if not burdened, by many histories": of past epidemics, of sexually transmitted diseases, of scientific investigations, of social hygiene, of social attitudes.[12]

Yet Sontag argues that, unlike tuberculosis and syphilis, AIDS has provoked no equivalent of the "compensatory mythology" that gave us the more positive images of the sexualized tubercular woman of La Traviata or the creative genius of Thomas Mann's syphilitic Doctor Faustus. Nor does she see any likelihood that this will ever happen: AIDS, she says, cannot be romanticized or sentimentalized; it is too "shameful or demeaning"—more like cholera.[13] However, the stage plays and musicals representing AIDS and HIV infection that are written by either gay artists or those close to them suggest quite the contrary. AIDS is not a disease of homosexual men alone, of course, but it is among this population that the "compensatory mythology" has certainly appeared, and for that reason this group will be the main concern of our final chapter. Given the importance of opera in this particular culture, it is likely that the full-scale AIDS-inspired operas may well come from there.

The process of *deliberately* constructing new meanings for disease is of course a more overt version of what cultural representations have always managed to do over time. With AIDS and its gay activist politics, the tone and tactics have changed: often consciously reversing the negative images of both AIDS and other associated diseases, this is mythology as *countermythology*. This taking control of the mechanisms of making meaning is often done openly, didactically, even outrageously—with irony and humor. It is also frequently eroticized, perhaps in an attempt to restore something of the hard-won liberation of the pre-AIDS sexual life.[14] And just as the gay Walt Whitman claimed he couldn't have written *Leaves of Grass* without opera, so perhaps these plays and performance pieces owe to what Herbert Lindenberger calls the "operatic principle" something of their verbal excesses, their playful use of fantasy, and their often histrionic verve.[15] As Susan Sontag herself noted back in the 1960s in her famous "Some Notes on 'Camp,'" certain parts of urban gay male culture have shown a strong iconoclastic streak. The work of these "aristocrats of taste," she claimed, has often been passionate, extravagant, yet playfully ironic.[16] In the recent gay plays about AIDS, there has been a move beyond the early but still powerful rage or elegiac mourning for the dead that obviously can never be dismissed; the new ironic twisting of a whole series of conventional social representations of disease and sexuality has an activist, educational intent and an often ironic, camp tone.[17] But it also works simultaneously to recall the history of other diseases and give new meanings to this one. We have come to think it likely that this complicated move may well affect the shape of any gay operas about AIDS to come.

It has been said that "AIDS is a nexus where multiple meanings, stories, and discourses intersect and overlap, reinforce, and subvert one another."[18] As such it serves as a fitting means to conclude this study of the operatic representation of disease in the past two centuries. If its meanings—medical, social, aesthetic—are as multiple and discontinuous as many have suggested they are, however, and if there is not yet a body of what we would conventionally call operas by which to limit our investigation, there is still a large group of stage productions—plays, Broadway musicals, performance pieces—that draw on many of the same conventions as opera and elicit some of the same responses from live audiences. The narrative devices and the verbal complexities of the text make these very similar to opera librettos *as scripts* on a literary level. These staged forms share that communal audience experience that all forms of drama provide, along with the direct immediacy of contact between live performer and spectator.[19] In addition, in the West at least, AIDS has been a "theatricalized" disease for some time, especially within gay culture (which is itself often extremely theatricalized to begin with): "performativity" and politicization have been connected through activist groups such as Queer Nation or ACT UP, with its ironized "die-ins" that function as a "hyperbolic display of death and injury to overwhelm the epistemological resistance to AIDS and to the graphics of suffering."[20]

In musicals like *Falsettos* or in performance works like Diamanda Galas's "Plague Mass," the power of music has been used in complex and very different ways, but ways that nonetheless recall the art of opera. Even *Angels in America* began as a commission to write a play with songs.[21] There have also been musical pieces—such as John Adams's "The Wound Dresser" and John Corigliano's Symphony no. 1—that have been inspired by the AIDS crisis. Unlike many of the television and Hollywood film representations, many of these have been produced from within what is usually referred to as the gay "community" and thus are deliberate *self*-representations.[22] In contrast to those operatic and literary images and stories of people suffering from tuberculosis or syphilis, these are told from the inside of an afflicted community. So are many of the novels, stories, and poems about AIDS, but that combination of literary text, narrative conventions, live performance, and the frequent use of music makes the stage performances the closer analogue to opera and may foretell more accurately some of the forms that operas about HIV infection or AIDS might take.[23] The struggle over the representation of a disease and those who contract it is on. From the inside, the chosen strategies are clear: "A wide range of cultural responses (pleasure, humour, eroticism, fantasy, and pathos) is important within a broad-based culture of resistance; . . . anger, denunciation, and reactive media critique cannot be the sole cultural diet of a community in for a long haul."[24]

The "Gay Plague": *Angels in America*

From the earliest days of the epidemic, apocalyptic rhetoric about AIDS as the "gay plague" has been a constant both in the media and on the stage.[25] In Larry Kramer's *The Normal Heart*, an early play about AIDS, Dr. Emma Brookner, herself in a wheelchair because of polio, puts this image in context: "There's always a plague. Of one kind or another. I've had it since I was a kid."[26] But as Prior's ancestor in *Angels in America* implied, it is usually the bubonic plague that is specifically called on in the analogy. Although many more people died, and died much more quickly and randomly, in the European plague epidemics, the parallels do exist in terms of social issues raised about "the obligations of physicians, the scapegoating of certain classes of persons, and the ease with which inferences are drawn between human catastrophe and divine retribution."[27] There are also medical parallels, of course. Like the plague, AIDS first appeared by surprise and seemed, at the start, to kill quickly (because it was diagnosed only in its late stages). Now, of course, we know that HIV is a slow-acting retrovirus, but that has not stopped the use of the plague rhetoric—with all its power to evoke the inescapability of arbitrary mass death, impotence, and horror—to refer to AIDS not only among the gay population in the West, but among heterosexuals too, especially in Asia, Africa, and other parts of the world where the epidemic is raging.[28]

The source of plague—like that of cholera and syphilis—is tradition-ally (and conveniently) seen as foreign: these are diseases that everyone (apparently no matter where they live) sees as coming from "elsewhere." In the case of AIDS in the West, the threat from "elsewhere" is some-times from Africa or Haiti or sometimes simply from the male homo-sexual population, figured as the "tainted community" that illness has judged: "Such is the extraordinary potency and efficacy of the plague metaphor: it allows a disease to be regarded both as something incurred by vulnerable 'others' and as (potentially) everyone's disease."[29] The scapegoating of the poor and the Jews in Rome in 1656, for instance, was sadly typical of social behavior in other places and other times.[30] It is no accident, then, that the image of the Holocaust recurs in essays (like those of Larry Kramer's *Reports from the Holocaust*) or plays about AIDS, a dis-ease whose new cases, in the West, are mainly among homosexual men and intravenous drug users. In the Broadway musical *Falsettos*, the PLWA, whose lover and family are Jews, ironically asks the doctor: "Tell me why was I chosen, / Why me of all men?"[31]

Tied to the seeming need to find a scapegoat for such medical and so-cial calamities is the fear—based on historical precedent—that disease will disrupt the social order. With AIDS, though, worries about the pre-sumed anarchy that would result from hedonism run rampant (as de-scribed by Edgar Allan Poe in his plague narrative "The Masque of the Red Death," for instance) are matched by a contrary "anhedonia" or fear of sex, for sex can now kill.[32] William M. Hoffman's *As Is* portrays the gay bars and clubs as seen through the eyes of a homosexual whose for-mer lover is infected: "They remind me of accounts of Europe during the Black Plague: groping in the dark, dancing till you drop. The New Wave is the corpse look."[33] In another play, Harvey Fierstein's *Safe Sex*, another gay man can feel only total panic at the thought of any sexual contact during "this devastating epidemic."[34] Like Stephen's worries about the "mean, and extremely dangerous streets" in *The Lisbon "Traviata,"* one of the characters in Harry Kondoleon's *Zero Positive* laments: "Everyone meets everyone else and suspects they're meeting their executioner, it makes the most casual overtures seem extinctionary . . . no, that's not a word . . . extinctive."[35] There is also a play within this play, one that, with deliberate echoes of *Oedipus Rex*, is about the pestilence that strikes a city "ripe with shame" (265).

As both Sophocles' play and those operas on the Oedipus theme suggest, that combination of social panic, medical anxiety, and moral blame is a very old and powerful one that feeds into the idea of plague as divine retribution for transgression. The Latin root of the word "plague," *plaga*, means wound, but it also means blow or stroke. According to the *Oxford English Dictionary*, a plague is an "affliction, calamity, evil 'scourge'; *esp.* a visitation of divine anger or justice, a divine punishment." The extension of this manifestation of godly fury to include an "infectious disease or epidemic attended with great mortality; a pestilence" does not diminish the potent religious and moral associations. Whereas the word "epidemic" has as its etymological root the relatively benign Greek word for "visit," the more violent notion of wound or stroke has always stood behind the idea of plague as serving a moral end—to cleanse the world of undesirables through divine punishment.[36] The capability these associations have of playing into existing social biases has been clear in the response of American religious fundamentalists such as Jerry Falwell and his Moral Majority, for whom AIDS is simply God's punishment for homosexuality.[37] How this can explain AIDS as a disease of hemophiliacs or of heterosexuals in Africa or Asia is less clear, though no doubt room can more easily be made for intravenous drug users in this particular moral scheme of things.

In *Zero Positive*, a woman gets AIDS from one of her lovers—a "married man" who spent his "time off" with some other "married men." She provides a somewhat different angle on the involvement of God with humankind and its diseases. She says that Christ called her once and said, "We're relocating, discontinue correspondence until further notice, . . . stop wondering until further notice" (262). If religion is no longer a comfort, if it cannot answer the worries and "wonderings" of those with AIDS, why should its moral judgments on the disease be internalized by those who contract it? As we discussed in the introduction, Sander Gilman has argued that it is precisely the internalizing of socially constructed images of disease that gives them their power.[38] One of the most powerful responses—because it is so very trangressive—to this specific question, in the context of the rise of the Christian Right in the United States, has been Tony Kushner's *Angels in America*, with its subtitle *A Gay Fantasia on National Themes*. Like nineteenth-century European opera, these two plays are about the nation as much as the individuals whose story they tell.[39] But instead of the more usual practice of promoting national(ist) values, these works criticize them, through one of the most daring examples of gay countermythology on the stage today: by giving new and utterly different meaning to the idea of AIDS as the plague sent by God as punishment upon the sexually sinful. Avoiding sentimentality, *Angels in America* mixes comedy with tragedy, historical with fictional characters, realism with fantasy, scenes in hospitals with scenes in heaven. Eight actors play some thirty roles, creating interrelations among characters that are often pointedly ironic, often unexpectedly appropriate. The most operatic of theatrical pieces, these plays, however, use humor instead of the romanticized pathos of *La Bohème* to move their audiences.

In *Perestroika*, Joe voices the Mormon teachings of his upbringing when he says that he expects "divine retribution" for having sex with a man for the first time. This is the conventional religious response that is about to be turned upside down. When Prior, the PLWA, appears on stage in a long black coat and a scarf shaped into a hood, the stage directions inform us that his "appearance is disconcerting, menacing and vaguely redolent of the Biblical" (41). With characteristic black humor, Prior himself reinforces this association, saying he is intended to look "like the Wrath of God" (42). In saying this he literalizes the countermythic joke that circulated among gays about the new acronym for AIDS: WOGS—standing for "wrath of God syndrome." This small detail of dress and its explanation together form a microcosmic version of what is a major ironic twisting of the Christian reading of AIDS. And it is this twisting that structures these plays, right from Prior's initial description of his first Kaposi's sarcoma lesion as the "wine-dark kiss of the angel of death" in *Millennium Approaches* (21).

Although angel imagery has appeared in many gay contexts—such as the anthology of homosexual verse titled *Angels of the Lyre*—in *Angels in America* its resonance is decidedly and specifically biblical: Judeo-

Christian culture is rich in images of the angel of death as the messenger of God (indeed, *angelos* in Greek means messenger), the one who announces his scourge to be wielded against the sinful.[40] In *Part One*, under the (clinical) sign of that "wine-dark kiss of the angel of death," we hear Joe use the story of Jacob wrestling with another angel as the analogue of his own struggle — "fierce, and unfair" — with his homosexuality (49). Louis, the lover who cannot bear to stay with Prior during his illness, is another whom the playwright has presented in these terms: "We live in a very bad time for the human body and this is a problem that all of us are going to have to face at a much younger age than our parents did. Louis wrestles with that particular angel and sometimes people are very upset by the choices he makes, but he's struggling tremendously with it."[41] It is also Louis who gives the plays their collective title and sets up the countermythological inversion they are based on: "There are no gods here, no ghosts and spirits in America, there are no angels in America, no spiritual past, no racial past, there's only the political." (92). But as Prior learns, for those who can look past the narrowly political there *are* angels in America — ones that literally come crashing through the ceiling of your room ("*Very* Steven Spielberg") to greet you as "Prophet" as the first play ends.[42]

The beginning of the "angelification" of AIDS is made possible through the choice of Mormonism as the conservative Christian — and indigenous American — theology of the plays. Its founder, Joseph Smith Jr., was led in 1827 by the angel Moroni to find golden plates from which he translated the Book of Mormon and founded his religion. But Prior's angel in *Perestroika* is rather different: she defines herself as his "Released Female Essence Ascendant" (48). The book she leads Prior to find — through a series of funny misadventures in his apartment — is also quite different, for instead of telling the Mormon story of the migration of the Hebrews from Jerusalem to America, this one is its direct parody: the Book of the Anti-Migratory Epistle. This is also an eroticized angel, whose ecstatic presence makes everyone orgasmic. As she puts it, "I am Utter Flesh, / Density of Desire" (47). In a rather unconventional sexualization of the religious, the erotic becomes the heavenly function of the angels: "Angelic orgasm makes protomatter, which fuels the Engine of

22. The angel of death striking during the plague of Rome.

23. The angel (Ellen McLaughlin) appearing to Prior Walter
(Stephen Spinella) in *Angels in America, Part Two: Perestroika,*
Walter Kerr Theatre.

Creation. They used to copulate *ceaselessly* before . . ." (49). These angels, it turns out, were made for God's pleasure—and thus are both "fabulous and dull all at once"—but their changelessness ended up boring him. For this reason God then created male and female and "unleashed / Sleeping Creation's Potential for Change" through imagination, thought, exploration, progress, migration: "In YOU the Virus of TIME began!" (49). But with each change, each progression and migration, we learn, tremors rocked heaven—described as "a City Much Like San Francisco" (50)— until, echoing the actions of the god Wotan in Wagner's *Der Ring des Nibelungen*, God became restless:

> *Bored with His Angels, Bewitched by Humanity,*
> *In Mortifying Imitation of You, his least creation,*
> *He would sail off on Voyages, no knowing where.*
> *Quake follows quake,*
> *Absence follows Absence:*
> *Nasty Chastity and Disorganization:*
> *Loss of Libido. (50–51)*

On 18 April 1906—the day of the great San Francisco earthquake—God left, never (yet) to return.

The angel has come to Prior to get him to stop human destructiveness and change: "Turn back. Undo. / Till HE returns again" (53). She ominously remarks: "On you in you in your blood we write have written: / STASIS! / The END" (54). The implication is that AIDS is not therefore the scourge of God against the sexually deviant, but the sign of God's absence and abandonment of heaven. The resulting "Nasty Chastity" of the "AGE OF ANOMIE" (56) in a very sexualized heaven is Kushner's countermythological response to the Christian Right's confident assertions of AIDS as divine retribution. The angel here is obviously metaphoric: Joe's mother, Hannah, explains to Prior that an "angel is just a belief, with wings and arms that can carry you. It's naught to be afraid of. If it lets you down, reject it. Seek for something new" (105). But Hannah also says that Joseph Smith's angel was "real"—"His desire made prayer. His prayer made an angel" (103)—and so too is Prior's angel a "real" one with whom he must literally wrestle.

In act 5, titled "Heaven, I'm in Heaven," Prior ascends to a dispiriting and desolate place that looks not unlike San Francisco after the quake.[43] He goes there to explain to the angels that humans cannot stop moving and changing — as the angels wish them to — and the reason is what he calls "desire." So he must return their "Anti-Migratory" book to them. As for God: "If He ever *dared* to show His face . . . if after all this destruction, if after all the terrible days of this terrible century He returned to see . . . how much suffering His abandonment had created, if He did come back you should *sue* the bastard. . . . Sue the bastard for walking out" (133). So much for AIDS as the scourge of God; this is AIDS as the sign of the desertion, not retribution, of the divine. Not surprisingly, when Prior asks the angels to stop "this plague. . . . In me and everywhere. Make it go away" (133), they have to reply:

> Oh We *have tried.*
> We *suffer with You but*
> We *do not know.* We
> Do *not know how. (133–34)*

The plague may not go away, but its meaning has been changed irrevocably by this countermyth that redistributes the moral blame and undoes the sexual shame. In the epilogue to the aptly named *Perestroika*, set in 1990, the characters sit near the angel Bethesda's fountain in New York's Central Park. This angelic commemoration of the Civil War dead figured earlier in the play as a metaphor to explain the tendency to distance oneself "too far off the earth to pick out the details," a tendency rife in an America that is described as "terminal, crazy and mean" (96). This time, with Prior still alive after five years with AIDS, the statuary angel still commemorates death but also suggests "a world without dying" (147). Louis — who is Jewish — tells the story of this angel who descended in Temple Square in Jerusalem. Where she touched the earth a fountain sprang up, one whose waters healed — stopping suffering in body and spirit, washing them "clean of pain" — but it dried up when the Romans destroyed the Temple. The hope is that it will flow again when the millennium comes. It is February and the Central Park fountain has ceased to flow, but Prior intends to be alive when it is turned on again in summer. Yet this is not Violetta's heartbreaking "spes phthisica," the vain delusion of recovery at the moment of death. Having given new meanings to AIDS and those who have it, these plays can end with both defiance and compassion, with both hope and elegy: "This disease will be the end of many of us, but not nearly all, and the dead will be commemorated and will struggle on with the living, and we are not going away. We won't die secret deaths anymore" (148).

The healing waters of Bethesda that will flow again recall the other, global healing metaphor of the plays. Early in *Millennium Approaches*, Joe's Valium-addicted wife, Harper, had a vision of the threatened ozone layer being saved by a "gift from God . . . guardian angels, hands linked, make a spherical net, a blue-green nesting orb, a shell of safety for life itself" in the face of "systems of defense giving away" (16–17). HIV infection as a metaphor for ecological dangers is both recalled and put into historical context by Harper's final vision, from an airplane heading to San Francisco, where the guardian angels become the human dead in a version of the Mormon millennium, when bodies are regenerated: "Souls were rising, from the earth far below, souls of the dead, of people who had perished, from famine, from war, from the plague, and they floated up . . . [and] clasped ankles, and formed a web, a great net of souls, and the souls were three-atom oxygen molecules, of the stuff of ozone, and the outer rim absorbed them, and was repaired" (144). Suffering and death have been given new meaning, and now there can be what Harper calls "a kind of painful progress" (144). This is certainly one way to fight back against social stigma, and a way that any gay opera on the subject of AIDS may well decide to use to turn the weapons of prejudice back on their bearers. The widespread appeal of such a tactic can be seen already: a New York–based volunteer organization that delivers meals to homebound PLWAS is named, with appropriate and typically countermythological irony, "God's Love We Deliver."

The Logic of Contagion: Cholera and AIDS

In Albert Innaurato's 1984 novel *Coming of Age in Soho*, a character creates a *Death in Venice* video game "involving a chase between an old man, a young boy, and cholera. The game is a reflection of his life in the age of

AIDS."[44] Though Thomas Mann's novella and Myfanwy Piper's libretto for Benjamin Britten's opera avoided the indignities of cholera's diarrhea and vomiting and most of its quick wizening and other dehydrating horrors in their versions of *Death in Venice*, Susan Sontag is right to see medical and social analogies between the "dehumanizing" of the homosexual man who contracts AIDS and the one who succumbs to cholera. Both diseases are seen as epidemics that come from foreign and exotic lands.[45] Both have provoked the desire to scapegoat and lay blame, and this in turn has induced suspicions on the part of the stricken communities and individuals that the disease was being spread deliberately to wipe them out, be they the urban poor of the nineteenth-century European and North American cholera epidemics or, in the United States today, gay men or African Americans.[46] But you don't need to believe in conspiracy to see that, even when miasma theories of the environmental origins of cholera prevailed, it was a disease believed to hit those whose constitution was already weakened by dietary deficiencies, "excessive" consumption of alcohol, or other kinds of "behavior uncontrolled."[47] Since the bourgeois middle classes saw these failings as characterizing the poor, they were able to consider themselves "innocent" victims if they contracted cholera.[48] The analogies today, of course, are with what the media have called the "innocent" victims of AIDS — such as those who had the misfortune of requiring blood transfusions before the availability of blood-screening tests. Among those most often presented as the "guilty" when it comes to AIDS are not exactly cholera's economically marginalized but the sexually different and those addicted to intravenous drugs. But as we have seen, homosexuality and cholera were also associated with one another in a powerful way in *Death in Venice*. Recalling this and making a further link to AIDS, John Greyson, in his diverting countermythological "A Fake Video Script," resets *Death in Venice* at Venice Beach, California, and has a narrating African Green Monkey introduce the gay "dandy in its habitat" — Aschenbach.[49]

It was with historically and culturally accurate logic, however, that both Mann and Piper had their Aschenbach call upon his bourgeois background and his middle-class habits of life and work in his attempt to set up for himself a kind of bulwark against his homosexual attraction to the boy Tadzio — an attraction the boy's mother senses as a threat to her family. The heterosexual family has long been held up as the bourgeois moral model. It too has been given new meanings in the gay counter-mythologizing that AIDS has induced. William Finn and James Lapine's Broadway musical *Falsettos* presents Marvin, a gay male who was once married and has fathered a son, but who wants to have it all, both the conventional family *and* his male lover: "But I want a tight-knit family. / I want a group that harmonizes" (12). But his divorced wife, Trina, marries his psychiatrist, Mendel, and his lover, Whizzer, gets AIDS. The "lesbian next door," Dr. Charlotte, has worried that:

> *Something bad is happening.*
> *Something very bad is happening.*
> *Something stinks.*
> *Something immoral,*
> *Something so bad that words*
> *Have lost their meaning.*
> *Rumors fly and tales abound.* (141)

Refusing to abandon or be turned off by his infected lover, Marvin crawls into Whizzer's hospital bed, announcing "Here I am / By your side / One old horny lover" (157), even though Dr. Charlotte now knows that the "something bad" that is contagious and kills is spread "from one man to another" (162). Marvin's son, Jason, prays to God to save Whizzer's life, while the PLWA himself eroticizes death in ways that recall *Angels in America*:

> *Death's a funny pal*
> *With a weird sort of talent.*
> *He puts his arms around my neck and walks me to the bed.*
> *He pins me up against the wall and kisses me like crazy.*
> *The many stupid things I thought about with dread*
> *Now delight.* (164)

Reversing the Moral Majority's denunciations against homosexuality as the destruction of the family, *Falsettos* ends in Whizzer's hospital room with the bar mitzvah of Jason — "Son of Abraham, Isaac, and Jacob. / Son of Marvin, son of Trina, son of Whizzer, son of Mendel, / And godchild to the lesbians from next door" (170). The nuclear family is ironically re-configured in this moving and funny scene, as Marvin and Whizzer sing of their undying friendship and testify to no regret, no matter what the fatal consequences. The countermythologizing here tackles and reverses yet another of the cultural representations of AIDS, this time as the threat to middle-class morality. There is no sign here of Violetta's surrender to the bourgeois Germont senior's familial demands.

From 1832 on, cholera too was figured as a disease that threatened the bourgeois family. It is important to recall one final time that it had been the reports of public health physicians in England (following the first cholera epidemic there) that allowed the middle classes to discover and be duly shocked not only by the state of the slums but by the correlation between disease and "incest and other practices abhorrent to the reign-ing domestic ideal."[50] The linking of epidemics, filthy and overcrowded living conditions, urban poverty, dissipation, and moral failings fueled the Christian temperance movement as much as it did the sanitary re-forms. Although much has been written about the negative effects of the increased surveillance in the name of public health since the first cholera epidemics, with AIDS it has been that very surveillance—by the Centers for Disease Control and other agencies—that has made it possi-ble to collect the necessary information to identify the disease and its spread. The difference lies in what it is that is being watched—and con-trolled: "It is probably fair to say that no one objects to the control and eradication of the causative agent(s) of AIDS, but AIDS control policy has been much more and has inevitably raised the question of the supervi-sion and regulation of sexuality."[51] The social, moral, and ideological framework that has made possible what Arthur Kroker calls "Body Mc-Carthyism"—with its checking of the purity of bodily fluids—was set up, however, with cholera.[52]

Like that earlier epidemic, AIDS too has been perceived in the West not only in moral terms, but specifically as a disease of cities, the "tradi-tional harbors of disease and degeneration" since Sodom and Gomorrah, if not before.[53] The title of *Death in Venice*, of course, brings together too the fatal result of cholera and what is presented as a decadent and com-mercially driven city. And today the same rhetoric of contagion has resulted in familiar anxieties and familiar demands, often from the Christian Right, for regulatory control: the rise of Protestant evangelism in 1832 in the northeast and midwest of the United States has been directly tied to the cholera epidemic, blamed on the Irish Catholic poor in the city slums.[54] Because of the connection between AIDS and what is seen as "erotic excess," there is talk of mandatory HIV testing and even threats of tattooing and quarantine for gay men. By what has been called the "logic of contagion," the anxiety created by the need for social control and surveillance is used to justify specific regulations and legislation.[55] But it is likely the fact of the sexual transmission of AIDS that has intensified even more the moralizing process that accompanies such attempts at control of sexuality, as the history of syphilis has made all too clear.

"Polluted Blood": Syphilis and AIDS

AIDS is not *only* a sexually transmitted disease, of course, but it can be and has been spread that way within the male homosexual community. That is all that has been needed to fuel homophobic reaction in some quarters. Many of the AIDS plays have fought the kind of obsession with causality and origin that has led to seeing the "cause" of the disease not as the HIV retrovirus but as its perceived mode of transmission: non-procreative, multiple-partner male-male sex.[56] Just as syphilis became a metaphor for nineteenth-century anxieties about contagion, sexuality, and social organization, as discussed in chapter 3, so AIDS has raised contemporary worries about hygiene, contamination, and social as well as sexual "pollution." The two diseases have provoked not only similar social debates (medical, moral, sexual), but also similar misconceptions in public perception.[57] So when Prior (in *Millennium Approaches*) says, "My heart is pumping polluted blood. I feel dirty" (34), he is drawing on the sociocultural associations of earlier venereal disease as well, associations that can account for some of the power of Wagner's *Parsifal* too, as we have argued. The fear of anarchy in the Grail realm, whose leader has been stigmatized by his sexually connected wound that will not heal, is comparable to the social panic surrounding AIDS. In terms of fear of infection, the syphilophobia of the nineteenth century is matched by AIDS phobia today. In both cases the meanings given to venereal diseases tend to be "entangled with our ideas about the social meanings and moral evaluations of sexual behaviors."[58] And in both eras the middle-class norm has been the monogamous heterosexual marital relationship and the safest of sex, abstinence.[59] In *Falsettos*, it is when Marvin comes out of the closet that he gives his wife syphilis, which is treatable by this time; but his male lover, Whizzer, is the one who dies of AIDS. A certain Christian interpretation might want to make the analogy here with Kundry, Wagner's prostitute figure, who must die; the male Spear must be reunited with the female Grail if the chaste Grail realm is to be restored to spiritual wholeness. But in "Falsettoland" that is not how things turn out.

Think of the sexualized angel's remark in *Perestroika* about "Nasty Chastity": as we have seen, one countermythological response to AIDS's problematic inheritance of the historical and biomedical contexts of venereal disease, in plays like *Angels in America*, is to give new and very different meanings to the notion of disease as divine retribution, for syphilis too was seen as a "plague" sent to punish specifically sexual transgression. In *Laughing Wild*, Christopher Durang deals directly with the biblical injunction that men who lie with other men must be punished. This male monologue *confronts* even more than it *addresses* the views of Christians who think "that God is so disgusted by the sexual activities of homosexuals that He created AIDS to punish them, apparently waiting until 1978 or so to do this, even though homosexual acts have been going on for considerably longer than that, at least since . . . 1956."[60] The ironic speaker then imagines God telling the angel Gabriel that he's going to give "disgusting" homosexuals (as well as drug addicts and hemophiliacs) a "really horrifying disease" because "I'm all-powerful and can do everything 'cause I'm God" but he's also "too tired today to figure out how to connect the disease to the bloodstream and *not* affect hemophiliacs. Besides, the suffering will be good for them" (181). The kind of redemption of the sinner through suffering that *Parsifal* took seriously is here made ironic and thereby called into question. When the angel asks a few too many difficult questions of this God, however, he is condemned to be a man with the words, "I give you suffering and death; I give you psychological pain; I give you AIDS, your immune system will shut down totally. . . . I hereby revoke penicillin. Anyone out there who has ever been exposed to syphilis will suffer and die just like they used to — as a side issue, I love to connect sex and death . . . I want those who disobey me to die a horrible death from AIDS and syphilis and God knows what else" (181). Does God know what else? asks the countermyth.

As Durang's play suggests, the person who has contracted AIDS is liable to be associated with what Sander Gilman calls one of the most potent in the repertory of images of the stigmatized patient — the syphilitic. In his long and detailed study of the visual history of representations of syphilitics and the analogies with images of persons with AIDS, Gilman shows how those of AIDS conflate the figures of the isolated male sufferer (like Amfortas) with that of the corrupting, infecting female source (like Kundry) into the single image of the gay male, at once victim and source of his own infection.[61] Many have pointed to the analogies between the scapegoating of the prostitute as the contaminated cause of disease and that of the infected gay male, as well as to the comparable threats to the civil liberties of both: just as thirty thousand prostitutes were detained in United States government institutions during the First World War — to protect the health of the fighting men — so there has been talk of quarantine and detention centers for the HIV positive.[62] The "Flower Maidens" have always been constructed as the threat, but this time so have those "soldiers."

The connection examined in earlier chapters between the history of the spread of syphilis and the military (through the movements of soldiers) makes an ironic, if fitting, background against which to look at the military metaphors that have proliferated in AIDS discourse: when the body's immunological defenses are down disease can invade, and so one must struggle, fight, combat, and so on. As Sontag has pointed out, there are exact analogies here with the language of syphilis education.[63] Perhaps this is not surprising, at least from a medical perspective. There has been a marked increase in the incidence of syphilis with the sexual liberation of recent decades, of course, and this has generated a lot of attention in the medical literature.[64] But just as striking, perhaps, are the similarities in the clinical properties of the two diseases: both are what Sontag calls diseases of time — slow, chronic, progressive — though both were at first perceived as rapid and virulent. The difference here is that syphilis changed from the deadly, rapid killer it was in its first decades to being a chronic and staged disease. With AIDS it has been our knowledge of the disease that has changed, not the disease itself: it looked as if it killed quickly at first because it wasn't being diagnosed until its end stages. Both these venereal diseases have skin manifestations, however, and both have major neurological consequences (AIDS dementia and general paresis of the insane). In other words, it isn't hard to imagine *The Rake's Progress* being staged today as an AIDS opera, with Mother Goose in drag.

In a new chapter on AIDS added to the reissue of his book *No Magic Bullet: A Social History of Venereal Disease in the United States since 1880*, Allan M. Brandt points out what the history of these two diseases also share in social terms, at least in the United States: "the pervasive fear of contagion; concerns about casual transmission; the stigmatization of victims; the conflicts between protecting public health and assuring civil liberties; the search for magic bullets."[65] In a study of certain French fin-de-siècle works on syphilis and writing on AIDS, Emily Apter notes parallel "discourses of disease and difference, of bodies erotically and socially marked, [that] articulate ways in which eroticism and death collaborate on the dissolution of the subject."[66] Given the focus on Wagner earlier in this book, even more interesting may be Sander Gilman's study of German fiction about syphilis from 1939 and fiction about AIDS published in 1989: "In Germany the evocation of a socially stigmatizing disease seems to be difficult without the evocation of past metaphors of disease and political persecution."[67] The constant invocation of images of the Holocaust in gay drama and musicals about AIDS echoes in this way back through history. But when Tony Kushner says that AIDS reminds us that "compassion has to do with passion," we cannot help thinking of Wagner's similar (and yet very different) wordplay on compassion (*Mitleid*) and suffering (*Leid*).[68] The reeroticizing that substitutes passion for suffering is part of the countermythologizing process: an ironic answer to the Christianized view of syphilophobic victimhood in *Parsifal* and a protest against the identification of the sick person with the disease. Ronald O. Valdiserri, a physician who watched his twin brother die of AIDS, articulates what we might call the Amfortas syndrome: "Disease does more than rob the body of function: it also chips away at identity."[69] It is precisely this that the countermyths seek to resist.

"Aesthetic" Epidemics: Tuberculosis and AIDS

Remarking on the recent explosion of plays, novels, films, and television shows about AIDS, one critic has noted that "not even tuberculosis, that most 'aesthetic' of epidemics, produced a comparable outpouring in so short a time."[70] What the two illnesses share, beyond their artistic fruitfulness, is a similar set of medical associations: their victims are seen to be the young, cut off in their prime; as chronic degenerative diseases, they are both diseases of emaciation; neither has many other external signs—the tubercular cough and the Kaposi's sarcoma lesion are the most perceivable beyond the wasting away of the body.[71] It may not be inappropriate, then, that there have been at least two modernized versions of Verdi's *La Traviata* that have recoded Violetta's consumption into AIDS-related disease: Nicholas Muni's production at the New York City Opera and Esquire Jauchem's for Opera New England.

Gay culture has long had a fascination with this tubercular operatic heroine, as suggested by *The Lisbon "Traviata"* or by Charles Ludlam's travesty performance of Garbo's film portrayal of Camille, the "Dame aux camélias." John Clum's reading of the opera's source text, Dumas's play version of the story, as a gay narrative that places "sexually active characters within the realm of disease as well as that of the normative discourse of sexual morality," is significant in its pointing to the sexualization of tuberculosis, but it depends for its argument on the idea that consumption was in fact a coded term for venereal disease, "a respectable contagious disease figuring the results of pollution of body and spirit."[72] As seen in chapter 2, however, when Dumas wrote the play tuberculosis was not known to be a contagious disease. In fact its sexualization probably depended precisely on the *lack* of such knowledge: by the time of *La Bohème*, when it was known, the response began to change.

We will return to this (actually quite common) misreading of the meaning of tuberculosis later, but it certainly is true that the *Traviata* narrative core of a life of sexual "indulgence," illness, social stigmatization, lovers' separation, and their tearful reunion does reappear often in AIDS dramas—and melodramas.[73] There are deathbed reconciliations, even marriages of sorts—most notably at the end of Larry Kramer's *The Normal Heart*. But AIDS offers none of the tragic ironies of the tubercular's "spes phthisica," the physically experienced hope that life will return just at the moment of death. Yet though the lovers' bedside "marriage" in Kramer's play may end in Felix's death, it does also mark the play's positive resolution: Ned's first real commitment to another person and the prelude to his reconciliation with his brother, who has never until now been able to accept his homosexuality as "normal." And these positive results rebound back on the meanings of the disease and death from it.

Analogies with the narrative details of *La Bohème*, the opera that came *after* Koch's discovery of the tubercle bacillus, can be found as well in the plays about AIDS, in two particular ways: in the stress on the clinical physicality of the disease and in the fear of contagion. Just as Rodolfo leaves Mimì after a night of her incessant coughing, so Louis in Kushner's *Millennium Approaches* leaves Prior in his moment of greatest need, despite his love for him, because he can not "incorporate sickness into his sense of how things are supposed to be," because he is afraid of "vomit . . . and sores and disease" and "isn't so good with death" (25). Like Rodolfo, Louis is tortured by the knowledge that he cannot bear to be with the one he loves in his illness: he leaves Prior alone in the hospital, simply saying to the nurse, "Tell him I had to go" (52). Prior's caustic remark about the apartment's being too small for three—"Louis and Prior and Prior's Disease" (78)—recalls in detail if not tone Mimì's account of Rodolfo's abandoning her. But like his Parisian model, Louis misses Prior, feeling cold and miserable, yet fears for his own health: "I miss him so much but then . . . those sores, and the smell and . . . I could be . . . I could be sick too" (99). Ned in *The Normal Heart* puts the dilemma succinctly: "I'm afraid to be with him. I'm afraid to be without him" (47).

Like Violetta and Mimì, Prior laments his physical decline—though with typical countermythological camp humor: "I look like a corpse. A corpsette" (31). He too fears being alone in his illness, as so many PLWAS are, according to the Hospice Worker in Hoffman's *As Is*, and as both of the opera's tubercular women are, at least until the final moments of reconciliation with their lovers. Interestingly, from the critic who described so extensively the visual iconography of tuberculosis in *Illness as Metaphor* and who has argued for the need to combat the negative images surrounding AIDS in *AIDS and Its Metaphors* has come the transposition of the "glittering eyes" and the "ivory pallor" of the beautiful and sexually attractive consumptive to the person with AIDS. Susan Sontag's story "The Way We Live Now" and its stage adaptation by Edward Parone are in this way part of the counter-mythology of AIDS writing, different in tone if not in final impact.[74]

Richard Goldstein puts his finger on a major difference between the cultural representations of tuberculosis — created from the outside — and those of AIDS — from the inside. AIDS, he feels, has led to a recovery of romanticism,

> much as tuberculosis fueled operatic masques of purity amid pollution. Once again, death sanctions love and gives it a tragic edge. Once again, a disease is thought to single out the abnormally passionate, creative, and effete. But it is hard to imagine the contemporary gay man as a latter-day Dame aux Camélias. The confrontational stance of today's gay culture gives the bond between people with *AIDS* in fictional works a more insistent edge.[75]

But it is precisely that edge — sharpened sometimes by outrageous humor, sometimes by erotic transgression — that has made it possible to countermythologize even the "Dame aux Camélias."

Gay Countermythologies

In North American and European AIDS education films, videotapes, and photos after about 1985, there has been a comparable eroticization of "safe sex" that has been intended as a "counterdiscourse" to or a "dissident vernacular" of the dominant representations of gay sexuality in the mainstream media, science, and medicine.[76] As a protest against what has been called the "sadistically punitive gaze" turned on the gay male body with AIDS, the image of the "victim" has been resisted on many fronts.[77] The images of skeletal, passive AIDS patients, reduced and yet aestheticized by the documentary camera of Rosalind Solomon or Nicholas Nixon, have been challenged in many different but equally countermythological ways. Andy Fabo sexualized Michelangelo's "slave" images of the male body; the trio of artists known as General Idea ironized both the concept and the reality of "victimage" through one of the iconic tradition's favorite images of utter helplessness: they stranded three (stuffed) baby seals—their own self-images as gay men, some of whom were at the time HIV positive—on an ice floe made of polystyrene sheets.[78] Moving through rage and elegiac lament and even the need to bear witness, gay stage productions today are also just as likely to startle either by their erotic content or by their humor. This is certainly one way to combat the increasing acceptance of AIDS as somehow normal rather than as a crisis. In an article written in 1993 while he was dying of AIDS, Jeffrey Schmalz pointed out that "once AIDS was a hot topic in America—promising treatments on the horizon, intense media interest, a political battlefield. Now, 12 years after it was first recognized as a new disease, AIDS has become normalized, part of the landscape."[79] The activist theatrical energies of ACT UP and Queer Nation have found their countermythic analogues—in terms of effect and impact—in the ironic and sexualized angelification of disease in *Angels in America* or in the combination of satiric verve and elegy in Paula Vogel's *The Baltimore Waltz*—in which a single schoolteacher gets ATD (acquired toilet disease) from her young charges as her gay brother dies of AIDS.

The more outrageous the ironic inversion of dominant myths, the more powerful, perhaps, the impact. For instance, it is one thing to use the image of AIDS—a disease of the blood—as a vampire that could manifest itself in many forms and seem impossible to track down.[80] But it is quite another thing to literalize the image, as Greg Kramer has done in his *Lies of the Vampire*. Arriving on stage in a long white gown, he addressed the audience: "Good evening. This is an allegory about AIDS. I was human once but I acquired a disease. And now I am The Vampire." Black comedy may demystify the horror of AIDS, but drawing upon everything from film to fiction (most notably, we suspect, that of Anne Rice), this one-man show also eroticized and sexualized both vampires and the disease. The countermythological effect was not unlike that achieved when new meanings are given to the bourgeois family—said to be threatened by homosexuality—by a musical like *Falsettos*. These are all examples of ways of taking control of the means of giving meaning to diseases and those who get them. Their proactive and didactic intent and the fact that they are being constructed from the "inside" make them different from the representations of other diseases in opera that we have studied here. They also suggest that the AIDS operas to come might well be recognizable in detail but new in tone and impact, for they too may well partake of that attempt to "wrest from the dominant culture the wholly negative if not annihilative representation of HIV infection and AIDS, and to construct in its stead a discourse of empowerment, meaning, and possibility."[81]

Certainly a number of independent films — again made within the gay community — have moved in this direction, and music has figured in important ways in several of them. Bill Sherwood's 1986 *Parting Glances* presents a PLWA defined by excess: a rock singer who retains a sexual energy that makes AIDS into "exuberant expenditure," not loss, into "another factor in a dance marked equally by death and desire."[82] More provocatively, John Greyson's 1993 film *Zero Patience* (with music by Glenn Schellenberg) cannot be dismissed as kitsch or camp, even if at times it depends on both for its comedy. Frankly sexual and very funny, it suggests that both eroticism and humor may be important affirmative responses to the gay male body represented on screen. This is a musical about the facts and myths that surround HIV infection and AIDS and about the creation of scapegoats — from the African green monkey to gay men. It is also an open countering of Randy Shilts's portrayal in *And the Band Played On* of Gaetan Dugas, the Québécois flight attendant and supposed "Patient Zero" of the epidemic.[83] In the film, Dugas returns to life to clear his name, singing:

> We were boys who loved our bodies
> Playing hard and deep
> Boys who thought we'd live forever
> Didn't know that we were playing for keeps.

Though he comes back from the dead in the bathhouse he once frequented, no one can actually see his ghostly form — a very eroticized and sexually attractive form (and not at all a victimized, wasted one) — except Richard Burton, the Victorian sexologist and explorer who, it seems, *did* find the fountain of youth on one of his trips. Still a handsome young man though 170 years old, Burton works in the Natural History Museum and is involved in a project called the "Hall of Contagion." When budget cuts stop his plague-rat exhibit, he decides to feature Patient Zero and AIDS instead. The subsequent love affair of Zero and Burton is a sort of allegory of science in the age of AIDS: despite technological advances, the remnants of Victorian sexual hangups remain. In what may be the most bizarrely transgressive scene in the film, the "Butthole Duet," Burton's sphincter sings:

> But Freud said we have a death wish
> Getting buggered is getting killed
> Is this ghastly epidemic
> Something our subconscious willed?

Fantasy, dream sequences, and self-conscious artifice meet science. As Zero and Burton (also the translator of *The Arabian Nights*) look at Zero's infected blood under a microscope, an anthropomorphized "Miss HIV" floats into their sight, singing: "Tell a story of a virus . . . / A tale that's cruel and sad. / Weep for me, Scheherazade." The use of the conventions of the musical is at once defamiliarizing—given what is being sung about—and at the same time the means to a broader audience appeal, something that is important for a film that wants to challenge the myths about AIDS and the moral blame that goes with them. Like Kushner's linking of compassion and passion, *Zero Patience* calls on countermythological eroticism as well as humor and wit to take a step beyond mourning to celebrate the lives of those living with and dying from AIDS.

Operas about other diseases have rarely been this funny, however. The pathos and tragedy of illness and death are sometimes not to be denied or transcended. The closest thing to prefiguring a conventional AIDS opera in this vein may be *Masque of the Red Death*, a work by the unconventional performance artist Diamanda Galas. Called a "Plague Mass" about AIDS, this confronts many of the issues we have already seen in the plays and musicals, in particular the Christian Right's reading of the disease as the scourge of God against the sexually sinning. This is a trilogy of very different musical parts, each of which uses Galas's multioctaved voice in different and equally astonishing ways, with some electronic manipulation and echoing. The first part, titled "The Divine Punishment," presents Galas chanting, moaning, wailing, and cackling, in powerful rhythmic ways, Old Testament texts from Leviticus and the Psalms that deal with "uncleanness" laws, sexual behavior, bodily disintegration, and despair. In juxtaposing these judgmental words with the touching prayers of the suffering, Galas too takes on the Christian reading of AIDS, this time not with humor or erotic transgression but with moving angry denunciation.

The organ overture of the second part, "Saint of the Pit," suggests the liturgical context of this Christianized reading, a context shared by the syphilophobic discourses of the nineteenth century and earlier. This is precisely the historical connection made by the texts of this section, taken from Baudelaire's *Les Fleurs du mal* and other French nineteenth-century romantic and "decadent" sources. With its focus on the sufferer's cries for love and mercy, this section contrasts sharply with the third and final one, "You Must Be Certain of the Devil." Here the musical idioms are those of the contemporary United States. From its opening "Swing Low Sweet Chariot" on, this section moves toward counter-mythological inversion of the conventions of American gospel music, as well as fundamentalist logic and rhetoric. But this time it is with anger and pain, urging violence in response to violence. This is not AIDS as *God's* curse—quite the contrary:

> *The Devil has designed my death*
> *and he's waiting to be sure*
> *that plenty of his black sheep die*
> *before he finds a cure.*

The recorded version of this performance piece ends in a way that is excruciatingly painful to listen to, as Galas gasps out Psalm 23 ("*The Lord is my shepherd . . .*") and footsteps recede. The printed lyrics end with an added passage, repeated on the back of the compact disc cover, that is comparable to the epilogue of *Angels in America* in its imagery and even in its message, though offered with more fierce confrontation than generous hope:

LISTEN MAN

IT MAY SOON BE TIME

FOR YOU TO GUARD A DYING MAN

UNTIL THE ANGELS COME

LET'S NOT CHAT ABOUT DESPAIR

IF YOU ARE A MAN (AND NOT A COWARD)

YOU WILL GRASP THE HAND OF HIM DENIED BY MERCY

UNTIL HIS BREATH BECOMES YOUR OWN.

His breath does become her gasping breath at the end; symbolically, she "accompanies the dying as they plumb the depths of solitude and reports back the emotions and sensations, the fears and the why-me anger afflicting them."[84]

A "Plague Mass" of this force and unconventionality is not an opera, but it does have important and obvious connections — thematic and formal — with those "plague operas" from *Oedipus Rex* and *Oedipe* through to *Death in Venice*. So too did the 1991 performance project in Houston called *Ad Mortem*, a video, dance, voice, and music oratorio about "sexuality, dying, mourning, and healing" that also directly confronted the taboos and political conflicts around AIDS.[85]

In Europe and North America we tend to forget that diseases like syphilis, cholera, and tuberculosis are still raging today, especially in the non-Western world; so too is AIDS, but we may know of its power firsthand and close to home.[86] When friends or family die, we tend to pay more attention. This amnesia about the past — even the recent past — may well be characteristic of our postmodern culture at large, but it is also disturbing for what it may predict. How much of the current suffering and death from AIDS will we forget? And how soon?

As we've just seen, tuberculosis offers one easily traced marker of just how much (and how quickly) we are capable of forgetting, and of the effect such forgetfulness can have on how the representations of disease are understood (and misunderstood). In *Violetta and Her Sisters*, a recent collection of responses to the myth of the "Lady of the Camellias," the editor notes that, unlike cholera, consumption *did not attack a whole community. Consumption singled out its victims, and they acquired an interesting individuality; the decline refined them in suffering, and they suffered the prototype of a passive death, consumed by an inner, unseen passion. Far from the clinical reality of foul breath and emaciation, it was portrayed as a death of aesthetic beauty, directly allied to spiritual innocence.*[87]

So far so good. But suddenly that historical amnesia strikes, for the next step is to claim that Alfredo's attraction to Violetta in La Traviata is based on the very fact that her days are numbered and that he knows his own "infection may be the terrible price to be paid for desire." But what is here interpreted as "perverse sexuality" is in fact nothing of the kind, because in Dumas's and Verdi's day consumption was thought to be primarily a hereditary disease and not a contagious one. These works both predate Koch's discovery of its infectious nature. Violetta's appeal does indeed reside in her feverish beauty and short life, but not in the supposed danger that Alfredo will face in being near her. That was the plot of that later, post-Koch opera, La Bohème.

If this example were an isolated one, there would be no point to our singling it out. But it is not, as we have already seen. Even the most scholarly of accounts are prone to either over- or underinterpret the signs of tuberculosis in opera and literature. One recent, meticulously researched study of the French medical and literary culture of Dumas's time calls consumption "that nineteenth-century euphemism for syphilis."[88] How easily are forgotten the particular symptoms and significance of the disease that, at the time, was the single most frequent cause of death in Paris. Another commentator, writing on La Traviata, moves in the other direction, reading the symptoms of consumption in very general terms: as the signs of "what we now recognize as a peculiarly nineteenth-century way of symbolizing human frailty."[89] Perhaps. But tuberculosis was also a very real disease, suffered by real people. The nineteenth-century audiences of these operas and plays knew that, even if advances in medical science have given us the luxury of forgetting it today.

Our argument in this book has been that Theodor Adorno's famous theory—that opera constituted a "bourgeois vacation spot" with "little involvement in the social conflicts of the nineteenth-century"—is far from historically accurate.⁹⁰ Such an interpretation ignores the complex power that composers and librettists could and did draw on when they chose to represent certain diseases on the operatic stage at that time. All diseases are both biomedical and social entities, and these particular ones were diseases with a continuing history of anxiety, for none had yet been cured. All were still major causes of worry and thus loaded with meanings for members of the audience—as opera creators knew well. However, that we have been fortunate enough to be allowed not to have these worries, and sometimes to forget those meanings, has often hampered our ability to understand even the most familiar of canonical operas today. It may be rhetorically effective to claim that the pleasure of opera "leads us astray to chimerical shores where we become the toys of a powerful bewitchment," because, as an art form, it is so forgetful of "the demands of reality."⁹¹ But that is a seriously misleading and ahistorical claim, forgetful of "the demands of reality" of those who suffered from or feared contracting very real diseases. Time and science have mercifully allowed us distance; but in the age of AIDS we might want to be suspicious of how easily and how quickly amnesia can set in.

None of the diseases discussed in this book—from tuberculosis to AIDS—is really a finished chapter in medical or social history. Just as we have learned much about past societies by studying how they conceptualized and represented diseases, so we can continue to learn much about our own, and even to change the shape of its knowledge, in part through the recovery of memory. The ways medicine comes to understand disease will continue to affect the way the general culture portrays it; but it is also true that medical knowledge will always be affected in turn by the social and cultural meanings given to disease. To be made self-conscious about the process of how meanings are given—one of the aims of gay countermythologizing—is one step on the way to being more active, daily, in combating stereotyping, stigmatizing, and discrimination. To be made historically aware of the emotional and intellectual force of operatic presentations of disease and sexuality (and of their consequences)—one of the aims of this book—is perhaps another step in helping us understand the particular power of cultural representations, not only in the past but in the present.

Notes

Prologue

1. The editions of the librettos used are always the standard ones unless otherwise specified.
2. Ellen Rosand, "Criticism and the Undoing of Opera," *Nineteenth-Century Music* 14 (1990): 77.
3. See Nelly Furman, "Opera, or The Staging of the Voice," *Cambridge Opera Journal* 3, 3 (1991): 303–6.

1. Melodies and Maladies

1. Charles E. Rosenberg, "Framing Disease: Illness, Society, and History," in *Framing Disease: Studies in Cultural History*, ed. Charles E. Rosenberg and Janet Golden (New Brunswick: Rutgers University Press, 1992), xiv.
2. See Charles E. Rosenberg, "Disease and Social Order in America: Perceptions and Expectations," in *AIDS: The Burdens of History*, ed. Elizabeth Fee and Daniel M. Fox (Berkeley: University of California Press, 1988), 17–19.
3. Allan M. Brandt, "AIDS: From Social History to Social Policy," in Fee and Fox, *AIDS: The Burdens of History*, 147.
4. See Herbert Lindenberger, *Opera: The Extravagant Art* (Ithaca: Cornell University Press, 1984), 239.
5. See Jeremy Tambling, *Opera, Ideology and Film* (Manchester: Manchester University Press, 1987), on films of operas and their democratizing potential.
6. See Michel Noiray, "L'Opéra de la Révolution (1790–1794): Un 'Tapage de chien'?" in *La Carmagnole des muses: L'Homme de lettres et l'artiste dans la Révolution*, ed. Jean-Claude Bonnet (Paris: Armand Colin, 1988), 359–79.
7. Lindenberger, *Opera*, 238. See also Barry Emslie, "Woman as Image and Narrative in Wagner's *Parsifal*: A Case Study," *Cambridge Opera Journal* 3, 2 (1991): 109; David Levin, "Introduction," in *Opera through Other Eyes*, ed. David Levin (Stanford: Stanford University Press, 1994), 14.
8. Theodor Adorno, "Bourgeois Opera," reprinted in Levin, *Opera through Other Eyes*, 30.
9. For an extended discussion of opera and national identity, see Anthony Arblaster, *Viva la Libertà! Politics in Opera* (New York: Verso, 1992).
10. See Lindenberger, *Opera*, 17; Paul Robinson, *Opera and Ideas: From Mozart to Strauss* (Ithaca: Cornell University Press, 1985), 264.

11. Marc Angenot, in *1889: Un Etat du discours social* (Longueuil: Préambule, 1989), 13, defines "social discourse" as all the rules of organizing the "sayable" (the narratable and the verisimilar), as well as all that is written and stated by a given society.

12. Lawrence Kramer, *Music as Cultural Practice, 1800–1900* (Berkeley: University of California Press, 1990), xii.

13. Richard Leppert and Susan McClary, in their introduction to *Music and Society: The Politics of Composition, Performance and Reception*, ed. Richard Leppert and Susan McClary (Cambridge: Cambridge University Press, 1987), xi; see Joseph Kerman, *Contemplating Music: Challenges to Musicology* (Cambridge: Harvard University Press, 1985), on the entrenchment of formalism in musical thinking and teaching.

14. Lindenberger, *Opera*; Catherine Clément, *Opera, or The Undoing of Women*, trans. Betsy Wing (Minneapolis: University of Minnesota Press, 1988); Peter Conrad, *Romantic Opera and Literary Form* (Berkeley: University of California Press, 1977), and idem, *A Song of Love and Death: The Meaning of Opera* (New York: Poseidon, 1987); Wayne Koestenbaum, *The Queen's Throat: Opera, Homosexuality, and the Mystery of Desire* (New York: Poseidon, 1993); Arthur Groos and Roger Parker, eds., *Reading Opera* (Princeton: Princeton University Press, 1988); Levin, *Opera through Other Eyes*.

15. See Lawrence Kramer, "Culture and Musical Hermeneutics: The Salome Complex," *Cambridge Opera Journal* 2 (1990): 269. His note 1 provides an excellent bibliography of the move in music studies from formalism to a concern with semantic and expressive aspects.

16. See Ellen Rosand, "Criticism and the Undoing of Opera," *Nineteenth-Century Music* 14 (1990): 76–77 on the two texts of opera.

17. Lindenberger, *Opera*, 56.

18. Gary Schmidgall, *Literature as Opera* (New York: Oxford University Press, 1977); Joseph Kerman, *Opera as Drama* (New York: Knopf, 1956).

19. On the complex structural relations between music written for a text and a text designed to be put to music, see Carolyn Roberts Finlay, "Structural Paradigms: A Semiotic Approach to the Opera Text," *Yearbook of Comparative and General Literature* 35 (1986): 25.

20. John Eaton, "Stories That Break into Song: Choosing Plots for Opera," *Kenyon Review* 4, 3 (1982): 73.

21. See Paul Robinson, "A Deconstructive Postscript: Reading Libretti and Misreading Opera," in Groos and Parker, *Reading Opera*, 328–46.

22. Patrick J. Smith, *The Tenth Muse: A Historical Study of the Opera Libretto* (London: Victor Gollancz, 1971), xviii. On the related conventions of prose librettos

and the debates over them, see Hugh MacDonal, "The Prose Libretto," *Cambridge Opera Journal* 1, 2 (1989): 155–66.

23. Levin, "Introduction," in *Opera through Other Eyes*, 18 (our emphasis).

24. Smith, *Tenth Muse*, xviii.

25. Virgil Thomson, "On Writing Operas and Staging Them," *Parnassus: Poetry in Review*, fall–winter 1982, 6.

26. Levin, "Introduction," 14; Adorno, "Bourgeois Opera," 34.

27. Lindenberger, *Opera*, 167.

28. For an analysis of how this is done, see Carolyn Roberts Finlay, "Syntagmatic and Paradigmatic Structures of Text and Score in Opera" (Ph.D. diss., University of Toronto, 1984).

29. See Schmidgall, *Literature as Opera*, 12.

30. See Peter Brooks, *Reading for the Plot: Design and Intention in Narrative* (New York: Columbia University Press, 1984), 7. Peter J. Rabinowitz argues in "Outside the Culture, Outside the Music: Bizet's Carmen and Narrative Resistance," paper presented at the annual conference of the Society for the Study of Narrative Literature, Vancouver, 22 April 1994, that nineteenth-century opera is a narrative genre even more than a dramatic genre, but perhaps to separate them in this way in general is misleading, though it is fruitful in this particular case of *Carmen*.

31. See, for example, Friedrich Kittler, "World-Breath: On Wagner's Media Technology," in Levin, *Opera through Other Eyes*, 221–22 especially; Peter Branscombe, "The Dramatic Texts," in *Wagner Handbook*, ed. Ulrich Müller and Peter Wapnewski, trans. John Deathridge (Cambridge: Harvard University Press, 1992), 269–86.

32. Carl Dahlhaus, *Nineteenth-Century Music*, trans. J. Bradford Robinson (Berkeley: University of California Press, 1989), 280.

33. Richard Klein, *Cigarettes Are Sublime* (Durham: Duke University Press, 1993), 107.

34. This combination is likely what has attracted semiologists to the study of opera. See, for example, Ilie Balea, "Vers une Sémiologie de l'opéra: Systèmes—structures—interférences sémiologiques," *Etudes Littéraires* 13, 3 (1980): 437–59. It is also what has upset aesthetic purists for centuries. See Lindenberger's discussion of this in *Opera*, 201.

35. See Jean-Jacques Nattiez, *Music and Discourse: Toward a Semiology of Music*, trans. Carolyn Abbate (Princeton: Princeton University Press, 1990), ix.

36. Marc A. Weiner, *Richard Wagner and the Anti-Semitic Imagination* (Lincoln: University of Nebraska Press, 1994).

37. Peter Brooks, *Body Work: Objects of Desire in Modern Narrative* (Cambridge: Harvard University Press, 1993), xi. The subsequent citation is from p. 1.

38. Sander L. Gilman, *Disease and Representation: Images of Illness from Madness to AIDS* (Ithaca: Cornell University Press, 1988), 155.

39. For relevant and related analyses of representations of death and women in Western culture, see Elisabeth Bronfen, *Over Her Dead Body: Death, Femininity and the Aesthetic* (New York: Routledge, 1992), and for opera in particular, Michel Poizat, *The Angel's Cry: Beyond the Pleasure Principle in Opera*, trans. Arthur Denner (Ithaca: Cornell University Press, 1992). Poizat's focus is on voice and the powerful emotional response to it that he associates with both the erotic and the divine, connecting the two in the image of woman suffering and dying.

40. Poizat, *Angel's Cry*, 134.

41. See Howard Brody, *Stories of Sickness* (New Haven: Yale University Press, 1987); Arthur Kleinman, *The Illness Narratives: Suffering, Healing, and the Human Condition* (New York: Basic Books, 1988); Eric Cassell, *The Nature of Suffering and the Goals of Medicine* (New York: Oxford University Press, 1991).

42. Elaine Scarry, *The Body in Pain: The Making and Unmaking of the World* (New York: Oxford University Press, 1985), 3.

43. David B. Morris, *The Culture of Pain* (Berkeley: University of California Press, 1991), 248.

44. Gottfried Ephraim Lessing, *Werke in drei Bänden*, ed. Herbert G. Göpfert (München: Carl Hanser, 1982), 31: "Zudem ist der körperliche Schmerz überhaupt des Mitleidens nicht fähig, welches andere Übel erwecken."

45. See Jeffrey Weeks, "AIDS and the Regulation of Sexuality," in *AIDS and Contemporary History*, ed. Virginia Berridge and Philip Strong (Cambridge: Cambridge University Press, 1993), 18–19.

46. Kramer, *Music as Cultural Practice*, 136.

47. For more on the debate over sexuality and its social construction, see Edward Stein, ed., *Forms of Desire: Sexual Orientation and the Social Constructionist Controversy* (New York: Routledge, 1992).

48. On the complex (and often confused) meanings given to "desire," see the special issue of *Textual Practice* 7, 3 (1994), and Jay Clayton's detailed survey in "Narrative and Theories of Desire," *Critical Inquiry* 16 (1989): 33–53.

49. Mosco Carner, *Puccini: A Critical Biography*, 2d ed. (London: Duckworth, 1974), 258, where he is writing of *verismo* opera's "uninhibited inflation of every dramatic and emotional moment": "Characters are presented over-life-size and are swept along in a whirlwind of passions in which sex becomes the driving force. Erotic desire is always thwarted and thus leads to acts of insensate jealousy and savage revenge." See also Peter Conrad, *Song*, 13, where he calls opera the realm of "emotional atavism," the "empire of irresistible, coercive impulse," where the libido rules. His chapter "Eros" (42–54) ex-

pands on this hedonistic, sensual drive in opera. Realist opera, he argues, is the domain of "pathological desire" (191).

50. See Julien S. Murphy, "The AIDS Epidemic: A Phenomenological Analysis of the Infectious Body," in *The Meaning of AIDS: Implications for Medical Science, Clinical Practice, and Public Health Policy*, ed. Eric T. Juengst and Barbara A. Koenig (New York: Praeger, 1989), 55; Brian Inglis, *The Diseases of Civilization* (London: Hodder and Stoughton, 1981), 150; Owsei Temkin, *"The Double Face of Janus" and Other Essays in the History of Medicine* (Baltimore: Johns Hopkins University Press, 1977), 460.

51. See Giovanni Boccaccio, *Il Decamerone* (1353; Milano: Ulrico Hoepli, 1965), 5–12. The operetta *Boccaccio* by Franz Suppé/F. Zell and Richard Genée omits the plague frame completely and concentrates on the stories of amorous intrigue told by the young people.

52. For an extended analysis, see David Steele, "Plague Writing: From Boccaccio to Camus," *Journal of European Studies* 11 (1981): 88–110.

53. George Deaux, *The Black Death 1347* (London: Hamish Hamilton, 1969), 6.

54. Günter B. Risse, "Epidemics and History: Ecological Perspectives and Social Responses," in Fee and Fox, *AIDS: The Burdens of History*, 40; Johannes Hohl, *The Black Death: A Chronicle of the Plague*, trans. C. H. Clarke (London: Allen and Unwin, 1926), chapter 8, "Persecution of the Jews," 181–206; Deaux, *Black Death*, 22.

55. Paul Slack, *The Impact of Plague in Tudor and Stuart England* (London: Routledge and Kegan Paul, 1985), 3.

56. Murphy, "AIDS Epidemic," 52.

57. René Girard, "The Plague in Literature and Myth," *Texas Studies in Literature and Language* 15, 5 (1974): 846.

58. Igor Stravinsky, cited in Roman Vlad, *Stravinsky*, trans. Frederick Fuller, 3d ed. (Oxford: Oxford University Press, 1978), 113.

59. Stravinsky, in Robert Craft, ed., *Stravinsky: Selected Correspondence* (London: Faber and Faber, 1982), 1:94.

60. See Eric Walter White, *Stravinsky: The Composer and His Works*, 2d ed. (Berkeley: University of California Press, 1979), 329.

61. Conrad, *Song*, 76.

62. Stephen Walsh, *Stravinsky: Oedipus Rex* (Cambridge: Cambridge University Press, 1993), 34.

63. Gilman, *Disease and Representation*, 7; Elizabeth Fee, "Sin versus Science: Venereal Disease in Twentieth-Century Baltimore," in Fee and Fox, *AIDS: The Burdens of History*, 121.

64. There has recently been considerable interest in the intersection of medicine and opera, though most of it is on the level of thematic concerns (doctor figures in opera) or the causes of death of either composers or famous

singers. See, for a particularly germane example, the special issue of the *Tribuna Médica: Revista Latinoamericana de Educación Médica Continuada* 88, 6 (December 1993). On the relation of music to medicine and the idea of music's therapeutic functions, see A. Markoff, *La Musique, les musiciens, la fonction musicale: Essai thérapeutique, anthropologique, anatomo-clinique* (Toulouse: Université de Toulouse, 1937); Erhard Völkel, *Die spekulative Musiktherapie zur Zeit der Romantik: Ihre Tradition und ihr Fortwirken* (Düsseldorf: Triltsch, 1979); Raoul Blondel, *Propos variés de musique et de médecine* (Paris: Editions d'Art et de Médecine, n.d.); Simin Baradaran-Chassemi, *"Der musikalische Arzt" von Peter Lichtenthal* (Düsseldorf: Medizinischen Akademie, 1965); Dorothy M. Schullian and Max Schön, eds., *Music and Medicine* (New York: Henry Schuman, 1948).

65. Jacques Vallin, "Mortality in Europe from 1720–1914: Long Term Trends and Changes in Patterns by Age and Sex," in *The Decline of Mortality in Europe*, ed. R. Schofield, D. Reher, and A. Bideau (Oxford: Clarendon, 1991), 43. See too James C. Riley, *Sickness, Recovery and Death: A History and Forecast of Ill Health* (London: Macmillan, 1989), 159, on the post-1850 statistical trend toward recovery: "The proportion of sickness episodes resolved in death in the short run declined, and the quantity of sickness, especially protracted sickness, increased at every age."

66. William H. McNeill, *Plagues and Peoples* (Garden City: Anchor/Doubleday, 1976), 261.

67. Abdul R. Omran, "Epidemiologic Transition in the U.S.," *Population Bulletin* (Population Reference Bureau, Washington DC) 32, 2 (1977): 9.

68. Graziella Caselli, "Health Transition and Cause-Specific Mortality," in Schofield, Reher, and Bideau, *Decline of Mortality in Europe*, 79.

69. Gilman, *Disease and Representation*, 2.

70. Robert S. Gottfried, *The Black Death: Natural and Human Disaster in Medieval Europe* (London: Robert Hale, 1983), 77.

71. Slack, *Impact of Plague in Tudor and Stuart England*, 17–19. See also Randolph Starn, "Foreword to the English-Language Edition," in Giulia Calvi, *Histories of a Plague Year: The Social and the Imaginary in Baroque Florence*, trans. Dario Biocca and Bryant T. Ragan Jr. (Berkeley: University of California Press, 1989), x.

72. Cecilia C. Mettler, *History of Medicine* (Philadelphia: Blakiston, 1947), 424.

73. Rosenberg, "Disease and Social Order in America," 20.

74. Randall M. Packard, *White Plague, Black Labor: Tuberculosis and the Political Economy of Health and Disease in South Africa* (Berkeley: University of California Press, 1989), xix.

75. Susan Sontag, *Illness as Metaphor* (New York: Farrar, Straus and Giroux, 1978); see also Pierre Guillaume, *Du Désespoir au salut: Les Tuberculeux aux 19e et 20e siècles* (Paris: Aubier, 1986), 97.

76. Jean Delumeau and Yves Lequin, eds., *Les Malheurs des temps: Histoire des fléaux et des calamités en France* (Paris: Larousse, 1987), 426.

77. For a typical, if rather ironic, late nineteenth-century view of syphilis, see F. Buret, *Syphilis in Ancient and Prehistoric Times*, trans. A. H. Ohmann-Dumesnil (Philadelphia: F. A. Davis, 1891), 210: "Syphilis, the daughter of Prostitution, was born as soon as Commerce, chasing Love, presided over the exchange of caresses. The venereal virus must have marked the first step of the human race on the highway of civilization."

78. Laura Engelstein, "Syphilis, Historical and Actual: Cultural Geography of a Disease," *Reviews of Infectious Diseases* 8, 6 (1986): 1037.

79. Girard, "Plague in Literature and Myth," 834.

80. See Frank Mort, *Dangerous Sexualities: Medico-moral Politics in England since 1830* (New York: Routledge and Kegan Paul, 1987); Alan M. Kraut, *Silent Travelers: Germs, Genes, and the "Immigrant Menace"* (New York: Basic Books, 1994), 33–37, shows how the cholera epidemics in the United States fed into religious and ethnic prejudices as well as class ones, with the scapegoating of the Irish Catholic poor.

81. Lindenberger, *Opera*, 65.

82. Gilman, *Disease and Representation*, 4.

83. See Virginia Berridge, "AIDS and Contemporary History," in Berridge and Strong, *AIDS and Contemporary History*, 2.

84. Rosenberg, "Disease and Social Order in America," 28.

2. Famous Last Breaths

1. See R. T. H. Laënnec, *A Treatise on the Diseases of the Chest and on Mediate Ausculta-tion*, trans. John Forbes (1819; New York, 1838).

2. E. T. A. Hoffmann, "Rat Krespel," in *Meistererzählungen* (Zürich: Manesse, 1948), 81. Subsequent references are to this edition.

3. On the adaptation see P. Walter Jacob, *Jacques Offenbach in Selbstzeugnissen und Bilddokumenten* (Reinbeck bei Hamburg: Rowohlt, 1969), and Louis Schneider, *Offenbach* (Paris: Perrin, 1923), 225–26. On the play's reception, see Claude Dufresne, *Offenbach, ou La Gaîté parisienne* (Paris: Criterion, 1992), 276–77. On Offenbach's manifest interest in the topic, see Alexander Faris, *Jacques Offenbach* (London: Faber and Faber, 1980), 196.

4. There are major difficulties in deciding which text to use to study both the music and the libretto, since Offenbach died four months before the first performance, leaving it not quite finished. Ernest Guirand rearranged it, cutting one act completely; others added music and incidents. After the Second World War, new manuscript evidence has led to yet other versions. In short, there is no "definitive" text of this opera. We have used the 1881 version, published in Paris by Calmann Lévy. On the disputed order of the

three stories, see David Rissin, *Offenbach, ou Le Rire en musique* (Paris: Fayard, 1980), 330, who argues that Antonia should be the third, the buildup to tragedy, after which only the love of the Muse can remain.

5. Faris, *Jacques Offenbach*, 213.

6. On the "restored" text (based on manuscripts found by Antonio Almeida), see Bruce Alan Brown, "*Contes d'Hoffmann*," entry in *The New Grove Dictionary of Opera*, ed. Stanley Sadie (London: Macmillan, 1992), 1:925.

7. On the emotional tension of the scene, see Faris, *Jacques Offenbach*, 214, and Edouard Hanslick in *Jacques Offenbach, "Hoffmanns Erzählungen": Texte, Materialien, Kommentare*, ed. Attila Csampai and Dieter Holland (Reinbeck bei Hamburg: Rowoht, 1984), 241.

8. For discussions on the theory of tuberculosis and physical chest types, see F. B. Smith, *The Retreat of Tuberculosis, 1850–1950* (London: Croom Helm, 1988), 26; René Dubos and Jean Dubos, *The White Plague: Tuberculosis, Man, and Society* (1952; rpt. New Brunswick: Rutgers University Press, 1987), 123.

9. Gabrielle Brandstetter, "Die Stimme und das Instrument Mesmerismus als Poetik, in E. T. A. Hoffmanns 'Rat Krespel,'" in *Jacques Offenbachs "Hoffmanns Erzählungen": Konzeption, Rezeption, Dokumentation*, ed. Gabrielle Brandstetter (Laaber: Laaber Verlag, 1988), 21–29, argues the case for functional illness (i.e., with a psychological or situational, but not physical cause) from the E. T. A. Hoffmann source text rather than from the opera. According to this interpretation, the father-daughter relationship is one of patriarchal power: it is Krespel who first articulates Antonie's illness (the doctor merely corroborates his diagnosis) and who repeatedly makes the connection between the symptoms and the danger to her life. Antonie's mysterious illness might thus result from a situational double bind: she is caught between the demands of art and bourgeois life, but any choice is made impossible by incestuous love: the daughter Antonie replaces the difficult wife Angela, not as repetition but as final fulfillment of Krespel's desire. In short, Krespel invents her illness and silencing to keep her with him, to prevent her both from singing on the stage and from being married. That her singing cannot be fatal, it might be argued, is clear from the fact that in the story she collapses when Krespel forces her to say farewell forever to her fiancé—not when they sing together for the last time—and from the text's evidence that she dies without singing at all. Krespel simply imagines it in a dream. Although such an interpretation is in some ways convincing, it cannot account for her actual death: even if it was believed in the nineteenth century that death from strong emotions was a possibility, double binds rarely strangle. Such a reading also applies only to the literary version of the tale; in the opera, although paternal love is clearly important, its power is displaced. The demonic action and even

images of the source text are transferred from Krespel to a new character, Dr. Miracle.

10. In this reading Dr. Miracle would be a demonic external image not of patriarchal power but of Antonia's own inner desires. After all, she does ask who will save her from the demon that is herself: "Qui me sauvera du démon, de moi-même." Here Antonia would be the emblematic figure of the hysteric and artist. Caught between what Freudian psychology might call instinct and sublimation, she is also trapped into making a choice between love and art, desire and discipline and, thanks to Crespel, sexuality and celibacy. Hers is the situation of the dependent female trapped by male power, as analyzed in general terms in Michel Foucault's work (in *The History of Sexuality*) on the "hystericization" of the female body, saturated with sexuality, in the nineteenth century. Antonia too has been "pathologized" through medical practices and "socialized" through family dynamics, as Foucault might have argued. The voice of the mother offers her both power and professional wish fulfillment, but it too is under the obvious control of the male. Dr. Miracle is thus merely the continuation of the power of the bourgeois male, seen earlier in Crespel and then in Hoffmann—who both forbid her to sing in the name of her health. Antonia acutely had noted that her lover had become her father's accomplice. But this view of Antonia as hysteric still cannot account for her death. See Gerhard Heumann, "Der Erzählakt als Oper: Jules Barbier-Michel Carré, Drama und Libretto 'Les Contes d'Hoffmann,'" in Brandstetter, *Jacques Offenbachs "Hoffmanns Erzählungen,"* 74–87 especially.

11. Cardiac disease—in particular a narrowing of the mitral valve of the heart (mitral stenosis)—could also account for her red cheeks ("mitral facies") and her rapid and irregular pulse (implying atrial fibrillation).

12. See Smith, *Retreat of Tuberculosis,* 98.

13. Thomas Bartlett, *Consumption: Its Causes, Prevention and Cure* (London: Baillière, 1855), 17.

14. Susan Sontag, *Illness as Metaphor* (New York: Farrar, Straus and Giroux, 1978), 13.

15. A heart condition like mitral stenosis, however, is acquired, and the other cardiac possibilities that *are* hereditary fail to account for her physical appearance. See L. G. Dauber, "Death in Opera: A Case Study, *Tales of Hoffmann*—Antonia," *American Journal of Cardiology* 70, 7 (1992): 838–40. It has also been suggested that Mimì suffers from mitral stenosis. See John Collee, "Music and the Myocardium," *Cardiovascular Research* 27 (1993): 2087–88.

16. Reginald E. Thompson, *The Different Aspects of Family Phthisis in Relation Especially to Heredity and Life Assurance* (London: Smith, Elder, 1884), 13: "From an early period in the history of medicine, physicians have held the opinion that consumption is hereditary"; H. Lebert, *Traité clinique et pratique de la phthisie*

pulmonaire et des maladies tuberculeuses des divers organes (Paris: Delahaye, 1879), 35: "Cette hérédité engendre une constitution faible"; Jean-Louis-Simon Joly, *De la Phthisie pulmonaire et de sa curabilité* (Paris: Ballière, 1881), 42: "L'hérédité de la phthisie pulmonaire est manifeste: elle est démontrée par un nombre considérable de traits, et l'on peut dire que la plupart des enfants nés de parents phthisiques sont emportés un jour ou l'autre par la tuberculose"; William Heberden, *Commentaries on the History and Cure of Diseases* (1802; rpt Birmingham: Classics of Medicine Library, Gryphon, 1982), 377: "Persons most subject to pulmonary phthisis are those who are born of consumptive parents." See also Wilhelm Loeffler, "Rückblick auf die Therapie," in *Handbuch der Tuberkulose*, ed. J. Klein, H. Kleinschmidt, and E. Uehlinger (Stuttgart: Thieme, 1958), 50–54, and Charles Coury, *Grandeur et déclin d'une maladie: La Tuberculose au cours des âges* (Suresnes: Lepetit, 1972), 168–70, on the heredity arguments.

17. Bartlett, *Consumption*, 2. The quotation following this is from p.11.

18. Isabelle Grellet and Caroline Kruse, *Histoires de la tuberculose: Les Fièvres de l'âme 1800–1940* (Paris: Ramsay, 1983), 53; J. Ruffié and J.-C. Sournia, *Les Epidémies dans l'histoire de l'homme* (Paris: Flammarion, 1984), 166.

19. Theophilus Thompson, *Clinical Lectures on Pulmonary Consumption* (London: John Churchill, 1863), 175.

20. Selman A. Waksman, *The Conquest of Tuberculosis* (Berkeley: University of California Press, 1964), 29. Dubos and Dubos suggest that among the other possible "substances" that might have influenced some of the artists was the opium used in treatment of consumption "to quiet cough and diarrhea and to ease mental anguish" (*White Plague*, 63). On the association of artistic genius and tuberculosis, see Lewis J. Moorman, *Tuberculosis and Genius* (Chicago: University of Chicago Press, 1940); on the questioning of this association, see Harley Williams, *Requiem for a Great Killer: The Story of Tuberculosis* (London: Health Horizon, 1973), 27, and Andrew Nikiforuk, *The Fourth Horseman: A Short History of Epidemics, Plagues, Famine and Other Scourges* (Toronto: Viking, 1991), 129.

21. Siegfried Kracauer, *Orpheus in Paris: Offenbach and the Paris of His Time*, trans. Gwenda David and Eric Mosbacher (New York: Knopf, 1938), 355.

22. The quotation is from Kracauer, *Orpheus in Paris*, 346. He also claims that Meilhac, Halévy and Wolff, when visiting, would "often hear tunes from *The Tales of Hoffmann* floating upstairs, mixed with terrible attacks of coughing" (358). Dr. Harriet Rhys-Davies, in "Cause of Offenbach's Death—a Medical Comment," printed in Faris, *Jacques Offenbach*, 233, agrees that he had tuberculosis but is not convinced that he died of it.

23. See Alain Décaus, *Offenbach: Roi du Second Empire* (Paris: Librairie Académique Perrin, 1966), 244 and 257.

24. Nevertheless, various critical sources do assume (and mention only in passing) that Antonia is tubercular. See the *Oxford Dictionary of Opera*, ed. John Warrack and Ewan West (Oxford: Oxford University Press, 1992), 155; Peter Conrad, in *A Song of Love and Death: The Meaning of Opera* (New York: Poseidon, 1987), 26; and Julian Budden, in his discussion of *La Traviata* in *The Operas of Verdi: From "Il Trovatore" to "La Forza del Destino"* (London: Cassell, 1978), 121.

25. Richard Payne Cotton, *The Nature, Symptoms and Treatment of Consumption* (London: John Churchill, 1852), 70.

26. Smith, *Retreat of Tuberculosis*, 26.

27. Sontag, *Illness as Metaphor*, 13. Her "still is" here is supported by Smith's contention that even in the 1930s and 1940s people in sanatoriums talked mostly about sex and disease: women spoke "about the men and TB" and men about "sex and TB" (*Retreat of Tuberculosis*, 119).

28. Dubos and Dubos, *White Plague*, 9.

29. See Leopoldo Cortejoso, "Realismo ed espressionismo nella rappresentazione artistica della tubercolosi," *Castalia* 21 (1965): 153. Wilhelm Roloff's *Tuberkuloselexikon* (1949) still lists this as part of a *medical* description; see Vera Pohland, "From Positive-Stigma to Negative-Stigma: A Shift of the Literary and Medical Representation of Consumption in German Culture," in *Disease and Medicine in Modern German Culture*, ed. Rudolf Käser and Vera Pohland, *Cornell Studies in International Affairs, Western Societies Papers*, no. 30 (1990): 148.

30. Sontag, *Illness as Metaphor*, 25 and 26.

31. Cited in Moorman, *Tuberculosis and Genius*, x. See also Gérard Briche, "Entre Phthisie et tuberculose: L'Ecriture de Jules Laforgue," *Revue des Sciences Humaines* 79, 208 (1987): 145.

32. In her recent study *Living in the Shadow of Death: Tuberculosis and the Social Experience of Illness in American History* (New York: Basic Books, 1994), Sheila M. Rothman claims the disease was known as consumption before 1882 and tuberculosis after that; but in fact "consumption" continued to be used afterward, and "tuberculosis" was first coined as a term for the disease in 1839 by Schönlein. Although correct in pointing out the different cultural associations with the two words, she is again not accurate in her derivation of the word *tuberculosis*. Consumption is indeed associated with its dramatic symbol, the body being consumed (16), but tuberculosis was not named after *Mycobacterium tuberculosis*, the bacillus that could be viewed only under a microscope at a distance (160); the reverse was true. The 1839 designation had been derived from the Latin *tuberculum*, meaning "small growth," a term that had been in common use since at least the sixteenth century.

33. Dubos and Dubos, *White Plague*, 102. See especially F. Loeffler, "Zum 25 Jährigen Gedenktage der Entdeckung des Tuberkelbacillus," *Deutsche Medizinische*

Wochenschrift 33 (1907): 449–51, on the excitement felt by the audience who heard Koch's lecture. The published version, "Die Ätiologie der Tuberkulose," appeared on 10 April in the *Berliner Klinische Wochenschrift* 19 (1882): 221–30. Appropriately, it began by citing previous evidence of the transmissibility of tuberculosis.

34. See Thomas D. Brock, *Robert Koch: A Life in Medicine and Bacteriology* (Berlin: Springer-Verlag, 1988), 132, and Williams, *Requiem*, 30: "The news of Robert Koch's discovery spread quickly over the world in medical journals and was a message of hope for every consumptive patient. Within two or three weeks it was reported in *The New York World*." See *Lancet* 1 (22 April 1882): 655–56; 1 (29 April 1882): 694–95, and 1 (24 June 1882): 1041–43; and William Pirrie's "Address on the Infectiveness of Tubercle with Special Reference to Tubercular Consumption," *Lancet* 2 (5 August 1882): 171–73.

35. W. Watson Cheyne, "Report to the Association for the Advancement of Medicine by Research on the Relation of Micro-organisms to Tuberculosis," *Practitioner*, April 1883, 243. Clearly, though Smith argues that "general acceptance of germ causation of tuberculosis by infection did not come in Britain until after 1890" (*Retreat of Tuberculosis*, 49), there is evidence of extensive discussion of Koch's discovery, to the point, as Brock states, that "despite a few exceptions, his work was rapidly accepted" (*Robert Koch*, 132). In fact, by 1890 G. A. Heron, *Evidences of the Communicability of Consumption* (London: Longmans, Green, 1890), 3, writes: "No doubt, the bulk of the medical profession today believe[s] that tubercular disease is caused by a living organism, and that organism is Koch's bacillus of tubercle."

36. From the *British Medical Journal*, 22 November 1890, as cited in Brock, *Robert Koch*, 196.

37. See Alberto Vedrani, *Le più belle pagine di storia della medicina* (Genova: Scientia Veterum, 1963), 145–47, on the work of Augusto Murri on the consequences of Koch's discovery and the impact of his textbooks in Italy; Vicenzo Busacchi, *Storia della medicina* (Bologna: Patron, 1973), on the earlier but related biological research by Spallanzani, Bassi, Acerbi, and others (263–64), as well as Forlanini's 1882 advocating of pneumothorax as treatment (284); Arturo Castiglioni, *Storia della tubercolosi* (Milano: Vallardi, 1931), 54–55, on the early research of Luciano Armanni in his *Sulla specificità e virulenze delle sostanze caseose e tubercolose* (1872); C. Fossati, "Cenni sulla storia della tubercolosi," *Atti del XVI Congresso Nazionale di Storia della Medicina (Bologna-Ravenna)*, May 1959, 321–24 and Ercole Vittorio Ferraro, "Il problema della tubercolosi nel secolo XIX," *Castalia* 18, 1 (1962): 16, on the importance of the work of other Italian scientists.

38. Arturo Castiglioni, *Italian Medicine*, trans. E. B. Krumbhaar (New York: Hoeber, 1932), 75.

39. See Giorgio Cosmacini, *Storia della medicina e della sanità in Italia: Dalla peste europea alla guerra mondiale, 1328–1918* (Roma: Laterza, 1987), 362; with the 1885 work of Angelo Celli, *Igiene della tubercolosi secondo le moderne concezioni etiologiche*, Koch's discovery became part of the "patrimonio acquisito della scienze medica italiana." On the translation of Koch's work, see Arnaldo Cherubini and Francesca Vannozzi, *Previdenze di malattia e malattie sociali dall'unità alla prima guerra mondiale* (Perugia: Istituto Italiano di Medicina Sociale, 1990), 103.

40. Statisticians and analysts are careful to point out the limitations of these data because of the various names under which tuberculosis was recorded ("tisi, etisia, tisi tubercolare, tubercolosi, tabe, tabe polmonare, cachessia, consunzione, atrofia, bronchite cronica o lente, caseosi polmonare, broncopneumonite caseosa, bronco-alveaolite cronica, granulosi") and because not all deaths (especially those of the lower classes) would have been recorded. See Chiara Borro Saporiti, "L'endemia tubercolare nel secolo XIX: Ipotesi per ripensare un mito," in *Storia d'Italia*, vol. 7, *Malattia e medicina*, ed. Ranco Della Peruta (Torino: Einaudi, 1984), 846–50.

41. Budden, *Operas of Verdi*, 128. See also Denis Arnold, "'La Traviata': From Real Life to Opera," in *La Traviata* (London: John Calder; New York: Riverrun, 1981), 19.

42. Arnold, "'La Traviata,'" 19.

43. See Dubos and Dubos, *White Plague*, 198: "Since tuberculosis was then almost exclusively an urban disease, there was ground for the universal belief that susceptibility to it was increased by the artificialities of city life." And of course the first sanatorium opens, in the country, in 1859. See also Grellet and Kruse, *Histoires de la tuberculose*, 75 ff., on the city as dangerous, especially after the 1830s cholera epidemics.

44. Alexandre Parent-Duchâtelet, *De la Prostitution dans la ville de Paris*, 2d ed. (1836; Paris: Ballière, 1837), 1:176.

45. Charles Bernheimer, *Figures of Ill Repute: Representing Prostitution in Nineteenth-Century France* (Cambridge: Harvard University Press, 1989), 27. See also Jann Matlock, *Scenes of Seduction: Prostitution, Hysteria, and Reading Difference in Nineteenth-Century France* (New York: Columbia University Press, 1994), 106–12, on the Dumas text and contemporary economic and political conditions that determined the views of courtesans and their threat to the family fortune as well as the individual's health.

46. See Allan C. Barnes, "La Traviata," *Journal of the American Medical Association* 208 (1969): 93: "Physicians were often the custodians of disease processes, rather than the master of diseases."

47. Budden, *Operas of Verdi*, 157.

48. Conrad, *Song of Love and Death*, 155.

49. In "Genre and Content in Mid-century Verdi: 'Addio, del Passato' (La Traviata, act III)," Cambridge Opera Journal 1, 3 (1989): 259, James A. Hepokoski wonders (in parentheses) if this echo was intended and if Germont is meant to be "the voice of conscience, natural simplicity and so on." There are other more sinister — and obvious — ways to interpret this echo, however.

50. Hepokoski, "Genre and Content," 269.

51. Arnold, "'La Traviata,'" 28.

52. Superintendent Durborow, Annual Report of the Philadelphia Protestant Episcopal City Mission 18 (1888): 28; quoted in Barbara Bates, Bargaining for Life: A Social History of Tuberculosis, 1876–1937 (Philadelphia: University of Pennsylvania Press, 1992), 68. See too Cotton, Nature, Symptoms and Treatment of Consumption, 233: "Mental life which, in bidding adieu to this world, sometimes presents a brilliancy which, however transient, is sometimes usefully employed by the dying, and thankfully remembered by the living"; Bartlett, Consumption, 19: "It has repeatedly been noticed that patients have been hopeful of cure but a short time before dissolution, and when recovery was obviously an impossibility." See also Waksman, Conquest of Tuberculosis, 43, citing Moorman and also Jeannette Marks, Genius and Disaster (New York: Adelphi, 1925).

53. Charles Osborne, The Complete Operas of Verdi (London: Gollancz, 1969), 276.

54. Budden, Operas of Verdi, 162–63.

55. La Dame aux camélias (Paris: Calmann-Lévy, n.d.). Subsequent references are to this edition.

56. See April FitzLyon, "Alexandre Dumas the Younger and 'La Dame aux Camélias,'" in La Traviata, 29, and Arnold, "'La Traviata,'" 17.

57. Cited in Budden, Operas of Verdi, 118. See also Barnes, "'La Traviata,'" 93.

58. Rothman, Living in the Shadow, 8.

59. La Dame aux camélias, pièce en cinq actes, mêlée de chants (Bruxelles: J.-A. Lelong, 1852), 132. Subsequent references are to this edition.

60. Sontag, Illness as Metaphor, 63.

61. Catherine Clément, Opera, or The Undoing of Women, trans. Betsy Wing (London: Virago, 1989), 62 and 64. See also Gerrit J. Fonk, "Le Drame aux camélias," in Littérature et opéra, ed. Philippe Berthier and Kurt Ringger, Colloque de Cerisy, 1985 (Grenoble: Presses Universitaires de Grenoble, 1987), 93.

62. Respectively, Elizabeth Wilson, "Bohemians, Grisettes and Demi-mondaines," in Violetta and Her Sisters: The Lady of the Camellias, Responses to the Myth, ed. Nicholas John (London: Faber and Faber, 1994), 29; and in the same volume, Naomi Segal, "Our Lady of the Flowers," 164.

63. See, for a longer discussion, Jean Sgard, "Manon avec ou sans camélias," in Berthier and Ringger, Littérature et opéra, 84–85.

64. This is from his review of the 1897 Vienna premiere, translated and cited

in Arthur Groos and Roger Parker, *Giacomo Puccini: "La Bohème"* (Cambridge: Cambridge University Press, 1986), 133. The next two quotations are from p. 134.

65. Camille Bellaigue, in the *Revue des Deux Mondes* in 1898, cited in Groos and Parker, *Giacomo Puccini*, 136.

66. Henry Murger, *Scènes de la vie de bohème* (Paris: Calmann Lévy, 1884). Subsequent references are to this edition. Puccini, because of competition with Leoncavallo, who was also writing on this theme at the same time, inquired about getting unique copyright. He discovered that the novel was free (Murger had died without heirs) but the play was still under copyright. See Groos and Parker, *Giacomo Puccini*, 33. On the condensations and transpositions, see Gaston Knosp, *G. Puccini* (Bruxelles: Schott, 1937), 67–70.

67. Jerrold Seigel, "The Rise of Bohemia," in Groos and Parker, *Giacomo Puccini*, 4.

68. For details see Mosco Carner, *Puccini: A Critical Biography*, 2d ed. (London: Duckworth, 1974), 329–32.

69. Cherubini and Vannozzi, *Previdenze di malattie*, 113, cite many Italian newspaper articles at the time about these problems of industrialization. On textile workers, see Cosmacini, *Storia della medicina*, 356. On nutrition, see Saporiti, "L'endemia," 874, on the results of the increase in food prices and the lack of increase in wages in the 1880s in northern Italian cities. On housing, see Cherubini and Vannozzi again, 112; Dubos and Dubos, *White Plague*, 140; Smith, *Retreat of Tuberculosis*, 168. On tuberculosis and poverty in general, see again Smith, 19. Of course if poverty begot the disease, as Smith says (13) and as we mentioned in the introduction, the disease continued to beget poverty. See Pohland, "From Positive-Stigma," 152, on tuberculosis as "rooted in the miserable hygienic conditions of the underclasses."

70. Bartlett, *Consumption*, 30.

71. See Ariane Thomalla, *Die 'femme fragile': Ein literarischer Frauentypus der Jahrhundertwende* (Düsseldorf: Literatur in der Gesellschaft, 1972).

72. Groos and Parker, *Giacomo Puccini*, 73. On the associations of "fanciulla," see p. 69.

73. See Dante del Fiorentino, *Immortal Bohemian: An Intimate Memoir of Giacomo Puccini* (New York: Prentice-Hall, 1952), 82. On the differences between the two Mimi characters in particular, and on the arguments between Illica and Puccini on this topic, see Howard Greenfeld, *Puccini: A Biography* (New York: Putnam's Sons, 1980), 85–86.

74. Clément, *Opera, or The Undoing of Women*, 86.

75. On the music here, see William Mann, "Puccini's La Bohème," in *Giacomo Puccini, "La Bohème,"* Metropolitan Opera Classics Library (Boston: Little, Brown, 1983), 10 and 18.

76. The two quotations are from Mann, "Puccini's *La Bohème*," 18, and Groos and Parker, *Giacomo Puccini*, 25. However, Marcello's verbose chiding of Rodolfo ("Collerico, lunatico, imbevuto / di pregiudizi, noioso, cocciuto!") is accompanied by a "sinister chromatic scale — the inevitable *topos* of jealousy, at least since Verdi's *Otello*" (Groos and Parker, 24).

77. Groos and Parker, *Giacomo Puccini*, 25. See also Mann, "Puccini's *La Bohème*," 19: "The continuation ('Una terribil tosse') brings back Puccini octaves and close harmony with claustrophobic oppressive sweetness (the smell of a chest ward in a hospital)."

78. See Ruffié and Sournia, *Les Épidémies*, 164–65.

79. Dubos and Dubos, *White Plague*, 29. Also of musical interest is that Paganini was turned out of a house in Naples in 1818 because of the landlord's concern about his consumption (31). George Sand related that she and Chopin were also evicted, with the owner demanding that they pay for the replastering of his house after their contamination of it (32). See also the editorial "The Contagiousness of Consumption from a Historical Point of View," *British Medical Journal*, 19 May 1900, 1259–60.

80. The rejected act is reprinted in the appendix to Groos and Parker, *Giacomo Puccini*, 152–81. For Puccini's insistence on Mimì's death as the most important focus, see his letters in Giuseppe Adami, ed., *Letters of Giacomo Puccini*, trans. Ena Makin (London: Harrap, 1931), 90, 91, 96–97. In the novel Mimi does die of consumption as well, having returned to Rodolphe in poverty with her "chest on fire" and the "corruption of death in her body" (308). Certain details of the opera's death scene are related to this version (selling the coat; sending for the doctor), but this Mimi dies in the hospital, alone. The opera plot also contains many details from the story (214–37) of the short, doomed love of the faithful Francine and her lover, Jacques: the extinguished candle, the fainting, the lost key, the muff to warm her hands, and of course her death by consumption as well. It is worth noting that, just as the more negative aspects of Murger's Mimi's personality are left behind in the opera, so too is Rodolfo's character less frivolous, fickle, and "expert" in his seduction — if no less jealous.

81. Groos and Parker, *Giacomo Puccini*, 28.

82. William Drabkin, "The Musical Language of *La Bohème*," in Groos and Parker, *Giacomo Puccini*, 87.

83. Drabkin, "The Musical Language," 95.

84. Groos and Parker, *Giacomo Puccini*, 30. On the use of the harp, see William Ashbrook, *The Operas of Puccini* (Oxford: Oxford University Press, 1985), 63.

85. Quoted and translated in Groos and Parker, *Giacomo Puccini*, 75.

86. Clément, *Opera, or The Undoing of Women*, 19.

87. Clément, *Opera, or The Undoing of Women*, 20.

88. Groos and Parker, *Giacomo Puccini*, 75.

89. See Pierre Guillaume, *Du Désespoir au salut: Les Tuberculeux aux 19e et 20e siècles* (Paris: Aubier, 1986), 9, 22, 81–82, on the literary presentation of tuberculosis, especially in France.

90. See Briche, "Entre Phthisie et tuberculose," 142; Pohland, "From Positive-Stigma," 153.

91. Quoted in Bates, *Bargaining for Life*, 57.

92. See, for instance, Bates, *Bargaining for Life*. Often there were protests against the presence of the sick in certain neighborhoods. See Godfrey L. Gale, *The Changing Years: The Story of Toronto Hospital and the Fight against Tuberculosis* (Toronto: University of Toronto Press for West Park Hospital, 1979), 9–10.

93. Thaddeus A. Browne, "The White Plague," in *"The White Plague" and Other Poems* (Toronto: William Briggs, 1909), 9 and 10.

94. On the link between the *femme fragile* and the femme fatale, see Carola Hilmes, *Die Femme Fatale: Ein Weiblichkeitstypus in der nachromantischen Literatur* (Stuttgart: J. B. Metzler, 1990), 28–30.

95. See Peter F. Barnes and Susan A. Barrows, "Tuberculosis in the 1990s," *Annals of Internal Medicine* 119 (1993): 400–410.

3. Syphilis, Suffering, and the Social Order

1. In 1845 Wagner read Wolfram's Parzifal and Titurel poems in the Simrock and San-Marte versions. See Barry Millington, "Parsifal," in *The New Grove Dictionary of Opera*, ed. Stanley Sadie (London: Macmillan, 1992), 3:890. On the Fisher King myths, see J. G. Frazer, *The Golden Bough: A Study in Magic and Religion*, abridged ed. (London: Macmillan, 1922), chapters 29–33, and Jesse L. Weston, *The Legend of Sir Perceval: Studies upon Its Origin, Development, and Position in the Arthurian Cycle* (London: David Nutt, 1906), 1:330–33. T. S. Eliot cites Verlaine's "Parsifal" poem in *The Waste Land* and refers his readers to Weston's work on the Fisher King in his infamous notes to the poem. At other points he also cites from others of Wagner's operas. See William Blissett, "Wagner in *The Waste Land*," in *The Practical Vision: Essays in English Literature in Honour of Flora Ray*, ed J. Campbell and J. Doyle (Waterloo: Wilfrid Laurier University Press, 1978), and Stoddart Martin, *Wagner to "The Waste Land": A Study of the Relationship of Wagner to English Literature* (London, 1982).

2. See Arthur Groos, "Appropriation in Wagner's *Tristan* Libretto," in *Reading Opera*, ed. Arthur Groos and Roger Parker (Princeton: Princeton University Press, 1988).

3. See M. Amelia Klenke, *Chrétien de Troyes and Le Conte del Graal: A Study of Sources and Symbolism* (Madrid: José Porrua Turanzas, Studia Humanitatis, 1981), 7–

22. On the javelin and the placing of the wound, see Leonardo Olschki, *The Grail Castle and Its Mysteries*, trans. J. A. Scott, ed. Eugene Vinaver (Manchester: Manchester University Press, 1966), 32, and C. Brunel, "Les Hanches du roi pêcheur," *Romania* 81 (1960): 37 ff, who notes that "parmi les hanches ambe-deus" was known to mean "genitalia" at the time.

4. Wolfram von Eschenbach, *Parzival*, trans. A. T. Hatto (London: Penguin, 1980), 244 and 241. The subsequent quotation is from p. 244.

5. See Dieter Borchmeyer, "Recapitulation of a Lifetime," in *Parsifal* (London: Calder; New York: Riverrun Press, 1986), 20, for classical echoes of Amfortas's wound that will not close (like Prometheus's) but is finally healed by the spear that caused it (Achilles healing Telephos). Other echoes are in Ovid's *Metamorphoses* 13.171–72; it is also a commonplace in the medieval rhetorical tradition and in lyrics—as in Petrarch's *Rime* 75.1–2, 159.12, 164.78. Our thanks to Rachel Jakoff for this information.

6. Carolyn Abbate, in "'Parsifal': Words and Music," in *Parsifal*, notes that all the stories in act 1 (Kundry's, Amfortas's, Titurel's, Klingsor's) "generate a temporal circle that will constantly and inevitably turn back to a single event. This event is Klingsor's wounding of Amfortas, a moment laden with mythic significance" (48). It is also laden, as we will argue, with meanings related to both social order and sexual illness.

7. See Mary A. Cicora, *"Parsifal" Reception in the "Bayreuther Blätter"* (New York: Peter Lang, 1987), 5; Lucy Beckett, *Richard Wagner: "Parsifal"* (Cambridge: Cambridge University Press, 1981), 103 ff.

8. Friedrich Nietzsche, *On the Genealogy of Morals*, trans. Walter Kaufmann (New York: Vintage, 1967), 100; see idem, *Ecce Homo*, trans. Walter Kaufmann (New York: Vintage, 1967), 288.

9. On art and religion, see Richard Wagner, "Religion und Kunst," *Bayreuther Blätter*, October 1880, in *Sämtliche Schriften und Dichtungen* (Leipzig, 1911–16), 10: 211–52.

10. Peter Conrad, in *A Song of Love and Death: The Meaning of Opera* (New York: Poseidon, 1987), puts the emphasis on the Easter setting and its connection to both the "pagan rite of spring and a Christian promise of resurrection" (185). Although the libretto does mention this, it is Parsifal himself who reminds us of the day of suffering that made it all possible.

11. See Byron Nelson, "Wagner, Schopenhauer, and Nietzsche: On the Value of Human Action," *Opera Quarterly* 6, 4 (1989): 30–31; Constantin Floros, "Studien zur Parsifal-Rezeption," in *Richard Wagner, Parsifal, Musik-Konzepte 25*, ed. Heinz-Klaus Metzger and Rainer Riehn (München: Text und Kritik, 1982), 17, 21–22.

12. See Cicora, *"Parsifal" Reception*, 75.

13. Eric Cassell, *The Nature of Suffering and the Goals of Medicine* (New York: Oxford University Press, 1991), especially chapter 3, "The Nature of Suffering."

14. Borchmeyer, "Recapitulation," 22: it is "an *imitatio perversa*" of Christ's wound.

15. Robin Holloway, "Experiencing Music and Imagery in 'Parsifal'" in *Parsifal*, 40.

16. Appia, the Swiss designer who influenced Wieland Wagner's conception of *Parsifal*, is cited in Beckett, *Richard Wagner: "Parsifal,"* 100.

17. See Frazer, *Golden Bough*, 56, on the idea of sympathetic magic and the relationship between the man and the weapon that wounds him.

18. Conrad, *Song of Love and Death*, 173. An interesting subtext in Thomas Mann's famous 1933 essay "The Sorrows and Grandeur of Richard Wagner" and in his 1951 review of the published letters of Wagner (both included in Thomas Mann, *Pro and Contra Wagner*, trans. Allan Blunden [London: Faber and Faber, 1985]) links disease to art in Wagner's own mind. Citing Wagner's letters about his nerves being "in an advanced state of decay" (114), Mann talks about what he calls "one of those medically indeterminate ailments" that plagued the composer, arguing that Wagner "does not omit to establish a causal connection between his suffering and his practice of art, viewing art and disease as one and the same affliction" (115).

19. Beckett, *Richard Wagner: "Parsifal,"* 25. The subsequent citations are from pp. 26 and 34.

20. The other adjective (besides "healing") that is used by musicologists to describe this music is, significantly, "chaste." Barry Millington notes that when Kundry kisses Parsifal, "by a clever twist of its tail, the theme associated with sorcery gradually reveals part of the chaste opening theme of the work" ("Parsifal," 894).

21. Arnold Whittall, "The Music," in Beckett, *Richard Wagner: "Parsifal,"* 70.

22. Mike Ashman, "A Very Human Epic," in *Parsifal*, 9–10. Peter Wapnewski further argues that "Wagner always suffered in a sense from Amfortas's wound. That is, he was never able to tame the sexual urge with socially approved norms" ("The Operas as Literary Works," in *Wagner Handbook*, ed. Ulrich Müller and Peter Wapnewski, trans. and ed. John Deathridge [Cambridge: Harvard University Press, 1992], 92). He goes on to suggest that Wagner's love for Judith Gautier at this time makes *Parsifal* into a kind of "purification exercise" whereby Wagner tried to "tame and chastise the strongest of urges, and to guard against its destructive potential" (93).

23. For an example of what happens in this fortunate condition of medical-cultural forgetfulness, see Barry Emslie, "Woman as Image and Narrative in Wagner's *Parsifal*: A Case Study," *Cambridge Opera Journal* 3, 2 (1991): 109–24. Here Amfortas's wound is seen as symbolic of feminizing menstrual "torment,"

that is, as periodic bleeding that can stop at the end because Amfortas's "virginity" has been recovered.

24. D. Zeissl, *Lehrbuch der Syphilis*, vol. 2 (Stuttgart: Enke, 1875), 230; current textbooks of dermatology agree with this description: see Harry Arnold Jr., Richard B. Odom, and William D. James, *Andrews' Diseases of the Skin: Clinical Dermatology*, 8th ed. (Philadelphia: Harcourt Brace Jovanovich and W. B. Saunders, 1990), 422.

25. See Claude Quétel, *History of Syphilis*, trans. Judith Braddock and Brian Pike (Cambridge: Polity, 1990), 57, for a summary of Fernel's findings.

26. This is Wynne-Finch's 1935 prose translation, cited in James Cleugh, *Secret Enemy: The Story of a Disease* (New York: Thames and Hudson, 1954), 66. See also Juan de Vigo's 1514 description as paraphrased by Quétel: "The patient experiences intense pains in his limbs and joints. A year or more later, purulent tumours appear, along with bone-like callosities which are so painful at night that they make the sufferer scream" (*History of Syphilis*, 26).

27. Alfred Fournier's commentary on Jean de Vigo, *Le Mal français*, trans. Alfred Fournier (Paris: Masson, 1872), here cited in the English translation by Wallace B. Hamby (St. Louis MO: Warren H. Green, 1979), 59, n.

28. Benedetto, quoted in Quétel, *History of Syphilis*, 10. This particular vision of the power of syphilis on the body persisted into the seventeenth century in the writings of "the British Hippocrates," Thomas Sydenham, *The Works of Thomas Sydenham*, M.D. (London: Sydenham Society, 1848), 2:281.

29. Sir William Osler, *The Principles and Practice of Medicine* (New York: D. Appleton, 1892), 169. See also, for a much earlier version of the same observation, Fracastorius, *De contagione* 1, quoted in Geoffrey Marks and William K. Beatty, *Epidemics* (New York: Scribner's Sons, 1976), 118.

30. Sander L. Gilman, *Difference and Pathology: Stereotypes of Sexuality, Race, and Madness* (Ithaca: Cornell University Press, 1985), 211.

31. See Owsei Temkin, *"The Double Face of Janus" and Other Essays in the History of Medicine* (Baltimore: Johns Hopkins University Press, 1977), 466–68.

32. The recent exhumation of a sixteenth-century Neapolitan mummy has shown that the woman (Maria d'Aragona) suffered from a syphilitic ulcer to which had been applied a balsam of vegetable filaments immersed in sulfur. See Gino Fornaciari et al., "Syphilis in a Renaissance Italian Mummy," *Lancet*, 9 September 1989, 614. On the Arab origins of mercury ointments, see Charles E. Winslow, *The Conquest of Epidemic Disease* (Princeton: Princeton University Press, 1944), 125.

33. At the risk of simplifying complex arguments, we present the three major rival theories of the origins of syphilis: it is an ancient disease, traceable through descriptions of genital afflictions in the texts of antiquity, and it is

therefore often linked to leprosy, a disease that declined as syphilis raged; it was brought to Europe by Columbus's sailors returning from the Americas in 1492; and according to a "unitarian" hypothesis, it was present in both Old and New Worlds with different manifestations that evolved over time depending on varying social and environmental factors. Since this last theory is more recent, articulated only in the 1960s, the terms of the debate in Germany in Wagner's time involved only the first two. For instance, see Friedrich Wilhelm Müller, *Die venerischen Krankheiten in Alterthum: Quällenmässige Erörterungen zur Geschichte der Syphilis* (Erlangen: Enke, 1873), and especially J. K. Proksch, *Die Geschichte der venerischen Krankheiten*, 2 vols. (Bonn: Peter Hanstein, 1895). Other summaries of the debates include E. Jeanselme, *Histoire de la syphilis* (Paris: G. Doin, 1931), 3–9; Richmond C. Holcomb and C. S. Butler, *Who Gave the World Syphilis? The Haitian Myth* (New York: Froben Press, 1937); J. R. Whitwell, *Syphilis in Earlier Days* (London: H. K. Lewis, 1940); William Allen Pusey, *The History and Epidemiology of Syphilis* (Springfield IL: Charles C Thomas, 1933), 5–13 especially. For a more recent and comprehensive overview of the issues and all three theories, see Brenda J. Baker and George J. Armelagos, "The Origin and Antiquity of Syphilis," *Current Anthropology* 29, 5 (1988): 703–20. See too Quétel's chapter, "A Much-Disputed Origin," in *History of Syphilis*, 33–49.

34. The first citation is from Parvi Rosaefontani, *Chronicon Johannis Regis Daniae* (1560), cited in Quétel, *History of Syphilis*, 16. The one from von Hutten was used as the epigraph to Oscar Panizza's "syphilis" tragedy, *The Council of Love* (1895), which will be discussed in the next chapter, and is also cited in Quétel, 45. Emperor Maximilian I's "Edict on the Sins against God" linked syphilis to blasphemy as well as sexual activity. See Rahel Hahn, "The Wood, the Word, and the Cure: Ulrich von Hutten's Self-Presentation as a Healed Syphilitic," in *Disease and Medicine in Modern German Culture*, ed. Rudolf Käser and Vera Pohland, *Cornell Studies in International Affairs, Western Societies Papers*, no. 30 (1990): 30.

35. See Temkin, "*Double Face*," 475, and Quétel, *History of Syphilis*, 54. See also Henry E. Sigerist, *Civilization and Disease* (Chicago: University of Chicago Press, 1943), 76. Consult Quétel, *History of Syphilis*, 59, for a fuller discussion of Béthencourt's 1527 *Nova penitentialis Quadragesima, nec non purgatorium in morbum Gallicum, sive venereum*.

36. Jean-Baptiste Lalli, *La Franceide, ou Le Mal français, poème burlesque* (1629), quoted and translated in Quétel, *History of Syphilis*, 74.

37. Ambroise Paré, *Workes*, trans. Th. Johnson (London, 1634), 724.

38. Greg W. Bentley, *Shakespeare and the New Disease: The Dramatic Function of Syphilis in "Troilus and Cressida," "Measure for Measure," and "Timon of Athens"* (New York: Peter Lang, 1989), 7.

39. Sigerist, *Civilization and Disease*, 78.

40. See L. Fleck, *Genesis and Development of a Scientific Fact* (1935; Chicago: University of Chicago Press, 1979) for a detailed discussion of the shift in medical theories from a concern for the astrological origins of syphilis to a move to consider it as an ethical-religious issue (of the "carnal scourge") and finally, by the nineteenth century, to seeing it as what he calls an empirical-therapeutic and an experimental-pathological disease.

41. Sigerist, *Civilization and Disease*, 77, and see further George L. Mosse, *Nationalism and Sexuality: Respectability and Abnormal Sexuality in Modern Europe* (New York: Fertig, 1985), 5 and 9. See also Elaine Showalter, "Syphilis, Sexuality, and Fiction of the Fin de Siècle," in *Sex, Politics, and Science in the Nineteenth-Century Novel*, ed. Ruth Bernard Yeazell (Baltimore: Johns Hopkins University Press, 1986), 89: "Whereas in the Renaissance, syphilis functioned as a religious symbol of the disease in the spirit, and during the Restoration became a political metaphor for the disease in the state, fin-de-siècle English culture treats it as a symbol of the disease in the family." Wagner's opera treats it as all three, in a kind of summa of these historically validated responses to syphilis.

42. Patrick Wald Lasowski, *Syphilis: Essai sur la littérature française du XIXe siècle* (Paris: Gallimard, 1982), 17; see Quétel, *History of Syphilis*, 127–30.

43. See Proksch, *Die Geschichte*, 2:765–881.

44. Showalter, "Syphilis," 92. For a contemporaneous American equivalent, see the (1830) venereal disease entry in *Gunn's Domestic Medicine: A Facsimile of the First Edition* (Knoxville: University of Tennessee Press, 1986), 260–61 especially.

45. Cited in Floros, "Studien," 18. It is also tempting to make a biographical link here between Amfortas and a real king—Ludwig II of Bavaria, Wagner's patron and the opera's first viewer. We thank Raymond Grant for providing the evidence about Ludwig as a possible syphilitic.

46. Holloway, "Experiencing Music," 32. For the tension-creating argument, see Ashman, "Very Human Epic," 13.

47. See Sir William Holdsworth, *A History of English Law* (Boston: Little, Brown, 1962), 8:347–49.

48. Baudelaire wrote admiringly to Wagner on 17 February 1860 (and his article on him appeared in the *Revue Européenne* in April 1861); Wagner was delighted to find in Baudelaire a man of "most extraordinary understanding." See Gerald D. Turbow, "Art and Politics: Wagnerism in France," in *Wagnerism in European Culture and Politics*, ed. David C. Large and William Weber (Ithaca: Cornell University Press, 1984), 144–45.

   See especially J.-K. Huysmans, *A Rebours*, published as *Against Nature*, trans. Robert Baldick (London: Penguin, 1959). Des Esseintes, a jaded youth, "had recourse to the perilous caresses of the professional virtuosos, but the only effect was to impair his health" (23). He admires Baudelaire for having "finally reached those districts of the soul where the monstrous *vegetations* of the *sick* mind flourish" (146; our emphasis). In chapter 8, Des Esseintes collects "monstrous" and "sickly" artificial-looking hothouse flowers that are described in terms of fleshy wounds, body parts and fluids: "Most of them, as if ravaged by syphilis or leprosy, displayed livid patches of flesh" (98). He realizes, looking at the "rotting flesh" of the blossoms, that "it all comes down to syphilis in the end" (101). His subsequent nightmare of what can be read as a congenital syphilitic woman, with whom he feels an "inexplicable yet undeniable liaison," and their flight from the apocalyptic horse-riding "image of the Pox" (103) fades into a vision of "the Flower"—his link between vegetation and virus (105)—toward which/whom he is irresistibly drawn despite his terror of the sexual "hideous flesh-wound of this plant" (106). As Charles Bernheimer notes in his *Figures of Ill Repute: Representing Prostitution in Nineteenth-Century France* (Cambridge: Harvard University Press, 1989), 246, this is an image of the castrating and castrated female sexual organs as flowers of evil, of woman as "diseased phallic flower."

Zola's prostitute heroine in *Nana* (1880) begins working in a workshop making artificial flowers—like Puccini's Mimì. As Bernheimer remarks, Nana does die of smallpox, but this can be read as a displacement or "sublimating pun": "Given Nana's promiscuity, it is not surprising that many readers remember her as dying from the pox, syphilis. The same wordplay is possible in French: 'la petite vérole' means smallpox; 'la grande vérole,' or simply 'la vérole,' means syphilis" (224). For plot purposes, Nana has to die more quickly than syphilis would have allowed, but the description of her is in terms of that disease, according to Sander L. Gilman in *Sexuality: An Illustrated History* (New York: John Wiley, 1989), 306. See also Jill Warren, "Zola's View of Prostitution in *Nana*," in *The Image of the Prostitute in Modern Literature*, ed. Pierre L. Horn and Mary Beth Pringle (New York: Ungar, 1984), 37.

49. The quotations are from Beckett, *Richard Wagner: Parsifal*, 38.

50. Theodor Adorno, *In Search of Wagner*, trans. Rodney Livingstone (London: Verso, 1981), 94 and 93–94. See also Emslie, "Woman as Image," 114: Kundry is called the "most splendid of whores in the most magical of brothels."

51. Whittall, "Music," 66.

52. Abbate, "'Parsifal,'" 52. There are other textual connections in the libretto too. For example, Parsifal is called the same thing—"Frevler,"wrongdoer— by both the knights (when he kills the swan) and the Maidens (when he injures their lovers). In both cases the word is repeated twice; both times, the groups seek some sort of revenge on him for his transgression.

53. Temkin, *"Double Face,"* 477. For the American perspective on syphilis and the

military in the two world wars, especially, see Allan M. Brandt, *No Magic Bullet: A Social History of Venereal Disease in the United States since 1880* (New York: Oxford University Press, 1985). The next chapter will examine more closely twentieth-century (and American) cultural and social constructions of syphilis.

54. David de Planis-Campy, *La Vérole reconnue, combattue et abattue sans suer et sans tenir chambre, avec tous les accidents, le tout selon l'ancienne et moderne médecine* . . . (Paris, 1623), quoted in Quétel, *History of Syphilis*, 44.

55. See Alfred Jay Bollet, *Plagues and Poxes: The Rise and Fall of Epidemic Disease* (New York: Demos, 1987), 9–10.

56. See Elizabeth Fee, "Venereal Disease: The Wages of Sin?" in *Passion and Power: Sexuality in History*, ed. Kathy Peiss and Christina Simmons with Robert A. Padgug (Philadelphia: Temple University Press, 1989), 179.

57. Klaus Theweleit, *Male Fantasies*, vol. 2, *Male Bodies: Psychoanalyzing the White Terror*, trans. Erica Carter and Chris Turner (Minneapolis: University of Minnesota Press, 1989), 17.

58. See Quétel, *History of Syphilis*, 6 and 230. See also Judith R. Walkowitz, *Prostitution and Victorian Society: Women, Class, and the State* (Cambridge: Cambridge University Press, 1980), 49, and Jeffery Weeks, *Sex, Politics and Society: The Regulation of Sexuality since 1800*, 2d ed. (New York: Longman, 1989), 85. The response in England was the Contagious Diseases Acts of the 1860s, which regulated prostitutes as the major source of the problem.

59. Cited in Temkin, *Double Face*, 478.

60. That the French decadents and symbolists were enraptured by what they saw as Wagner's sensual, even erotic, works is a matter of historical record, and proof of it includes the founding by Edouard Dujardin of the *Revue Wagnerienne* in 1885. See Richard Sieburth, "1885, February: The Music of the Future," in *A New History of French Literature*, ed. Denis Hollier (Cambridge: Harvard University Press, 1989), 789–98; Elaine Brody, "Wagner in France and France in Wagner," in her *Paris: The Musical Kaleidoscope, 1870–1925* (New York: Braziller, 1987); Walter Pache, "Ludwig II. von Bayern in der Literatur der europäische Dekadenz," *Jahrbuch der Universität Augsburg*, 1989, 226–30.

61. Robert W. Gutman, *Richard Wagner: The Man, His Mind, and His Music* (1968; rpt. New York: Harcourt Brace Jovanovich, 1990), 438; Showalter, "Syphilis," 99–101. See more generally Sander L. Gilman, *The Jew's Body* (New York: Routledge, 1991), on syphilophobia and the femme fatale's "vampiric power to control the male's rationality" (109). On vampirism and the fear of sexuality related to monstrosity, see Christopher Craft, "'Kiss Me with Those Red Lips': Gender and Inversion in Bram Stoker's *Dracula*," *Representations* 8 (1984): 107–33.

62. Gutman, *Richard Wagner*, 438; Showalter, "Syphilis," 88.

63. Mary Ann Doane, *Femmes Fatales: Feminism, Film Theory, Psychoanalysis* (New York: Routledge, 1991), 262.

64. Peter Gay, *The Bourgeois Experience: Victoria to Freud*, vol. 1, *Education of the Senses* (New York: Oxford University Press, 1984), 326. Although *Ghosts* and *Parsifal* are contemporaneous works, Ibsen's play was not translated into German until 1884.

65. Doane, *Femmes Fatales*, 263.

66. In *Critical Inquiry* 12, 1 (1985): 232 especially.

67. Gutman, *Richard Wagner*, 427; Paul Lawrence Rose, *Wagner: Race and Revolution* (New Haven: Yale University Press, 1992), 164. On the non-Christian woman as erotic "other," see David Biale, *Eros and the Jews: From Biblical Israel to Contemporary America* (New York: Basic Books, 1992).

68. On the link to the Wandering Jew, see Timothy P. Martin, "Joyce, Wagner, and the Wandering Jew," *Comparative Literature* 42, 1 (1990): 50. This stereotype of the mocking laughter is also related to Schopenhauer's notion of "Schadenfreude" in Beckett, *Richard Wagner: Parsifal*, 12. On Kundry's split identity, see Livia Bitton-Jackson, *Madonna or Courtesan? The Jewish Woman in Christian Literature* (New York: Seabury, 1982), 1. See too Gunther Jarfe, "Die Abdankung des Subjekts oder 'Die Schrecken der Liebe': Überlegungen zu Identitätsproblemen einiger Gestalten Richard Wagners," in *Die Modernisierung des Ich: Studien zur Subjektkonstitution in der Vor- und Frühmoderne*, ed. Manfred Pfister (Passau: Rothe, 1989), 215–16, on Kundry's split personality as appropriate in a world of either/or—that is, salvation/loss. Thomas Mann saw her split as part of her "mythical pathology" and thus her modernity. See Floros, "Studien," 34–35.

69. By 1888 Seidl had already read Kundry as representative of the Old Testament Jew versus Parsifal's New Testament Aryan German identity. See Floros, "Studien," 27. Gutman, in *Richard Wagner*, links the sexual relations of Kundry and Amfortas to "criminal miscegenation" and calls Klingsor's garden a symbol of Jewish luxury (427). Klingsor, like Beckmesser, is also read as Jewish in terms of the music (428). Rose calls Klingsor "in spirit a Jew" in his search for material power, like "those Germans who have surrendered to Judaism [and] have cut themselves off from the idealism of Germanness" (163). Wagner himself, however, linked Klingsor to the Jesuits (see Floros, "Studien," 31). Adorno saw the "glorified blood-brotherhood" of *Parsifal* as Nazilike (*In Search of Wagner*, 140), but it is worth recalling that the opera was not put on at Bayreuth from 1940 to 1944.

70. Marc A. Weiner, *Richard Wagner and the Anti-Semitic Imagination* (Lincoln: University of Nebraska Press, 1994).

71. Paracelsus, in *Sämtliche Werke*, ed. Karl Sudhoff (München: Otto Wilhelm Barth, 1923), 7:14–15, links Jews with supposed cures as well as causes of syphilis; Hitler's *Mein Kampf*, trans. Ralph Mannheim (Boston: Houghton Mifflin, 1943), 247, saw Jews and prostitutes as commercially exploitative and thus as causing plagues. See also Gilman, *Jew's Body*, 97–98; Edmond Bassereau, *Origine de la syphilis* (Paris: Ballière, 1873), 38–39; Heinrich Singer, *Allgemeine und spezielle Krankheitslehre der Juden* (Leipzig: Konegen, 1904); M. J. Guttmann, *Über den heutigen Stand der Rasse- und Krankheitsfrage der Juden* (München: Müller und Steinicke, 1920).

72. Gay, *Education*, 327. In the work of Lombroso and Weininger, among others, female degeneration and anti-Semitism were connected even more strongly (see Bernheimer, *Figures*, 260). See too Sue Zomka, "Wagner's Opera of Redemption: *Parsifal* at Bayreuth," *Criticism* 27, 3 (1985): 273–74 on racial impurity and Amfortas's sinful blood and redemption.

73. Writing about German *Freikorps* members not long after this, Theweleit, *Male Fantasies*, 2:16, notes: "'Syphilis' is *one name only* for the dissolution to which a man falls prey if he comes into contact with the external incarnation of his devouring, dead unconscious. But it is a particularly apposite name, a rich code, containing as it does the corrosions of femininity, Jewishness, epidemic disease, criminality . . . and emasculating death."

74. Rose, *Wagner*, 164. See also Anthony Arblaster, *Viva la Libertà: Politics in Opera* (New York: Verso, 1992), 187.

75. We are responding here, all too briefly, to Weiner's long and complex argument in chapter 2 of his *Richard Wagner and the Anti-Semitic Imagination*. In a related move, Michel Poizat, in *The Angel's Cry: Beyond the Pleasure Principle in Opera*, trans. Arthur Denner (Ithaca: Cornell University Press, 1992), 193–95, reads the opera in terms of the suffering Amfortas as tragic hero and sacrificed god because of his "clearly designated desire and [symbolic] castration."

76. Wagner merged Orgeluse, who seduced Anfortas and is loved and redeemed by Gawan, with Sigune and Cundrie. Of course there's not a little of Mary Magdalene and Circe in there too. That Wagner saw Wolfram primarily as a courtly love ~~poet and not a~~ poet of sexual passion might be inferred from his portrayal of Wolfram in his earlier opera *Tannhäuser*, as Volker Mertens suggests in "Wagner's Middle Ages," in Müller and Wapnewski, *Wagner Handbook*, 267.

77. Mann, *Pro and Contra Wagner*, 99. He links Wagner to Zola based on the "affinity of their minds, intentions and artistic resources" (93) as well as on the grounds of their shared "naturalism." He implicitly connects Kundry to Zola's Nana, that "Astarte of the French Second Empire" (93), also a prostitute, of course. See note 48, this chapter.

   In *Doktor Faustus* (*Doctor Faustus: The Life of the German Composer Adrian Lever-*

kühn as Told by a Friend, trans. H. T. Lowe-Parker [1947; Harmondsworth: Penguin, 1968]), Mann's own novel about a composer (of operas, among other things), the protagonist, Adrian Leverkühn, has been read as a parodic anti-Parsifal who does not resist—indeed who, like Amfortas, seeks out—the snares of a prostitute, Esmeralda, who admits to him that she is infected with syphilis. The narrator of the novel calls her a "witch" and a "brown wench" and rails against the "deliberate, reckless tempting of God": "What compulsion to comprise the punishment of the sin, finally what deep, deeply mysterious longing for daemonic conception, for a deathly unchaining of chemical change in his nature was at work, that having been warned he despised the warning and insisted upon possession of this flesh?" (151). What follows are detailed clinical descriptions of the stages of Adrian's syphilis and of his vain attempts to cure himself. Like *Parsifal*, *Doktor Faustus* is a late work of its creator, and in both there are parallel concerns with German society in a state of decay and crisis, though different messages about the possibility of redemption. But it is the intertextual linking of Kundry with the syphilitic prostitute in this reading of the novel that is particularly suggestive. See also Mary A. Cicora, "Wagner Parody in *Doktor Faustus*," *Germanic Review* 63, 3 (1988): 133–39.

78. Gilman, *Disease and Representation: Images of Illness from Madness to AIDS* (Ithaca: Cornell University Press, 1988), 256.

79. Lasowski, *Syphilis*, 47.

80. Laurence Kramer, *Music as Cultural Practice, 1800–1900* (Berkeley: University of California Press, 1990), 138. Kramer here is basing his argument on that of Michel Foucault in *The History of Sexuality*, vol. 1, *An Introduction*, trans. Robert Hurley (New York: Vintage, 1978).

81. James F. Poag, *Wolfram von Eschenbach* (New York: Twayne, 1972), 86.

82. Thomas Laqueur, *Making Sex: Body and Gender from the Greeks to Freud* (Cambridge: Harvard University Press, 1990), 1.

83. See Bentley, *Shakespeare and the New Disease*, 4.

84. Brandt, *No Magic Bullet*, 5.

85. Whittall, "Music," 69–70. Subsequent references are from pp. 76–77.

86. The opening of act 2, as Abbate points out ("'Parsifal,'" 51), is in B minor tone color and in the eighteenth and nineteenth centuries this would have been associated with magic, the supernatural, and even evil. It is Beethoven's "schwarze Tonart" and is the iconic key for Wagner's other cursed and cursing figures: the Dutchman, Hagen, and Alberich. It is also interesting that Klingsor's music here is strikingly energetic and dissonant, in comparison with the more static and even crudely rhythmic music of the Grail knights' march in the previous act.

87. Beckett, *Richard Wagner: "Parsifal,"* 56.

88. See Cicora, *"Parsifal" Reception,* 153, 18–19, 25–27. The Nazis did not seem to like the opera's message of "pacifism, reconciliation, and compassion" (58).

89. Showalter, "Syphilis," 88.

90. See Jacques Chailley, *"Parsifal" de Richard Wagner: Opéra initiatique* (Paris: Buchet-Chastel, 1979), 23–27 on the universal resonances gained by the male-female symbolism.

91. Victor E. Frankl, *Man's Search for Meaning* (New York: Washington Square Press, 1959, 1962, 1984), 135.

92. However, Syberberg's alternative interpretation is equally plausible. Although he uses an adult male voice for Parsifal throughout his film, he engages two actors to actually play the role: a young male (for the foolish and feisty Parsifal of the first half) and a young woman for the "feminized savior" of the second after Kundry's kiss. The male and female meet in the ultimate symbolic union. See Conrad, *Song of Love and Death,* 273, and Oskar Sahlberg, "Wagner heute: Syberbergs 'Parsifal,'" *Neue Deutsche Hefte* 30, 2 (1983): 342, who argues that Kundry's kiss awakens Parsifal to a presexual, narcissistic mother identification and so a woman should play the role while a man continues to sing it. At the end, Syberberg shows us a healed father figure (Amfortas) lying in state with a saved mother figure (Kundry).

93. The term is that of Peter Conrad in *Romantic Opera and Literary Form* (Berkeley: University of California Press, 1977), 165. Some critics merely present the Parsifal story, in general, as that of a masculine initiation to women and love, as the subtitle of Claudio Risé's *"Parsifal": L'iniziazione maschile alla donna e l'amore* (Como: Ed. RED, 1988) suggests.

94. For representative psychological interpretations, see Slavoj Žižek's Lacanian psychoanalytic reading in "'The Wound Is Healed Only by the Spear That Smote You': The Operatic Subject and Its Vicissitudes," in *Opera through Other Eyes,* ed. David J. Levin (Stanford: Stanford University Press, 1994), 177–214; Hans Alfred Grunsky's depth-psychological reading in "'Parsifal' im Lichte der Tiefenpsychologie," in *Programmhefte der Bayreuther Festspiele: "Parsifal,"* 1951, 6–28, which reads Parsifal as the androgynous connection of the male Spear and the female Grail (27); Peter Canzler's Oedipal reading in "Parsifal und das Mitleiden des Psychoanalytikers," *Jahrbuch der Psychoanalyse* (ed. H. Beland, F.-W Eickhoff, W. Loch, et al.) 21 (1987), 33–57; Otto Mensendieck, *Bayreuther Blätter,* 1915, on the characters as realistic of the psychic processes of the two sexes and of the dangers of desire. One influential philosophical reading is that of Robert Bosshart, *Bayreuther Blätter,* 1930, which sees the wound as a wound of dualism and thus of unredeemed mankind. For these last two see Cicora, *"Parsifal" Reception,* 51 especially.

95. Mann, *Pro and Contra Wagner*, 120.

96. Mann, *Pro and Contra Wagner*, 128–29.

97. Respectively, Gutman, *Richard Wagner*, 433, and Beckett, *Richard Wagner: "Parsifal,"* 132. Wapnewski ("Operas," 87–88) has read this as a conflict between Wagner's version and the Wolfram source text. Floros ("Studien," 18) explores the complexity of the other heterogeneous components too: Christian and Buddhist thought, Schopenhauer, social utopianism, and so on.

98. For example, John Deathridge and Carl Dahlhaus, *The New Grove Wagner* (New York: Norton, 1984), 163–64.

99. Mann, *Pro and Contra Wagner*, 129.

100. Mann, *Pro and Contra Wagner*, 129. Mann sees Kundry as having a split personality that was "the decisive inspiration and allurement, the source of his [Wagner's] most secret delight in this whole wondrous undertaking" (48–49).

101. See Borchmeyer ("Recapitulation," 17–18) on the intertexts suggested here, including Eugène Sue's *Le Juif errant* (1844), where Herodias accompanies Ahasuerus, the Wandering Jew; Heinrich Heine's *Atta Troll* (1843) and Mallarmé's *Hérodiade*, which merge Herodias and her daughter, Salome; traces of Oscar Wilde and Villiers d'Isle-Adam; Nikolaus Lenau's ballad about the Wandering Jew. He also suggests connections to *Tannhäuser*'s Venus and the biblical Eve.

102. As noted earlier, Parsifal is repeatedly called "Frevler" by the Grail knights when he kills the swan in act 1 and by the Flower Maidens when he injures their lovers in act 2. He calls himself by this name in act 3 for not getting back to the Grail world in time to save Titurel's life, blaming his own "Frevels Schuld." Klingsor is also said to have turned his own "Frevlerhand" against himself in his self-castration. He is supposed to have sinned ("gesündigt") and for this reason sought release from passion by castration; Parsifal, in killing the swan, is said to have committed a sin ("Sündentat"), but he finds redemption by resisting passion in a different way. Again, the connection and contrast are established on the verbal level.

103. It is not surprising, perhaps, that Gerd Rienacker should therefore hear echoes of Bach's *St. Matthew Passion* in *Parsifal*: "As Amfortas and, later, Parsifal suffer the Saviour's wounds and experience his [*sic*] cry they take over His pain; the musical language of Bach comes to their aid" ("Discursions into the Dramaturgy of 'Parsifal,'" in *Parsifal*, 70).

104. The Old French *pescheor* comes from the Latin *piscatore*, giving the modern French for fisherman, *pêcheur*, while *pecheor* derives from *peccatore*, giving the modern *pécheur* or sinner. See Olschki, *Grail Castle*, 35.

105. In act 1 he had made a play on words that relates directly to this. He says that the pure fool, the "reine *Tor*," he awaits is named "*Tod*" or death. The knights are given a punning aural play on the idea of Amfortas doing the Grail office

for the Last Time—"zum letzten Male"—since that office involves the act of communion in which the bread and wine of the Last Supper—"des letzten Mahles"—offers sustenance, both spiritual and physical.

106. Christa Wolf, *Patterns of Childhood*, trans. Ursule Molinaro and Hedwig Rappolt (New York: Farrar, Straus and Giroux, 1980), 288.

107. Klingsor awakens Kundry at the start of act 2, telling her that once again she will fall under the enslaving spell of his power: "Meinem Banne wieder *verfallen* heut." *Verfallen* also means to devolve upon, as when Titurel's job as protector of the Grail devolves upon his son. And indeed, Amfortas refers to the "Wehvolles Erbe, dem ich *verfallen*."

108. Holloway, "Experiencing," 26.

109. Carl Dahlhaus, *Richard Wagner's Music Dramas*, trans. M. Whittall (Cambridge: Cambridge University Press, 1979), 151; Boulez is quoted in Whittall, "Music," 61.

110. Adorno, *In Search of Wagner*, 43.

111. Carolyn Abbate suggests a related argument in terms of the relation of libretto to music when she describes Wagner's music as "pulled awry by a text with which it cannot be at peace," in Carolyn Abbate and Roger Parker, eds., *Analyzing Opera: Verdi and Wagner* (Berkeley: University of California Press, 1989), 95.

112. Conrad, *Song of Love and Death*, 183.

113. Marianne Wynn, "Mittelalterliche Literatur in der Rezeption: Richard Wagner und Wolframs Parzival," *Archiv für Kulturgeschichte* 65, 2 (1983): 433–34.

114. Our thanks to Arthur Groos for his clarification of and insight into the Wolfram text in his forthcoming *Romancing the Grail*.

115. Mann, *Pro and Contra Wagner*, 128.

4. The Pox Revisited

1. Claude Quétel, *History of Syphilis*, trans. Judith Braddock and Brian Pike (Baltimore: Johns Hopkins University Press, 1990), 2.

2. Susan McClary, *Georges Bizet: Carmen* (Cambridge: Cambridge University Press, 1992), 41; see also Andrew Nikiforuk, *The Fourth Horseman: A Short History of Epidemics, Plagues, Famine and Other Scourges* (Toronto: Viking, 1991), 106.

3. Sander L. Gilman, *Sexuality: An Illustrated History* (New York: John Wiley, 1989), 80. The quotations that follow are from pp. 80 and 83.

4. Oskar Panizza, *Das Liebeskonzil: The Council of Love, a Celestial Tragedy in Five Acts*, trans. Oreste F. Pucciani, intro. André Breton (New York: Viking, 1973), 121 and 124.

5. Alfred Fournier, *Syphilis and Marriage*, trans. Alfred Lingard (London: David Bogue, 1881). See also Harry C. Solomon and Maida Herman Solomon, *Syphilis of the Innocent: A Study of the Social Effects of Syphilis on the Family and the Commu-*

nity (Washington DC: United States Interdepartmental Social Hygiene Board, 1922). Predating both these, however, and proving that these issues were of major concern, see the Report of the Select Committee of the House of Lords on the Contagious Diseases Act, 1866, that was printed on 2 July 1868: "The medical discoveries of late years have proved that this fearful disease not only affects immediately, and in its own form, the man, too often the innocent wife and his offspring, but that, as stated by some witnesses, even to the third and fourth generation, a train of diseases result from it, of which the source has till lately been unsuspected, affecting the liver, the sight, the brain, the lungs, and the vital powers generally, so that actual degeneracy of the race, failing preventive measures, is continually increasing" (ix).

6. Jay Cassel, *The Secret Plague: Venereal Disease in Canada, 1838–1939* (Toronto: University of Toronto Press, 1987), 19.

7. For the background of the London of *Lulu*'s last act, see Elaine Showalter, "Syphilis, Sexuality, and Fiction of the Fin de Siècle," in *Sex, Politics, and Science in the Nineteenth-Century Novel*, ed. Ruth Bernard Yeazell (Baltimore: Johns Hopkins University Press, 1986), 88–115.

8. Alban Berg, cited in Rudolph Sabor, *The Real Wagner* (Harmondsworth: Penguin, 1987), 359–60.

9. Constantin Floros, "Studien zur *Parsifal*-Rezeption," in *Richard Wagner, Parsifal, Musik-Konzepte 25*, ed. Heinz-Klaus Metzger and Rainer Riehn (München: Text und Kritik, 1982), 14–57.

10. See Frank Mort, *Dangerous Sexualities: Medico-moral Politics in England since 1830* (New York: Routledge and Kegan Paul, 1987), 76–79, on female active, autonomous sexuality as deviant. See too Cassel, *Secret Plague*, 80.

11. Douglas Jarman, *Alban Berg: "Lulu"* (Cambridge: Cambridge University Press, 1991), 91.

12. Jarman, *Alban Berg: "Lulu,"* 43.

13. For a summary, see William E. Grim, "Das Ewig-weibliche zieht uns zurück: Berg's Lulu as Anti-Faust," *Opera Journal* 22, 1 (1989): 21.

14. See Leo Treitler, *Music and the Historical Imagination* (Cambridge: Harvard University Press, 1989), 283–84, and Grim, "Das Ewig-weibliche," 26. On Lulu as "die Urgestalt des Weibes," see J. L. Hibberd, "The Spirit of the Flesh: Wedekind's Lulu," *Modern Language Review* 79, 2 (1984): 340–41.

15. Thomas Elsaesser, "Lulu and the Meter Man: Pabst's *Pandora's Box*," in *German Film and Literature: Adaptations and Transformations*, ed. Eric Rentschler (New York: Methuen, 1986), 40.

16. Frank Wedekind, *Pandora's Box*, in *The Lulu Plays*, trans. Steve Gooch (Bath: Absolute Classics, 1990), 58.

17. For a summary of the debate here, see David Midgley, "Wedekind's *Lulu*: From 'Schauertragödie' to Social Comedy," *German Life and Letters* 38, 3 (1985): 205.

18. Cited in Treitler, *Music and the Historical Imagination*, 268.

19. On this quality in *The Rake's Progress*, see Mikhail Druskin, *Igor Stravinsky: His Life, Works and Views*, trans. Martin Cooper (Cambridge: Cambridge University Press, 1983), 68. On specific parallels between the two operas see, for example, Paul Griffiths, *Igor Stravinsky: "The Rake's Progress"* (Cambridge: Cambridge University Press, 1982), 92.

20. Diane Beyer Perett, "Ethics and Error: The Dispute between Ricord and Auzias-Turenne over Syphilization, 1845–70" (Ph.D. diss., Stanford University, 1977), iv.

21. Igor Stravinsky and Robert Craft, *Memories and Commentaries* (Garden City NY: Doubleday, 1960), 144.

22. Dereck Cooke, "'The Rake' and the 18th Century," *Musical Times* 103 (1962): 20–23, argues that Stravinsky profoundly misunderstood eighteenth-century music; on the contrary, Druskin, *Igor Stravinsky*, 110, sees the parody as creating an important Brechtian alienation effect that is crucial to the opera's success.

23. Mary Webster, *Hogarth* (London: Cassell, Studio Vista, 1979), 36.

24. See Ronald Paulson, *Hogarth: His Life, Art, and Times* (New Haven: Yale University Press, 1971), 1:254.

25. One of these fashions is opera: at the harpsichord in the second image sits a figure playing through an opera identified as *The Rape of the Sabines* by F. H. (Frederick Handel?).

26. Paulson, *Hogarth*, 1:325.

27. In Stravinsky and Craft, *Memories*, 145. See also Stravinsky's letter to Auden of 6 October 1947, reprinted in W. H. Auden and Chester Kallman, *Libretti and Other Dramatic Writings, 1939–1973*, in *The Complete Works of W. H. Auden*, ed. Edward Mendelson (Princeton: Princeton University Press, 1993), 578.

28. This is Auden's articulation, in a BBC broadcast, 28 August 1953, reprinted in *Libretti*, 621.

29. Webster, *Hogarth*, 52, puts it most strongly: Tom is "already rotting physically."

30. Georg Christoph Lichtenberg, *Lichtenberg's Commentaries on Hogarth's Engravings*, trans. Innes Herden and Gustav Herdan (1784–96; rpt. London: Cresset, 1966), 221. For more context on these contemporary commentaries, see Frederick Burwick, "The Hermeneutics of Lichtenberg's Interpretation of Hogarth," *Lessing Yearbook/Jahrbuch* 19 (1987): 167–91.

31. Paulson, *Hogarth*, 333.

32. Paulson, *Hogarth*, 543 n. 46.

33. See Quétel, *History of Syphilis*, 162.

34. H. Noguchi and J. W. Moore, "A Demonstration of *Treponema pallidum* in the Brains of Cases of General Paresis," *Journal of Experimental Medicine* 17 (1913): 232–38.

35. See M. Moore and H. H. Merritt, "Role of Syphilis of the Nervous System in the Production of Mental Disease," *Journal of the American Medical Association* 107 (1936): 1292–93; Allan M. Brandt, *No Magic Bullet: A Social History of Venereal Disease in the United States since 1880*, rev. ed. (New York: Oxford University Press, 1987), 129; Cassel, *Secret Plague*, 19.

36. On Charming Betty Careless, see *Lichtenberg's Commentaries*, 268. On baldness, see Greg W. Bentley, *Shakespeare and the New Disease: The Dramatic Function of Syphilis in "Troilus and Cressida," "Measure for Measure," and "Timon of Athens"* (New York: Peter Lang, 1989), 197, citing Thomas Nash's *Pierce Penilesse* on the "balde pates" and "close periwig" that hides "all the sinnes of an olde whore-master" who suffers from the "old boan-ach."

37. Gilman, *Sexuality*, 217.

38. For more on the eighteenth-century inspiration, see Joseph Kiermeier-Debre, "Wie Bilder Laufen lernen: Hogarths Graphikzyklen und ihre poetischen Um-Malungen durch H. v. Hofmannsthal und W. H. Auden," *Maske und Kothurn: Internazionale Beitrage zur Theaterwissenschaft* 31, 1–4 (1985): 212.

39. Quétel, *History of Syphilis*, 192.

40. Cited in Brandt, *No Magic Bullet*, 62.

41. Quétel, *History of Syphilis*, 62.

42. See Brandt, *No Magic Bullet*, 161–63.

43. Griffiths, *Igor Stravinsky*, 35.

44. Griffiths, *Igor Stravinsky*, 46.

45. See M. Chimenes, "Une Production de l'opéra de Glyndbourne: Les Décors et costumes de David Hockney, la mise en scène de John Cox," in *The Rake's Progress*, ed. J.-M. Vaccaro (Paris: CNRS, 1990), 166.

46. See Curtis Price, "*Venus and Adonis*," in *The New Grove Dictionary of Opera*, ed. Stanley Sadie (London: Macmillan, 1992), 4:923.

47. See Stravinsky and Craft, *Memories*, 164–65.

48. See, for example, Frieder Busch, "'The Rake's Progress' von Hogarth zu Strawinsky: Festschrift für Dietrich Rolle zum 60. Geburtstag," in *Scholastic Midwifery: Studien zum Satirischen in der englischen Literatur, 1600–1800*, ed. Jan Eden Peters and Thomas Michael Stein (Tübingen: Narr, 1989), 166.

49. Lord Harewood, in a review of the first performance in *Opera* 2 (1951): 613, found Nick "musically more Leporello than Mephistopheles"; Eric Walter White, in *Stravinsky: The Composer and His Works*, 2d ed. (Berkeley: University of California Press, 1979), 455, found him a mix of *Faust*'s Mephistopheles, Mr.

Hyde, and the Admirable Crichton. Auden himself later (1953) called Shadow "a Mephisto disguised as a Leporello," in *Libretti*, 618.

50. C. G. Jung, *Psyche and Symbol*, ed. Violet S. de Laszlo, trans. Cary Baynes and F. C. R. Hull (New York: Doubleday/Anchor, 1958), 7.

51. See Noguchi and Moore, "Demonstration of *Treponema pallidum*," 235–36.

52. On the comparison of the music of the two descents into hell, see Joseph N. Straus, *Remaking the Past: Musical Modernism and the Influence of the Tonal Tradition* (Cambridge: Harvard University Press, 1990), 156–61 especially. In 1953 Auden noted that Hogarth's rake was "not a demonically passionate man like Don Giovanni but a self-indulgent one." See *Libretti*, 617.

53. Arnold Whittall, *Music since the First World War* (London: Dent, 1977), 66.

54. Charles Clayton Dennie, *A History of Syphilis* (Springfield IL: Charles C Thomas, 1962), 30.

55. Joseph Kerman, "Opera à la Mode," *Hudson Review*, winter 1954, 561. He even goes so far as to suggest that the opera be rewritten to enable the last scene to incorporate some sort of redemption (577). For a related but more complex Kierkegaardian interpretation of the ending, see Geoffrey Chew, "Pastoral and Neoclassicism: A Reinterpretation of Auden's and Stravinsky's *Rake's Progress*," *Cambridge Opera Journal* 5, 3 (1993): 239–63.

56. Neil Tierney, *The Unknown Country: A Life of Igor Stravinsky* (London: Robert Hale, 1977), 157.

57. Fournier, *Syphilis and Marriage*, 79–80.

58. See Michael Anthony Waugh, "History of Clinical Developments in Sexually Transmitted Diseases," in *Sexually Transmitted Diseases* (New York: McGraw-Hill, 1990), 11–13.

59. See Jean Jacquot's remarks in "L'Opéra 'The Rake's Progress': Naissance et formation d'un récit dramatique," in Vaccaro, *Rake's Progress*, 64.

60. *John Gay's "The Beggar's Opera" and Other Eighteenth-Century Plays*, selected by John Hampden (1928; rpt. London: Dent; New York: Dutton, 1968), 112, 117, 121.

61. Voltaire, *Candide, or Optimism*, trans. John Butt (London: Penguin, 1947), 27–28. For typical descriptions of this collection of symptoms see, in one of the earliest and best-known instances, *Hieronymus Fracastorius and His Poetical and Prose Works on Syphilis*, trans. William Renwick Riddell (Toronto: Canadian Social Hygiene Council, 1928), 9: "In some the lips are consumed, in some the nose"; for later confirmation of these symptoms as syphilitic, see Philippe Ricord, *Practical Treatise on Venereal Diseases* (1838; Birmingham, AL: Classics of Medicine Library, Gryphon Editions, 1988), 265; for a summary discussion of signs such as nose disfigurement, see James Cleugh, *Secret Enemy: The Story of a Disease* (New York: Thomas and Hudson, 1954), 47.

62. Voltaire, *Candide*, 29.

63. Quétel, *History of Syphilis*, 7.

64. Thomas Parran, *Shadow on the Land: Syphilis* (1937; New York: Reynal and Hitchcock, 1971), 33, suggested that Columbus himself may have died of syphilis.

65. For a more extensive bibliography, see chapter 3, note 33.

66. Voltaire, *Candide*, 30.

5. "Acoustic Contagion"

1. Randolph Starn, Foreword to the English-language edition of Giulia Calvi, *Histories of a Plague Year: The Social and the Imaginary in Baroque Florence*, trans. Dario Biocca and Bryant T. Ragan Jr. (Berkeley: University of California Press, 1989), x.

2. See Paul Slack, *The Impact of Plague in Tudor and Stuart England* (London: Routledge and Kegan Paul, 1985), 4.

3. See Raymond Crawfurd, *Plague and Pestilence in Literature and Art* (Oxford: Clarendon, 1914).

4. See Charles E. Rosenberg, "Disease and Social Order in America: Perceptions and Expectations," in *AIDS: The Burdens of History*, ed. Elizabeth Fee and Daniel M. Fox (Berkeley: University of California Press, 1988), 18.

5. Richard J. Evans, *Death in Hamburg: Society and Politics in the Cholera Years, 1830–1910* (London: Penguin, 1987), 229. Subsequent citations are all from p. 230.

6. On cholera in various art forms, see Patrice Bourdelais and Jean-Yves Raulot, *Une Peur bleue: Histoire du choléra en France, 1832–1854* (Paris: Payot, 1987), on Berlioz's *Symphonie fantastique* (221) and on the work of Gérard de Nerval (who was a medical student during one of the epidemics in France), Eugène Sue (*Le Juif errant*), Jean Giono (*Hussard sur le toit*), and Roger Carrière (*La Grotte des pestiférés*) (245). On the visual iconography of cholera, see 245–46, 222.

7. See the entire first part of Frank Mort's *Dangerous Sexualities: Medico-moral Politics in England since 1830* (New York: Routledge and Kegan Paul, 1987).

8. Dhiman Barua, "History of Cholera," in *Cholera*, ed. Dhiman Barua and William B. Greenough III, Current Topics in Infectious Disease (New York: Plenum Medical Book Co., 1992), 9.

9. Oscar Felsenfeld, *The Cholera Problem* (St. Louis MO: W. H. Green, 1967), 4.

10. William H. McNeill, *Plagues and Peoples* (Garden City NY: Doubleday/Anchor, 1976), 261.

11. More recently, new concepts suggest that cholera may also have a free-living cycle and may be transmitted by other than fecal-oral means, such as by eating bivalves. See Barua, "History of Cholera," 130.

12. See Slack, *Impact of Plague*, 6.

13. Vivian Nutton, "The Seeds of Disease: An Explanation of Contagion and Infection from the Greeks to the Renaissance," *Medical History* 27 (1983): 1–34.

14. McNeill, *Plagues and Peoples*, 265.

15. See Charles E. Rosenberg, *The Cholera Years: The United States in 1832, 1849, and 1866* (1962; rpt. Chicago: University of Chicago Press, 1987), 42.

16. See Asa Briggs, "Cholera and Society in the Nineteenth Century," *Past and Present* 19 (1961): 76.

17. See McNeill, *Plagues and Peoples*, 275.

18. Norman Longmate, *King Cholera: The Biography of a Disease* (London: Hamish Hamilton, 1966), 113.

19. François Delaporte, *Disease and Civilization: The Cholera in Paris, 1832*, trans. Arthur Goldhammer (Cambridge: MIT Press, 1986), 86.

20. This is the situation in Paris, according to Delaporte in *Disease*, 40. See also p. 38: "There is no doubt that the masses of the poor were looked upon as dangerous carriers. They were believed to be responsible for spreading the disease, which in the tragic spring of 1832 was their principal possession." For the situation in England, see Mort (*Dangerous Sexualities*, 16) on the isolation and inspection and detention powers of authorities, combined with "propaganda to educate the poor into a regime of cleanliness and morality." Rosenberg, in "Disease and Social Order," 19, notes: "With no consensus regarding the pathology of the disease . . . social variables necessarily played a prominent role in fashioning a usable framework that enabled regularly trained physicians and their middle-class patients to cope with the disease."

21. See Longmate, *King Cholera*, 4; Delaporte, *Disease*, 54.

22. Longmate, *King Cholera*, 144.

23. See Mort, *Dangerous Sexualities*, 22–28.

24. Mort, *Dangerous Sexualities*, 39, citing a nineteenth-century report. See too Delaporte, *Disease*, 19, for an 1875 report on cholera in Paris in 1832.

25. Mort, *Dangerous Sexualities*, 26.

26. Wedekind is quoted in Douglas Jarman, *Alban Berg: "Lulu"* (Cambridge: Cambridge University Press, 1991), 115.

27. In a 1988 production at the Théâtre de la Monnaie in Brussels, Ruth Berghaus used a projection of Lulu and Geschwitz in bed together, having consummated their relationship. This is not indicated in specific terms in the texts, however. See Jarman, *Alban Berg*, 54.

28. This link between the endings of Wagner's *Tristan und Isolde* and *Lulu* has often been made. For a recent version, see Michel Poizat, *The Angel's Cry: Beyond the Pleasure Principle in Opera*, trans. Arthur Denner (Ithaca: Cornell University Press, 1992), 204.

29. These two points are made by, respectively, Leo Treitler, *Music and the Historical Imagination* (Cambridge: Cambridge University Press, 1989), 294, and Karl Kraus, quoted in Jarman, *Alban Berg*, 105.

30. See J. L. Hibberd, "The Spirit of the Flesh: Wedekind's Lulu," *Modern Language Review* 79, 2 (1984): 346–47, and Thomas Elsaesser, "Lulu and the Meter Man: Pabst's Pandora's Box (1929)," in *German Film and Literature: Adaptations and Transformations,* ed. Eric Rentschler (New York: Methuen, 1986), 40.

31. George Perle, "Some Thoughts on an Ideal Production of *Lulu,*" *Journal of Musicology* 7, 2 (1989): 244–53.

32. See Sander L. Gilman, *Difference and Pathology: Stereotypes of Sexuality, Race and Madness* (Ithaca: Cornell University Press, 1985), 70. On Nana, see Charles Bernheimer, *Figures of Ill Repute: Representing Prostitution in Nineteenth-Century France* (Cambridge: Harvard University Press, 1989), 226, and also chapter 3, note 48, above.

33. Discussed in Jarman, *Alban Berg,* 113–14.

34. Richard Gallagher, *Diseases That Plague Modern Man: A History of Ten Communicable Diseases* (Dobbs Ferry NY: Oceana, 1969), 23.

35. See Bourdelais and Raulot, *Une Peur Bleue,* 69, 129, 133.

36. See T. J. Reed, "Mann and His Novella: 'Death in Venice,'" in *Benjamin Britten: "Death in Venice,"* ed. Donald Mitchell (Cambridge: Cambridge University Press, 1987), 165: "The epidemic which reached Venice in 1911 came from India. So, it was thought, did the cult of the alien god Dionysus which once swept like an epidemic through ancient Greece."

37. Throughout we will continue to quote from this English translation—not only because the libretto is in English, but because it is consciously derived from the familiar H. T. Lowe-Porter translation available in (and here quoted) *"Death in Venice" and Seven Other Stories* (1930; New York: Vintage, 1989), 5–6. All further references will be to this edition.

38. See Andrew Nikiforuk, *The Fourth Horseman: A Short History of Epidemics, Plagues, Famine and Other Scourges* (Toronto: Viking, 1991), 60, on the "brisk trade" of microbes and on the deaths of a third of the population in the plagues of 1575 and 1630.

39. See Ulrich Müller, "Wagner in Literature and Film," in *Wagner Handbook,* ed. Ulrich Müller and Peter Wapnewski, trans. John Deathridge (Cambridge: Harvard University Press, 1992), 378 and 384. The role of Venice in early seventeenth-century opera is said to have inspired Britten to restore recitative in his work. See Eric Walter White, *Benjamin Britten: His Life and Operas,* 2d ed., ed. John Evans (London: Faber and Faber, 1983), 269.

40. See Naomi Ritter, "*Death in Venice* and the Tradition of European Decadence," in *Approaches to Teaching Mann's "Death in Venice" and Other Short Fiction,* ed. Jeffrey B. Berlin (New York: MLA, 1992), 90.

41. See Robert K. Martin, "Gender, Sexuality, and Identity in Mann's Short Fiction," in Berlin, *Approaches,* 65.

42. Gerald Gillespie, "Mann and the Modernist Tradition," in Berlin, *Approaches*, 100.

43. Edward W. Said, *Musical Elaborations* (New York: Columbia University Press, 1991), 52.

44. For greater detail on these oppositions, see Gary Schmidgall, *Literature as Opera* (New York: Oxford University Press, 1977), 325, and James Allen Feldman, "The Musical Portrayal of Gustav von Aschenbach in Benjamin Britten's *Death in Venice*" (Ph.D. diss., Kent State University, 1987), part 2. See too Eugene Lunn, "Tales of Liberal Disquiet: Mann's *Mario and the Magician* and Interpretations of Fascism," *Literature and History* 11, 1 (1985): 80.

45. Adorno, quoted in Schmidgall, *Literature as Opera*, 355; Arnold Whittall, "Death in Venice," in *The New Grove Dictionary of Opera*, ed. Stanley Sadie (London: Macmillan, 1992), 1:1096 and 1095.

46. Schmidgall, *Literature as Opera*, 347, sees his "monkishness" enacted through the preclassical vocal line that "hints at ancient Greek hymn, the melisma of Schütz's *Passions*, and the chaste qualities of plainsong." Peter Pears, for whom the role was written, had sung the *Passions* while Britten was writing the opera, and hearing this might have been the reason the composer changed his mind: he had originally wanted to have Aschenbach's lines spoken.

47. Respectively by Patrick Carnegy, "The Novella Transformed: Thomas Mann as Opera," in Mitchell, *Benjamin Britten*, 174; Peter Evans, "Synopsis: The Story, the Music Not Excluded," in the same volume, 77; Eric Roseberry, "Tonal Ambiguity in 'Death in Venice': A Symphonic View," also in this volume, 89.

48. Christopher Palmer, "Benjamin Britten, *Death in Venice*," liner notes to the 1974 Decca London compact disc (#425670-2), 16.

49. Roseberry, "Tonal Ambiguity," 89.

50. See Christopher Palmer, "Britten's Venice Orchestra," in Mitchell, *Benjamin Britten*, especially 131–39.

51. See Carnegy, "Novella Transformed," 175: This "A major-ish theme with its prominent major seventh, A–G♯, scored for vibraphone and other percussion is quite literally a shimmering, vibrant and vibrating sound aura." On the earlier use of this technique see Humphrey Carpenter, *Benjamin Britten: A Biography* (London: Faber and Faber, 1992), 552.

52. The dance was choreographed, in the first performance, by Frederick Ashton. On the dramatic and symbolic function of the ballet, see Carolyn Roberts Finlay, "Literary Analysis of Opera: Three Recent Publications," *Canadian Review of Comparative Literature* 8, 4 (1981): 529, and Myfanwy Piper's own comments in "The Libretto," in Mitchell, *Benjamin Britten*, 47. Some critics have expressed serious reservations about the aesthetic effectiveness of this particular marking of difference—that is, having the Poles be dancers. See, for

instance, Schmidgall, *Literature as Opera*, 350–52. The odd irony of stylized dance representing the physical world of the body is matched by the "oddly disembodied" effect of the music here, as discussed by Evans, "Synopsis," 79. In general, however, the simple fact that Aschenbach is a singer and Tadzio a dancer embodies on stage the permanent inability of the two to communicate.

53. Frederick Beharriell, in "'Never without Freud': Freud's Influence on Mann," in *Thomas Mann in Context: Papers of the Clark University Centennial Colloquium* (Worcester MA: Clark University, 1978), 1–15, argues that even in 1911 Mann was influenced by Freudian notions of sexual repression, sublimation, and the unconscious, even though he did not write on Freud until the mid-1920s.

54. Evans, "Synopsis," 82.

55. Tadzio's key is A major; C major and minor are used as the basis of the plague motive. See Roseberry, "Tonal Ambiguity," 89–95.

56. Evans, "Synopsis," 82.

57. See Briggs, "Cholera and Society," 88, on the role of rumor and suspicion in cholera epidemics. To this is added the more venal reason for the suppression of truthful information: fear of losing the tourist trade.

58. Palmer, "Benjamin Britten, *Death in Venice*," 16.

59. On the fear of fruit's spreading cholera in Italy, see Paolo Sorcinelli, "Uomini ed epidemie nel primo Ottocento: Comportamenti, reazioni e paure nello Stato pontificio," in *Storia d'Italia*, vol. 7, *Malattia e medicina*, ed. Franco Della Peruta (Torino: Einaudi, 1984), 498.

60. The quotations are from Evans, "Synopsis," 84, and Whittall, "*Death in Venice*," 1096.

61. Schmidgall, *Literature as Opera*, 330.

62. Friedrich Nietzsche, "*The Birth of Tragedy*" and "*The Genealogy of Morals*," trans. Francis Golffing (Garden City: Doubleday/Anchor, 1956), 56–57. Subsequent references are to this translation and edition.

63. On the importance and symbolic meanings of music in Mann's text, see Marc A. Weiner, "Silence, Sound, and Song in *Der Tod in Venedig*: A Study in Psycho-social Repression," *Seminar* 23, 2 (1987): 137–55.

64. Kenneth Burke, *Counter-statement* (1931, 1953; Berkeley: University of California Press, 1968), 95.

65. Britten's homosexuality was well known, of course. See Mitchell, *Benjamin Britten*, 21: "*Death in Venice* embodies unequivocally the powerful sexual drive that was Britten's toward the young (and sometimes very young) male." See also Ned Rorem, "Britten's Venice," in Mitchell, *Benjamin Britten*, 187: "His human fixations are chiefly aquaphilic and pedophilic." Mann's widow claimed

that the sexual dimension of the narrative was purely imaginary (in Carpenter, *Benjamin Britten*, 552), and Mann himself claimed that his real subject was passion "as confusion and as a stripping of dignity," a position many critics have supported (see, for example, Schmidgall, *Literature as Opera*, 330). On the autobiographical elements of the story, see Herbert Lehnert, "Thomas Mann's Interpretations of *Death in Venice* and Their Reliability," *Rice University Studies* 50 (fall 1964): 41–60. See also Martin, "Gender," 58, on Mann's love for his schoolmate Armin Martens and the painter Paul Ehrenberg.

66. Myfanwy Piper, in "The Libretto" (in Mitchell, *Benjamin Britten*, 45), cites Mann's letter about the sensational interest that had been displayed in what Mann himself called the story's "pathological subject matter." See also Michael Kennedy, *Britten* (London: Dent, 1981), 255–56.

67. Susan Sontag, *Illness as Metaphor* (Harmondsworth: Penguin, 1983), 41, where she argues that tuberculosis individualizes and cholera does not.

68. See Adrian Del Caro, "Philosophizing and Poetic Licence in Mann's Early Fiction," in Berlin, *Approaches*, 44. Eugene Goodheart, in his chapter "The Art of Ambivalence: Mann's *Death in Venice*," in *Desire and Its Discontents* (New York: Columbia University Press, 1991), 46, argues that "bourgeois artist" is in fact oxymoronic.

69. Briggs, "Cholera and Society," 76.

70. Martin, "Gender," 65.

71. Roderick Stackelberg, "Teaching Mann's Short Fiction: A Historian's Perspective," in Berlin, *Approaches*, 32.

72. Several operas have been made of this story, but most concentrate only on the theatrical second half. The Somers/Anderson opera works with the entire novella and for this reason has been chosen as the focus of the discussion.

73. On the repression of nature, see Edward Timms, "*Death in Venice* as Psychohistory," in Berlin, *Approaches*, 135–36, where he argues that the Prussian ethos that suppressed emotional impulses is clear not only in Aschenbach but in the subject of one of his books: Frederick the Great. On the allegory of the narcissism of empire, see Ritter, "*Death in Venice*," 89.

74. René Girard, "The Plague in Literature and Myth," *Texas Studies in Literature and Language* 15 (1974): 837.

75. Again, because the libretto is closely based on the Lowe-Porter translation, we will cite from the novella in that translation: *Mario and the Magician*, in "*Death in Venice*" and *Seven Other Stories*, trans. H. T. Lowe-Porter (1930; New York: Vintage, 1989), 133. Subsequent references are to this translation and edition.

76. That, through Mussolini, Mann might have been expressing his earliest fears

about Hitler would be supported by the historical argument that Hitler was a German version of Il Duce. See Wolfgang Sauer, "National Socialism: Totalitarianism or Fascism?" *American Historical Review* 73 (1967): 404–22.

77. On Mussolini's oratory, see Denis Mack Smith, *Mussolini's Roman Empire* (New York: Viking, 1976). The opera, written in the 1990s in full knowledge of historical events Mann could not have known about in 1929, makes Stefan into an antifascist (like the later Mann himself) even before Hitler's real rise to power. It is perhaps also for this reason that Anderson has made the rather pompous and elitist narrator of the novella into a much more sympathetic stage character.

78. Our thanks to Eva Geulen for sharing with us her work in progress on "Theories of Resistance," where she makes the Boccaccio connection to Mann's story in a most convincing manner.

79. Lunn, "Tales," 87.

80. Rod Anderson, "*Mario* and the Medium: Necessary Liberties," essay for press release, Canadian Opera Company (1992), 1.

81. Lunn, "Tales," 91–92.

82. George L. Mosse, *Nationalism and Sexuality: Respectability and Abnormal Sexuality in Modern Europe* (New York: Fertig, 1985), 23.

83. See Barbara Spackman, *Decadent Genealogies: The Rhetoric of Sickness from Baudelaire to D'Annunzio* (Ithaca: Cornell University Press, 1989), 9.

84. Sontag, *Illness as Metaphor*, 41.

6. Where There's Smoke, There's . . .

1. Arthur Imhof, "From the Old Mortality Pattern to the New: Implications of a Radical Change from the Sixteenth to the Twentieth Century," *Bulletin of the History of Medicine* 59 (1985): 1–29.

2. R. Schofield, D. Reher, and A. Bideau, *The Decline of Mortality in Europe* (Oxford: Clarendon, 1991), 1–8 especially.

3. John Slade, "The Tobacco Epidemic: Lessons from History," *Journal of Psychoactive Drugs* 21, 3 (1989): 281.

4. See the statistics presented in Slade, "Tobacco Epidemic," 282.

5. It should be said that there was a kind of "exchange" involved between the Old and the New Worlds: alcohol, smallpox, and perhaps tuberculosis entered the Americas, and the potato, corn, tobacco, and maybe syphilis went the other way. On the aboriginal use of tobacco smoking, see Count Egon Caesar Corti, *A History of Smoking*, trans. Paul England (London: Harrap, 1931), 28; Sarah Augusta Dickson, *Panacea or Precious Bane: Tobacco in Sixteenth Century Literature* (New York: New York Public Library, 1954), chapter 1; Jerome E.

Brooks, *Tobacco: Its History Illustrated by the Books, Manuscripts and Engravings in the Library of George Arents, Jr.* (New York: Rosenbach , 1937), 1:13.

6. See Brooks, *Tobacco*, 1:83.

7. Johnson's remark is typically pointed: "Smoaking has gone out. To be sure, it is a shocking thing, blowing smoak out of our mouths into other peoples mouths, eyes, and noses, and having the same thing done to us. Yet I cannot account why a thing which requires so little exertion, and yet preserves the mind from total vacuity, should have gone out." Quoted in David Krogh, *Smoking: The Artificial Passion* (New York: Freeman, 1991), 12.

8. See Corti, *History*, 220–22.

9. Croker, quoted in G. L. Apperson, *The Social History of Smoking* (London: Martin Secker, 1914), 139.

10. See Georg A. Brongers, *Nicotiana Tabacum: The History of Tobacco and Tobacco Smoking in the Netherlands* (Amsterdam: Becht's; Groningen: Niemeyer, 1964), 228; Corti, *History*, 252.

11. See Slade, "Tobacco Epidemic," 283–84.

12. See Ned Rival, *Tabac, miroir du temps* (n.p.: Librairie Académique Perrin, 1981), 27 and 34.

13. See *Encyclopédie du tabac et des fumeurs* (Paris: Les Grandes Encyclopédies Internationales Le Temps, 1975), 373; see also Brooks, *Tobacco*, 1:31, where the forms and uses of tobacco at the time are listed as "powders, gargles, unguents, etc.; as antiseptics, vulneraries, disinfectants, cathartics, emetics, collyriums, inhalations, expectorants, clysters, styptics, dentifrices, etc."

14. See Corti, *History*, 58; Victor G. Kiernan, *Tobacco: A History* (London: Hutchinson Radius, 1991), 20, quotes a 1595 claim that "venereal disease was only one of the many ailments it [tobacco] could set right"; see also Grégoire Ramniceanu, *Quelques Considérations sur le tabac et sur son emploi en thérapeutique* (Paris: A. Parent, 1869).

15. On constipation, see F. W. Fairholt, *Tobacco: Its History and Associations* (London: Chapman and Hall, 1859), chapter 6; on drowning, see Brongers, *Nicotiana Tabacum*, 29.

16. Cited in Apperson, *Social History of Smoking*, 77.

17. Howel (1646), quoted in Apperson, *Social History of Smoking*, 75.

18. For Berlin, see Corti, *History*, 228–32; for England, see Kiernan, *Tobacco*, 206.

19. Quoted in Corti, *History*, 83; see also Brooks, *Tobacco*, 59–60: "Those who engaged in the wanton pleasure of 'drinking' tobacco were earnestly assured that they were shortening their days, and that those 'sooty fumes' had the effect eventually of blinding, deafening or weakening them incurably."

20. H.-A. Depierris, *La Vérité sur le tabac, le plus violent des poisons, la nicotine* (Paris: Dentu et Ballière, 1880), 5 and 29.

21. On the nineteenth-century French antitobacco leagues, see Rival, *Tabac*, 206–12.

22. Fairholt, *Tobacco*, 68. The close relation between tobacco and empire is explored by Rival, *Tabac*, 64–65.

23. See *Encyclopédie*, 356; on the aboriginal smoking traditions picked up by Columbus, see Brooks, *Tobacco*, 1:17: "That ancient gesture, thus first observed by Europeans, was a common sign of amity with all Americans wherever tobacco was known. The white strangers soon adopted it and it was the only manifestation of Indian etiquette which became, in various forms, a part of the social rites of civilized man, developing into an almost universal sign of fellowship."

24. Apperson, *Social History*, 217. He also quotes Dickens's response to a trip to Geneva in 1846: "But I never was so surprised, so ridiculously taken aback, in my life; for in all my experience of 'ladies' of one kind and another, I never saw a woman—not a basket woman or a gypsy—smoke before!" (219).

25. Quoted in *Encyclopédie*, 357.

26. See Leo Tolstoy, "*Why Do Men Stupify Themselves?*" *and Other Writings*, trans. Aylmer Maude (Hankins NY: Strength Books, 1975), 55–56: "Why among women do those who lead a regular life smoke least? Why do prostitutes and madmen all smoke?" See also Kiernan, *Tobacco*, 92, who quotes Oscar Wilde's "The Harlot's House": "Sometimes a horrible marionette / Came out, and smoked its cigarette / Upon the steps like a living thing." On courtesans, see *Encyclopédie*, 357; Richard Klein, in *Cigarettes Are Sublime* (Durham: Duke University Press, 1993), 117, claims that "among women, smoking began with those who got paid for staging their sexuality: the actress, the gypsy, the whore." See also pp. 159–60 on women smoking.

27. *Les Fumeurs de Paris* (Paris: Gustave Havard, 1856), 86.

28. Fairholt, *Tobacco*, 147–48.

29. See *Encyclopédie*, 357, on the necessary technology.

30. Quoted by Ross Chambers, "Le Poète fumeur," *Australian Journal of French Studies* 16, 2 (1979): 141. On Baudelaire's orientalist fantasies in "La Pipe," see Chambers, 141, and Klein, *Cigarettes*, 6, 55, 59. Klein's chapters 2, 3, and 4 are extended discussions of the literary representations of smoking cigarettes in particular.

31. Klein, *Cigarettes*, 2. Odile Lesourne, in *Le Grand Fumeur et sa passion* (Paris: Presses Universitaires de France, 1984), 64–76, argues—through a psychoanalytic case study—that smoking today is associated with both sexual pleasure and danger for *women* as well as men.

32. *John Gay's "The Beggar's Opera" and Other Eighteenth-Century Plays*, ed. John Hampden (1928; rpt. London: Dent; New York: Dutton, 1968), 126.

33. Rival, *Tabac*, 166, claims that to ask for a light from another's cigar was in itself a social demand not to be refused. This is what created, he says, the grand fraternity of smokers.

34. Kiernan, *Tobacco*, 48.

35. This is, in fact, a kind of Puccini commonplace: in *La Bohème*, Schaunard appears in act 1 with wood, cigars, and wine for the Christmas celebrations. Puccini, of course, smoked several packs of cigarettes a day himself and, sadly, died of laryngeal cancer. See Howard Greenfeld, *Puccini: A Biography* (New York: Putnam's Sons, 1980), 273.

36. Klein, *Cigarettes*, 20–21; see also his chapter 5, "The Soldier's Friend," 135–56.

37. Krogh, *Smoking*, 53–56; Klein, *Cigarettes*, 144.

38. Antonio Gramsci, cited in Kiernan, *Tobacco*, 164, from a letter to his sister-in-law in 1931.

39. Thomas Mann, "Mario and the Magician," in *"Death in Venice" and Seven Other Stories*, trans. H. T. Lowe-Porter (1930; rpt. New York: Vintage, 1989), 170.

40. Quoted in Kiernan, *Tobacco*, 48.

41. On Gil as a comic Othello, see Ernst Leopold Stahl, *Ermanno Wolf-Ferrari* (Salzburg: Kiesel, 1936), 39. Raffaello De Rensis, in a speech in 1948, "In memoria di Ermanno Wolf-Ferrari," published in the *Quaderni dell'Accademia Chigiana* 17 (1948): 25, calls this opera "Falstaffian," however.

42. John C. G. Waterhouse, in *The New Grove Dictionary of Opera*, ed. Stanley Sadie (London: Macmillan, 1992), 3:300.

43. See Mosco Carner, *Puccini: A Critical Biography*, 2d ed. (London: Duckworth, 1974), 422; William Ashbrook, *The Operas of Puccini* (Oxford: Oxford University Press, 1985), 178.

44. Carner, *Puccini*, 431.

45. Catherine Clément, *Opera, or The Undoing of Women*, trans. Betsy Wing (Minneapolis: University of Minnesota Press, 1988; London: Virago, 1989), 48.

46. There are, in fact, many sources for details of the Carmen narrative, including a story told to Mérimée by a Spanish friend, Mme de Montiljo; his own travels in Spain in 1830 and 1840 (and the letters written on "Les Voleurs en Espagne" and on "Sorcières espagnoles" in his *Lettres d'Espagne*); and Cervantes' stories of Don Quixote and Roque Guinart and of "La Gitanilla" in the *Exemplary Tales*.

47. See Dominique Maingueneau, *Carmen: Les Racines d'un mythe* (Paris: Sorbier, 1984), 101.

48. Hugh Macdonald, "Carmen," in *The New Grove Dictionary of Opera*, 1:735. See also p. 738 on "the outrageous behaviour of the cigarette girls."

49. Rival, *Tabac*, 67, points out that the factory was built by the Spanish royal ministry of finances—which obviously knew a good revenue-producing thing

when it saw it. Brooks, *Tobacco*, 143, notes that, given the Spanish import duty established by 1611, all Cuban tobacco that was not consumed on the island had to be sent to Seville. This is how the city became the center for the manufacture of cigars and snuff.

50. See José Perez Vidal, *España en la historia del tabaco* (Madrid: Centro de Estudios de Etnologia Peninsular, 1959), 237.

51. Maingueneau, *Carmen*, 95.

52. Théophile Gautier, *Voyage en Espagne* (1845; Oxford: Clarendon, 1905), 159.

53. See the discussions in Maingueneau, *Carmen*, 96, and Vidal, *España*, 273–76.

54. See, for example, Pierre Louÿs, *La Femme et le pantin: Roman espagnol* (1898; Paris: Charpentier et Fasquelle, 1916), 77–78: "Les plus vêtues n'avaient que leur chemise autour du corps (c'étaient les prudes); presque toutes travaillaient le torse nu, avec un simple jupon de toile désserré de la ceinture et parfois retroussé jusqu'au milieu des cuisses. Le spectacle était mélangé. . . . Il y avait de tout dans cette foule nue, excepté des vièrges, probablement."

55. See Rival, *Tabac*, 167, and Vidal, *España*, 268, on the disappointment of those who mistakenly came in cooler weather and missed "las semidesnudeces estivales."

56. Louÿs, *La Femme et le pantin*, 81.

57. Maurice Barrès, *Du Sang, de la volupté et de la mort* (Paris: Charpentier, 1894), 135.

58. See Henry Malherbe, *Carmen* (Paris: Albin Michel, 1951), 241: "Rien de plus léger, de plus malicieux que cet ensemble, dans son alanguissement. Sous forme enjouée, la musique dévoile la basse coquetterie et le charme onduleux des frivoles compagnes d'atelier de Carmen. Désabusées, elles répondent avec nonchalance aux compliments madrigalesques de leurs adorateurs, tout en fumant des cigarettes. Clarinettes, flutes, altos, aidés des cordes amorties par les sourdines, retracent les spirales indécises et flottantes de la fumée du tabac. Spirales qui s'envolent dans l'air et disparaissent comme les propos, les transports et les serments d'amour."

59. The French is, "Elle s'avançait en se balançant sur ses hanches comme une pouliche du haras de Cordoue." Prosper Mérimée, *Carmen* (Paris: Larousse, 1975), 98. All further page references will be to this edition. See Maingueneau, *Carmen*, 49–50, for more on the images of sex and horses associated with Spain in contemporaneous French poetry.

60. See Vidal, *España*, 258, where he quotes what we take to be an eerily apt piece of evidence of this realism: a decree against a certain Maria del Carmen Garcia, "hija de *José y Carmen*, natural de Sevilla" (our emphasis), for attacking a colleague in the factory in Seville: "Por decreto 12 de agosto de 1825 es expulsada para siempre por haber proferido palabras insultantes a las companeras, y escandalosas, y tirando las tijeras a Concepción Vegue, y di-

versos atados de tabaco que halló a mano, atemorizando a la maestra con su furia."

61. See Peter Robinson's "Mérimée's *Carmen*," in *Georges Bizet, "Carmen*," ed. Susan McClary (Cambridge: Cambridge University Press, 1992), 11, for more on the male or phallic symbolism of both the blunderbuss José carries and the narrator's cigars.

62. See Vidal, *España*, 269.

63. On the common practice of allowing a condemned person a last smoke and for nineteenth-century Spanish examples, see Kiernan, *Tobacco*, 170–71.

64. The French text allows for an interesting visual punning involving lovers and connected to fishing *(pêche)* and sin *(péché)* that we have seen to have a long history dating back to Chrétien de Troyes and those Fisher King myths. Here are added puns on poison *(poison)* and fish *(poisson)* and on lowering *(baisser)* and kissing *(baiser)*. Mérimée writes, "Les amateurs, à cette pêche-là, n'ont qu'à se baisser pour prendre le poisson" (97); but the image can be rewritten with little change to read, "les amants, à ce péché-là, n'ont qu'à baiser pour prendre le poison."

65. Cited by McClary, *Georges Bizet, "Carmen*," 16. For a statistically complex sociological and historical study of who went to this opera house and others in Paris up to this time, see Steven Huebner, "Paris Opera Audiences, 1830–1870," *Music and Letters* 70 (1989): 206–25.

66. For the opera, see the review by "F. de L." in the *Revue des Deux Mondes*, 2 (1875): 475–80. The Larousse edition of the novella from which we have been quoting reprints a piece by the music critic of *Le Temps*, Félix Clément, which appeared in his 1885 *Historie de la musique*: "Je ne rangerai pas *Carmen*, de Bizet, parmi les ouvrages . . . qui doivent rester au répertoire, parce que la musique, fût-elle aussi intéressante qu'elle est inégale et de facture hybride, ne pourrait racheter la honte d'un pareil sujet, lequel, depuis deux siècles, n'avait jamais déshonoré une scène destinée aux plaisirs délicats et aux divertissements de bonnes compagnies" (70). See too August Dupouy, *"Carmen" de Mérimée* (Paris: Société Française d'Editions Littéraires et Techniques, 1930), 136–38.

67. The censor had the power to ban a work that was felt to threaten public morality, order, or political propriety. Flaubert's *Madame Bovary*, of course, was banned on precisely these grounds. See Lesley A. Wright, "A New Source for *Carmen*," *Nineteenth-Century Music* 2, 1 (1978): 61–71.

68. Susan McClary, *Feminine Endings: Music, Gender, and Sexuality* (Minneapolis: University of Minnesota Press, 1991), 56. In *Georges Bizet, "Carmen*," 46, she points out that Bizet may have given in to convention and pressure, to some extent, in using the typical Opéra-Comique heroine (Micaëla), but he certainly rel-

egates her to the margins of his drama. Others disagree: Peter Brook, in his stage and film investigation of the story in *La Tragédie de Carmen*, made Micaëla into a strong rival to Carmen for José's love as a way of dramatizing and being faithful to what he saw as the spirit of Mérimée's text, in which there is no Micaëla figure but in which Don José's Basque background (which she represents) is an important factor in his character. See interview with Glen Loney, "The *Carmen* Connection," *Opera News* 48, 3 (1983): 12. Carl Dahlhaus, in *Nineteenth-Century Music*, trans. J. Bradford Robinson (Berkeley: University of California Press, 1989), 280, agrees that Micaëla personifies José's past.

69. By act 2 Don José's music also shows signs of chromatic slippage. This is all the more noticeable because he seems to lack any real signature theme of his own. See McClary, *Georges Bizet, "Carmen,"* 42, 136.

70. Jeremy Tambling, *Opera, Ideology and Film* (Manchester: University of Manchester Press, 1987), 37; McClary, *Feminine Endings*, 57.

71. See that 1875 review in the *Revue des Deux Mondes*: "Voulez-vous du pittoresque et voir revivre en chansons l'Espagne de Zamacoïs et de Fortuni" (477).

72. Winton Dean, *Bizet* (London: Dent, 1948), 192.

73. For further reference, see chapter 3; see also Peter Gay, *Education of the Senses: The Bourgeois Experience, Victoria to Freud* (New York: Oxford University Press, 1984), 197–213. See also Sander Gilman, *Difference and Pathology: Stereotypes of Sexuality, Race, and Madness* (Ithaca: Cornell University Press, 1985), 39–58, and Bram Dijkstra, *Idols of Perversity: Fantasies of Feminine Evil in Fin-de-Siècle Culture* (New York: Oxford University Press, 1986).

74. See Franco Fornari, *Carmen Adorata: Psicoanalisi della donna demoniaca* (Milano: Longanesi, 1985), for the long history of demonic women in the religious and literary, as well as musical, traditions.

75. This profile is drawn from the following texts: Kathleen H. Hofeller, *Battered Women, Shattered Lives* (Palo Alto CA: R and E Research Associates, 1983); Jennifer Baker Fleming, *Stopping Wife Abuse* (Garden City NY: Anchor/Doubleday, 1979); Sandra Horley, *Love and Pain: A Survival Handbook for Women* (London: Bedford Square, 1988); Kersti Yllo and Michele Bograd, eds., *Feminist Perspectives on Wife Abuse* (Newbury Park CA: Sage, 1988); Edward W. Gondolf, *Man against Woman: What Every Woman Should Know about Violent Men* (Blue Ridge Summit PA: Tab Books, 1989).

76. McClary, *Feminine Endings*, 152. She also argues that Carmen "arouses desire; and because she apparently has the power to deliver or withhold gratification of the desires she instills, she is immediately marked as a potential victimizer" (57). Klein, in *Cigarettes*, 112, writes of the figurative "irresistible violence of her charms" but never remarks on José's literal violence.

77. McClary, *Feminine Endings*, 62; Peter J. Rabinowitz, in "Outside the Culture,

Outside the Music: Bizet's *Carmen* and Narrative Resistance," paper presented at the annual conference of the Society for the Study of Narrative Literature, Vancouver, 22 April 1994, argues against McClary's reading and in favor of a conflict between our desire for formal closure on the level of the music and our ethical desire for Carmen to survive on the level of the narrative.

78. McClary, *Feminine Endings*, 63.

79. An example of the critical position we are arguing against here is John Louis DiGaetani, *An Invitation to the Opera* (New York: Doubleday, 1986), 223: "*Carmen* has an eternal quality because of its basis in the male-versus-female conflict and its tragic ending, and because of Bizet's music." This should be contrasted with the feminist views of Clément and McClary.

80. Stephen Heath, *The Sexual Fix* (New York: Schocken, 1982), 3.

81. For more detail, see Maingueneau, *Carmen*, 20–22, 49–53, 58–60. On Gitanes cigarettes, see Klein, *Cigarettes*, 107–8.

82. "F. de L.," *Revue des Deux Mondes*, 480.

83. "F. de L.," 479.

84. Director Peter Brook may be right, therefore, when he claims that "Bizet was working at a time when public taste prevented him from going as far on the opera stage as Mérimée did in print. What was only *just* possible in literature was not permissible at all on the stage." See interview in Loney, "*Carmen* Connection," 12.

85. On "Orientalism," see Edward Said, *Orientalism* (New York: Vintage, 1979). Christopher L. Miller, "1847, 23 December: Orientalism, Colonialism," in *A New History of French Literature*, ed. Denis Hollier (Cambridge: Harvard University Press, 1989), 700, notes that "Orientalism was a *discourse*, a body of linguistic and extralinguistic expressions capable of shaping the perception of reality." On Orientalist opera, in particular, see the entry "Exoticism" in *New Grove Dictionary of Opera*, 2:96.

86. The Greek puns on, and thereby sets up the relation between, *thalamos* (chamber—here translated as bed) and *thanatos* (death).

87. See Dupouy, "*Carmen*" *de Mérimée*, 131, 134.

88. McClary, *Georges Bizet, "Carmen"*, 22; for a challenge to this view, see Rabinowitz, "Outside the Culture," where he argues convincingly in favor of Carmen's physical and moral agency and choice.

89. See McClary, *Georges Bizet, "Carmen,"* 66.

90. See Mina Curtiss, *Bizet and His World* (New York: Knopf, 1958), 407.

91. On the nondomestic appeal, see Maingueneau, *Carmen*, 111. On smoking, see T. de Ferrière, *Les Romans et le mariage* (Paris: Fournier, 1827), 1:97, where there is a description of a gypsy orgy of wine, women, and song, plus smoking:

"les femmes souriantes et à demi nues, l'amour dans les yeux, le cigare à la bouche."

92. McClary, *Georges Bizet, "Carmen,"* 57, 65–66, 104; Rabinowitz, "Outside the Culture," 10, notes that the prelude's ominous "fate motif" also turns on the augmented second.

93. See McClary, *Georges Bizet, "Carmen"*, 34. One of the librettists and Bizet's brother-in-law, Halévy, was himself Jewish, but McClary's argument can be supported by the 1875 review in the *Revue des Deux Mondes* discussed earlier. Contrast this to the dehistoricized interpretation of Robert Wangermée in "L'opéra sur scène et à l'écran: A Propos de 'Carmen,'" in *Approches de l'opéra*, ed. André Helbo, Actes du Colloque AISS, Royaumont, September 1984 (Paris: Didier, 1986), 252: "Carmen est une femme fatale, farouchement attachée à sa liberté, mais elle est d'un autre monde, c'est une bohémienne: elle ne pouvait inquiéter la bourgeoisie bien pensante que dans un imaginaire sans conséquence."

94. The fourth chapter of the novella, added in 1847, is a pedantic disquisition on gypsies, based largely on the work of Borrow and Pott, but the focus is on the light morals of gypsy women, their sneakiness and superstition. Robinson ("Mérimée's *Carmen*," 14) reads this chapter as the French narrator's assertion of his authority over Carmen's language, in an act that duplicates José's male control over her body. This he connects to the French male response to the emancipated female (e.g., George Sand) and to renewed feminist activity in the nineteenth century. For a full analysis of the multiple and even contradictory associations with the "magic and malevolence" associated with gypsies, see Katie Trumpener, "The Time of the Gypsies: A 'People without History' in the Narratives of the West," *Critical Inquiry* 18, 4 (1992): 843–84.

95. Clément, *Opera, or The Undoing of Women*, 49.

96. Klaus Theweleit, *Male Fantasies*, vol. 1, *Women, Floods, Bodies, History*, trans. Stephen Conway (Minneapolis: University of Minnesota Press, 1987), 79. Theweleit here is studying the fantasies of the German *Freikorps* members who went from being regular soldiers in World War I to being irregulars between the wars and finally SA members in the Second World War.

97. For the association of the proletarian woman with the whore and, further, of the erotic woman with perverted nature and thus with fascist conceptions of class and race, see Theweleit, *Women*, 68, 79, and 171 especially.

98. It is no doubt significant that in Latin Carmen's name means both song and charm, both music and prophecy; there may also be a punning play on the Latin *carmin*, red—the color associated with passion and with Carmen throughout. Emphasizing even more Carmen's marginal position, in Andalu-

sia a *carmen* is a country house "between culture and nature," explains Nelly Furman in "The Languages of Love in *Carmen*," in *Reading Opera*, ed. Arthur Groos and Roger Parker (Princeton: Princeton University Press, 1988), 174.

99. McClary, *Feminine Endings*, 65.

100. See McClary's long discussion of these issues in *Feminine Endings*, 63–65.

101. See Vera Pohland, "From Positive-Stigma to Negative-Stigma: A Shift of the Literary and Medical Representation of Consumption in German Culture," in *Disease and Medicine in Modern German Culture*, ed. Rudolf Käser and Vera Pohland, *Cornell Studies in International Affairs*, *Western Societies Papers*, no. 15 (1990): 153 and 163, n. 19.

102. Krogh, *Smoking*, 12–13; see also Klein, *Cigarettes*, 182: cigarette smoking is a "wordless but eloquent form of expression. It is a fully coded, rhetorically complex, narratively articulated discourse with a vast repertoire of well-understood conventions that are implicated, intertextually, in the whole literary, philosophical, cultural history of smoking."

Epilogue

1. Wayne Koestenbaum, *The Queen's Throat: Opera, Homosexuality, and the Mystery of Desire* (New York: Poseidon, 1993).

2. Terrence McNally, *The Lisbon "Traviata"* (New York: Plume, 1990), 20. All further references will be to this edition.

3. The Loren Linnard/Donald Briggs opera *Least of My Children* is said to be about two lovers, one of whom has AIDS. See Bruce-Michael Gelbert, "Gay Themes in Opera," *Christopher Street* 220 (1994): 17. An opera based on Sarah Schulman's novel *People in Trouble* (New York: Dutton, 1990)—about a woman, her husband, and her female lover, set against a backdrop of AIDS—was scheduled for production by the Houston Grand Opera in 1993. See Judith Laurence Pastore, "What Are the Responsibilities of Representing AIDS?" in *Confronting AIDS through Literature: The Responsibilities of Representation*, ed. Judith Laurence Pastore (Urbana: University of Illinois Press, 1993), 23. We have not been able to see or to locate the text of either opera.

4. Mirko D. Grmek, *History of AIDS: Emergence and Origin of a Modern Pandemic*, trans. Russell C. Maulitz and Jacalyn Duffin (Princeton: Princeton University Press, 1990), xii.

5. Susan Sontag, *AIDS and Its Metaphors* (New York: Farrar, Straus and Giroux, 1988), 94.

6. The phrase quoted is from Charles E. Rosenberg, "Disease and Social Order in America: Perceptions and Expectations," in *AIDS: The Burdens of History*, ed. Elizabeth Fee and Daniel M. Fox (Berkeley: University of California Press, 1988), 28. See also his "Framing Disease: Illness, Society, and History," in *Fram-*

ing Disease: Studies in Cultural History, ed. Charles E. Rosenberg and Janet Golden (New Brunswick: Rutgers University Press, 1992), xx: "Disease is irrevocably a social actor, that is, a factor in a structured configuration of social interactions. But the boundaries within which it can play its social role are often shaped by its biological character."

7. Barry D. Adam, "The State, Public Policy, and AIDS Discourse," in *Fluid Exchanges: Artists and Critics in the AIDS Crisis*, ed. James Miller (Toronto: University of Toronto Press, 1992), 306–7.

8. Respectively, Paula Treichler, "AIDS, Homophobia, and Biomedical Discourse: An Epidemic of Signification," *October* 43 (1987): 31–70, and Lee Edelman, "The Plague of Discourse: Politics, Literary Theory, and AIDS," in *Displacing Homophobia*, ed. Ron Butters, John Clum, and Michael Moon (Durham: Duke University Press, 1989), 289–305. See also Douglas Crimp, "AIDS: Cultural Analysis/Cultural Activism," in *AIDS: Cultural Analysis/Cultural Activism*, ed. Douglas Crimp (Cambridge: MIT Press, 1987), 3.

9. For examples of the limitation of these metaphors to the 1980s, see Dorothy Nelkin, David P. Willis, and Scott V. Parris, "Introduction: A Disease of Society," in their edition of *A Disease of Society: Cultural and Institutional Responses to AIDS* (Cambridge: Cambridge University Press, 1991), 4; for the "unprecedented sexual threat," see Leo Bersani, "Is the Rectum a Grave?" *October* 43 (winter 1987): 198; for the "unparalleled scale," see Simon Watney, *Policing Desire: Pornography, AIDS, and the Media* (Minneapolis: University of Minnesota Press, 1987), 9. See too Mark A. Wainberg, "Why Are There So Many Myths about AIDS?" *Canadian Medical Association Journal* 148, 5 (1993): 745: "No other disease has been written about in a way that combines tragic details with sexual innuendoes that both enrapture and confound the public."

10. Patricia W. Dideriksen and John A. Bartlett, *New England Journal of Medicine* 322, 6 (1990): 415.

11. Tony Kushner, *Part Two: Perestroika* (New York: Theatre Communications Group, 1992), 55, and idem, *Part One: Millennium Approaches* (New York: Theatre Communications Group, 1992), 86. Subsequent references are to these editions.

12. Jeffrey Weeks, "AIDS and the Regulation of Sexuality," in *AIDS and Contemporary History*, ed. Virginia Berridge and Philip Strong (Cambridge: Cambridge University Press, 1993), 17. On the discursive complexities of AIDS outside the West, see Paula A. Treichler, "AIDS and HIV Infection in the Third World: A First World Chronicle," in *Remaking History*, ed. Barbara Kruger and Phil Mariani (Seattle: Bay, 1989), 31–86; Jeff O'Malley, "The Representation of AIDS in Third World Development Discourse," in Miller, *Fluid Exchanges*, 169–76.

13. Sontag, *AIDS and Its Metaphors*, 38–39.

14. See Michael Denneny, "AIDS Writing and the Creation of a Gay Culture," in Pastore, *Confronting AIDS through Literature*, 36.

15. This was discussed at the end of chapter 1; see Herbert Lindenberger, *Opera: The Extravagant Art* (Ithaca: Cornell University Press, 1984), 65, on Whitman and on the "operatic principle."

16. See Susan Sontag, "Some Notes on 'Camp,'" in her *"Against Interpretation" and Other Essays* (New York: Ferrar, Straus and Giroux, 1966), 275–92.

17. See Eric Savoy, "You Can't Go Homo Again: Queer Theory and the Foreclosure of Gay Studies," *English Studies in Canada* 20, 2 (1994): 129–52, on queer theory and ironized discourse as capable of "destabilizing coherence, disrupting category, fostering doubleness" (131).

18. Treichler, "AIDS, Homophobia, and Biomedical Discourse," 42. See also Cindy Patton, *Inventing AIDS* (New York: Routledge, 1990), 1.

19. See Joseph Cady and Kathryn Montgomery Hunter, "Making Contact: The AIDS Plays," in *The Meaning of AIDS: Implications for Medical Science, Clinical Practice, and Public Health Policy*, ed. Eric T. Juengst and Barbara A. Koenig (New York: Praeger, 1989), 42.

20. Judith Butler, *Bodies That Matter: On the Discursive Limits of "Sex"* (New York: Routledge, 1993), 233. See also Eve Sedgwick, "Queer Performativity," in *GLQ* 1, 1 (1993). The relationship of AIDS performativity and traditions of cross-dressing and drag is also discussed in both. On the movement Queer Nation, see Lauren Berlant and Elizabeth Freeman, "Queer Nationality," *boundary 2* 19 (1992): 149–80.

21. Tony Kushner in an interview with Adam Mars Jones, 24 January 1992, published in *Platform Papers 2: On "Angels in America"* (London: Royal National Theatre, 1992), 15.

22. On television and film representations of AIDS, see Paula A. Treichler, "AIDS Narratives on Television: Whose Story?" in *Writing AIDS: Gay Literature, Language, and Analysis*, ed. Timothy F. Murphy and Suzanne Poirier (New York: Columbia University Press, 1993), 161–99; John M. Clum, "'And Once I Had It All': AIDS Narratives and Memories of an American Dream," in the same volume, 200–224; John J. O'Connor, "Gay Images: TV's Mixed Signals," *New York Times*, 19 May 1991, H1 and H32; Stephen Farber, "A Decade into the AIDS Epidemic, the TV Networks Are Still Nervous," *New York Times*, 30 April 1991, C13 and C18; Bart Beaty, "The Syndrome Is the System: A Political Reading of *Longtime Companion*," in Miller, *Fluid Exchanges*, 111–21.

   The difference between a story told from the inside and one told from the outside has been addressed in other terms by Arthur Kleinman in *The Illness Narratives: Suffering, Healing, and the Human Condition* (New York: Basic Books,

1988), where he contrasts the personal, intimate, emotional "illness narrative" with the clinical, cold medical case history.

23. For bibliographies on AIDS literature in general and plays in particular, see Franklin Brooks and Timothy F. Murphy, "Annotated Bibliography of AIDS Literature, 1982–91," in Murphy and Poirier, *Writing AIDS*, 321–39; Joseph Cady, "AIDS on the National Stage," *Medical Humanities Review* 6 (1992): 20–26; Judith Laurence Pastore, "Annotated Bibliography," in Pastore, *Confronting AIDS through Literature*, 249–64.

24. Thomas Waugh, "Erotic Self-Images in the Gay Male AIDS Melodrama," in Miller, *Fluid Exchanges*, 134.

25. On the importance of apocalyptic AIDS rhetoric in general, see Peter Dickinson, "'Go-Go Dancing on the Brink of Apocalypse': Representing AIDS — an Essay in Seven Epigraphs," *English Studies in Canada* 20, 2 (1994): 227–47. The particular theatrical echoes of plague imagery include Antonin Artaud's "Le Théâtre de la peste," *Nouvelle Revue Française*, 1 October 1934, 481–99, in which plague victims are seen as driven, by the psychic and physical pain of a life-threatening disease, to freedom and extravagant behavior. For Artaud this situation resembled the theater, with what he saw as its contagious epidemic of delirium.

26. Larry Kramer, *The Normal Heart* (London: Methuen, 1985), 11. Subsequent references are to this edition.

27. Albert R. Jonsen, "Foreword," in Juengst and Koenig, *Meaning of AIDS*, xiii. See also Jennifer O'Flaherty, "The AIDS Patient: A Historical Perspective on the Physician's Obligation to Treat," *Pharos*, summer 1991, 13–16.

28. See Laurel Brodsley, "Teaching about AIDS and Plagues: A Reading List from the Humanities," in Pastore, *Confronting AIDS through Literature*, 199; contrast this to earlier discussions such as those of Frederick P. Siegal and Marta Siegal, *AIDS: The Medical Mystery* (New York: Grove, 1983), and David Black, *The Plague Years: A Chronicle of AIDS, the Epidemic of Our Time* (New York: Simon and Schuster, 1985).

29. Sontag, *AIDS and Its Metaphors*, 64.

30. On the scapegoating during the European plagues, see the earlier discussion in chapter 1. See also Guenther B. Risse, "Epidemics and History: Ecological Perspective and Social Responses," in Fee and Fox, *AIDS: The Burdens of History*, 40; Barbara Tuchman's chapter "This Is the End of the World: The Black Death," in *A Distant Mirror* (New York: Knopf, 1978); William H. McNeill, *Plagues and People* (Garden City NY: Doubleday, 1976), chapters 1 and 2; Philip Ziegler, *The Black Death* (New York: Harper and Row, 1969), 96–108; Edwin M. Stieve, "Medical and Moral Interpretations of Plague and Pestilence in Late Middle English Texts" (Ph.D. diss., Michigan State University, 1988).

On the analogies with AIDS and its scapegoating, see Sander L. Gilman,

Difference and Pathology: Stereotypes of Sexuality, Race, and Madness (Ithaca: Cornell University Press, 1985), 24; Ken Plummer, "Organizing AIDS," in *Social Aspects of AIDS*, ed. Peter Aggleton and Hilary Homans (Philadelphia: Falmer, 1988), 33; Simon Watney, "The Spectacle of AIDS," *October* 43 (1987): 74. For a different reading of scapegoating and AIDS in drama, see George Newtown, "Sex, Death, and the Drama of AIDS," *Antioch Review* 47, 2 (1989): 209–22.

31. William Finn and James Lapine, *Falsettos*, part 2, *Falsettoland* (New York: Plume, 1993), 163. Subsequent references are to this edition.

32. See Richard D. Slick, "Poe's 'The Masque of the Red Death,'" *Explicator* 47, 2 (1989): 24–26.

33. William M. Hoffman, *As Is*, in *The Way We Live Now: American Plays and the AIDS Crisis*, ed. Elizabeth M. Osborn (New York: Theatre Communications Group, 1990), 12. Subsequent references are to this edition.

34. Harvey Fierstein, *Safe Sex*, in Osborn, *Way We Live Now*, 82. Subsequent references are to this edition.

35. Harry Kondoleon, *Zero Positive*, in Osborn, *Way We Live Now*, 247. Subsequent references are to this edition.

36. See Julien S. Murphy, "The AIDS Epidemic: A Phenomenological Analysis of the Infectious Body," in Juengst and Koenig, *Meaning of AIDS*, 55.

37. See Graham Hancock and Enver Carim, *AIDS: The Deadly Epidemic* (London: Gollancz, 1986), 40.

38. Sander L. Gilman, *Disease and Representation: Images of Illness from Madness to AIDS* (Ithaca: Cornell University Press, 1988), 4.

39. On opera and nationalism, see Anthony Arblaster, *Viva la Libertà: Politics in Opera* (New York: Verso, 1992), 63–146, 193–224.

40. Angels have become a kind of postmodern commonplace, as Brian McHale notes in his *Constructing Postmodernism* (New York: Routledge, 1992), 200. He claims that "from epoch to epoch, the angels have always served immediate ideological needs dictated by the times in which they find themselves. Appropriated and reappropriated by different and often incompatible systems of thought, they have functioned as a kind of secondary language in which angelologists could conduct coded discussions of a range of this-worldly issues" (202). Prior's angel, however, draws specifically on that long tradition of Jewish as well as Christian associations, using them to subvert the religious Right's interpretation of AIDS.

41. Kushner, in the interview with Adam Mars Jones, 13.

42. We thank Russell Kilbourn for pointing out that (the tubercular) Franz Kafka, in his diaries, records the arrival of an angel, likewise through his ceiling, as "a vision intended for my liberation." See *The Diaries of Franz Kafka, 1914–1923*, ed. Max Brod, trans. Martin Greenberg (New York: Schocken, 1949), 63.

43. This portrayal of heaven suggests that powerfully transgressive image of a heaven where everything is falling apart (including the aged, blind God) in Oskar Panizza's scandalous satirical play about syphilis, *The Council of Love: A Celestial Tragedy in Five Acts*, trans. Oreste F. Pucciani (1895; New York: Viking, 1973). Panizza is also as clinically forthright in his portrayal of this venereal disease as Kushner is in his stage presentation of AIDS.

44. John M. Clum, *Acting Gay: Male Homosexuality in Modern Drama*, rev. ed. (New York: Columbia University Press, 1992), 263.

45. Sontag, *AIDS and Its Metaphors*, 39. For AIDS, the African green monkey is among the many claimed sources of the virus, for instance.

46. See Judith Laurence Pastore, "What Are the Responsibilities of Representing AIDS?" 27–28.

47. Rosenberg, "Disease and Social Order," 29.

48. See Risse, "Epidemics and History," 46.

49. John Greyson, "Parma Violets for Wayland Flowers," in Miller, *Fluid Exchanges*, 139–45.

50. See Nancy Aycock Metz, "Discovering a World of Suffering: Fiction and the Rhetoric of Sanitary Reform — 1840–1860," *Nineteenth-Century Contexts* 15, 1 (1991): 65.

51. Adam, "State, Public Policy, and AIDS Discourse," 306.

52. Arthur Kroker, "Sacrificial Sex," in Miller, *Fluid Exchanges*, 325.

53. Gilman, *Disease and Representation*, 266.

54. See Alan M. Kraut, *Silent Travelers: Germs, Genes, and the "Immigrant Menace"* (New York: Basic Books, 1994), 33–34.

55. See Linda Singer, *Erotic Welfare: Sexual Theory and Politics in the Age of Epidemic*, ed. and intro. Judith Butler and Maureen MacGrogan (New York: Routledge, 1993), 29; Watney, *Policing Desire*, 3.

56. See Clum, *Acting Gay*, 46.

57. Allan M. Brandt, "AIDS: From Social History to Social Policy," in Fee and Fox, *AIDS: The Burdens of History*, 150–53.

58. Elizabeth Fee, "Sin versus Science: Venereal Disease in Twentieth-Century Baltimore," in Fee and Fox, *AIDS: The Burdens of History*, 122. This link is also suggested by Barbara Fass Leavy's analysis of the echoes of Ibsen's syphilitic morality tale, *Ghosts*, in William Hoffman's AIDS play *As Is*. See her *To Blight with Plague: Studies in a Literary Theme* (New York: New York University Press, 1992), 102–10.

59. Allison Fraiberg, "Of AIDS, Cyborgs, and Other Indiscretions: Resurfacing the Body in the Postmodern," in *Essays in Postmodern Culture*, ed. Eyal Amiran and John Unsworth (New York: Oxford University Press, 1993), 47. On the fear of infection and the attempt of plays to break the power of that fear,

see James W. Jones, "The Sick Homosexual: AIDS and Gays on the American Stage and Screen," in Pastore, *Confronting AIDS through Literature*, 106–7.

60. Christopher Durang, *Laughing Wild*, the male monologue central section of *Seeking Wild*, excerpted in Osborn, *Way We Live Now*, 181. Subsequent references are to this edition.

61. For this long discussion, see Gilman, *Disease and Representation*, 247–62 especially.

62. See Brandt, "AIDS: From Social History to Social Policy," 152; Fee, "Sin versus Science," 123; Watney, *Policing Desire*, 33; Roy Porter, "History Says No to the Policeman's Response to AIDS," *British Medical Journal* 293, 6562 (1986): 1589–90. Porter pointedly notes, "It is a misfortune, not a crime, to contract a disease" (1590).

63. Sontag, *AIDS and Its Metaphors*, 9–11. See also Michael S. Sherry, "The Language of War in AIDS Discourse," in Murphy and Poirier, *Writing AIDS*, 39–53.

64. For an overview of this, see Edward W. Hook III and Christine M. Marra, "Acquired Syphilis in Adults," *New England Journal of Medicine* 326, 16 (1992): 1060–69.

65. Allan M. Brandt, *No Magic Bullet: A Social History of Venereal Disease in the United States since 1880* (New York: Oxford University Press, 1987), 199.

66. Emily Apter, "Fantom Images: Hervé Guibert and the Writing of 'SIDA' in France," in Murphy and Poirier, *Writing AIDS,* 89. However, the 1989 "Against Nature" exhibition in Los Angeles deliberately took on the French decadent syphilitic scenario of Huysmans's *A Rebour* (often translated as *Against Nature*), recoding it into an AIDS context and framing it in "the ironic, campy perspective of latter-day dandies" (Greyson, "Parma Violets," 136). On Huysmans and syphilis, see chapter 3, note 48.

67. Sander L. Gilman, "Plague in Germany, 1939/1989: Cultural Images of Race, Space, and Disease," in Murphy and Poirier, *Writing AIDS,* 77.

68. Tony Kushner, cited in *Economist* 322 (22 February 1992): 88.

69. Ronald O. Valdiserri, *Gardening in Clay: Reflections on AIDS* (Ithaca: Cornell University Press, 1994), 9.

70. Richard Goldstein, "The Implicated and the Immune: Responses to AIDS in the Arts and Popular Culture," in Nelkin, Willis, and Parris, *Disease of Society*, 17. John Greyson, in "Parma Violets," 135, talks of this explosion of work: "We make AIDS art to heal, to mourn, to rage, to engage, to change," and therefore, he says, the response of artists is going to be "urgent, vital, and voluminous."

71. People in the United States (as elsewhere) with AIDS have faced the same social prejudices in recent years that those with tuberculosis faced earlier: problems with insurance companies, difficulties in getting hired if their di-

agnosis was known, not to mention general fear and panic over contagion. See, on tuberculosis, Sheila M. Rothman, *Living in the Shadow of Death: Tuberculosis and the Social Experience of Illness in American History* (New York: Basic Books, 1994), 189.

72. Clum, *Acting Gay*, 48 and 52. See also Everett Quinton, "Tootaloo Marguerite!" in *Violetta and Her Sisters: The Lady of the Camellias, Responses to the Myth*, ed. Nicholas John (London: Faber and Faber, 1994), 151–53, for an argument for the *non*-gender-specific nature of Dumas's universal oppressed heroine.

73. See Waugh, "Erotic Self-Images," on the importance of melodrama's conventions to AIDS films and videos.

74. Susan Sontag, with Edward Parone, "The Way We Live Now," in Osborn *Way We Live Now*, 125 and 124.

75. Richard Goldstein, "Implicated and the Immune," 31.

76. The terms are, respectively, those of Jan Zita Grover, "Visible Lesions," *Afterimage* 17, 1 (1989): 13, and Patton, *Inventing AIDS*. Simon Watney writes of the "counterdiscourse of gay identity" in a somewhat different sense of the term, in "The Possibilities of Permutation: Pleasure, Proliferation, and the Politics of Gay Identity in the Age of AIDS," in Miller, *Fluid Exchanges*, 352.

77. The phrase is that of Simon Watney, "The Spectacle of AIDS," *October* 43 (1987): 78. See also Douglas Crimp, "How to Have Promiscuity in an Epidemic," in Crimp, *AIDS: Cultural Analysis/Cultural Activism*, 237–71; Michael Callan, *Surviving and Thriving with AIDS: Collected Wisdom*, 2 vols. (New York: People with AIDS Coalition, 1987).

78. On Fabo's art, see David White, " 'The Soul Is the Prison of the Body': Fabo on Foucault," in Miller, *Fluid Exchanges*, 65–86. On General Idea, see John Bentley Mays, "Illness as Metaphor," *Globe and Mail*, 20 March 1993, C13. On the negative reaction to Nixon's show at the Museum of Modern Art in New York, see "Art about AIDS: Two Voices—Multiple Contexts," a dialogue between Thomas Sokolowski and Robert Atkins, guest curators of "From Media to Metaphor: Art about AIDS," a 1992–93 traveling exhibition. The dialogue is in the catalog, pp. 10–12.

79. Jeffrey Schmalz, "Whatever Happened to AIDS?" *New York Times Magazine*, 28 November 1993, 58.

80. Black, *Plague Years*, 61.

81. Thomas Yingling, "Wittgenstein's Tumour: AIDS and the National Body," *Textual Practice* 8, 1 (1994): 101.

82. Ibid., 106.

83. On Dugas, see Randy Shilts, *And the Band Played On: Politics, People, and the AIDS Epidemic* (New York: St. Martin's Press, 1987), 21 ff.

84. Diamanda Galas, statement included with the compact disc of *Masque of the Red Death*, MUTE Records, 1986.

85. See Johannes Birringer, "*Ad Mortem*, an AIDS Performance Project," *Theatre Topics* 2, 2 (1992): 135–48. The work was created by Johannes Birringer, Isabelle Ganz (mezzo-soprano), Richard Nunemaker (bass clarinet), and Deborah Hay (dancer).

86. For a powerful analysis of "First World" perceptions of "Third World" AIDS, see Treichler, "AIDS and HIV Infection in the Third World."

87. Nicholas John, "Introduction," in *Violetta and Her Sisters*, 11. The subsequent quotation is from the same page.

88. Jann Matlock, *Scenes of Seduction: Prostitution, Hysteria, and Reading Difference in Nineteenth-Century France* (New York: Columbia University Press, 1994), 110.

89. Lindenberger, *Opera*, 267. Barbara Fass Leavy, in *To Blight with Plague*, 90, also notes that it is a commonplace of criticism on Ibsen's *Ghosts* to read the work's syphilis as only a metaphor for a "sick society that stifled the individual." But this too was a real disease, even if it also took on symbolic meanings.

90. Theodor Adorno, "Bourgeois Opera," in *Opera through Other Eyes*, ed. David Levin (Stanford: Stanford University Press, 1994), 36.

91. The quotations are from Jean Starobinski, "Opera and Enchantresses," in Levin, *Opera through Other Eyes*, 20.

Photo Credits

1. Photo by Michael Cooper. Canadian Opera Company Archives (87-1048-#8).
2. Photo by Michael Cooper. Canadian Opera Company Archives (87-1048-#19).
3. Photo by Michael Cooper. Canadian Opera Company Archives (91-626-#24-24A).
4. Photo by Michael Cooper. Canadian Opera Company Archives (91-832-#23).
5. Metropolitan Opera Archives.
6. From Franz Mracek, *Atlas of Syphilis and the Venereal Diseases* (London: The Rebman Publishing Co., 1898), plate 53. Wellcome Institute Library, London (L0023387B00).
7. From Karl Sudhoff, *Graphische und typographische Erstlinge der Syphilisliteratur aus den Jahren 1495 und 1496* (München, 1912), table 10. Wellcome Institute Library, London (L0023388B00).
8. "The Rake's Progress," engraving 3. Fisher Library, Rare Books and Special Collections, John P. Robarts Library, University of Toronto.
9. The Rake's Progress," engraving 8. Fisher Library, Rare Books and Special Collections, John P. Robarts Library, University of Toronto.
10. Metropolitan Opera Archives.
11. Metropolitan Opera Archives.
12. Photo by Michael Cooper. Canadian Opera Company Archives (91-306-#2).
13. Photo by Robert C. Ragsdale. Canadian Opera Company Archives (PX7000-84-XXTIF-21).
14. Photo by Michael Cooper. Canadian Opera Company Archives (92-107-#134-14).
15. Photo by Michael Cooper. Canadian Opera Company Archives (92-103-#11A).
16. "Elegant Preventive of the Cholera," from F. W. Fairholt, *Tobacco: Its History and Association* (London, 1859), vol. 1. Arents Collections, The New York Public Library, Astor, Lenox and Tilden Foundations (Arents 3248).
17. From J. Balde, *Die Truckene Trunkenheit* (Nuremberg, 1658). Arents Collections, The New York Public Library, Astor, Lenox and Tilden Foundations (Arents 3283).
18. "Pipes as Works of Art," Arents Collection *Catalog*, Arents Collections, The New York Public Library, Astor, Lenox and Tilden Foundations.
19. "Enjoying a Friend," from F. W. Fairholt, *Tobacco: Its History and Association* (London, 1859), vol. 2. Arents Collections, The New York Public Library, Astor, Lenox and Tilden Foundations (Arents 3249).

20. Metropolitan Opera Archives.
21. Metropolitan Opera Archives.
22. Engraving by Levasseur after J. Delaunay (n.d.). Wellcome Institute Library, London (V0010664B00).
23. Photo by Joan Marcus.

Index

Abbate, Carolyn, 78, 246 n.6, 255 n.86, 258 n.111

Adorno, Theodor, 77, 87, 92, 226–27, 229 n.8

AIDS: and cholera, 24, 26, 196, 203, 210–14; countermythology about, 27, 200–202, 205, 206, 208–10, 212–13, 215–16, 218, 220–25, 227; medical history of, 2, 19, 197–99, 216–17; and plague, 26, 96, 198, 199, 202–10, 215, 223–25; religious interpretation of, 27, 204–5, 206, 208–10, 214, 215–16, 223–25; stage and musical representations of, 17, 26–27, 195–227; and syphilis, 26, 61, 121, 196, 198–99, 200, 202, 203, 214–18; and tuberculosis, 26, 196, 198, 200, 202, 218–20, 225. See also *Angels in America* (Kushner)

Anderson, Rod. See *Mario and the Magician* (Somers/Anderson)

Angels in America (Kushner), 26–27, 199, 201, 202–10, 212, 214, 215, 219, 224

antisemitism. *See* Judaism

As Is (Hoffman), 203, 219

Auden, W. H. See *The Rake's Progress* (Stravinsky/Auden and Kallmann)

The Baltimore Waltz (Vogel), 221

Barbier, Jules. See *Les Contes d'Hoffmann* (Offenbach/Barbier and Carrière)

Barrès, Maurice, 181, 188

Bartlett, Thomas, 36, 50

Baudelaire, Charles, 74, 77, 79, 224, 250 n.48

Bayle, Gaspard L., 21, 30

The Beggar's Opera (Gay), 117–18, 168

Berg, Alban. See *Lulu* (Berg/Wedekind)

Bernheimer, Charles, 241 n.45, 251 n.48, 254 n.72, 265 n.32

Bernstein, Leonard, 23, 118–19

Bizet, Georges. See *Carmen* (Bizet/Meilhac and Halévy)

Black Death. *See* plague

Boccaccio, Giovanni, 15, 152–53

La Bohème (Puccini/Giacosa and Illica), xiv, 12, 21–22, 29, 38, 39, 40, 48–59, 128, 177, 194, 205, 218, 219, 226, 272 n.35

Boulez, Pierre, 92, 99

Brandt, Allan M., 217, 229 n.3, 252 n.53, 255 n.84, 283 n.57, 284 n.62 n.65

Britten, Benjamin. See *Death in Venice* (Britten/Piper)

Brooks, Peter, 8, 10

Candide (Bernstein), 23, 117–20

Candide (Voltaire), 118–19

Carmen (Bizet/Meilhac and Halévy), 8, 9, 11, 25–26, 48, 80, 165, 178–92, 194, 195

Carmen (Mérimée), 179–80, 181, 184, 188–89, 190–91

Cassell, Eric, 64–65, 149

cholera: and homosexuality, 23–24, 130–33, 134, 138, 141–44, 159–60; medical history of, 18–19, 21, 23–25, 123–30, 134–35; miasma theory of, 128, 133, 135, 136, 143, 151, 164; operatic representations of, 17, 23–24, 130–49; social context of, 24, 123, 124–30, 149, 159–60, 164, 165, 214, 235 n.80; symptoms of, 24, 124, 125, 129, 135–36

Civinini, Guelfo. See *La Fanciulla del West* (Puccini/Civinini and Zangarini) class, social, 4, 15, 22, 24, 42, 47, 48–49, 57–58, 74–75, 80, 128–30, 191, 211, 213, 215, 226–27, 235 n.80

Clément, Catherine, 5, 11–12, 13, 47, 57–58, 179, 191, 243 n.74

Cocteau, Jean, 16. See also *Oedipus Rex*

Conrad, Peter, 5, 93, 232 n.14, 241 n.48, 246 n.10, 247 n.18, 256 n.92 n.93

consumption. See tuberculosis

Les Contes d'Hoffmann (Offenbach/Barbier and Carrière), 21, 29, 30–37, 40, 59, 170

countermythology. See AIDS: counter-mythology about

Dahlhaus, Carl, 9, 92, 275 n.68

La Dame aux camélias (Dumas), 29, 44–48, 52, 54, 218, 220

Dean, Winton, 186

Death in Venice (Britten/Piper), 15, 23–24, 128, 134–49, 151, 159, 210–11, 213–14, 225

Death in Venice (Mann). See Mann, Thomas: *Der Tod in Venedig*

Debussy, Claude, 14

Delaporte, François, 264 n.19 n.20 n.24

disease: eroticization of, 24, 38–39, 77, 148, 200, 217; interventions, phar-maceutical, 19, 25, 108, 117, 121; and medical historical changes, 18–21, 126–28, 234 n.65; and poverty, 22, 24, 40, 48, 49–50, 52, 54–55, 58, 59, 128–30, 213; public health measures and surveillance, 23, 24, 25, 27, 107–8, 128–30, 159–60, 213–14, 216–17; social and cultural construc-tion of, v, 1–3, 13–14, 17–19, 21, 24, 26–27, 38–39, 57, 58–59, 150–51, 199–202, 220–25, 226–27, 233 n.64. See also AIDS; cholera; plague; sexuality; stigmatizing; syphilis; tuberculosis

Doane, Mary Ann, 80

Dumas, Alexandre, fils. See *La Dame aux camélias* (Dumas)

Durang, Christopher, 215–16

Enescu, George, 17. See also *Oedipe* (Enescu/Fleg)

eroticization. See disease: eroticiza-tion of

Evans, Richard J., 124

Falsettos (Finn and Lapine), 201, 203, 212–13, 215, 221

La Fanciulla del West (Puccini/Civinini and Zangarini), 9, 25, 170–72

fascism, 25, 149, 150, 153–55, 158–59, 160, 193

feminist interpretations of opera, 11–12, 57–58, 96, 191–92. See also Clé-ment, Catherine; McClary, Susan

femme fatale, 59, 79, 95, 189, 277 n.93

Fernel, Jean, 69

Fierstein, Harvey, 203

Finn, William. See *Falsettos* (Finn and Lapine)

Fisher King, 62, 85, 88, 90

Fleg, Edmond, 17

flower images in opera, 49, 52, 54–55, 64, 77, 79, 140

Fournier, Alfred, 71, 97, 106, 107, 116–17

Fracastorius, Hieronymus, 54, 71, 72, 109, 152, 248 n.29, 262 n.61

Galas, Diamanda, 201, 223–25

Gautier, Théophile, 54, 180

Gay, John, 117

Gay, Peter, 80, 254 n.72, 275 n.73

gender, 12, 57, 96, 99, 236 n.9, 237 n.10. See also feminist interpretations of opera; prostitution; tuberculosis

Giacosa, Giuseppe. See *La Bohème* (Puc-cini/Giacosa and Illica)

Gilman, Sander L., 10–11, 18, 26, 80, 82,

96, 133, 204, 216, 217, 251 n.48, 252
n.61, 254 n.71, 265 n.32, 275 n.73, 281
n.30, 283 n.53, 284 n.61

Girard, René, 150, 233 n.57

Goldstein, Richard, 220

Golisciani, Enrico. See Il segreto di Susanna (Wolf-Ferrari/Golisciani)

Götterdämmerung (Wagner), 48

Greyson, John, 211, 222–23, 284 n.70

Groos, Arthur, 245 n.2, 258 n.114

Gutman, Robert, 79

gypsies. See race; smoking

Halévy, Ludovic. See Carmen
(Bizet/Meilhac and Halévy)

Hanslick, Edward, 48–49, 76

Hepokoski, James A., 242 n.49

HIV infection. See AIDS

Hoffman, William M., 203, 219

Hoffmann, E. T. A., 30–37, 59, 170

Hogarth, William: "The Harlot's
Progress," 102, 105; "The Rake's
Progress," 23, 101, 102–6, 111, 116, 117

Holloway, Robin, 92

homosexuality, 22–25, 26–27, 130–33,
134, 138, 141–49, 155–60

Huysmans, J.-K., 74, 77, 79, 140, 250
n.48, 284 n.66

Illica, Luigi. See La Bohème (Puccini/Gia-
cosa and Illica)

interdisciplinarity, xiii–xvi

Jarman, Douglas, 259 n.11 n.12

jealousy, 52, 53, 55, 59, 174–76, 177–78,
184, 186–87, 189, 194, 244 n.76. See
also violence

Judaism, 15, 80–82, 99, 188, 190–91. See
also race

Kallmann, Chester. See The Rake's Progress
(Stravinsky/Auden and Kallmann)

Kerman, Joseph, 6, 116, 230 n.13

Klein, Richard, 161, 168, 231 n.13 n.18,
271 n.26 n.30 n.31, 272 n.36, 275 n.76,
278 n.102

Koch, Robert, 39–40, 58, 59, 126, 219,
226

Koestenbaum, Wayne, 5, 195

Kondoleon, Harry, 203

Kracauer, Siegfried, 37

Kramer, Greg, 221

Kramer, Larry, 219

Kramer, Lawrence, 5, 13, 230 n.12, 255
n.80

Kushner, Tony. See Angels in America
(Kushner)

Laënnec, René-Théophile-Hyacinthe,
21, 30

Lapine, James. See Falsettos (Finn and
Lapine)

Laughing Wild (Durang), 215–16

Levin, David, 7

Lindenberger, Herbert, 4, 5, 6, 26, 200,
231 n.27, 286 n.89

The Lisbon "Traviata" (McNally), 195–96,
203, 218

Louÿs, Pierre, 181

Lulu (Berg/Wedekind), 23, 95, 96–100,
101, 119, 130–33, 134

Maeterlinck, Maurice, 14

Mann, Thomas: Doktor Faustus, 200,
254 n.77; Mario und der Zauberer,
149–59; Der Tod in Venedig, 24, 128,
134–49, 267 n.65; on Wagner, 82, 87,
88, 93, 247 n.18, 253 n.68, 254 n.77,
257 n.100

Mario and the Magician (Somers/Ander-
son), 24–25, 149–59, 173, 193

Matlock, Jann, 241 n.45, 286 n.88

Maupassant, Guy de, 74, 78–79

McClary, Susan, 5, 185, 187, 189, 258
n.2, 277 n.92 n.93, 278 n.99 n.100

McNally, Terrence, 195

McNeill, William, 18–19, 263 n.10 n.14, 264 n.17
medical history. See AIDS; cholera; disease; plague; syphilis; tuberculosis
Meilhac, Henri. See Carmen (Bizet/Meilhac and Halévy)
Mérimée, Prosper. See Carmen (Mérimée)
miasma. See cholera
Morris, David B., 12
Mosse, George L., 158–59
Murger, Henry. See Scènes de la vie de Bohème (Murger)

nationalism, 4, 150, 152, 153–55, 158–59, 229 n.9
Nietzsche, Friedrich, 5, 16, 63, 86, 143, 146, 147–48, 154
The Normal Heart (Kramer), 219

Oedipe (Enescu/Fleg), 17, 225
Oedipus Rex (Sophocles), 14, 148, 203–4
Oedipus Rex (Stravinsky/Cocteau), 16–17, 225
Offenbach, Jacques. See Les Contes d'Hoffmann (Offenbach/Barbier and Carrière)
opera: complexity of, xiv–xvi, 1–2, 3–11, 230 n.19, 231 n.34; history of, 3, 11–12; libretto, importance of, xiv, 5–10; power of, 3–11, 227, 232 n.39 n.40; and sexuality (see sexuality; and individual operas by name)
Osler, Sir William, 71

pale spirochete. See syphilis
Palmer, Christopher, 140–41, 266 n.50, 267 n.58
Panizza, Oskar, 95, 96, 97, 283 n.43
Paré, Ambroise, 74
Parent-Duchâtelet, Alexandre, 42
Parran, Thomas, 107–8, 263 n.64

Parsifal (Syberberg), 67, 256 n.92
Parsifal (Wagner), xiv, 7, 13, 15, 22–23, 61–93, 96, 98, 101, 107, 116, 186, 190, 192, 214–15, 217
Parzifal. See Wolfram von Eschenbach
Paulson, Ronald, 102–3, 104–5
Pelléas et Mélisande (Debussy/Maeterlinck), 14
phthisis. See tuberculosis
Piave, Francesco Maria. See La Traviata (Verdi/Piave)
Piper, Myfanwy. See Death in Venice (Britten/Piper)
plague, 2, 14–17, 18, 19–20, 22, 23, 24, 77, 123–26, 139–40, 145, 150, 159, 164, 202–10, 223–25
Poizat, Michel, 12, 232 n.39, 254 n.75, 264 n.28
pox. See syphilis
Proksch, J. K., 75, 249 n.33, 250 n.43
prostitution, 22–23, 42, 43, 47–48, 77, 78–80, 82–83, 96–99, 102–4, 109–10, 112–13, 117–18, 130, 133, 216
Puccini, Giacomo. See La Bohème; La Fanciulla del West; Il tabarro

Quétel, Claude, 95, 107, 119, 248 n.25 n.26 n.28, 249 n.33 n.34, 252 n.58, 261 n.33 n.39 n.41

Rabinowitz, Peter J., 231 n.30, 275 n.77, 277 n.92
race, 15, 80, 95, 183, 186, 188–91, 192. See also Judaism; scapegoating
The Rake's Progress (Stravinsky/Auden and Kallmann), 23, 100–102, 103, 106–17, 119, 120, 217
Ricord, Philippe, 22–23, 75, 262 n.61
Der Ring des Nibelungen (Wagner), 76, 208; wordplay in, 87–92, 217.
Rose, Paul, 81
Rosenberg, Charles E., 21, 27, 229 n.1 n.2, 263 n.4, 264 n.15 n.20, 283 n.47

Safe Sex (Fierstein), 203

Said, Edward, 266 n.43, 276 n.85

scapegoating, 15, 17, 86, 126, 203–4, 211, 216, 281 n.30

Scary, Elaine, 12

Scènes de la vie de Bohème (Murger), 49–50, 52, 55, 58

Schmidgall, Gary, 6, 268 n.65

Schopenhauer, Arthur, 64, 67, 85, 149, 253 n.68, 257 n.97

Il segreto di Susanna (Wolf-Ferrari/Golisciani), 9, 25, 173–76, 182, 183, 192

sexuality, 4, 10, 13–17, 19, 23–24, 25–26, 59, 63–64, 76–80, 86, 93, 98–99, 102, 124, 129–30, 131–33, 141–49, 195, 227, 232 n.49. *See also* AIDS; cholera; homosexuality; syphilis; tuberculosis

Shilts, Randy, 222

Showalter, Elaine, 75, 79, 250 n.41 n.44, 259 n.7

Siegel, Jerrold, 49

Siegfried (Wagner), 14

Smith, Patrick J., 7

smoking: and disease, 19, 26, 161–62, 192–93; double meaning of, 9, 25, 162–68, 171, 173, 192; and gender, 167–71, 174–76, 179–83, 191–92; and gypsies, 26, 183–85, 187–91; history of, 161–68, 180, 192–93; operatic representations of, 9, 25–26, 168–94; and sexuality, 25–26, 167–68, 170–71, 174–92, 194

Somers, Harry. *See Mario and the Magician* (Somers/Anderson)

Sontag, Susan, v, 21, 38, 39, 60, 148, 150, 159, 197, 199–200, 211, 216, 220, 237 n.14, 284 n.63

spes phthisica. See tuberculosis

stigmatizing, 38–39, 59, 108, 210, 216, 217, 218, 239 n.29

Stravinsky, Igor. *See Oedipus Rex* (Stravinsky/Cocteau); *The Rake's Progress* (Stravinsky/Auden and Kallmann)

suffering, 10, 11–13, 22, 46–47, 61, 64–68, 76, 86, 89, 90, 91, 93, 96, 118, 148–49, 201, 216, 217, 223–25

Syberberg, Hans-Jürgen, 67, 256 n.92

syphilis: Christian interpretations of, 17, 22, 24, 61, 72–73, 74, 76, 87, 93, 124–25; and insanity, 23, 97, 100, 102–6, 108, 112–17, 217, 258 n.5; medical history of, 18, 19, 21, 22, 25, 69–76, 81, 97, 99, 101, 105–8, 115–17, 119–21, 225, 227, 239 n.32, 248 n.33; and the military, 72, 78–79, 83, 109–10, 119–20, 216; operatic representations of, 17, 22–23, 61–93, 95–121, 124; and prostitution, 22–23, 42, 77, 78–80, 82–83, 96–99, 102, 103–4, 109–10, 112–13, 117–18, 130, 133; and sexuality, 18, 22–23, 68–69, 71, 76, 77–78, 87, 93, 95, 106, 117, 124, 126, 235 n.77; symptoms of, xiv, 2, 22, 68–71, 75–76; syphilophobia, 22–23, 77, 87, 96, 99, 107, 109, 217

Il tabarro (Puccini), 9, 176–78

Theweleit, Klaus, 191, 252 n.57, 254 n.73, 277 n.96 n.97

tobacco. *See* smoking

La Traviata (Verdi/Piave), xiv, 8, 21–22, 29, 38, 39, 40–48, 49, 57, 59, 128, 186, 196, 210, 213, 218, 226

tuberculosis: contagiousness of, 39–40, 50, 53–54, 58–59, 218, 226, 244 n.79; cultural representations of, 17, 21–22, 193, 225–26; and feminine beauty, 22, 32, 36–38, 40–41, 45, 50, 52, 59, 220–26; hereditary theory of, 32, 36, 38, 40, 59, 226, 237 n.16; medical history of, 18, 19, 21, 25, 29–30, 34, 36, 38, 39–40, 49–50, 54, 58–59, 126, 218, 225–26; operatic images of, xiv, 8, 21–22, 29–59, 225–26; and poverty, 22, 40, 48, 49–50, 52, 54–55, 58, 59; sanatorium movement,

tuberculosis (*cont.*)
54, 59; and sexuality, 22, 31, 38, 40–43, 47–48, 52, 58, 126, 226; "spes phthisica", 44, 45, 46, 56, 210, 219; symptoms of, xiv, 31–32, 34, 36–38, 41, 43–44, 45–46, 50, 53–54, 135–36, 218, 226

venereal disease. *See* syphilis
violence, 25, 150, 174–75, 177–78, 179, 183, 184–85, 186–87, 189, 192, 194, 195–96
Vogel, Paula, 221
Voltaire. See *Candide* (Voltaire)

Wagner, Richard. See *Götterdämmerung; Parsifal; Der Ring des Niebelungen; Siegfried; Die Walküre*

Die Walküre (Wagner), 14
Wapnewski, Peter, 247 n.22, 257 n.97
Wedekind, Frank, 97–100, 131, 133
Weiner, Marc A., 10, 81, 254 n.75, 267 n.63
Whittal, Arnold, 84, 115, 139, 247 n.21, 251 n.51, 267 n.60
Wolf-Ferrari, Ermanno. See *Il segreto di Susanna* (Wolf-Ferrari/Golisciani)
Wolfram von Eschenbach: *Parzifal*, 62, 82, 86, 87, 93, 257 n.97, 258 n.114
women. *See* gender; prostitution; violence

Zangarini, Carlo. See *La fanciulla del West*
Zeissl, D., 69, 248 n.24
Zero Positive (Kondoleon), 203, 204

In the *Texts and Contexts* series

Volume 1
Inscribing the Other
By Sander L. Gilman

Volume 2
Crack Wars: Literature,
Addiction, Mania
By Avital Ronell

Volume 3
Madness and Art: The Life
and Works of Adolf Wölfli
By Walter Morgenthaler
Translated and with
an introduction by
Aaron H. Esman

Volume 4
Serenity in Crisis: A Preface
to Paul de Man, 1939–1960
By Ortwin de Graef

Volume 5
The Mirror and the Word
Modernism, Literary
Theory, and Georg Trakl
By Eric B. Williams

Volume 6
Undertones of Insurrection
Music, Politics, and the
Social Sphere in the Modern
German Narrative
By Marc A. Weiner

Volume 7
Herbarium, Verbarium
The Discourse of Flowers
By Claudette Sartiliot

Volume 8
Finitude's Score
Essays for the End of the
Millennium
By Avital Ronell

Volume 9
The Imaginary Jew
By Alain Finkielkraut
Translated by Kevin O'Neill
and David Suchoff

Volume 10
Antisemitism, Misogyny, and the
Logic of Cultural Difference
Cesare Lombroso and Matilde Serao
By Nancy A. Harrowitz

Volume 11
Organic Memory: History and
the Body in the Late Nineteenth
and Early Twentieth Centuries
By Laura Otis

Volume 12
Richard Wagner and
the Anti-Semitic Imagination
By Marc A. Weiner

Volume 13
Titanic Light: Paul de Man's
Post-Romanticism, 1960–1969
By Ortwin de Graef

Volume 14
The Jews and Germany: From the
"Judeo-German Symbiosis" to the
Memory of Auschwitz
By Enzo Traverso; Translated
by Daniel Weissbort

Volume 15
Poetic Process
By W. G. Kudszus

Volume 16
Sojourners: The Return of German
Jews and the Question of Identity
By John Borneman
and Jeffrey M. Peck

Volume 17
Opera: Desire, Disease, Death
By Linda Hutcheon and
Michael Hutcheon